Anna Noveroske
Au Sable Grad Fellow

Ravished by Beauty

Ravished by Beauty

The Surprising Legacy of Reformed Spirituality

BELDEN C. LANE

UNIVERSITY PRESS

Oxford University Press, Inc., publishes works that further
Oxford University's objective of excellence
in research, scholarship, and education.

Oxford New York
Auckland Cape Town Dar es Salaam Hong Kong Karachi
Kuala Lumpur Madrid Melbourne Mexico City Nairobi
New Delhi Shanghai Taipei Toronto

With offices in
Argentina Austria Brazil Chile Czech Republic France Greece
Guatemala Hungary Italy Japan Poland Portugal Singapore
South Korea Switzerland Thailand Turkey Ukraine Vietnam

Published by Oxford University Press, Inc.
198 Madison Avenue, New York, New York 10016

www.oup.com

Library of Congress Cataloging-in-Publication Data

Lane, Belden C., 1943–
Ravished by beauty : the surprising legacy of reformed spirituality / Belden C. Lane.
p. cm.
ISBN 978-0-19-975508-0
1. Nature—Religious aspects—Christianity. 2. Reformed Church—Doctrines. I. Title.
BT695.5.L36 2011
231.7—dc22 2010019023

1 3 5 7 9 8 6 4 2
Printed in the United States of America
on acid-free paper

Contents

Permissions

A very different version of chapter 2 appeared as "Spirituality as the Performance of Desire: Calvin on the World as a Theatre of God's Glory," in *Spiritus: A Journal of Christian Spirituality* I:1 (Spring 2001).

Much of "The Whole World Singing: A Journey to Iona and Taizé" was originally published in *The Christian Century* 117:10 (March 22–29, 2000).

An earlier version of Chapter 3 appeared as "Two Schools of Desire: Nature and Marriage in Seventeenth-Century Puritanism," in *Church History* 69:2 (June 2000).

"Open the Kingdom for a Cottonwood Tree" appeared in an earlier form in *The Christian Century* 114:30 (October 29, 1997).

Sections of chapter 4 were presented at the Third Congregational Symposium of the National Association of Congregational Christian Churches in Los Angeles in January 2002. They appeared in the published proceedings of those lectures, entitled *Yet More Light and Truth: Congregationalism, Covenant and Community*, ed. Steven A. Peay (Milwaukee, WI: Congregational Press, 2003).

"Biodiversity and the Holy Trinity" was published in a shortened form in *America* 185:20 (December 17, 2001).

An earlier version of chapter 5, "Jonathan Edwards on Beauty, Desire, and the Sensory World" appeared in *Theological Studies* 65:1 (March 2004).

"Can We Chant Psalms with All God's Creatures?" originated as an invited lecture at the Vancouver School of Theology on July 22, 1998. A subsequent version of this and other parts of the book were given as the Schaff Lectures at Pittsburgh Theological Seminary on March 10–12, 2008.

Beauty, Desire for God, and Delight in Creation

"Spirituality is what we do with the fire inside of us, about how we channel our eros."

—Ronald Rolheiser, *The Holy Longing* (1999)

"The human soul needs beauty even more than it needs bread."

—D. H. Lawrence, "Nottingham and the Mining Country" (1929)

"Beauty is the source of all things. . . . It is the great creating cause which bestirs the world and holds all things in existence by the longing inside them to have beauty . . . It is the longing for beauty which actually brings them into being."

—Pseudo-Dionysius the Areopagite, *The Divine Names* (sixth century)

"The doctrine of the Trinity is . . . the source of the rhythmically dancing and vibrating worlds."

—Jürgen Moltmann, *God in Creation* (1991)

"In a vision . . . I beheld and comprehended the whole creation, that is, what is on this side and what is beyond the sea, the abyss, the sea itself, and everything else. . . . And my soul in an excess of wonder cried out: 'This world is pregnant with God!'"

—Angela of Foligno, *Book of Visions and Instructions* (thirteenth century)

"God is beautiful. Beautiful . . . as a fact and as a force in the manner in which he asserts himself as the one who arouses pleasure, creates desire for himself, and rewards with delight . . . , the one who as God is both lovely and loveworthy."

—Karl Barth, *Church Dogmatics*, II/1 (1970)

"Beauty is . . . the blazing forth of the primal, protological and eschatological splendour of creation even in this age of death, in which redeemed man is admitted to participation in God's act of praising himself in his creation."

—Hans Urs von Balthasar, *The Glory of the Lord* (1983)

"The soul is accepted not because of what it has done, but because of what it has desired."

—Macarius the Syrian, *Homilies* (fourth century)

"Do anything to me, God, just never cease to take pleasure in me."

—Elizabeth Rowe, *Devout Exercises of the Heart* (1796)

"His desire gives rise to yours."

—Bernard of Clairvaux, Sermon 57 on the Song of Songs (twelfth century)

"There are pleasures that are able to save people."

—*The Shepherd of Hermas*, III.vi.5 (second century)

"God truly waits for us in things. . . . By means of all created things, without exception, the divine assails us, penetrates us, and moulds us. . . . Matter contains the spur or allurement to be our accomplice towards heightened being."

—Teilhard de Chardin, *The Divine Milieu* (1960)

"Here bee [*sic*] millions of Ministers and Apostles sent by God into the world, to preach unto men the inexhaust[ible] treasures of their Lords goodness, wisdome, and power."

—Thomas Taylor, *Meditations from the Creatures* (1635)

"God's glory in creation appears in various degrees and ways. An insect and a star, the mildew on the wall and the cedar in Lebanon, a common labourer and a man like Augustine, are all creatures of God; yet how dissimilar they are and how varied their ways of glorifying God."

—Abraham Kuyper, *The Work of the Holy Spirit* (1900)

"If a doctrine of creation is to be ecological, it must try to get away from analytical thinking, with its distinctions between subject and object, and must strive to learn a new, communicative and integrating way of thought."

—Jürgen Moltmann, *God in Creation* (1991)

"There cannot be such a thing as true life without praise. Praising and no longer praising are related to each other as are living and no longer living."

—Claus Westermann, *The Praise of God in the Psalms* (1965)

"The experience [of God] is one of intense longing. It is distinguished from other longings by two things. In the first place, though the sense of want is acute and even painful, yet the mere wanting is felt to be somehow a delight. Other desires are felt as pleasures only if satisfaction is expected in the near future. . . . But this desire, even when there is no hope of possible satisfaction, continues to be prized, and even to be preferred to anything else in the world, by those who have once felt it."

—C. S. Lewis, *The Pilgrim's Regress* (1944)

"Come, for you are yourself the desire within me. Come, for you are my breath and my life."

—Simeon, the New Theologian (tenth century)

"My Lord God, I have no idea where I am going. I don't see the road ahead of me. . . . The fact that I think I am following your will does not mean that I am actually doing so. But I believe that the desire to please you does in fact please you. And I hope I have that desire for all that I am doing. . . . And I know that if I do this you will lead me by the right road, though I may know nothing about it."

—Thomas Merton, *Thoughts in Solitude* (1956)

"Metaphysical desire. . . can not be satisfied. . . . It desires beyond everything that can simply complete it. It is like goodness—the Desired does not fulfill it, but deepens it. Desire nourishes itself, one might say, with its hunger. . . ."

—Emmanuel Levinas, *Totality and Infinity* (1969)

"The thirst in our souls is the attraction put out by the water itself. . . . In fact, all the particles of the world are in love and looking for lovers."

—Jelaluddin Rumi, *The Mathnawi* (thirteenth century)

"In the jungle, during one night in each month, the moths did not come to lanterns; through the black reaches of the outer night, so it was said, they flew toward the full moon. He could not recall where he had heard it, or from whom; it had been somewhere on the rivers of Brazil. . . . Yet the idea of the moths in the high darkness, straining upward, filled him with longing, and at these times he would know that he had not found what he was looking for."

—Peter Matthiessen, *At Play in the Fields of the Lord*

Illustrations

Abbreviations

CO The Works of John Calvin, *Ioannis Calvini opera quae supersunt omnia*, in 59 volumes, eds. Wilhelm Baum, Edward Cunitz, and Edward Reuss, *Corpus Reformatorum* (Brunswick: A. Schwetchke and Son [M. Bruhn], 1863–1900).

Comm. The Commentaries of John Calvin on the Old and New Testaments, translated in CNTC and CTS below.

CR *Corpus Reformatorum*, the title given to the collected writings of Philip Melanchthon, John Calvin, and Ulrich Zwingli, begun by editor Karl G. Bretschneider in 1834. Within its 101 volumes, volumes 29–87 contain the writings of Calvin, also referred to above as CO.

CNTC *Calvin's New Testament Commentaries*, a twentieth-century English translation in 12 volumes, eds. David W. Torrance and Thomas F. Torrance (Grand Rapids, MI: Eerdmans, 1959–1972).

CTS John Calvin's Commentaries on the Bible, translated into English by various translators of the Calvin Translation Society in 45 volumes, 1843–1848. These have been reprinted as *Calvin's Commentaries* in 22 volumes (Grand Rapids, MI: Baker Books, 2005). Volume numbers refer to this 2005 edition.

Inst. John Calvin, *Institutes of the Christian Religion*, *Institutio Christianae Religionis* (1559), in 2 volumes, ed. John T. McNeill, trans. Ford Lewis Battles (Philadelphia: Westminster Press, 1960).

OS The Selected Works of John Calvin, *Calvini Ioannis Opera Selecta*, in 5 volumes, eds. Peter Barth, Wilhelm Niesel, and Donna Scheuner, (Munich: Chr. Kaiser, 1926–1959).

YE *The Works of Jonathan Edwards*, in 25 volumes, general editor, Perry Miller (New Haven: Yale University Press, 1957–2006).

Ravished by Beauty

Prologue

Ring Lake Ranch, Wyoming

From this cabin in the Wind River Range of the Rockies I look out onto a landscape of desire. In these recent years of drought everything longs for rain. My wife and I woke up to three inches of late snow a few days ago and mountain bluebells, delighted at the unexpected moisture, have suddenly appeared in a brief riot of color across the meadow.

On Glacier Trail up by the falls yesterday I noticed a patch of green moss growing under the exposed roots of an old fir tree, straining in the shadows for what little sunlight it could find. Rain isn't the only object of desire here. Everything hungers for something. Last night a band of bighorn sheep passed through, heading up Whiskey Basin toward the high country for the lambing season. A year-old male was making advances on some of the ewes. He too failed. In a landscape that pulses with desire, failure is often more common than fulfillment. Yearning is constant.

That's why I've come in late spring to a lonely cabin in the high desert country of western Wyoming. Desire for God, for the wife I love, and for the healing of the earth all converge here. Theological and environmental concerns mesh with my own confused longings in a place of such beauty. This is a good place for reflecting on the arousal and relinquishment of desire, on what seventeenth-century Puritans spoke of as a spirituality of ravishment and the role that "weaned affections" play in achieving its purity. To learn desire one necessarily sits at the feet of those who are thirsty. The satisfied never make good teachers. It isn't the mastery of truth, but a relentless longing for it that qualifies those who become trusted guides for others. Mark it down as a rule: the desert alone possesses the secret knowledge of water.

Only what we deeply long for do we ever really know, says nature writer Craig Childs. Absence sharpens attention to a fine edge. Oddly enough, the desert is the best place to study water. Its landscape is defined by the memory of rain, etched into the land at every turn. Its surface "is carved into canyons, arroyos, cañoncitos, ravines, narrows, washes, and chasms. The anatomy of [the] place has no other profession but the moving of water."[1] A remembrance of flow lingers in the shadow of every rock. This is how the desert knows water—achingly, desperately, with a passion bordering on dread. It's the only way we ever know God as well.

I've come to this unforgiving terrain to write about the often-maligned Calvinist spirituality that, for better or worse, has formed my American Presbyterian way of thinking about God and the world. I'm here to ask how my religious roots relate to such a landscape. How does a Reformed spirituality of desire resonate with the energies of this place? What are the resources in a tradition like mine for addressing the ecological concerns that arise from the land?

This book is about beauty and desire, the capacity of the earth to mirror God's splendor, and the importance of forging a bond between human longing and the rest of creation. It recognizes the need for solid religious underpinnings of a viable environmental ethic. My particular way of approaching such concerns is rooted in the heritage of John Calvin, a figure not generally associated with beauty, desire, or the earth. Yet they all come together here in the high-desert terrain of western Wyoming where global warming, as elsewhere, has begun to take its toll.

The Reformed tradition[2] came across the Atlantic in the early seventeenth century from ports in Britain and the Netherlands to the rocky, wind-swept coast of New England. It had thrived earlier in the harsh landscapes of Scotland and Northern Ireland, and before that in the mountainous enclaves of Zurich and Geneva in Switzerland. Calvinism emerged geographically out of the same fierce terrain once occupied by the ancient Celts in northern Europe. The Celts and Calvinists alike were fascinated with eternal mysteries, the wonders of creation, a rigorous discipline, and the harsh, stubborn realities of life.

Calvinism was, in part, the product of a landscape of desire—hardened by affliction, toughened by geography, yet driven by the earth's wild beauty to a God of matchless splendor. Leon Kellner emphasizes the hard edges of its mystique when he writes that:

> Calvinism is the natural theology of the disinherited; it never flourished, therefore, anywhere as it did in the barren hills of Scotland and in the wilds of North America. The Calvinist feels himself surrounded by naught but hostile powers; his

> is a perpetual conflict from his very birth. The farmer who has to keep up a constant struggle against untoward phenomena, against the refractory soil, against drought and frost, against caterpillars and a host of other insect plagues . . . is naturally inclined to the belief from the outset that God, who created the world, is a well-meaning but unquestionably a rigorous, cold being who rules the world with some great purpose unknown to the inhabitants of the earth.[3]

This is a half-truth at best. Kellner missed the deeper realization of the Reformed tradition that God dances in thunderstorm and shadow, luring the world to a breathtaking beauty through the power of unquenched thirst. Calvin knew that desire is the great teacher, and sustained desire the path to holiness.

One learns this quickly at Ring Lake Ranch. Everything here participates in longing; fulfillment is irregular at best. There were no mountain bluebells last year. The late snow never came. In places throughout the Greater Yellowstone ecosystem, fir trees are dying because of the drought. Their frustrated desire has reached its peak, yielding to something beyond itself. But insects thrive in the dead wood, and that's good news for the hairy woodpeckers. Loss and gain are ever-changing and hard to measure here. Yet longing endures in a landscape of desire—through death, defeat, and on rare occasions ecstasy. This gives passion its edge, its compelling fortitude.

Reformed Spirituality and The Dilemma of Desire

I hadn't wanted to hear any of this during my time in that remote Wyoming cabin a few years ago. I'd come with an eager anticipation of writing this book, arriving with every expectation of realized delight. But I encountered frustrated desire instead. After churning out the first page or two, I wasn't able to write another word. To my chagrin, I first had to live my way more fully into the truth I was trying to express, passing (with the terrain) through an experience of Puritan "desertion" before being able to write about it.

I'd come there to work out of an intensity of desire—doing what I loved, capturing the lineaments of a Reformed spirituality of longing, speaking for the earth in calling others to its beauty, recovering my theological roots. The place was perfect for such work. My wife had brought along her quilting and I my laptop. We were there to celebrate our thirty-fifth wedding anniversary, the blue-eyed girl of my youth and I. We built a fire each morning in the wood stove, worked side by side as we sewed and tried to write, and took daily walks along the creek or up the ridge. In the evening, we'd sit on the front porch watching the snow-covered peaks of the Absaroka Range to the north. I should have thought we'd died and gone to heaven.

But I'd brought with me a misplaced passion to *produce*—and I was miserable. There I was in paradise, at an ideal site to work on a book about the ecstatic fulfillment of desire, and I couldn't string two sentences together. It was pathetic. I'm ashamed to admit I hadn't come primarily to celebrate our marriage, to delight in my wife and the wild beauty of the place, to meet God in its terrible and glorious silence. I was there to *write*, to weave words together with magic, to exercise control over the subject of Reformed desire. I received, instead, what the tradition (and the landscape) gives best—an excruciating deconstruction (and transformation) of desire.

After venting my anger with God one night, trudging up the ridge through snow flurries driven by a hard north wind, I came back, half-frozen, to the cabin. There my wife told me a story. She'd been given an image of a father and son walking together through an extraordinarily beautiful wilderness. The father longed for nothing but the son's enjoyment, simply delighting in their time together. The son, however, was so anxious for the father's approval, he could think of nothing but finishing the book he'd been given to write. They were missing each other altogether as a result. The tears in her eyes said it all.

Instead of sitting down to the meal set before me, I'd been trying to write out a perfect menu. Only as I submitted to what the landscape wanted to teach me about longing and the abandonment of desire could I give up my compulsion to write for the sake of the deeper desires before me—the gift of my wife, the surrounding wilderness, and a God of love who refused to be captured by words. For the next three weeks I wrote nothing, giving myself instead to what mattered most. Some of us have to be dragged kicking and screaming into what we truly desire. It was a lesson, I learned, that summarizes much of the mystery of Reformed spirituality. Its path toward holiness involves an awakening of desire, the relinquishing of what initially may have seemed so important, a subsequent longing for God alone, and a discovery that what was sought had been there all along.

The theological heart of the Reformed tradition can, at its best, be summarized in five vigorous convictions:

1. A response of awe before a grand and powerful God, seen in the majesty of sky and sea, and in the transformed lives of those whose stories are recounted in Scripture.
2. An amazement that this same God is full of grace and love, evoking a response of gratitude, even adoration.
3. A need to probe the intellectual mysteries of faith, while recognizing the metaphorical, accommodating, and limited nature of all theological language.
4. A concern to carry theological reflection to its completion in the transformation of culture and the exercise of justice in society.
5. A view of the church as an organic and interdependent unity of diverse peoples, knit by Word and Sacrament into the body of Christ.[4]

All of these were reinforced for me in the high desert country of the upper plains. A holy longing nourishes each of them.

The centrality of desire in this book is rooted in the awareness that a misplaced yearning lies at the heart of the current ecological crisis. Our craving for an endless supply of imagined "goods" drives the engines of a consumer-oriented society. Desire is killing us, along with our planet. It underlies our problems of obesity and impoverishment, the endless thirst for new and improved goods, the disposal of waste, the passion for unlimited economic growth, and the global effects of a free-market economy, each of them paid for at the expense of the poor and the environment. Ecology and spirituality, the fragile balance of the earth's resources and the mistaken hungers of the soul, converge at precisely this point. The result is a desperate need for a new paradigm—for what in the language of the church is called repentance and conversion.

The manufactured desires of a consumer culture turn creation into a cafeteria line of consumable resources. We're trapped in a cultural cage devoted to the relentless consumption of beauty, the continual acquisition (and eventual discarding) of all the things that attract us. The Reformed tradition offers in response, like Carmelite and Buddhist traditions before it, an ironic reminder that the only desire truly able to satisfy is a desire which cannot be filled. Our deepest human longing is to linger with a mystery we aren't able to fathom. We stand in awe before the extravagant wonder of an irreducible "other."

The ultimate Other, of course, is God—a reality never fully grasped, provoking a thirst that remains blissfully unfulfilled. Our greatest joy lies in what we can't possess. This is true of all our relationships: from God to each other to the earth itself. Only in wonder do we ever encounter any of them. Every experience of beauty involves the joyous agony of a desire unattained.

The Reformed tradition seeks to nurture this incurable longing of the heart after God. The Puritans, for example, were a people of fervent desire as well as rigorous discipline. It may surprise us how much they used the bold language of the Song of Songs to express their zealous passion. They spoke unashamedly of "lusting after God." Yet the God of beauty they desired was always more than they could grasp. Hence, they wrote perpetually of their struggles with longings unfulfilled, a sense of God's absence provoking an ever deeper yearning. When the flames of God's consuming presence burned low in their lives, they refused to despair, blowing on the embers to keep their desire alive.

One seventeenth-century Puritan divine, Matthew Sylvester, spoke of severe "consternations of spirit" coming to the most spiritual of saints, even David himself, "a man after God's own heart." "Dreadful afflictions and dismal apprehensions," he explained, "are incident to the holiest and best men [and women]." Such experiences toughen the human spirit, provoke the relinquishment of lesser desires, and point to the subtleties of God's deeper ways of loving. They spur "a consequent emboldening of the heart and face toward God, others, and themselves."[5]

Puritans recognized the need for a purgative testing of intense longing. They knew that all desires had to be judged. Being stripped of what ultimately cannot be held is inevitably painful, but not without its benefits. One experiences God in loss even more powerfully than in attainment. Joseph Symonds, in a book typical of Puritan spirituality, cautioned that "Desertions are not the interruption of God's love, but of the acts of his love; his affection is the same, but the expression is varied."[6] He pointed to the "absences of God" as occasions for encountering a love more subtle and profound. Once they gain this insight, "the faithful usually find their worst days their best days. . . . The capacity of the soul is widened, and enlarged in affliction. . . . He that is most athirst, drinks most."[7]

Hence, loss and gain, a desire left incomplete and a delight finally attained became a never-ending tension in Puritan spiritual life. "Desire," as Symonds defined it, is a wintry discipline, trusting in a faithfulness it cannot see. "Delight" is a summer activity, reveling in God's gracious open-handedness. "By desire . . . love extends it self towards God as absent: by delight she enjoyes him as present: desire is love in motion, delight is love in rest." In God's strange habit of rewarding the dearest lovers of God with the subtlest signs of grace, therefore, "He keeps the cistern empty, that we may look to the Clouds above."[8]

The Making of a Calvinist

This book is a story of going home again. Growing up in the South reading Thomas Wolfe, I know that's impossible. One only returns to a home he never really knew. That's as true for me as it was for George Webber, longing for his hometown of Libya Hill in the Piedmont region of Old Catawba (North Carolina).

Mine is a tale of a boy raised in a fundamentalist, Calvinist tradition in the swamp-filled pinelands of central Florida, chafing under its harsh image of an angry God. Yet that's where desire was first planted in him—a longing for something as alluringly beautiful as it was awesome and demanding. Growing up, he marveled at underwater snakes and white cranes in the lake behind his house, even as the lusty, heartfelt singing of "Amazing Grace" stirred him in Sunday night services. This desire for (and fear of) a God grander than anything he could imagine led to his becoming a Presbyterian minister himself. He later found in Karl Barth a softer, more appealing version of the Calvinism he had reacted to in the past.[9]

But Barth, despite his gloriously theocentric theology, didn't prove entirely satisfying either. The Swiss Reformed theologian's God was so "Wholly Other," it was hard to imagine such a deity delighting in water moccasins and great blue herons.[10] The boy needed a God wild enough to tromp through water hyacinths, searching for crayfish, laughing at dragonflies. After finishing doctoral work at Princeton, he began teaching theology at a Catholic, Jesuit University in Saint Louis. Through the years there he warmed to the rich sacramentality of the Roman Catholic tradition, delighting in its ability to affirm everything earthly. He reacted to Barth's dismissal of the Catholic effort to join nature and God (through an analogy of being) as an "invention of Antichrist."[11] Swamp water continued to flow in his veins, as he sought on Ozark trails what he had once found in marshlands of cypress and palmettos. He thought at times of converting to Mother Church, but something still drew him to his roots in the Calvinist tradition.

The longing led, at last, to the writing of this book—trying to recover the passionate, nature-loving spirituality he had dimly sensed, but never realized, in his distant past. A re-reading of John Calvin, seventeenth-century Puritans, and Jonathan Edwards awakened within him a half-forgotten desire for a God able to exult in wilderness. The possibility of grounding an ardent commitment to environmental ethics in a re-reading of the Reformed theology of his youth was intriguing. He found himself returning to a home he'd never really known, delighting in it for the first time. The pages that follow are a result of that work.

This book is not an autobiographical project, despite the self-disclosing narratives that frame it. It contains no "confessions of a lapsed Calvinist snatched from the jaws of Rome."

Nor does it try to articulate a full-fledged environmental ethic in the Reformed tradition. Its concern is rather to provide a historical and theological foundation for doing so. It hopes to stir in the reader a desire for God's glory, glimpsed so vividly in creation that one's work for ecological justice becomes a natural extension of praise. Reformed spirituality necessarily begins with a stunning vision of God's grandeur. That's where my own journey began.

What I experienced as a child growing up in the South wasn't a full-blown Calvinism, so much as an amalgam of fundamentalist thought and fragments of Reformed theology. Such is often the case in the American experience. The Baptist churches I attended were more Calvinist than Arminian in their sympathies, more drawn to Calvin's God of sovereign power than to Methodist notions of free will. People knew in the depths of their souls the awful, enduring impact of original sin. Theirs was a Calvinism shaped by Southern revivalism and a separatist mentality, fearful of involvement with the world. In many ways, Calvin would hardly have recognized it.

Yet they held the doctrine of human depravity in high esteem. I remember stories told of a traveling evangelist whose object lesson for children scared the hell out of everyone. He pulled a rotten egg from under the pulpit, telling the children gathered around him that he had left it out of his refrigerator for two weeks and that it represented each of them as rotten sinners. It smelled something awful. He then reached under the pulpit for a hammer which, he said, represented God's holiness and almighty power. Such a God could have nothing to do with sin, of course, and was naturally inclined to smash rotten eggs to smithereens. But just as the hammer was raised over his head to come down with all its force on the hapless egg, the minister reached under the pulpit yet again to retrieve a tin can. This he quickly placed over the egg as the hammer fell and the can absorbed its vicious blow. The tin can, the minister explained to the children, was Jesus, who accepted God's anger on their behalf. I suspected, even then, that being chosen and "saved" by such a God offered precious little comfort.

Only later would I learn that even Calvin had refused to define the human person exclusively in terms of sin.[12] The human soul is turned back on itself, twisted by selfishness; nonetheless, God's image remains apparent. Creation, therefore, needs to be revitalized, not destroyed. The first thing to be said about us is not our monstrous distortion of God's image, but our reflection of its glory. Sin may be an "infection" of our being, but not the "essence" of who we are.[13] This is a liberating truth that it took me years to appreciate as fully Reformed.

Despite the harshness of my religious upbringing, however, there was a primitive, archetypal energy about it that fascinated me. Associating God with danger and violence wasn't necessarily appalling to an eleven-year-old boy with a new Daisy pump-action BB gun. I spent much of my time with other kids roaming through wilderness, trapping raccoons and shooting squirrels with the neighbor's .410 shotgun. Ostensibly we were protecting his orange grove from predators, but we pretty much shot at anything that moved. I cringe now in thinking of it, but at the time a love of wilderness, a readiness to take life, and a God of awesome power were inextricably intertwined in my inchoate Calvinist imagination. My need, ever since, has been to know how to retain a God of feral and untamed beauty while affirming a moral universe where all of life is sacred.

Every childhood requires the nurturing of desire. My Calvinist, fundamentalist past, despite its faults, was able to do that for me. In a setting of rural poverty, where education was not especially prized, I fell in love with a God I'd first learned to fear. In the Reformed tradition, knowing oneself to be chosen (and loved) by a God of infinite power means having nothing else to fear. Being chosen, adopted out of abject poverty as a son or daughter of the King, gives one an extraordinary sense of self, a freedom to move through the world with fearless abandon. In my upbringing, Calvinist images of royalty were oddly juxtaposed with notions of undeserving insignificance.[14] To be chosen and loved was everything.

This was a God, then, preeminently able to evoke desire. At the age of ten, I began to write my first book in response to such wonder. On the wide-lined pages of a spiral school binder, I told the story of Christ's death and resurrection, amazed at a selfless love that included me. I marveled at the God whom Isaiah had met in speechless awe, his lips touched by fire as he responded to the divine call. Through images of hot coals, crowns of thorns, nails driven into flesh, and angels crying "Holy, Holy, Holy," I knew myself for the first time as unaccountably loved. Not by a mother whose nervous breakdowns mirrored a history of abuse. Nor by a father whose suicide would provide his only escape from torment. But by a God of glory who encompassed wildness and loss, yet loved indiscriminately. It was the same God I had met in stunning Florida sunsets and the crashing surf of the Atlantic coast.

I knew myself chosen and loved by a God who roared through the pages of the King James Bible, danced in passing hurricanes, and sang in the blue eyes of the girl with light brown hair in the church youth group (the woman I later married). Such a God was never "safe," but always good, as Lucy learned from Mr. Beaver in C. S. Lewis's *The Lion, the Witch, and the Wardrobe*.[15] This was a God of wild beauty, very different from the God of savage predictability I occasionally encountered at church.

In the hybrid Calvinism that I experienced growing up, the sense of chosenness I've described was generally anchored in the famous five points of Calvinist doctrine. Five-point Calvinism (also known as Tulip Calvinism) was not preached from the pulpit or articulated very clearly by church pastors, but it underlay much of the spirituality of my youth. Drawn from the Dutch Reformed tradition, this theological acronym emphasized:

- The ***T***otal Depravity of sinners
- God's ***U***nconditional Election of those chosen to be saved
- The ***L***imited Atonement accomplished by Christ's death on the cross (applying only to the elect)
- God's ***I***rresistible Grace (inevitably drawing the chosen to repentance)
- The ***P***erseverance of the Saints (guaranteeing the salvation of the elect).[16]

It was a sober theology, to say the least, and one not inclined to value creation. Though it suggested an extraordinary sense of self for those who knew themselves chosen by a God of immeasurable glory, it took a narrow view of most everything else.

What bothered me about such an exclusivist theology was the accompanying doctrine of double predestination that served to explain the enormous numbers of those who were *not* chosen. This tenet declared that even before the fall of humanity in Adam and Eve, God had foreseen what would happen and decreed the fate of each individual—predestining the few (the elect) to blessedness and justly consigning all the rest (the reprobate) to hell. It was a logic I found inexorable but terrifying, contradicting the God I had discovered in the wonders of nature and Scripture alike.[17]

My spiritual journey, ever since, has been an effort to recover God's wild and winsome splendor, making demands on my life, rollicking in fresh falling rain, fiercely affirming the whole of creation as unaccountably good, and stirring desire at every turn. Yearning for such a God requires a willingness to abandon previous conceptions of a rigid deity, a willingness to be surprised by grace. As I discovered when I began to write this book, a letting go (a release of control) is, at some point, what every true longing entails. God is always more than we wish for and certainly more than we can understand. Desire has to submit to discernment, even as glib explanations of God's eternal decrees must yield to the mystery of God's unfathomable love.

Desire for God can be a dangerous thing in the hands of an unrestrained ego, exercised by those who glibly identify themselves as divinely "chosen." It led Puritans in seventeenth-century Massachusetts to wreak their will on the surrounding wilderness, eradicating native peoples (the Wampanoags and Pequots) like eleven-year-olds with a new gun.[18] Authentic desire for God must pass through the same fire that purged Isaiah's lips, bringing reckless action to a halt and closing one's mouth in awe before a God of beauty and power who declares all things loved. It means challenging every shadow tendency toward self-delusion, exclusivism, and violence. Only as the soul is empty enough can true desire safely fill it.

Disclosures and Acknowledgements

Being honest about the bias that an author brings to his work is a small but important debt owed the reader. Hence, I acknowledge more specifically two influences that govern my approach to this work. I am a church historian, formed by the Reformed tradition (the Presbyterian Church, U.S.A.), who has taught for thirty years on a Roman Catholic, Jesuit, faculty. I've been deeply molded by the Great Tradition, testing my thinking as a Reformed Christian against the wider stream of Catholic and Orthodox Christianity, and other faith traditions as well. Ignatian spirituality has been an important tool to this end, continually offering connections and corrections to my own confessional approach to the spiritual life.

The second influence on my thought has been a lifelong fascination with wilderness and the natural world. My teaching and writing have focused primarily on connections between spirituality and geography or place. I've regularly used camping and canoeing trips to introduce students to the "book of creation," alongside other texts in the history of spirituality. Most of my spiritual retreats have been solo backpacking trips into wilderness areas of the Ozarks. Seeking ethical grounds in the Reformed tradition for valuing the earth emerges as a natural expression of this passion.

My goal in this book is to lift up a hidden, but retrievable tradition in Reformed piety, advancing an earthy and impassioned spirituality that few might initially recognize as Calvinist. The quest for a tradition I can affirm as my own has drawn me to hundreds of Puritan sermons and countless volumes of Calvin and Edwards, generously referenced here.

This thoroughness is necessary if the book is to substantiate its claim for a new and revitalized reading of Reformed spirituality, rich in ecological sensitivity. It interacts with current scholarship on the history of the tradition, though I try to keep that as brief and undemanding as possible. Taking the tradition seriously requires a careful attentiveness to its development, the criticisms it has drawn, and the challenges it offers. Reformed piety insists on intellectual credibility.

Despite its scholarly treatment of the material, however, the book undertakes a lively engagement with the passion, delight in beauty, sexual innuendo, love of the natural world, and ecological activism that dances through the history of the tradition. Each of these is part of a mix that has ravished the Reformed mind and heart at times in the past, and increasingly my own in the present.The chapters that follow share a historical, theological, ethical, and even liturgical agenda. They attempt to articulate a spirituality of desire in the history of the Reformed tradition, asking how major figures from John Calvin to Jonathan Edwards have emphasized the beauty of the world as a way of contemplating the beauty of God. Chapter 1 introduces the irony of Reformed spirituality—its celebration of the earth's beauty juxtaposed with its own tragic exercise of misplaced desire. It lifts up the neglected significance of nature and desire in a tradition that more often emphasizes divine transcendence and power. Chapter 2 looks at Calvin's metaphor of the world as a theater of God's glory, disclosing a remarkably sensitive theology of nature in a theologian usually associated with transcendence alone.

Chapters 3 and 4 attend to the spirituality of seventeenth-century English and American Puritans, showing how the natural world functioned simultaneously as a "School of Desire" and "School of Affliction." It pointed the faithful to God while purifying them of lesser longings. Puritanism throughout this book becomes a primary test case for measuring the extent to which Reformed spiritual values have been put into practice. Jonathan Edwards is the subject of chapter 5. It probes his understanding of a new spiritual sense that allows believers a richer sensibility to the surrounding world. Finally, chapter 6 asks how an environmentally-sensitive way of perceiving the earth might flow from this highly aesthetic, affective, and deeply Trinitarian spirituality. It elicits some of the ethical implications of a Reformed spirituality of desire.

Between these larger historical and theological studies are personal essays that I have designated "Landscapes of Desire." They express my own individual struggle to relate threads of the tradition to experiences of the natural world. These include pilgrimage narratives, stories of personal encounters with nature, and reflections on the interdependence of species—all related to the author's lived experience. They try to bridge the distance between the understanding and the practice of Reformed piety.

A cottage industry of books on spirituality and desire has emerged in recent years. Much of this interest is due to a renewed historical attention to the role of desire in the spiritual life (from Augustine to medieval women mystics), to new work in theological aesthetics and the dynamics of attraction (from Hans Urs von Balthasar to Richard Viladesau and Frank Burch Brown), and to psychoanalytical studies of desire by post-Freudian interpreters like Jacques Lacan, Julia Kristeva, and Georges Bataille. But it also has roots in the attention given to desire, sexuality, and power among postmodern theorists like Michel Foucault and Emmanuel Levinas, responding to a consumer, capitalist culture endlessly focused on the manufacture of desire.[19]

The wide range of popular works exploring this theme have included Jon Piper's *Desiring God: Meditations of a Christian Hedonist* (Portland, OR: Multnomah Press, 1986), Philip Sheldrake's *Befriending Our Desires* (Notre Dame, IN: Ave Maria Press, 1994), Ronald Rolheiser's *The Holy Longing* (New York: Doubleday, 1999), John Eldredge's *The Journey of Desire* (Nashville: Thomas Nelson, 2000), Wendy Farley's *The Wounding and Healing of Desire* (Louisville, KY: Westminster John Knox, 2005), and Diarmuid O'Murchu's *The Transformation of Desire* (Maryknoll, New York: Orbis Books, 2007). This present book is historically focused on the spiritual function of longing in a theological tradition generally thought to be far too cerebral and transcendent to have any interest in desire at all.

The thesis argued here is nothing new, especially for people familiar with studies in Reformed historiography over the last generation or so. It builds on the work of Susan Schreiner in articulating Calvin's fascination with the world of nature, on studies by Janice Knight and William Dyrness in emphasizing multiple strains of spirituality in

Anglo-American Puritanism, on the efforts of Amanda Porterfield and others in reassessing Puritan notions of sexuality and marriage, and on Roland Delattre's retrieval of Edwards as a theologian of beauty *par excellence*.[20] Despite this extensive work in recovering Reformed spirituality as a vital and multifaceted tradition, however, the tendency to reduce Calvinism to a narrow, rigid, and other-worldly belief still thrives in cultural and academic circles.

"You've got to be kidding," a colleague said to me not long after I'd begun this book about nature and the celebration of desire in the Calvinist tradition. "You really think you can find this in people like Calvin and Edwards?" He had thought of Calvin as little more than the recalcitrant and narrow-minded pope of Geneva. He remembered Enlightenment historian Peter Gay having labeled Edwards a "pathetic" figure, "the last of the medieval Americans."[21] I told him he might be surprised, as I've been so many times myself in the process of the work.

This book would not have been possible without the encouragement (*and* provocative challenges) of many colleagues and friends. These include Larry Rasmussen of Union Seminary in New York, Marcus and Marianne Borg at Oregon State University and Trinity Cathedral in Portland, Douglas Burton-Christie at Loyola Marymount University, Philip Sheldrake at the University of Durham, Cynthia Read of Oxford University Press, Leanne Van Dyk at Western Theological Seminary, Alister McGrath of Wycliffe Hall, Oxford, Sandra Schneiders at the Jesuit School of Theology in Berkeley, Martha Robbins at Pittsburgh Theological Seminary, David Field at the University of Transkei in South Africa, Richard Rohr of the Center for Action and Contemplation in Albuquerque, Steven Peay of the First Congregational Church of Wauwatosa, Wisconsin, Joan Guntzelman of Ring Lake Ranch in Western Wyoming, and my colleagues at Saint Louis University. Environmental groups (of both scholars and activists) have also been a spur to my work, from the Religion and Ecology group of the American Academy of Religion to Presbyterians for Restoring Creation.

In addition, I'm indebted to the librarians at the Bodleian Library, Oxford; Speer Library at Princeton Theological Seminary; Sterling and Beinecke Libraries at Yale University; and Pius XII Library at Saint Louis University. Friends and graduate students who have helped in the research or offered important insights include Jack Renard, Mark Stoll, Tim Hessel-Robinson, Stephen Hatch, Rob Furey, Jay Kridel, George Faithful, Jonathan Koefoed, Ben Wagner, David Miros, Chris Evans, Hudson Davis, Michael Pahls, Joe Rivera, and Kyle Schenkewitz.

I dedicate the book, at last, to Patricia with the blue eyes and light brown hair, the joy of my life and (with Kate and Jon) the chief sacrament of my desire for God.

July 10, 2009
500th Anniversary of Calvin's Birth

· 1 ·

The Double Irony of Reformed Spirituality

Nature, Desire, and the Easily Diverted Quest for God's Beauty

> Tis thee, abstractly thee, God of uncreated Beauty, that I love, in thee my wishes are all terminated; in thee, as in their blissful centre, all my desires meet . . . The God of nature, and the original of all beauty, is my God.
>
> —Puritan poet Elizabeth Rowe, *Devout Exercises of the Heart* (1796)[1]

Nothing delights the Calvinist mind and heart so much as the glory of God. This alone is life's chief end. Giving praise to God comes as naturally to the Reformed believer as to the Jesuit scholastic writing the letters "A.M.D.G." at the top of his daily journal. *Ad Majorum Dei Gloriam*, Ignatius Loyola urged his brothers: Do everything to the greater glory of God. It is the same impulse that drives the Hasidic Jew, dancing ecstatically to the *Kavod Adonai* in a Shabbat night service, or the Muslim believer, praying fervently the ninety-nine names of Allah the Mighty and Glorious, or the Hindu devotee, performing *puja* before the stunning beauty of Lord Krishna. Giving God glory is a universal impulse of the human spirit.

We grasp something of the distinctive Calvinist need to glorify God in a novel like John Irving's *A Prayer for Owen Meany*. It celebrates the mystery of a broken universe where God still reigns, where little people may be called to great things. They live in wonderment before a God they cannot fully name. In Presbyterian and Congregationalist churches we hear these familiar words sung with passion to an old Welsh melody: "Immortal, invisible, God only wise,/with light inaccessible hid from our eyes,/most blessed, most glorious, the Ancient of Days,/almighty, victorious, thy great name we praise." Singing in the pews, the faithful participate in the pastime of the angels, ascribing glory to God. No one walks into St. Gile's Cathedral, the High Kirk of Scotland on the Royal Mile in downtown Edinburgh, or into the stately Cathédrale Saint-Pierre where

John Calvin preached in Reformation Geneva, without sensing the reverence these congregations have for a God of splendor, one "who rulest in might."

Wild landscapes best convey the sense of awe that Reformed piety seeks most to nurture. Nature's untamed beauty awakens in my own Reformed heart an atavistic need to praise, to shout back glory. I sense this in the northern woods of Maine where Thoreau discovered a deeply disconcerting wildness; in the desert terrain of Ghost Ranch, New Mexico, where Georgia O'Keeffe touched a primeval mystery in the land; on the windswept island of Iona off the west coast of Scotland, where Columba's coracle landed in the sixth century. These are thin places, where dread and wonder converge in an apprehension of the holy.

At the Iona Abbey, hymn-writer John Bell sings of the Celtic wild goose. It symbolizes a God as wild and glorious as the waves of the Atlantic crashing on the shore nearby. Storms there can be horrendous, with wind sometimes assuming the force and consistency of stone. Leaning into such a wind is like trusting one's weight to an old stone fence. George MacLeod, the Presbyterian founder of the modern Iona Community, customarily welcomed God's coming in the fury of southwesterly Atlantic gales. "Awake for us Thy presence in the very storm," he prayed.[2]

He knew, like Calvin, that God's voice echoes eloquently in thunder and wind. In squall lines racing down from the Swiss alps, the Genevan pastor heard God saying, "I must come to you in a dreadful manner and admonish you in a way that will make you feel, in spite of your murmuring, that you cannot escape the incomprehensible majesty in me." Everything on Iona speaks of this wild majesty, filled with its own astounding beauty. Yet in apprehending such glory, fear inexplicably dissolves into trust. An amazing insight of Celtic and Reformed spirituality is that even the wind completes itself in praise. "The world was founded for this purpose," said Calvin, "that it should be the sphere of the divine glory."[3]

This book deals with a recurring, but neglected, theme in the history of Reformed spirituality: the awakening of desire for a God of ravishing beauty mirrored so generously (and flagrantly) in the world of nature. John Calvin in sixteenth-century Geneva, English and American Puritans in the seventeenth century, and Jonathan Edwards in eighteenth-century Massachusetts all conceived of the world as a theater of God's glory. They commonly spoke of nature as a school of desire, an important means by which humans are trained in awe and longing for God. Given its role in facilitating such desire, the natural world assumes a dignity that ought to suggest human sensitivity to ecological concerns. But creation's beauty has not always led Calvinists to a reverence for God's handiwork. The very tradition that lavishly extols God's glory in creation has often failed to express itself in a serious environmental consciousness. Reformed Christianity possesses stunning resources for ecological justice, but has seldom lived up to its promise.

The Presbyterian Church (U.S.A.) adopted a "Call to Restore the Creation" in its 1990 General Assembly, affirming that "God's work in creation is too wonderful, too ancient, too beautiful, too good to be desecrated" and that "Restoring creation is God's own work in our time, in which God comes both to judge and to restore." Presbyterians for Restoring Creation was subsequently founded in 1995 as a national, grassroots organization working for environmental justice.[4] More recently, the World Alliance of Reformed Churches has given voice to "the cry of the earth in the face of mounting economic injustice and ecological destruction" in its Accra Confession, adopted at its General Council in Ghana in 2004.

Learning to delight in God may seem a strange foundation on which to build an ecological ethic, but the Reformed tradition (when true to itself) sees God's glory as a perfectly natural basis for valuing everything God has brought into being. Back in the early 1960s, well before the first Earth Day celebration and even before the Club of Rome report on the threat of human growth to the natural environment, Lutheran theologian Joseph Sittler issued one of the first theological calls for ecological awareness. He urged that environmental ethics take their cue from the opening question of the Westminster Catechism in the Calvinist tradition. What is the chief end of man and woman (and of all creation, for that matter)? The answer: to glorify God and *enjoy* God forever.[5]

The proper starting point for a Christian attentiveness to the ecological crisis, he argued, is the exercise of delight—the enjoyment of all the manifestations of God's glory in the natural world. *This* is the place to begin—not with paralyzing fear over the potential of ecological catastrophe (as real as that may be) and not with crippling guilt over the human abuse of creation (as awful as that is, too), but with enjoyment and delight. This is the wellspring of free and spontaneous human action. Drawing on Augustine's distinction between what we can properly "use" as human beings and what we should best "enjoy," Sittler insisted that in matters of ecological responsibility, "delight is the basis of right use."[6] Learning to delight in a God of wild beauty is the heart of this book's concern.

This opening chapter explores the ironies of a Reformed tradition that perceives the natural world as a sphere of God's glory even as it fosters a spirituality of desire easily deflected from its focus on the divine. The Puritans, for example, encouraged an ardent longing for God, delighting in (and actively honoring) the earth's reflection of God's beauty. But their desire for the holy could increasingly dissolve into a craving for possession, leading ultimately to the misuse of the earth's resources, a denigration of women, and the eradication of native peoples. The Reformed tradition is full of surprises in the way it articulates a spirituality that joins nature and desire, as well as in the way it expresses (or fails to express) that spirituality in practice. To grasp this, we first have to recognize the importance of creation for Reformed thought in general.

Glorifying God in the School of the Creatures

Richard Baxter drew on a significant theme in the Calvinist tradition when he urged believers to concentrate on "the delights of sense" as part of their daily meditation on holy things. "What a pleasure is it to dive into the secrets of nature," he exulted. "What a deal of the majesty of the great Creator doth shine in the face of this fabric of the world!" He encouraged the devout to attend carefully to the budding of trees, the melodies of songbirds, even the minutiae of physics, astronomy, and geometry. Those who become "most skilful in this gathering art" are also the ones who most fully possess a "spiritual sweetness."[7]

Similarly, English Puritan Thomas Taylor urged that "the voice of the creatures is not to be banished out of the church." Nature must be heard in all the various and colorful ways in which it speaks. He knew the Belgic Confession of 1561 to have spoken for Reformed Christians in affirming the book of nature, alongside the book of Scripture, as a reliable witness to God's infinite glory. "The world is God's book," Taylor affirmed, "no page is empty, but full of lines; every quality of the creature, is a several letter of this book, and no letter without a part of God's wisdom in it."[8]

This meticulous attention to the details of the natural world and their spiritual significance goes back to Calvin himself. He had argued that, "We have been placed here, as in a spacious theater, to behold the works of God, and there is no work of God so small that we ought to pass by it lightly, but all ought to be carefully and diligently observed."[9] In the *Institutes*, he added:

> There is no doubt that the Lord would have us uninterruptedly occupied in this holy meditation; that, while we contemplate in all creatures, as in mirrors, the immense riches of his wisdom, justice, goodness, and power, we should not merely run over them cursorily, and, so to speak, with a fleeting glance; but we should ponder them at length, turn them over in our minds seriously, and faithfully, and recollect them repeatedly.[10]

Viewed from this perspective, the Calvinist at prayer in the world is necessarily a naturalist. The earth is a meticulous and exacting teacher, Calvin observed. It absorbs all our senses in pointing us to a God who "clothes himself, so to speak, with the image of the world, in which he would present himself to our contemplation. . . . Therefore, as soon as the name of God sounds in our ears, or the thought of him occurs to our minds, *let the world become our school* if we desire rightly to know God."[11]

This rigorous scrutiny of the natural world in Calvin and the Reformed tradition has led some historians to speak of a Calvinist influence on the development of Western science. Alister McGrath, for example, suggests that Calvin's contributions to the rise of modern science include his positive encouragement of the scientific study of nature and his elimination of biblical literalism as a major obstacle to scientific investigation.[12] Calvin had encouraged Christian scholars to consult pagan philosophers and scientists, not hesitating to make use of what Origen described as the "gold of the Egyptians."[13] Others have observed that it was no mere coincidence that Puritans in seventeenth-century England were prominent members of the Royal Society of London.[14] The Puritans, said Perry Miller, were "completely hospitable to the revolutionizing discoveries made by physical science during the seventeenth century."[15]

Since the Reformation, then, people influenced by the Calvinist tradition have been taught to regard the world as a lit stage where natural wonders regularly transpire. From Francis Bacon's meticulous study of seventeenth-century science to young Jonathan Edwards's analysis of flying spiders on his father's Connecticut farm, from Cotton Mather's experiments with smallpox vaccinations to Annie Dillard's fascination with the 1,356 living creatures in a square foot of forest topsoil—they knew that praise is a matter of studying in minute detail the footprints of God in the world.

They were, in many ways, heirs of Bonaventure, the thirteenth-century Franciscan who found "vestiges" or "traces" of the Holy Trinity in buttes, butterflies, and buzzards everywhere. Nature points us through the "vestiges" of these concrete mysteries, he said, to the deeper "image" of God in our own created being—our human capacity for rational consciousness—and beyond even that to the "likeness" of God that we discover through the indwelling Christ. In this threefold way, every created being erupts into praise, leading us ultimately to Christ as Lord.[16] The world thus becomes a starting point for the recognition of glory after glory. Calvin expressed it this way: "The sun discovers to our eyes the most beautiful theater of the earth and heaven and the whole order of nature, but God has visibly displayed the chief glory of his work in his Son."[17] A Christocentric thrust necessarily lies at the heart of any genuinely Reformed theology of creation. The natural world points indelibly to the Image from which it is made.

Nature regularly appears in the Reformed tradition as a mirror (*speculum*), school (*schola*), dramatic representation (*theatrum*), painting (*tabula*), clothing (*vestis*), book (*liber*), compass (*circuitus*), or imprint (*impressio*) of God's astonishing glory.[18] Metaphors abound in its eagerness to describe how the world sacramentally points to the majesty of God's presence. For countless theologians and spiritual writers between Calvin and Edwards, the theme was pivotal. A careful attentiveness to the world of nature, as they saw it, never compromised, but only enhanced, their theology of God's grandeur.

They avowed that idolatry could easily creep into artistic representations drawn from a human imagination unchecked by Scripture. They remained wary of "images" used in worship and elegant pageantry in church life. But they perceived the art of creation, God's own aesthetic work in nature, as a pure and reliable witness to God's stunning beauty.[19] Human artistic forms may be contrived and self-referential; but God's own handiwork is an art untainted. When read in the light of Scripture and informed by the Holy Spirit, God's creatures naturally lead the believer to a contemplation of God's glory, full (as they are) of color, amazement, and boundless variety. Puritans like Richard Bernard, in his *Contemplative Pictures with Wholesome Precepts*, warned of the danger of "popish superstition" in the use of images, but celebrated the depiction of God's beauty readily apparent in nature. "The azured sky is his comely curtain" and "the earth his theater."[20]

The early Reformed suspicion of "image making," says William Dyrness, was motivated by its reaction to the "externalization of piety" in late medieval practice. Calvin's "war against the idols" attacked a hollow and perfunctory reverence for external things like relics and pilgrimages. The Reformed tradition, in contrast, actively encouraged a meditation on imagery drawn from Scripture and creation, viewing such images as important aids to the internalization of faith. This validation of an imagination focused on the increase of spiritual desire served, as a result, to legitimate the natural world as a basis for pious and aesthetic meditation.

"Calvin's strong doctrine of creation encouraged him to subordinate artistic activity to the order of creation. He always encouraged his readers to 'listen to creation' and thus felt the best art would 'follow nature.'"[21] He specifically mentioned landscape painting, for example, with its depiction of "animals, towns, and countryside," as a legitimate subject for artists. Some scholars, in fact, have discerned a direct connection between the Reformed conception of nature as a "second book" and the rise of realistic Dutch landscape art in the seventeenth century.[22] The Reformed appreciation of the natural world has been more far-reaching than most of us realize.

The Ironies of Reformed Piety

Given the dark and somber images associated with Calvinism, however, we do not generally think of Reformed piety as exercising spiritual passion or honoring the revelatory character of creation. We picture Presbyterians as caught up in questions of divine election, referring to them as "God's frozen chosen." We can't imagine them using erotic imagery in describing intimate union with Christ. Nor do we think of Christians influenced by Karl Barth as having much sympathy for "natural theology," lending itself too easily to idolatry. Any thoughts of passion or pantheism would seem to be the farthest things from the Calvinist mind.

Reformed theologians, in fact, have traditionally been wary of the very term "spirituality," as if it suggested individualistic experiences given to mystical flights of the imagination. They prefer the word "piety"—referring to a more practical, communal, and societal expression of obedience to Christ.

Yet in the two centuries between Calvin and Edwards we find an extraordinarily passionate, personal, and at times highly erotic longing for God in Reformed piety. We also discern a deep reverence for the earth's beauty as unequivocally revealing God's glory in creation. Through the history of the Reformed tradition, one traces a recurring emphasis on nature as a "school of desire," training the soul in a longing for God. Nature and desire are not at all inimical to the dynamic core of Reformed spirituality.

Calvin's own deepest concern in the spiritual life was with realizing the intimacy of union with Christ. He spoke of God "enticing us to desire," of the soul being "ravished" by God's beauty. The pastor of Geneva gave "the highest degree of importance" to "that joining together of Head and members, that indwelling of Christ in our hearts—in short, that mystical union" by which "we put on Christ and are engrafted into his body." He relished spousal imagery, as Puritans after him would do, speaking of "that sacred wedlock through which we are made flesh of his flesh and bone of his bone, and thus one with him."[23]

Following his lead, Puritans from Francis Rous and Richard Sibbes in England to John Cotton and Edward Taylor in New England rang all the changes on the erotic language of the Song of Songs. They described spiritual devotion as a matter of "lusting" after Christ as bridegroom. They pictured the heart as a marriage bed prepared for the divine lover. The language of foreplay and orgasm became as common in Puritan preaching as anything found in the bridal mysticism of Bernard of Clairvaux or Mechthild of Magdeburg and Teresa of Avila.

All this makes it clear, then, why the Puritans *had* to be so careful in cautioning themselves about the danger of sexual sins. It wasn't that they were sexually repressed, straight-laced prudes—eager to put a bright red

"A" on the dress of every Hester Prynne in the colonies. They simply had a spirituality which fostered so much interior passion that setting appropriate boundaries for their exterior behavior was absolutely necessary.

In a similar way, the Reformed tradition from Calvin to Edwards has expressed an extraordinary delight in nature's beauty as a training ground for desiring God. We don't usually think of Calvin as an exponent of "creation spirituality," yet in a rare excess of language, he could go so far as to say that "nature is God" in recognizing the degree to which the cosmos is utterly filled with God's glory.[24] He celebrated the divine presence in the created world to such an extent that his language could almost slide into pantheism. Jonathan Edwards pushed the same edges in using the Platonic language of emanation to describe God's relation to the world. He spoke of God's glory as a refulgence that flows from the divine being into the world and back again to its luminary. Perry Miller noted that the Puritans were "always verging so close to pantheism that it took all their ingenuity to restrain themselves from identifying God with the creation."[25] The Reformed tradition has persistently discerned God's glory filling the earth, even as it warns that God's being is never contained by anything within it. A panentheist amazement lies close to its heart.[26]

The followers of Calvin have adamantly maintained that the finite is never able to contain the infinite ("*finitum non capax infiniti*").[27] Nothing on earth can encompass God's grandeur, at least not apart from God's consent to be actively revealed in such a way. This insistence serves to protect God's transcendence (and avoid idolatry) in a tradition where the divine self-disclosure in creation is recognized as so generous and compelling. God's revelation in the world of nature accommodates itself to our human weakness, says Calvin. In the wonders of the creative world, God "lisps" to us as to little children, anxiously conveying in flower and falling rain what would otherwise remain entirely beyond our comprehension. Falling in love with the natural world is such a powerful experience, therefore, that it has to be fixed within appropriate limits.

Two great ironies appear in all of this. The Puritans (as Reformed believers) had to set clear boundaries about sexual behavior because of their passionate spirituality. They also had to caution themselves against the danger of pantheism because of the earthly spirituality they espoused—warning themselves against confusing the world's lesser beauty with

God's unique glory. Reformed Christians who seem prudish and proper are thus revealed to be a people of incredibly passionate desire. Calvinist believers who seem so focused on divine transcendence turn out to be closet nature mystics who exult in God's beauty everywhere in creation. This is the double irony of Reformed spirituality. Curiously, the tradition has come to be known more for its *cautions* against pantheism and passion than for its original emphases on nature and desire themselves.

To appreciate this irony we have to recognize Reformed Christianity as more than a monolithic tradition, more than the stereotypical image of the dour Calvinist focused on the next world more than this one. We have to be able to identify more than one way of extolling God's glory within the history of Reformed piety.

Alternative Strains of Reformed Spirituality

Reformed spirituality is generally perceived as a heady, abstract affair, hardly lending itself to beauty and desire, much less to ecological responsibility. But this has been due to an overemphasis on only one strain of the tradition. It highlights those theologians in the centuries following Calvin who developed a single side of his theology, focusing on the inscrutability of God's eternal decrees. Ignoring the Genevan Reformer's attention to creation, they pondered the impenetrable questions of divine sovereignty and predestination. One seventeenth-century Puritan divine, William Perkins, laid out a rigid doctrinal formula in his *Golden Chaine*, proclaiming the glory of God to be as equally served by the reprobation of the damned as by the salvation of the elect. Eighteenth-century New England Calvinists like Samuel Hopkins defined the highest attainment of the spiritual life as a willingness to be damned for the glory of God. This austere spirituality, anxious to exalt God's opaque and omnipotent splendor, represents an alternative—but by no means normative—expression of piety within the Reformed tradition. These Calvinists perceived God's glory as a matter of breath-taking *power* evoking a holy fear. They stood in transfixed awe before the majesty of the divine will.[28]

Others in the same tradition, however, much more readily identified God's glory as a matter of ravishing *beauty* evoking a fervent desire. They remembered Calvin defining "true piety" as that "which loves God as

Father as much as it fears and reverences Him as Lord." God is not only an awesome King, but a father "inclined to allure us to himself by gentle and loving means," one who created the world as a theater of God's glory, using beauty to attract God's children in every possible way.[29]

Seventeenth-century Puritans like Richard Sibbes and Francis Rous marveled at the mystery of God's incomparable love, eliciting the longing of the human heart and the whole of creation. They delighted in the adoration of the Psalmist: "One thing I have desired. . . . to gaze upon the beauty of the Lord" (Psalm 27:4). They found as much allurement as they did danger in apprehending the divine glory. They perceived a God of thunder and light most truly as bridegroom and lover. It was the latter half of the catechism's avowed purpose of the Christian life that gripped them most—the need not only to glorify God, but to *enjoy* God forever.

Scots Presbyterian Olympic champion Eric Liddell summarized their passion in a line from the 1981 film "Chariots of Fire." Responding to his sister's question as to why he spent so much time on running when the call to missionary work in China was far more pressing, he answered: "God made me fast, and when I run, I feel his pleasure." Taking delight in pleasuring God through the exercise of one's natural gifts—one's created being—was, for Calvin himself and many of those who followed him, a deeply held value.

So we find two strains of spirituality that weave in and out of the Reformed tradition in the two centuries between John Calvin's first edition of the *Institutes* and Jonathan Edwards's initial preaching in the Great Awakening. The one begins with a sense of awe at God's majesty, the other with a delight in God's beauty. We usually think of Reformed piety as a highly intellectual response to a transcendent God. Yet it lends itself to provocative sexual imagery in describing God's love and to intense delight in reading God's mysteries from the book of creation.

The genius of the Reformed tradition, in fact, is its ability to combine these seemingly contradictory themes. It knows that God's raw power (apart from God's beauty) can be cruelly destructive and that God's self-absorbed beauty (without the power to communicate it) becomes irrelevant and ineffectual. Calvin and Edwards joined the two in a way that few others in the tradition were able to do. The Genevan Reformer was intrigued by predestination, of course, but was just as fascinated by the world as a theater of God's glory. Edwards was famous for his Enfield sermon on "Sinners in the Hands of an Angry God," but he wrote with equal passion (and far greater frequency) about the wonders of creation.

God's sovereignty and God's beauty are self-correcting and mutually stimulating themes in the history of Reformed spirituality. If we stress only one side of the tradition, we make Theodore Beza's austere predestinarianism indicative of the whole. But if we emphasize only the other we wind up with Ralph Waldo Emerson's amorphous nature mysticism, cut off from any roots in the past. The truth is that both tendencies are part of the Reformed heritage.[30] The warm-hearted, creation-centered strain is important in developing the ecological consciousness we need today. Yet the more austere, transcendent strain is helpful in reminding us of God's wildness—the fact that creation is not solely focused on our anthropocentric needs. As James Gustafson insists, "Piety evoked by a powerful Deity is not always comforting to human beings."[31] It radically challenges human-centered values. Discovering the balance between divine power and divine allurement, then, requires our lifting up the lesser-known part of the tradition, fostering a spirituality of desire that completes and enriches a spirituality of awe.

Contrasting Views of Creation in Reformed Thought

Within these alternative strains of Reformed spirituality we can also identify very different views of the natural world. We see a marked contrast, for example, between earlier and later Reformed theologies of creation when we compare two institutes (or compendiums) of theology that exercised enormous influence among subsequent Calvinists. These are John Calvin's *Institutes of the Christian Religion*, addressed to the King of France in 1559, and Francis Turretin's *Institutes of Elenctic Theology*, written for students at the Geneva Academy by its professor of philosophy in the 1680s.[32] The one moved from the human experience of the created world to God; the other moved from the mystery of God's eternal will to the inexorable logic of human destiny.

Calvin began his *Institutes* with the question of how human beings are able to know God. We have a twofold knowledge of God's wisdom, power, and goodness, he said: one apparent in nature and the other in Scripture.

While the latter provides the "spectacles" by which we properly read the former, the undeniable evidence of God's grandeur lies in the symmetry and beauty of the created world.[33] We see it even in ourselves, for example, made as we are in God's image. Knowledge of God and knowledge of one's self are inseparable, Calvin declared in the opening lines of his *Institutes*.[34] To know oneself as a creature displaying the "imprint" of God's shining glory is to be stricken by a sense of "dread and wonder," undone before God and one's deepest self.[35] It is to recognize one's radiance as a microcosm of the universe made in God's image, as well as one's brokenness, being separated by sin from a loving Creator. Those who respond to the world around (and within) them thus stand in awe at God's greatness, "struck blind in such a dazzling theater," the theater of their own created being.[36]

The *opera Dei*, God's works in creation, clearly point us to Christ as the image of the invisible God, said Calvin. In a remarkable metaphor, he declared that the natural world offers us, as it were, the very "hands and feet" of Christ. If we know the *heart* of the risen Lord through the witness of the Holy Spirit in Scripture, we know his *hands and feet* ("the works of his which are displayed before our eyes") in the earth's wild beauty.[37] Calvin knew that human sin impedes one's ability to read the book of nature aright, but he honored at every turn the clarity of God's glory revealed in creation. In book I of the *Institutes*, he reached such heights in extolling God as Creator that a recent interpreter can say: "If Spinoza has been called 'the God-intoxicated philosopher,' then Calvin surely must be the creation-intoxicated theologian."[38]

Nor was his delight in creation merely an aesthetic or purely spiritual concern. Putting himself in the place of Israelite farmers working the hill country of ancient Canaan, Calvin insisted on ecological responsibility as a proper expression of gratitude to God. "If now I seek to despoil the land of what God has given it to sustain human beings," he argued, "then I am seeking as much as I can to do away with God's goodness." He cautioned people against "damaging trees" in particular, avowing that "*our Lord ordained the land to be as it were our nursing mother*, and when it opens its entrails to sustain us, we should know that this is just as if God extended his hand to us and handed us proofs of his goodness."[39] Honoring creation was for him a Eucharistic impulse, an act of profound thanksgiving for all the sensible ways in which God comes to us.

A century later, Francis Turretin, by contrast, began his *Institutes of Elenctic Theology* not with creation, but with a discourse on theological method, defining the study of "theology" after the pattern of scholastic inquiry. The term "elenctic" refers to a method of strict, logical refutation. In the years following Calvin, Reformed theology had developed under the influence of scholastic debate into a highly speculative exploration of the operations of the divine will. An effort to "unscrew the inscrutable" assumed precedence under Theodore Beza, Calvin's successor at Geneva. Beza, like the Westminster Confession after him, moved the discussion of predestination from a Christological concern about the believer's assurance (where Calvin had placed it) to an analysis of the doctrine of God in itself and the timeless enigma of the eternal decrees. In the process, the beauty of Christ's gracious assurance and the reliability of creation as a mirror of God's glory were subordinated to a fascination with the interior workings of the divine will. Why attend, after all, to the School of the Creatures if one can enter immediately into the hidden secrets of the mind of God?

As a result, the opening paragraph of Turretin's book begins with a scholastic focus on "the Philosopher" (Aristotle) and "the use and true sense of terms." He doesn't get to creation for another 430 pages, where he subsumes it under a discussion of "The Decrees of God in General and Predestination in Particular." He places the works of God in creation under the umbrella of the divine decrees, showing how in creation "[God] executes his decrees outside of himself."[40]

For Turretin, the phenomenal world diminishes in importance when compared to the naked majesty of the God who brings it into being.[41] He had little interest in the *duplex cognitio* (the twofold knowledge of God in creation and Scripture) that had occupied Calvin so much. His attention to the created world as a disclosure of God's grandeur was marginal at best. Calvin knew God (through wonder and delight) in the mirrored beauty of the world that God creates and redeems in Christ. Turretin sought God more directly (with awe and trepidation) in the interior mystery of God's predestinating will.

Puritans like William Perkins and William Ames subsequently followed Turretin's lead, articulating the doctrine of creation under the rubric of the "efficiency" of the divine decrees. They viewed creation (and the Fall) as means by which God "accomplishes predestination," extending God's predetermining power over everything in the world. Creation for them was not a function of God's restless desire to communicate the divine love and beauty to others, as it had been for Calvin and would later be for Edwards.[42] It became an empty field on which God plays out the mystery of God's transcendent will.

Calvin had himself been critical of efforts to approach the divine majesty directly through speculative inquiry, apart from the ordinary means by which God has chosen to be made manifest. He acknowledged that in knowing God through the contemplation of creation it is possible to err, excessively plumbing the secrets of the natural world. But he recognized an even greater threat in the effort to assault heaven through intellectual inquisitiveness.

> Men are commonly subject to these two extremes; namely, that some, forgetful of God, apply the whole force of their mind to the consideration of nature; and others, overlooking the *works* of God, aspire with a foolish and insane curiosity to inquire into his *Essence*.[43]

Calvin, like Luther, was ever wary of a "theology of glory," one that tries to grasp God's splendor through an immediate apprehension of theoretical insight. A "theology of the cross," in contrast, discerns God's presence hidden in the little things of the world, revealed most perfectly in the broken body of Christ on a hill outside Jerusalem.[44]

We find in the Reformed tradition, therefore, remarkably different perceptions of creation and its ability to stir a desire for God in the hearts of believers. Fascination with creation was clearly a part of the original Genevan heritage. While Calvin's descendents may not generally have grasped the implications of his creation theology for environmental justice and an earthy spirituality, some did. The seeds were present, waiting for later development.

Measuring the Impact of a Reformed Creation Spirituality

How, then, can we measure the ethical impact that this creation-centered spirituality may have had on the history of the tradition? Can we discern a significant difference in the way Reformed Christians responded to the natural world? Though it began largely as an urban movement, to what extent has Reformed piety been able to foster an ecological consciousness? We find an answer to this question in a case study of seventeenth-century Puritans on both sides of the Atlantic. There we discern a vigorous defense of the dignity of animal life and a concern for the ethical practice of horticulture that was remarkable for its time.

Environmental historian Keith Thomas shows how Puritans in England were at the forefront of the movement to end cruelty to animals in the early seventeenth century. Drawing on Calvin's own caution that when God placed the beasts "in subjection unto us, he did it with the condition that we should handle them gently," Puritans like Philip Stubbes spoke out against malicious animal sports, including cock-fighting and bear-baiting.[45]

> What Christian heart can take pleasure to see one poor beast to rent, tear and kill another? . . . Although they be bloody beasts to mankind and seek his destruction . . . , yet they are good creatures in their own nature and kind, and *made to set forth the glory and magnificence of the great God* . . . and therefore for his sake not to be abused.[46]

Sir Matthew Hale, a member of the Westminster Assembly, similarly urged compassion for wild creatures, given "the admirable powers of life and sense . . . in the birds and beasts. . . . All the men in the world could not give the like being to anything, nor restore that life and sense which is once taken from them."[47] Some Puritans even opposed hunting as a sport. In 1605, for example, Lord Sheffield complained that his former Puritan tutor, Thomas Bywater, "maintain[ed] to my face that both hawks and hounds, which I did then and do now moderately delight in, were not ordained by God for man's recreation, but for adorning the world."[48] George Hughes, Puritan vicar of Plymouth, spoke for many when he urged that man's dominion (in Genesis 1:28) was "subordinate and stewardly, not absolutely to do what he list to do with God's creatures."[49] It comes as no surprise, therefore, that the first modern legislation against animal cruelty was passed in Puritan Massachusetts in the year 1641.

Nathaniel Ward, a Puritan pastor in Agawam (Ipswich), Massachusetts, drafted a code of laws for the colony of Massachusetts in that year. Among its regulations were the restrictions that "No man shall exercise any Tirranny or Crueltie towards any bruite Creature which are usuallie kept for man's use" and that cattle not be driven over long distances without food and rest. These were incorporated into the "Body of Liberties" adopted by the colony in 1641.[50] We find a precedent for this sentiment in a slightly earlier piece of legislation presented to the Irish parliament in 1635. Thomas Wentworth, Lord Deputy of Ireland and a man of intense Puritan piety, had proposed an "Act Against Plowing by the Tayle, and Pulling the Wooll off Living Sheep." He attacked the "barbarous customes" of farmers attaching plows to horses's tales, sometimes pulling them off, and of sheepherders tearing the wool from the animals' skin instead of clipping it.[51] From these and other examples, we discern a significant Puritan influence on the modern development of animal rights.

The seventeenth-century Puritan condemnation of the mistreatment of animals was rooted in a willingness to question anthropocentrism and a conviction that the dignity of animal life depends on the creatures' own capacity to "set forth" God's glory. In a similar fashion, Puritans took a prominent role in horticultural reform and gardening. Ralph Austen, a Puritan horticulturist in Oxford, spoke of husbandry as a holy work designed "to procure a society and neere fellowship between heaven and earth, for the increase and benefit of trees and plants," as well as the mutual improvement of human life. A social reformer as well as agriculturalist, his vision was to address the nation's economic and social problems by means of a massive program of planting fruit trees.[52]

Developing skills in grafting and fertilizing fruit-bearing trees, propagating mulberry trees for local silk industries, planting timber trees, and even raising bees were all part of a plan by which Austen sought to relieve poverty in the process of establishing the kingdom of heaven on earth. He was a seventeenth-century "Johnny Appleseed," as it were, seeking to realize a fruitarian commonwealth, "another Canaan, flowing with milk and honey."[53]

In a treatise (see figure 1.1) offering an imagined dialogue between people and trees, Austen sounded as much like a Druid as a Puritan. He urged a vastly higher regard for trees, beyond the "temporall profit and pleasure" people usually take from them. Drawing on passages like Psalm 19 and Job 12:7–9, he argued that:

> Men must discourse with Fruit-trees, having learned to understand their Language which though it be not Articulate, and distinct to the outward sense of hearing, in the sound of words, yet they speake plainly, and distinctly to the inward sense. . . .

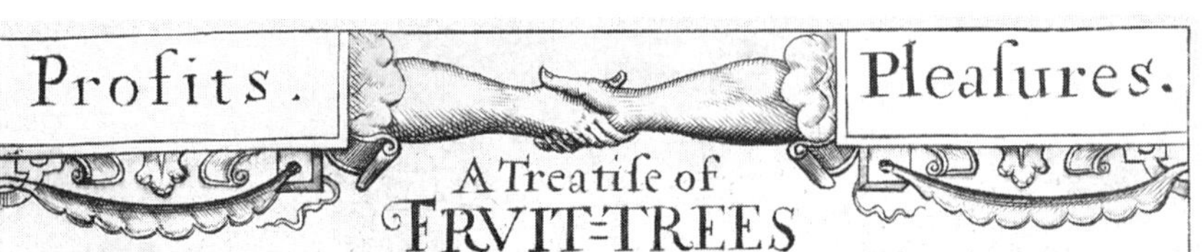

A Treatiſe of
FRVIT=TREES
Shewing the manner of Grafting, Setting, Pruning, and Ordering of them in all reſpects: According to divers new and easy Rules of experience; gathered in ye ſpace of Twenty yeares.
Whereby the value of Lands may be much improued, in a short time, by ſmall coſt, and little labour.
Also diſcovering ſome dangerous Errors, both in ye Theory and Practiſe of ye Art of Planting Fruit: trees.
With the Alimentall and Phyſicall vse of fruits.
Togeather with
The Spirituall vſe of an Orchard: Held forth in divers Similitudes be: tweene Naturall & Spirituall Fruit: trees: according to Scripture & Experiēce.
By RA: AUSTEN.
Practiſer in ye Art of Planting

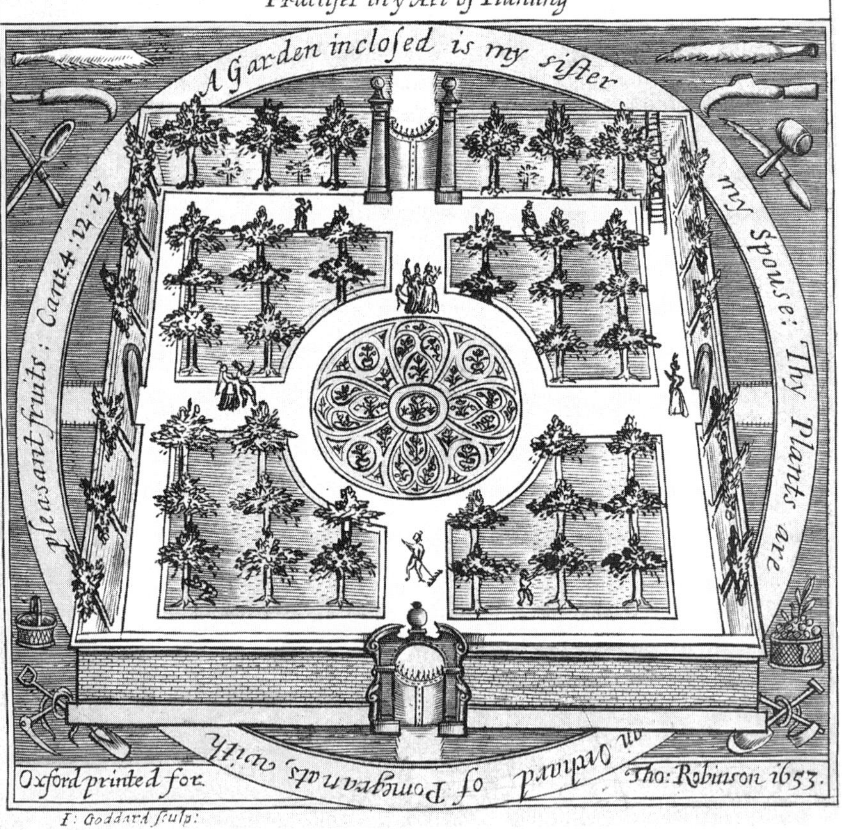

FIGURE 1.1. ©The British Library Board. E.701. (5,6).

> The trees . . . always speake Rationally, and Religiously; in every thing taking Gods part, speaking of his praise and glory; and for the instruction of all men.[54]

He observed that trees invite human beings to delight in their beauty, though they also complain that certain people "greedily pluck us, and tear us, and sometimes breake off some of our Branches to get our Fruits . . ." They "love us too much," he heard them lamenting, as the trees cautioned human beings against an exercise of untempered desire. "Too much love to Creatures abates love to God," they warned.[55]

Other Puritans, like William Lawson, extolled the virtues of gardening as an aid to spiritual reflection as well as a means of improving the quality of life shared with the rest of creation. He urged the faithful, each autumn, to "pause with your selfe, and view the end of all your labours in an Orchard: unspeakable pleasure, and infinite commodity." He cautioned that "although the yield will hopefully be profitable, the means is not all about the end."[56] Responsible agriculture creates a sensitivity to the interdependence of all living things.

In early-seventeenth-century New England, this moral consciousness expressed itself in restrictions regarding the unnecessary cutting down of trees, especially on common lands. In Cambridge, Massachusetts, for example, one Samuel Goffe was "convicted of disorderly falling and takeing away sundry loades of wood from the towne lott." As the century went on, however, and common fields became increasingly less frequent, Puritans were able to clear-cut forests without restraint. One historian of Puritan farming observes that "as the communal features of New England husbandry vanished, the need for common regulation went with them."[57] Taking pleasure in trees as a mirror of God's glory increasingly gave way to an emphasis on commodity alone.

Cecelia Tichi argues that the Puritans came to New England in the seventeenth century with a vision of environmental reform rooted in a vivid apocalyptic hope. They expected that the Christian millennium would originate in the New World and "that God intended Puritans to bear major responsibility for its site preparation."[58] Writers like Edward Johnson thus delighted in the fact that a "remote, rocky, barren, bushy, wild-woody wilderness" was being turned into "a second England for fertilness." He saw it becoming "the wonder of the world," with "neer a thousand acres of land planted for Orchards and Gardens" in Massachusetts, besides "fields filled with garden fruit."[59] What the New World offered in its natural beauty would pale in comparison to what it was becoming as a result of Puritan planting. But as the millennium tarried in its arrival, the task of turning the wilderness into a garden degenerated into a more immediate concern for increased fruit production and market potential. The harbingers of millennial peace and prosperity turned instead to measuring their success in the marketplace.

Initially, then, we discover a significant Puritan sensitivity to environmental concerns, a zealousness to protect and defend a world that echoes the divine image. But the holy desire that prompted this concern was gradually diverted from its original focus on delight in God's glory to an unrestrained use of creation as "serviceable goods" satisfying the needs of an expanding economy.

Women, Native Americans, and the Puritan Desire for Land

The refocusing of desire in colonial New England was deeply rooted in what emerged as a distinctively Puritan mythos of the land. This new mythology served to justify their laying claim to increasing amounts of landed property. As a result, an earlier vision of the world as a theater of God's glory was transformed into a subordinating or adversarial perception of nature as an object demanding possession. New World images of the land were deeply rooted in half-conscious fantasies and fears related to the mysterious allure of women and the ominous threat of Native Americans.

The daughters of Eve and the inhabitants of the dark forest came to represent two different typologies of the natural world, each of them drawn in part from biblical imagery. The Puritans perceived productive farmland, for instance, as exemplifying the feminine attributes of receptivity and fruitfulness, overflowing with abundance (after Psalm 65:9–10). They drew the image of the female body as an enclosed garden from Song of Songs 4:12 and figured that the reverse was true as well. The garden of the New World was a lovely female form inviting (and also requiring) enclosure.[60]

With respect to the dark, Satanic wilderness beyond the Puritan villages, the faithful saw nature as dominated by Native American attributes of chaos and violence. It had to be tamed and suppressed. Puritan preachers regularly compared Indian tribes to the Amalekites and Canaanites who were threatening God's New Israel.[61] Possessing their land was an inescapable part of God's call. Gradually this mythology of the land preempted earlier Puritan notions of the world as a mirror of God's grandeur. In a highly patriarchal society where sexual desire and the attractiveness of land came together in a volatile mix, the unleashed energies of holy longing proved hard to control.

A Reformed spirituality of nature and desire, therefore, could be transformed into an excuse for conquest and misuse. A piety that had spurred an appreciation of created life for some Puritans could evoke the shadow side of human sin for others. At the risk of oversimplifying the complexities of Puritan social thought, we can point to some of the ways by which women, Native Americans, and the land itself were increasingly colonized and turned into objects more readily controlled.

Feminist historian Annette Kolodny observes, for example, that New England Puritans were as inclined as other explorers to personify uncharted land as a woman waiting to be taken and "improved" by male conquerors. The image of the New World as a female body open to the plowshare of the bold husbandman became a dominant metaphor in colonial experience. Thomas Morton, in 1632, spoke of New England as "a faire virgin, longing to be sped, and meete her lover in a Nuptiall bed." William Strachey, in 1609, described the landscape of Maine as a female whose "fertility and pleasure" could be enhanced by "cleansing away her woods" and turning her into a "goodly meadow." In her double entendre of "the lay of the land," Kolodny thus identifies a tendency to objectify the land as woman (both to be used at will), tracing this through the subsequent history of American myth.[62]

Land, women, and sexual desire were also intertwined in the later history of the Salem witch trials. Most of the individuals accused of witchcraft in 1692 were young and single women, anxious about their prospects for marriage, reacting to "stifling gender and class hierarchies." Accusations of witchcraft were further fueled, however, by land disputes between two prominent families competing for access to expanding markets and by socioeconomic tensions between Salem Village and Salem Town.[63] As a result, a desire for land, a suspicion of young women as prone to sorcery and unrestrained passion, and interfamily hostilities all contributed to the subsequent frenzy in Salem, Massachusetts.[64]

Elizabeth Reis observes that Puritans commonly perceived the feminine soul (naturally inclined to insatiability, as they thought) to be an object of desire fought over by Christ and the devil. Consequently, it was easy to view women as particularly subject to being "defiled and deflowered" by Satan's wiles, uniquely inclined to the evils of witchcraft.[65] In this jumble of subliminal anxieties that made up the Puritan psyche, sexual desire was thus stripped of its power to communicate a deeper longing for God and projected onto aberrant women in the process of securing social stability and expanding the prospects for desirable land.

In a similar way, fascination and fear characterized early Puritan encounters with the indigenous peoples of New England. Tales of Native American sorcery and sexual promiscuity, for example, were joined with a Puritan thirst for land in sanctioning attacks on Indian settlements.[66] When William Bradford looked out onto the New England landscape, he saw a "hideous and desolate wilderness, full of wild beasts and wild men." It was, for him, a devilish place, the stronghold of Satan and his "hellish fiends" (referring to the original inhabitants).[67] Far from viewing creation as a mirror of God's glory and honoring indigenous people for their respect for God's handiwork, Bradford legitimated the confiscation of undeveloped Indian land. He saw it as a matter of God's chosen people overthrowing the insidious powers of darkness, exercising dominion in using fence and plow to master the world's wild, disordered state.[68]

Bradford thus justified attacks on native peoples as part of the necessary work of taming a devilish world. The Pequot War, for example, was fought to acquire Indian land along the Connecticut River Valley. Describing the Puritan massacre of Pequot men, women, and children near Mystic, Connecticut, in 1637, Bradford placidly observed:

> Those that escaped the fire were slain with the sword; some hewed to pieces, others run through with their rapiers, so that they were quickly dispatched and very few escaped. [The Puritan attackers] thus destroyed about 400 at this time. It was a fearful sight to see them thus frying in the fire . . . horrible was the stink and scent thereof, but the victory seemed a sweet sacrifice, and they gave the prayers thereof to God, who had wrought so wonderfully for them.

John Underhill, the Puritan military commander at the time, asked himself, "Should not Christians have [had] more mercy and compassion?" Yet he excused his actions by saying that since "sometimes the Scripture declareth women and children must perish with their parents. . . . We had sufficient light from the word of God for our proceedings."[69]

The Puritan ability to justify atrocities in the name of a divinely privileged social order was shocking. Their tendency to project onto aberrant women and fiendish Indians the dark forces of their own desire could lead to horrendous consequences. Making this even worse was a rapidly expanding thirst for land and market growth. In this turbulent combination of disordered passions, it became a matter of convention that nature itself required an exercise of dominion akin to the mastery of unruly women and native peoples. Land was assumed to be an "object" involving proprietary rights, no longer a "subject" mirroring divine beauty.

Consequently, later-seventeenth-century Puritans gave themselves to a reckless overuse of natural resources, as environmental historian William Cronon has shown. An earlier Puritan delight in the wonders of creation did not prevent New England settlers from stripping the land in the process of gathering "merchantable commodities" in a growing mercantile economy. Beavers were almost eliminated from New England in the quest for pelts. Ancient forests were clear-cut, with tall white pine trees taken for ship masts. Seemingly endless supplies of turkeys and passenger pigeons were exhausted. Enormous flocks of the latter were known to darken the sky as they passed over, expressing a "thick antichristian darkness" covering the land. They could be shot at will and eventually driven to extinction.[70]

By the end of the eighteenth century, Timothy Dwight (president of Yale and grandson of Jonathan Edwards) came to lament the "naked and bleak" landscape of New England, where "almost all the original forests of this country [have] been long since cut down." With the sad wisdom of hindsight, he mourned the loss of the great trees, saying, "there appears little reason to hope that they will ever grow again."[71]

The problem of deforestation had begun as a result of Puritan innovations in agriculture, bringing major changes to the New England landscape. Carolyn Merchant suggests that prior to the arrival of English colonists, agricultural practices of indigenous people had involved women assuming responsibility for planting corn in non-invasive ways that mimicked natural patterns. Agriculture among the Puritans, however, became a far more ambitious project, led by men engaged in clear-cutting trees, raising cattle, erecting fences, and planting cash crops useful in a mercantile economy. The "Puritan fathers" thus altered existing ecosystems in radically intrusive ways, displacing the "corn mothers," the earlier horticulturalists who had been deeply attuned to the land.[72] Puritan exploitation of the land proliferated in all sorts of ways as profitable use took precedence over spiritual delight.

What does one conclude from all of this? The stark, embarrassing irony I have to embrace as a Reformed Christian is that the tradition I claim—with all its passionate longing for God's beauty—possesses vast resources for deluding itself. While inclined to celebrate an awesome God amidst the wonders of the natural world, its desire to possess can be cruelly twisted, leading to patriarchal, racist, and anthropocentric attitudes of dominion toward the "other." The Reformed tradition, in short, has frequently failed to live out the implications of the best of its theology.

Analyzing the Character of Puritan Desire

How, then, do we understand a Puritan yearning for God's glory to have been so readily sidetracked by a desire for dominance? How do we make sense of the complicated engines of human desire in any time and place? Rene Girard and Emmanuel Levinas have explored the convoluted operations of longing in ways that I have found especially helpful in analyzing the Puritan dilemma.

Girard, in his study of sacred violence, argues that human desire is mimetic in its origin. We learn to desire what we see other people desiring. We make up for our own perceived lack or insufficiency by imitating the other, exercising an envy that eventually leads to violence. We simply want what the other has. This mimetic rivalry becomes contagious, ultimately threatening to destroy a society. Girard says that ancient cultures learned to focus the violent desires of the group onto a particular scapegoat. Eliminating this person (or this chosen minority) through an act of redemptive violence thus served to bring a catharsis to the system. It temporarily purged the destructive energies of desire as these were focused on a chosen victim.[73]

Girard might suggest, for example, that the Puritan desire for land was prompted in part by their envy of Native Americans' closeness to the earth in bringing forth its bounty and the uncanny power that witches drew from its dark wilderness. These energies elicited Puritan orthodoxy's own desire for mastery of the New World, leading to the elimination of all rivals. The Puritan social order required that devilish Native Americans and demonic women be singled out in the process of "purging" God's New Canaan of unmanaged desires.

Emmanuel Levinas, in his analysis of longing, suggests an important antidote to the process that Girard describes. He perceives the role of philosophy (or theology) as challenging the desire to possess the other, questioning the impulse toward domination that emerges so often in the human experience of wanting. Our need, instead, is to recognize our deepest human longing as a matter of appreciating the "distance" and unique character of what is different from us. Our profoundest desire, says Levinas, "tends toward something else entirely, toward the absolutely other." From this perspective, then, "possession" inevitably destroys, while true *eros* simply delights. It does not try to control what it cannot master. On the contrary, "Eros is awakened by the glimmering and disappearance of beings that remain perennially mysterious."[74] This is a truth that comes close to the heart of Puritan (and Reformed) spirituality, with its deep apophatic sense of a God who always remains beyond the grasp of human understanding.[75] Yet it is also what the Puritans could forget so easily.

In the end, I'm able to claim this Puritan/Reformed tradition, with all of its inconsistencies, as my own—delighting in the astonishing beauty of its vision as well as its occasional success in realizing its dreams. Despite the harsh image of a God who distinguishes so glibly between the reprobate and the elect, despite the early Reformed tradition's affinity to the spirit of capitalism (substituting a desire for goods for its desire for God), despite New England Puritans' deforestation of the land and decimation of indigenous peoples, despite Southern Presbyterians' defense of slavery in America and the Dutch Reformed Church's support of apartheid in South Africa, I acknowledge the sins, but still claim the hopes of those who have come before me. Perhaps we all have to trust, like Macarius of Syria, that God accepts us finally not because of what we do, but because of what we desire.

I've rediscovered in the Reformed tradition a boisterous celebration of the beauty of the natural world—underscoring the profound dignity of creation, urging that we attend to the School of the Creatures in learning environmental responsibility. Its appreciation of the world as a dazzling theater of God's glory is rooted, not in a shallow, "politically correct" ecological sensitivity, but in the mystery of God as Holy Trinity, the brokenness of the cross, and the liturgical power of communal praise. This gives me hope in the tradition, despite the errors of the past.

The Reformed Tradition and American Environmental Thought

How, then, can we finally judge the impact of Reformed spirituality on modern ecological thinking? Can a case be made, at least in part, for tracing the sources of the American environmental movement back to the influence of Calvin and his heirs? It is not accidental, I would argue, that a significant number of prominent naturalists in the history of American environmentalism, poets and activists alike, emerged out of roots in the Reformed tradition—whether English Congregationalist, Scots Presbyterian, Dutch Reformed, or Old School Baptist. These include an amazing range of figures—from Emerson, Thoreau, and John Burroughs to Theodore Roosevelt, Sigurd Olson, and Annie Dillard.[76]

Mountaineer and mystic John Muir memorized hundreds of Bible passages while growing up under the strict tutelage of his Scots Calvinist father. Gifford Pinchot, founder of the United States Forest Service, served as a Presbyterian Sunday School teacher in his youth. Frederick Law Olmsted, the "father of landscape architecture," came from deep Congregationalist roots in Connecticut, where he had been influenced by Horace Bushnell. Poet Wallace Stevens unhesitatingly insisted, out of his own Dutch Reformed background, that "the glory of God *is* the glory of the world."[77]

Louis Agassiz, the famous naturalist at Harvard, was the son of a Swiss Reformed pastor. Asa Gray, a Harvard botanist who became Darwin's foremost advocate in nineteenth-century America, was a committed New School Presbyterian. He claimed that "the Calvinistic doctrine of a calling heightened his determination to be a scientist."[78] Rachel Carson's mother, raised by a Presbyterian minister in Pennsylvania, did much to nurture her daughter's early love of the earth. The father of poet Robinson Jeffers was a professor of Old Testament at the Presbyterian seminary in Pittsburgh. Even the mother of Ed Abbey, that blustery desert writer of the American Southwest, was an organist and choir director at yet another Presbyterian church in Pennsylvania. All of these acquired a deep love of nature in their childhood, perhaps—to a greater or lesser extent—even *because* of their Reformed background.

The influx of American nature writing and nature sensitivity that began with the Transcendentalist movement in the 1830s was not an extraneous phenomenon, rooted solely in arcane notions of Eastern philosophy and European Romanticism. It grew directly out of an earlier New England Puritan tradition. Perry Miller was one of the first to identify a basic continuity, if not clear line of influence, between Jonathan Edwards's praise of God's glory in the natural world and Ralph Waldo Emerson's equally passionate love of nature as a source of mystical insight. He perceived in Edwards's "Dissertation on the End of Creation" a foreshadowing of Emerson's later manifesto on *Nature*. The Transcendentalist poet had come to reject orthodox Calvinism by the time of his Divinity School Address in 1838, but his love of nature drew more from the Reformed tradition than he might have realized.[79]

Emerson's turning his back on a Calvinist past was echoed by numerous others in the environmentalist movement who were equally as "turned off" by their Reformed heritage as they had been formed by it. People like Thoreau, Burroughs, Muir, and (more recently) Joanna Macy left the church of their fathers and mothers to embrace a wider nature mysticism, molded in some cases by Asian thought.[80] Others, like Stevens, Dillard, and (to some extent) Kathleen Norris would turn to the sacramental life of the Catholic Church in search of additional support for their love of the natural world.[81] The Reformed tradition may have been able to incite in them an early delight in the glories of nature. But they were soon put off by its alternative tendency to steer them away from the School of the Creatures lest they fall into idolatry, a Catholic dependence on "images," or a slide into pantheism. The fragmented faith of their childhood ultimately failed to provide the resources they needed for sustaining a vision of the world's beauty. The Reformed tradition, as a result, has the dubious distinction of being the most prevalent *ex*-religious commitment of all American nature writers and activists.[82]

Why have Reformed Christians had to go elsewhere at times to seek the mystical vitality or sacramental depth they found lacking in Reformed worship and piety? It has to do, in part, with the split character of

Reformed thought that I have described in comparing Calvin's and Turretin's theologies of creation. If one understands Reformed theology, after Turretin's model, as primarily absorbed with predestination and God's overwhelming work of redemption, viewing original sin as distorting every aspect of the created order, there is little reason to seek God in the natural world. If, on the other hand, one perceives Reformed theology (after Calvin) as *beginning* with creation, discerning God's glory in all its wonders despite the ravages of sin, there is every reason to take the world seriously.

Emerson and other nineteenth-century naturalists reared in the Reformed tradition often had more exposure to the former than to the latter strain of Calvinist spirituality. God's immanent beauty, illuminating the cosmos, may have been an initial theme in their formation, but God's transcendent power in destroying sin was far more emphasized in their subsequent experience. Nurtured in the school of Reformed spirituality that stressed its other-worldliness and severe theology of divine omnipotence, they lacked sufficient exposure to the creation-centered motifs of the other. They never realized, in short, all that the tradition had to offer.

This austere, one-sided emphasis of Reformed thought in New England life increased in the years following Jonathan Edwards's death. As with Turretin's shift in theological emphasis in the years after Calvin, Edwards's students—Samuel Hopkins, Joseph Bellamy, and Nathaniel Emmons—turned from their mentor's theocentric piety and focus on God's glory in creation, to a legalistic, anthropocentric moralism that highlighted divine omnipotence and the importance of justifying God's ways to the human mind.[83] Edwards's highly affective theology, which had relished an aesthetic taste for God's splendor, thus dissolved into a rationalistic effort to vindicate God's wisdom in the permission of sin. Honoring the world's beauty as a window onto God's glory degenerated into a narrow "obedience to the law of God."[84] Reactions to the dark severity of this "New Divinity," as it came to be known, were extremely pronounced in New England Unitarian circles where transcendentalists like Emerson and Thoreau had their beginnings. What they knew of a vibrant creation-sensitive Calvinism was profoundly limited.

In John Muir's case, it was his father's fierce commitment to the blustery Calvinism of John Knox that prevented him from readily discerning

Calvin's God of untamed magnificence and alluring beauty as filling the earth. The younger Muir hungered for a God as wild and beautiful as the wilderness with which he had fallen in love, but he found little to support that in his own little corner of the Church of Scotland.

"All wildness is finer than tameness," exclaimed the later John Muir, that inveterate post-Calvinist lover of the High Sierras.[85] Climbing tall trees in the midst of raging storms, dancing in flooded mountain streams, celebrating earthquakes, he exulted in the unrestrained world of nature about which his harsh Scots Presbyterian father had often warned him. Daniel Muir had considered his son's nature writing a worthless, even dangerous thing, telling him to give up his "cold icy-topped mountains" and come back to "our lovely Jesus."[86] As a young man, Muir turned his back on the family faith, but never gave up his love of the nature psalms. He read voraciously in Thomas Dick, a Scots Calvinist philosopher and astronomer who everywhere found "manifestations of God in the material universe."[87] This restless explorer of California's mountains came to recognize that the rocks themselves are alive. "Glaciers move in tides," he proclaimed. "So do mountains, so do all things."[88]

Remaining a deeper Calvinist than he knew, Muir insisted that, "Every particle of rock or water or air has God by its side leading it the way it should go. How else would it know where to go and what to do?"[89] He found God's glory written in "stormy sermons" preached relentlessly by towering clouds over Yosemite Valley and whispered by water-ouzels almost drowning themselves in ecstasy as they soar through torrents of white water. Muir's universe was wild because of the God he found revealed within it. "In God's wildness lies the hope of the world," he declared.[90]

The notion, urged by some, that John Muir could reverence wilderness only by renouncing his roots in the Reformed tradition comes from a very partial reading of the tradition itself, not to mention a failure to appreciate Muir's own continuing faith. References to God's glory filling the world around him echoed everywhere in his writings. His editor continually scolded him for his overuse of the word "glorious."[91]

The Reformed influence on American environmentalism, therefore, has not been insignificant. Donald Worster, in his study of the roots of the movement, traces back to Calvinist Protestantism a sense of moral activism, ascetic discipline, and aesthetic spirituality which, he says, has contributed to a developing ecological consciousness in the American mind. He does not hesitate to identify Jonathan Edwards (among others) as exemplifying the "nature-appreciating spirituality" that later flourished in activists and mystics like John Muir. From Edwards to Muir, there is an ever tightening connection between the aesthetic and the ethical, between an appreciation of the Connecticut Valley as a mirror of God's grandeur and a longing to preserve the Yosemite Valley as an expression of natural, even mystical beauty. Delighting in beauty leads naturally to the protecting of beauty in a Reformed theological aesthetic.

Through the centuries, then, Calvin's God of beauteous splendor has remained large (and wild) enough to capture the human imagination in ways that give distinct value to the earth. What started in sixteenth-century Geneva, came to bud in seventeenth-century Puritanism, and blossomed in Edwards's eighteenth-century thought would take new directions in the nineteenth-century work of Emerson, Nevin, Bushnell, Muir, and others. In the twentieth century, it went on to express an increased ethical responsibility, with writers like Jürgen Moltmann, George Hendry, Holmes Rolston III, Richard Cartwright Austin, Calvin DeWitt, and Steven Bouma-Prediger developing new environmental theologies out of the Reformed heritage. Even Sallie McFague has been deeply influenced by Karl Barth and Reinhold Niebuhr.[92] Over the last 450 years, all these figures have been in search of beauty, delighting (like Calvin) in a world that displayed the very "hands and feet" of God.

The Reformed tradition, in summary, recognizes desire for God's beauty as the proper starting point for theological reflection on environmental ethics. How we care for the planet depends upon how we perceive it. If we view the earth as a school, mirror, or theater of God's glory, we naturally desire its wholeness as a consequence of our amazement at its stunning beauty pointing us back to God. On the other hand, if we are distracted by the earth's loveliness as an end in itself, we bear witness to the perils of a desire that tries to possess its object rather than standing in awe before it. We end up betraying God and the creation as well.

The Whole World Singing: A Journey to Iona and Taizé

O hidden Mystery, Sun behind all suns,
Soul behind all souls, in everything we touch,
In everyone we meet, your presence is 'round us
And we give thanks.
But when we have not touched, but trampled you in creation,
When we have not met but missed you in one another,
When we have not received but rejected you in the poor,
Forgive us.

—Iona Communion Service Liturgy[1]

Standing beside Lake Geneva where the Rhone River begins its flow to the sea, I look up the hill toward the old cathedral where John Calvin preached in the sixteenth century. I try to imagine a conversation that he and Catholic Bishop Francis de Sales might have had if they had met here four centuries ago. These two humanist scholars were both trained in law, were both afire with the love of God, and both ended up in this lovely city of Geneva, though separated by a generation.[2]

Calvin and de Sales shared a common delight in the role played by all created beings in singing the glory of God. Calvin, in his Psalms commentaries, and de Sales, in his *Treatise on the Love of God*, emphasized a rich theology of divine providence. Their God was intimately involved in loving and sustaining the natural world. Calvin spoke of the world as a theater of God's glory; de Sales spoke of beauty as God's way of attracting the affection of all creation.[3]

Pausing between visits to two contemporary religious communities where both of these traditions are joined, I'm curious to ask what Catholic and Reformed spiritualities share in common. I'm on a pilgrimage of sorts, having spent my academic life as a Reformed theologian on a Roman Catholic faculty. I stand on the edge of the two traditions, loving both. The Taizé and Iona communities remind me how that remains possible.

A little over two hours by high speed train from Geneva is the Taizé Community, known around the world for the beauty of its chanted worship. This monastic community of a hundred Protestant, Roman Catholic, and Eastern Orthodox monks was founded in the early 1940s by Brother Roger Schutz, a Swiss Reformed pastor. Having launched a communal experiment among students at the University of Lausanne, Brother Roger sought a site for a more permanent community in eastern France. He chose the village of Taizé, not far from the border of the Nazi-occupied zone. There, in the midst of rural poverty, his community stirred controversy with its clandestine efforts to help Jewish refugees escape into Switzerland, its organization of a milk co-op among local farmers, and its use of the vacant Roman Catholic village church for daily prayer.

Seven hundred miles to the northwest along the rugged isles of Scotland's western coast, a restored Benedictine abbey is home to the Iona Community. It was founded by George MacLeod, a Church of Scotland pastor who organized unemployed stone masons and carpenters to rebuild the abbey in the 1930s. Here members of the community bear witness to the concerns of liturgical renewal, social justice, and ecumenical sharing. Here, too, the praise of God resounds in a daily pattern of prayer that echoes Columba's first journey to that remote island in the mid-sixth century.

Like Brother Roger, MacLeod sought to renew the church with a liturgically focused common life that embraced poverty. As a pastor he had responded to the plight of workers in the shipbuilding yards of Glasgow during the Depression. The community he founded on Iona became controversial for its strange mix of radical politics, a Catholic sense of the church and sacraments, and a call for reconciliation among Christians. Its members were accused of being crypto-Roman Catholics in Presbyterian guise.[4]

Both communities are based on a rule and a common life of prayer that joins work and worship in a Benedictine pattern. Morning prayer at Iona never concludes with a benediction; evening prayer never begins with a call to worship. Instead, the whole day becomes a continuation of the prayer that frames it at either end. Similarly, the three daily periods of prayer at Taizé lack any formal conclusion. Soft chanting persists as people gradually leave to attend to other activities. In each place, praise governs the order of the day.

Iona and Taizé are located at remote sites, places on the edge, where a concern for marginalized peoples expresses itself naturally. Both are determined to cross ethnic, economic, and ecclesial boundaries. Both reach out to the world while also reaching back to an earlier local tradition—Celtic in the one case, Cistercian in the other.

It is no accident that the two Reformed communities have identified so deeply with earlier spiritual traditions in the life of the church. These earlier strains of spirituality offer both support and correction for them. Reformed Christians echo the earlier Benedictine emphasis on *lectio*, for example, the diligent and reverent reading of Scripture. It is central to their charism, in preaching and practice alike. The Word stirs them to action, to involvement in the world. Yet Calvinists need to hear the Benedictine caution that *lectio divina* always finds its completion (and the recycling of its action) in contemplation. Presbyterians have never been especially good at silence.

Like the earlier Celtic tradition, Reformed Christians have also insisted on working out their faith in the world. Their relationship to Christ has to express itself in politics, economics, and social justice. Yet as urban-oriented Christians, awed by God's transcendence, they have been slower to recognize the revelatory character of the earth and its witness to God's presence in their midst. Celtic Christianity anchors them in the soil, reminding them of the importance of other creatures as partners in praise.

The two communities thus remain faithful to their roots in different ways. Taizé is a celibate, monastic community of men living under a common rule with Brother Roger as prior (until his tragic death in 2005).[5] It has smaller fraternities of brothers living among the poorest of the poor in Bangladesh, Calcutta, and Brazil, but the center of the community is Taizé. In contrast, the Iona community consists of 220 members spread all over the world, including laity and clergy, women and men, Protestant, Roman Catholic, and Eastern Orthodox. They too follow a rule that requires a daily practice of prayer and Bible study, the tithing of their money in support of common peace and justice concerns, and regular meetings with fellow members. Though a small contingent of members remains on Iona to help run programs and to welcome guests, the community in general follows the Celtic pattern of wandering missionaries launched on pilgrimage around the world.

Taizé appeals to the ear, while Iona more readily attracts the eye. People who return from Taizé invariably speak of the beauty of the chanted songs that constitute its worship. Those coming back from Iona mention the wild splendor of the island itself. But Iona is celebrated for its creative music as well (with John Bell, for example) and Taizé is surrounded by the beautiful vineyard-covered hills of Burgundy. Together they point to a common desire—a wish that the whole of creation break into song in awe of God's glory.

I was left with two dominant impressions from my encounter of these two communities. The one is an astounding sense of the adoration of God as still very much alive at the beginning of the twenty-first century. The other is an awareness of the breadth and diversity of the immense company engaged in this work of adoration.

The wind howled as I sat alone one afternoon in the great silence of the South Isle Chapel of the Abbey Church on Iona. My wife and I had made our way by two ferries and a bus from the distant harbor town of Oban. The wind beat on the wooden door nearby, rattling its iron latch, demanding entrance. From high above the nave a finger of wind had located a cracked window, whistling through it from time to time in a high soft scream. The wind was soon singing in multiple registers, like the voices of Tibetan monks chanting. I was aware of something going on in that place wholly apart from me—something I could only label as praise.

Suddenly two blackbirds entered the church, seeking shelter from the coming storm. Their songs echoed from the wooden ceiling and stone walls like a descant to the urgent melody of the wind. One of the birds walked up to me, stopping three feet away, and then turned to enter one of the choir stalls—as if to attend more properly to its singing. All this seemed natural in that place, as if nothing were more ordinary than a choir of blackbirds managing the psalms with exquisite beauty at the afternoon office.

Dare we imagine that the company of praise does not include the rest of creation? I asked that question again as I later sat beside the small, open window of the Abbey library and looked out across the sound toward the Isle of Mull. Sitting there was like being aboard a ship. The curved wood ceiling, shuttered wooden windows, and rough planked floors lent it a seaworthy air. My wife and I watched the sun rise from that window early one morning, listening to waves lapping on black rocks along the shore. The scene, framed by oak and foregrounded by walls of books, suggested John Scotus Eriugena's notion of the joining of the two sandals of Christ—Scripture and Nature—the latchets of which John the Baptist knew himself unworthy to loose.

From within the library, we looked out with eyes formed by the Word—Gaelic Bibles, works on Celtic spirituality, histories of the church in Scotland on nearby shelves. We gazed out at a "thin place," as MacLeod described it, a natural world as stark and simple as it is beautiful, hinting perhaps of other worlds beyond. In that one fragile moment at dawn we took our parts in a single community of praise—green grass lit by the rising sun, a gull's cry coming from across the water, two humans looking on with awe.

The journey to Taizé brought similar experiences. From Geneva, we made our way by train and bus to the welcome center at the small community north of Lyon, and then to the little room assigned us in an old farmhouse. Sitting that evening on the hard concrete floor of the Church of Reconciliation, I chanted songs alongside hundreds of others, watching candles flicker against the bright red-orange hangings stretched above the altar. Built on a hill beside the village of Taizé, this church is an unassuming building that can expand to shelter thousands of young people who come speaking dozens of languages. One would think the chasm between these individuals is impossible to bridge.

Yet something happens in the continual repetition of simple phrases put to song. The words and music, in French, Spanish, Polish, German, and Latin, are echoed over and over like a mantra. Sound and meaning are gradually internalized until repeating the words no longer requires conscious effort. People of many cultures find themselves praying in one language, with one heart.

The phrases tell of adoration and human longing, of God's tenderness and Teresa of ávila's consolation that, ultimately, nothing can trouble,

FIGURE 1.1X. The Restored Benedictine Abbey on the Island of Iona.

nothing can frighten. *Notre Dieu est tendresse. Nada te turbe, nada te espante.* Other chants exult in unrestrained joy: *Christus resurrexit.* Yet another melody celebrates the unity it extols: "Praise the Lord, all nations. Sing Allelulia." And not only all nations, but *omnia genera*—all species, too. From the red maples outside the church door to the yellow leaves of distant vineyards—even the nettles in nearby fields, once used by poor farmers to make soup. Everything is finally absorbed in praise.

We gathered in a circus tent for our daily meals (often just a bowl of soup and some bread) and for Bible study. Amidst the Babel-like diversity, Brother Wolfgang spoke alternately in German and in English, while others translated into Latvian, French, Italian, and Dutch. He laughed at one point about our confusion over a particular idiom, reflecting that, despite all the difficulties, "the problems of translation in our little European world are good. They require that we make sure nothing is forgotten, that no one is missed." He noted that in places like the United States, where everyone speaks a common language, it is easy to assume that everyone understands (and is understood), when that may not at all be the case. Carefully listening to each other's languages is prerequisite to any sense of common worship.[6]

FIGURE 1.2X. Inside the Church at Taizé.

Out of my experiences at Taizé and Iona, I thought of three theological insights that are common to both communities.

(1) *Dei gloriae.* The first is that the Reformed, Benedictine, and Celtic traditions to which these groups are indebted have always emphasized the praise of God's glory as the chief end of creation. Catholic historian Louis Bouyer celebrated the extraordinary importance that Calvin attributed to giving glory to God. He regarded the Reformed tradition as the most lucid and courageous attempt among the original Protestants to recover a sense of God's grandeur without minimizing the intimacy that God longs to maintain with all of creation.[7] He knew that Calvin shared this with Columba, Bernard of Clairvaux, and Ignatius Loyola as well.

They all emphasized that theology has to begin and end with doxology—a common vision of God's astounding beauty. Everything else flows from this. Action for social justice, for example, is simply the form that praise must assume in the marketplace and other corridors of power. If these energies do not flow naturally from the exercise of wonder, they have no life. If the church lacks clarity about its first love, then it has little to offer (from therapy to charity) that cannot be better provided by others.

Moreover, churches will not draw young people to their doors if they shy away with embarrassment from any mention of adoration. Thousands of young people come to Taizé *because* of a deep longing for contemplation, a desire to worship. There the adults are guests and the young people are teachers. I was stunned by their attentiveness to prayer. The whole earth shouts glory along with them, as George MacLeod would insist.

(2) *Sacramentum mundi.* A second theme arising from the two communities is the notion of the sacramental character of the world, the reminder that praise is always local, growing out of the specific memory and ecology of the world from which it rises. To rightly celebrate God's glory is to recognize the earth's dignity as a sacrament of God's presence. Bouyer identified the potential flaw in Calvin's grandiose vision as a tendency to reduce the creature to nothingness in the process of enhancing divine transcendence.[8] In contrast, worship at Iona and Taizé emphasizes the worth of every creature in glorifying God as Lord of creation.

When St. Columba chanted the three-fifties (all 150 psalms) down by the sea each morning before dawn, he did so with an awareness that the whole world joined him in benediction. He even claimed that a house fly often traced out the lines of the text for him at holy office so that he wouldn't lose his place. He knew that praise was natural to every created being. This sense of the world as celebrant of God's glory, witnessed also in the crops, farm animals, and grapevines around Taizé, underlies the call for ecological justice arising from both communities. They recognize the quest for a sustainable future as a natural extension of praise.

(3) *Peregrinatio perpetua.* A final theme drawn from the lives of these two communities has to do with the radically open-ended character of pilgrimage in the Celtic tradition. In its original form, this involved saints like Columba taking to his coracle (that bobbing teacup of a leather boat, without rudder or oars), trusting the waves to carry him wherever they might.

Such a spirit demands a readiness to travel light, a practice of living simply. It also nourishes sensitivity to the poor, an awareness of the tenuous life that involuntary pilgrims face, as well as an eagerness to learn the languages that facilitate the crossing of borders. Taizé expresses all of these characteristics in its stark simplicity of lifestyle and its extraordinary practice of hospitality. This is a community that not only helped Jewish refugees at the beginning of the war, but also fed German prisoners after it in a prison camp nearby. Compassion, as they knew it, is a wide land without partition.

Brother Roger thought this theme of ongoing pilgrimage should even challenge the church of the Reformation to examine its role as a permanently separate body in the Church of Christ. He said it should also prod Roman Catholics to embrace the Second Vatican Council's call to be a pilgrim church, always in movement. In the early days of Taizé, Marc Boegner, a Reformed pastor, had criticized Roger's efforts to advocate reconciliation with Rome. But near the end of his life, he wondered if Reformed Christians might best begin witnessing to reformation from within a universal church, rather than outside it. He asked Roger: "Should we now, after the Vatican Council, say that the brackets should be closed on Protestantism?" Roger's answer was startling: "Of course you should say so, because all the reforms sought after in the sixteenth century have been achieved and more!"[9]

His sanguine appraisal of reconciliation with Rome was undoubtedly rooted in his affection for Pope John XXIII, who had praised the Taizé experiment as "that little Springtime" in the church's life. The tendency of some in the Catholic Church to renege on the promises of Vatican II makes an undivided church harder to imagine today. Yet the hope for unity is one that we all have to share. The way toward reconciliation is never simply back. Reformed and Roman Catholic Christians have to journey together, as Karl Rahner said, to a home where none of us have been before.[10]

On the eve of October 31, 1999, my wife and I attended a service in the old Roman Catholic church down in the village of Taizé, celebrating the signing of the agreement between Roman Catholics and Lutherans on justification by faith the following day in Augsburg. In that small stone church where the community had originally begun, a Lutheran brother from Taizé celebrated a special Eucharist for a group of German Christians to which we were joined. With tears in our eyes, we sang the chants of Taizé and prayed for unity in the Church of Jesus Christ.

It was a foretaste of a community that John Calvin and Francis de Sales had already realized, a community that embraces Orthodox, Reformed, and Roman Catholic Christians in celebrating the differences we all bring to a common family identity. As Calvin and de Sales would remind us, it is a community that includes the rest of creation as well. It is evident that all creatures, said Calvin, from those in the heavens to those under the earth, are able to act as witnesses and messengers of God's glory.

That is what makes Iona and Taizé so compelling. Open to all the sundry languages of the human and more-than-human world, the two communities embrace all of creation in their praise. One of the petitions in the Communion Liturgy at Iona asks of God, "May we know that, in touching all bread, all matter, it is you that we touch." The liturgy concludes with a final benediction, saying: "With the whole realm of nature around us, with earth, sea and sky, we sing to you." That's a song that all of us who are on pilgrimage can sing together.

· 2 ·

John Calvin on the World as a Theater of God's Glory

> You cannot in one glance survey this most vast and beautiful system of the universe, in its wide expanse, without being completely overwhelmed by the boundless force of its brightness.
>
> —John Calvin, *Institutes of the Christian Religion*[1]

For a long time I've had a love-hate relationship with John Calvin. I love the undomesticated wildness of his great and glorious God. It puts to rout the sedate, housebroken deity that masquerades as God in so many churches today. I delight in the energetic power of his mind. He anchors theology in Scripture and tradition while demanding its practical application in transforming culture. I marvel at his embrace of paradox. His God of majesty, who causes the earth to tremble, is also a God who weeps, whose "astonishing warmth and tenderness of affection" is that of a mother giving birth, gasping in labor.[2] This is the Calvin I love.

Yet I also cringe at Calvin the polemicist, whose acid tongue harshly judged Roman Catholics and Anabaptists as monkeys, dogs, pigs, and wolves.[3] I shrink from his tendency to conceive of God as wrapped in words and stripped of liturgical imagery, logically held captive to his own horrible decree of double predestination. I wrestle with the Calvinist tradition I've inherited from him—with its long sermons and heady intellectualism, its bourgeois respectability and all-absorbing concern to do things "decently and in order." I am, at best, a reluctant Calvinist.

What warms me most to the Genevan Reformer, however, allowing me to forgive him so many other sins, is his delight in the natural world, his uninhibited celebration of creation. Calvin was as smitten by God's beauty as he was overwhelmed by God's power. His writings abound with creative images and metaphors. Like the Psalmist, he uses the language of nature to extol God's grandeur, admitting the limited capacity of human speech. He marvels at an entire world that exuberantly participates in praise.

Calvin's favorite metaphor in conveying the beauty of the natural world was to speak of it as a theater of God's glory. Every human being is "formed to be a spectator of the created world and given eyes that he might be led to its author by contemplating so beautiful a representation."[4] Moreover, God is the principal actor in this vast theatrical production, evoking desire by "showing himself in the visible splendor of his apparel."[5] As Calvin understood it, the contemplation of God's beauty on the great stage of nature is a performance of desire that incorporates the whole of creation. It is a cosmic as well as human impulse, resulting in transformative relationships at every level. All created reality, extending each moment from the hand of God, is shot through with longing. Shared praise is the end toward which everything is turned.[6]

It may seem strange to find John Calvin using the "theater" as a metaphor.[7] We do not associate positive images of theatrical life with sixteenth-century Geneva. Nor does his image of the "world as theater" fit the usual pattern of this literary trope in the history of Western thought. From Stoics (like Seneca and Marcus Aurelius) to patristic writers (like John Chrysostom and Augustine) to sixteenth-century Christian Platonists (like Ficino), the metaphor generally pictured humans as principal actors in a play determined by a divine playwright.[8] In this pattern, the *theatrum mundi* offered a reflection on the vanity of human life, the failure of human actors to play their parts well. Calvin, in contrast, conceived of the world as a theater for the contemplation of divine beauty, with *God* assuming the central role at the heart of the action on stage.

This chapter examines Calvin's metaphor of the world as theater, exploring his conception of worship as mimetic performance. He perceived the whole of creation as imitating God's beauty, absorbed in a desire for God's glory that adds luster and vitality to what it celebrates. Calvin was fascinated by how God allures (and instructs) us through the wonders of the natural world. The unselfconscious simplicity of the earth's creatures, mirroring God by their very being, invites the human heart to share in a common praise. This joint worship is a performative act, in Calvin's thinking, creating the world of wonder that it celebrates. The world is sustained in the process of giving glory to God.

The Metaphor of the Theater in Calvin's Thought

The Genevan reformer's theology was not characterized, as often thought, by a rigid "system" centered on the doctrine of predestination, but by "the constant reappearance of favorite images, metaphors, or figures of speech."[9] Calvin was formed by his training as a Renaissance humanist. His language was more rhetorical than dialectical. He made use of theatrical imagery to trace the entire course of salvation, for example. "In the vast theater of heaven and earth," Ford Lewis Battles says of Calvin's vision, "the divine playwright stages the ongoing drama of creation, alienation, return, and forgiveness for the teeming audience of humanity itself."[10] In the broadest sense, this theater is the entire created world, summoned to a common praise. But Calvin spoke more particularly of the church as a distinct company of players who have most fully grasped (and been grasped by) the drama enacted on stage.

The image of the theater became an organizing metaphor in Calvin's thought, putting worship at the heart of his theology.[11] The human adoration of God, as modeled in Scripture and echoed in creation, was the goal of his *Institutes of the Christian Religion*. His theological masterpiece should be read as a *summa pietatis* rather than as a *summa theologica*. In the long subtitle of the first edition of the *Institutes* (1536), Calvin described his book as "encompassing almost the whole sum of piety (*pietatis summam*) and whatever it is necessary to know about the doctrine of salvation, a work most worthy to be read by all who are zealous for piety."[12] Doxology was for him the chief goal and delight of all created beings.

Calvin employed a cluster of metaphors to describe the "spectacle" of God's glory that he found so apparent in nature. He spoke of the world as a "mirror" or "living likeness" of God.[13] It is a "painting" representing in stunning strokes the divine splendor, a "spacious and splendid house," a "book written in large enough letters," even a "compass" orienting people in their passage through life. "The contemplation of heaven and earth," he wrote, "is the very school of God's children."[14] Each of these images underscored the two principal roles played by the world as God's "glorious theater." Its purpose is to delight and to instruct, pointing its spectators to the wonder of God's sustaining presence. Even when Calvin used the metaphor of a “machine” to speak of the natural world, it is as if he had in mind the mechanisms used to operate the curtains and sets of a stage production.

> The whole machinery of the world would fall out of gear [*diffluerет tota mundi machina*: the whole frame would collapse] at almost every moment and all its parts fail in the sorrowful confusion which followed the fall of Adam, were they not borne up from elsewhere by some hidden support.[15]

The word *theatrum* itself appears at least seven times in the *Institutes* and dozens of times in Calvin’s sermons and biblical commentaries, especially in his commentaries on Genesis, Isaiah, and the Psalms.[16] He not infrequently resorted to the colorful imagery of dramatic performance in his writings. William Bouwsma observes that theatrical metaphors pervaded all of sixteenth-century discourse. It was not unusual, therefore, for Calvin to summarize his career in theatrical terms when he wrote to Melanchthon: “I am not ignorant of the position in his theater to which God has elevated me.” Speaking of the church in Geneva as God’s particular theater-of-choice for him, he said he was “satisfied with its approbation, though the whole world should hiss me, I shall never want courage.”[17]

Calvin stood in a historical tradition, stretching from Philo in the first century to Jean Bodin in the sixteenth, which perceived the natural world as a theater in which God’s providential hand is readily apparent. Philo, in his treatise *On the Creation of the World*, had presented the drama of creation as a way of stirring delight and causing people to marvel at God’s unexpected direction of events. His depiction of God as principal actor in the world theater and his emphasis on the twin goals of pleasing and instructing the audience would lay the foundation for Calvin’s later work.[18]

Moreover, when Calvin used the image of the world as theater, he drew on a long medieval tradition of liturgical drama as a means of delighting and instructing audiences.[19] He viewed the sudden Aristotelian reversal found at the heart of great tragedy and comedy alike as corresponding to the drama of the gospel. Aristotle had spoken of the unexpected “reversal” (*peripeteias*) found at the hinge of every good plot. This sudden change of fortune occasions a telling encounter for the principal character(s) of the play, effecting a change of heart and mind on the part of the audience as well.[20]

With the emergence of the medieval theater in the ninth and tenth centuries, an empty tomb and a crib were used as props in Benedictine monasteries at the Easter and Christmas liturgies. This practice gave rise to the *quem quaeritis* trope, a sung dialogue later expanded into a larger dramatic production. Actors portraying the shepherds meeting the angel in the field, or the three Marys with the angel at the tomb, responded in each case to the question: "Why do you seek him (*quem quaeritis*) in a manger, or in the tomb?" The great "reversal" of the gospel was captured in these twin mysteries of the incarnate Son of God being found (of all places) in a manger and the risen Lord no longer contained by the power of the grave. From these simple beginnings came the mystery and miracle plays of the later Middle Ages, as well as the popular theater that flourished in Strasbourg and Geneva on the eve of the Reformation.[21]

By the sixteenth century, these plays were featured in larger, non-liturgical settings, with the actors often performing satirical plays and farces on the same program. This mixing of sacred and secular motifs made drama increasingly suspect, particularly among some of the Protestant reformers. Calvin was critical of the popular theater on the grounds that "theaters resound with lying fictions," and that "the unlearned are carried away when they are persuaded that what they see represented in the theaters is true."[22] Yet plays were staged in Calvin's Geneva with his explicit approval. In 1546, for example, a controversy broke out over a drama based on the Acts of the Apostles, written by one of the local pastors. Calvin supported the production, even when Nicholas Cop—a fiery reformer—preached virulently against it.[23]

He also approved the performance of other plays, including one celebrating the new alliance of Geneva with Bern in 1558.[24] His attitude toward the theater was similar to that of Martin Bucer, his colleague at Strasbourg. In a treatise on the performance of theatrical works, Bucer defended the production of tragedies and comedies (especially those drawn from biblical figures), even when performed in the vernacular. Like Calvin, he saw the startling Aristotelian reversal of fortune—leading unexpectedly to a fall (in a tragedy) or to success (in a comedy)—as morally instructive, fostering faith in God.[25]

The theater, for Calvin, thus served as an apt metaphor of God's action in sustaining the world, luring all of creation back to its Maker.

If creation, as Calvin insisted, is a continuing event, ever unfolding from the hand of God, ever responding in praise of God's glory, the world as theater is an appropriate image for expressing a theology of nature intently focused on celebration.[26]

Calvin's Creation Theology

Calvin began his *Institutes* with the importance of God as Creator. Humans discern their earliest knowledge of God, he said, in the possibilities and limits of their own created being. As a microcosm of the world, they see God's glory mirrored in themselves, despite the tarnishing effects of sin.[27] Beginning, then, with the experience of creation, Calvin went on to speak of God as Trinity, the need for redemption, and the promise of a restored world. These three themes all emerge from the initial goodness of created life.

Trinity and Creation

In the first book of his *Institutes*, Calvin joined the beauty of a stunning cosmos with the mystery of God's inner life as Holy Trinity. As he understood it, the transcendent Creator of all things is at heart a sharing of persons bound together in inexplicable delight, reaching out in love to a world meant for relationship. To what end does "God by the power of his Word and Spirit create heaven and earth out of nothing?" asks Calvin. Why is there such "unlimited abundance, variety, and beauty of all things?" So that we might "take pious delight in the works of God open and manifest in this most beautiful theater," he answers.[28] The Trinity's joy is made complete in a creation that sings in response.

The impulse to create the world arises out of a loving dance of interrelationship within God's interior life. "Creation is a fruit of God's longing for 'his Other,'" says Jürgen Moltmann. It is a consequence of God's reaching out beyond the Trinity for ever more things to love. Calvin's Trinitarian theology is similar in this regard to Greek fathers like Gregory of Nazianzus who employed the Eastern Orthodox concept of *perichoresis* in relating the Trinity to creation. Like the dancing, interpenetrating lines of a Celtic knot, the persons of the Trinity reach for more and more dance partners in the ever-expanding celebration of God's glory.[29]

Calvin thought that all three persons of the Trinity were (and are) involved in the act of creation. They share in a common yearning, even as they assume different roles in the way they desire the world into being. "To the Father is attributed the beginning of activity and the fountain and wellspring of all things; to the Son wisdom, counsel and the ordered disposition of all things; but to the Spirit is assigned the power and efficacy of that activity."[30] In other words, the Father, as Calvin sees it, expresses a delight in being-in-general, bringing the world into undifferentiated existence. The Son desires that this creation take specific shape and form—calling forth the elegance of trees, for example. And the Spirit hungers for the lively individuality and intricacy of bristlecone pines, Japanese red maples, and coconut palms. The distinctive "beauty of the universe," says Calvin, "owes its strength to the power of the Spirit."[31] In each of these ways, God as Trinity takes pleasure in creating ever new possibilities for relationship in a ceaseless reflection and celebration of the divine splendor.

Human Sin, World Disorder, and Divine Providence

With Adam's sin, however, Calvin perceived the basic framework of the cosmos to have been thrown off kilter.[32] He thought the failure of human beings to delight in God's creation had significant cosmological effects. Calvin was surprised, for instance, that the stars do not collide in their movement across the heavens and that the sea is kept from flooding the earth. The fragile condition of the universe concerned him.[33] Moreover, he attributed the world's disordered state not only to the rebelliousness of human sin, but even more to the unresponsive "dullness" of the human family, their lack of gratitude in matching God's own delight.[34]

Given the earth's instability because of human sin, Calvin argued that God has to be more than a "momentary Creator." The Trinity must continually uphold the world through loving compassion, exercising "the bridle of divine providence" in restraining the powers of chaos. Providence, says Susan Schreiner, is a foundational doctrine for Calvin. It holds in check the severest threats posed by a world in disequilibrium.[35]

God's providential care prevents thunderstorms and earthquakes, drought and flood from destroying the earth. Under God's protectorship, these provide, instead, abundant occasions for repentance and the practice of faith. Nature serves as a school of affliction as well as a school of desire. It disrupts the ego, redirects misplaced longings, and teaches radical trust.[36] The earth's fury, as well as its beauty, drives the church to prayer. In fact, says Calvin, the performance of praise in the church (and throughout the theater of God's glory) is *itself* a contributor to God's providential care. The longing of the faithful shares in (and supports, as it were) God's own longing for a restored creation.

Recapitulation of All Things in Christ

God's redemption in Christ, then, is for Calvin a reaffirmation of creation itself, a reinvigoration of all that had been damaged by human sin. "In the resurrection," he says, "there is the restoration of all things, and thus it is the beginning of the second and new creation."[37] God's goal in the cross and resurrection is to restore the world to communion with the life of the Trinity. God "promises under the reign of Christ the complete restoration of a sound and well-constituted nature."[38]

He had no doubt that the eventual restoration of the world would include all of the natural order. In Calvin's covenant theology, the earth and its creatures are included in God's covenant with Noah (in Genesis 9:12). Hence, he affirmed that "the brute animals, and even inanimate creatures—even trees and stones—conscious of the emptiness of their present existence, *long* for the final day of resurrection, to be released from emptiness with the children of God."[39] Calvin echoes Irenaeus's doctrine of the recapitulation of all things in Christ, even though he holds back from speculating about the precise nature of the restored cosmos. He cautions against inquiring "with great curiosity into the future perfection of the beasts, plants, and metals," saying, "if we give rein to these speculations, where will they finally lead us?" Nonetheless, he was assured that "no appearance of deformity or impermanence will be seen" in the new creation.[40] The entire material order will, at last, redound to God's glory—a glory realized not simply above the world, but wholly within it as well.

The World's Fragility and the Necessity of Performative Praise

Calvin understood that the worship offered by the world as a theater of God's glory arises out of a deep sense of precariousness. From passages like

Psalm 104:5–9, he concluded that the world remains profoundly vulnerable, constantly on the verge of chaos as a result of human sin. God's providential hand is what holds back, at any moment, the threat of the waters of oblivion.[41] A medieval cosmology underlay his thinking here, convincing him that water is an element inherently lighter than earth. The natural tendency of the world's oceans, therefore, is to overwhelm the land. Only the continual commandment of God preserves the existence of dry earth as a virtual miracle from one moment to the next.[42]

No natural phenomenon engaged Calvin's imagination any more than the awesome power of the sea. He wrote of the ocean's "great surges and hideous waves," saying that "nothing is more terrifying than a tempestuous sea," a horror "so frightening that one's hair stands up on one's head." Only God's majesty is able to "compel the sea, which by its height seems to threaten the earth with continual destruction, to hang as if in mid-air."[43] Thunderstorms similarly occasioned the sense of numinous awe that he knew to lie at the heart of authentic religious experience. Storms on Lake Geneva rushing down from the Alps stirred his anxiety about the instability of the natural order. "We only praise God aright when we are filled and overwhelmed with an ecstatic admiration of the immensity of his power."[44]

Anxiety and praise were intimately connected in Calvin's experience. Bouwsma speaks of him as "a singularly anxious man," viewing human existence as a perpetual crisis of indecision, echoed in the contingencies of nature itself.[45] Throughout his life, Calvin searched for assurances of God's order in the fragile world around him. His mother had died when he was four years old. His father quickly remarried and shunted him off to a neighboring family where he received his earliest education. Exiled in later years from France, the country he loved most, he was never fully at home in Geneva. Moreover, he and his wife lost in infancy all three of the children born to them. His own personal world, like the entire cosmos, remained at risk.[46]

Calvin seldom wrote about his personal spiritual experience. But in the preface to his Psalms commentary he shared something of his private struggle as a way of inviting the reader into the intense and volatile world of the Psalmist. He spoke of the loneliness and abuse that his ministry had evoked, his desire for God honed by a sustained experience of loss.

He found in the Psalter "all the griefs, sorrows, fears, doubts, hopes, cares, perplexities, in short, all the distracting emotions with which the minds of men are wont to be agitated."[47] As if mirroring the turmoil of the Psalms, his own inner and outer worlds remained equally fragile.

All that keeps the universe from falling apart in any instant, said Calvin, is the immediate act of God's continual creation. "The glory of God [is] manifested in the stability of the earth." Apart from this sustaining act of divine intervention (and its celebration by the world), the earth would be "plunged into darkness, . . . thrown into a state of confusion and horrible disorder (*ataxia*) and misrule; for there can be no stability apart from God." Were God to withdraw his hand in any way—were the praise of God to cease in the world, "all things would immediately dissolve into nothing."[48]

As Calvin put it, "The stability of the world depends on the rejoicing of God in his works."[49] God sustains what he creates by the very act of taking delight in it. The Genevan reformer knew that, "Unless the Spirit of the Lord upholds everything, it all lapses back into nothingness."[50] The answer to anxiety, as he understood it, is found not only in the order that God establishes, but also in the desire that God expresses (and elicits from others). The latter makes possible the former. The world is a theater of desire, where the display of God's own continual hunger for relationship is met by the thunderous applause (and yearning) of creation itself. The role of human beings is to lead the rest of creation in praising the one for whom they all yearn, yet know they cannot possess. This, after all, is the nature of praise—a cry of ceaselessly unsatisfied longing, contributing to the very wholeness it seeks. The Psalmist urges believers to contribute to the rejoicing that maintains the universe, Calvin said, "because the end for which we are created is that the divine name may be celebrated by us on the earth."[51]

He could even say, "If on earth such praise of God does not come to pass . . . then the whole order of nature will be thrown into confusion and creation will be annihilated."[52] The continuity of the earth rests on the capacity of the created world to participate in the delight that God takes in all God has made. If God's creation of the universe is not consciously and deliberately celebrated, it remains radically at risk. From Calvin's perspective, then, what we call ecological viability depends upon the exercise of praise. The world is sustained by worship.

The praise of every creature in this theater contributes to the performative glue that joins everything together. The health and well-being of the biosphere is necessary for this praise to be sustained. The church has a responsibility in securing justice for the earth, even as it leads the rest of the world in the act of restorative worship. "The whole world is a theater for the display of the divine goodness, wisdom, justice and power; but the church is the *orchestra*, as it were—the most conspicuous part of it."[53] While the maintenance of the world does not rest solely on the prayers of the faithful, God solicits from them a prayerful longing for interconnectedness that tends to engender its own reality. Calvin observes that God's "deliverance of the church" is intended for nothing less than "an unparalleled renovation of the world." In extolling God's glory, the praise of the faithful helps restore the earth to its original order and wholeness.[54]

Catherine La Cugna observes that, "Words and gestures of praise are 'performative;' their utterance makes *actual* the glory of God to which they refer." Liturgical acts are intrinsically creative. Celebration is so basic to the inner life of the Trinity that God elicits a continuous praise which ever enhances God's glory in the world. Even though God does not *need* praise, there is nevertheless a sense in which "praise perfects perfection," La Cugna says. "Praise generates more praise; glory adds to glory. Praise works by overflow and contagion; it invites others to join in."[55] This is precisely what Calvin envisioned in his image of the theater of God's glory. In the act of worship, celebrants and celebrated are both enriched and enhanced.

This notion of the generative nature of praise, recognizing the power of desire to realize what it seeks, is rich in ecological significance—even if Calvin only slightly began to explore this himself. It suggests that *celebration* is as important to the well-being of the world as the physical and biological systems that contribute to its integrity. Contemporary naturalist and poet Pattiann Rogers asks in one of her poems, "Suppose praise had physical properties/and actually endured? . . . Suppose benevolent praise/ . . . had a separate existence, its purple or azure light/gathering in the upper reaches, affecting/the aura of morning haze over autumn fields?"[56] What if the act of giving glory were shown in some slight way to influence, even *maintain*, the natural world as we know it? Such a question, asked by a woman who grew up in the Reformed tradition herself, arises naturally out of Calvin's thought.

The Genevan Reformer's sense of God's intimate relation to the natural world was so intense—he perceived God's radiant glory to pervade the world so completely—that his thought bordered at times on pantheism. He warned of this danger, cautioning against the ancient notion of an *anima mundi*—as if the universe possessed its own spirit or "were its own creator." He scorned Virgil's idea of honeybees sharing in the divine mind and of God's Being suffusing all living things. Yet in the same paragraph he could resort to an extravagant stretch of language, daring to state:

> [I]t can be said reverently, provided that it proceeds from a reverent mind, that *nature is God*; but because it is a harsh and improper saying, since nature is rather the order prescribed by God, it is harmful in such weighty matters, in which special devotion is due, to involve God confusedly in the inferior course of his works.[57]

This bold language, though carefully qualified, demonstrates his concern to extol the divine grandeur he found so apparent in the cosmos.

The world, for John Calvin, is permeated with God's *shechinah* glory.[58] Though God's "unveiled essence" is never discerned in the external world, nature is shot through with evidences of God's "glory." This distinction between "essence" and "glory" is similar to the Eastern Orthodox distinction between "essence" and "energies" expressed by Gregory Palamas in the fourteenth century.[59] It allows people to speak of God's vivid presence in the physical universe without confusing the two. Calvin knew that direct experience of the divine glory would wholly obliterate us, hence we glimpse God only obliquely (though beautifully) through the mirror of God's works in the world.

Allurement and Instruction: Divine Performance and Human Response in the World as Theater

Calvin's metaphor of the world as theater involved all of creation in the act of performance. Oceans and mountains provide commanding sets that astound the theatergoers. Trees, birds, and animals serve as a Greek chorus, echoing the theme of God's glory. The audience ranges from humans in general, viewing the production with varying degrees of understanding, to the church down in the orchestra, singing along with the cast. All the while, God is the principal actor on stage, variously arrayed in garments of star-studded fabric, wearing masks that flash with the wild beauty of a storm at sea or the calm splendor of an alpine meadow.

These are images meant to attract—to stir desire as well as to instruct. Calvin was unremitting in his insistence that the enjoyment of God's glory is the chief end of creation.[60] "It is our nature to rejoice," he proclaimed in his commentary on David's dancing before the Lord when the Ark returned to Jerusalem.

> We are cold when it comes to rejoicing in God! Hence, we need to exercise ourselves in it and employ all our senses in it—our feet, our hands, our arms and all the rest—that they all might serve in the worship of God and so magnify him.[61]

God's purpose in putting on the costumes of nature's beauty is to awaken desire in those God loves, luring them back in ravishing delight. The language of longing recurs repeatedly in Calvin's references to the splendor of the natural world.

> That we may *enjoy* [*fruamur*] the sight of God, he must come forth to view with his clothing; that is to say, we must first cast our eyes upon the very beautiful fabric of the world in which he wishes to be seen by us. . . .
>
> For in this world God blesses us in such a way as to give us a mere foretaste of his kindness, and by that taste to *entice* us to *desire* heavenly blessings with which we may be satisfied [*tali gustu nos alliciat ad coelestium bonorum desiderium*].
>
> As soon as we acknowledge God to be the supreme architect, who has erected the beauteous fabric of the universe, our minds must necessarily be *ravished* [*rapi necesse est*] with wonder at his infinite goodness, wisdom, and power.[62]

This is an Augustinian language of intense longing. It aims at drawing the reader to that "Beauty so ancient and so new" which had captured the heart of the pastor of Geneva and the bishop of Hippo alike. What Margaret Miles says of Augustine, in analyzing the devices he used to enhance "the pleasure of the text," apply to Calvin as well.[63]

Calvin knew that human desire is a mirror of God's own desire for relationship. "For God cannot either more gently allure, or more effectually incite us to obedience, than by inviting and exhorting us to the imitation of himself."[64] The world as a theatrical performance follows a "script," instructing performers in their practice of praise. But it is also a garden of the senses, awakening yearning within them. As Calvin says:

> We see, indeed, the world with our eyes, we tread the earth with our feet, we touch innumerable kinds of God's works with our hands, we inhale a sweet and pleasant fragrance from herbs and flowers, we enjoy boundless benefits; but in those very

> things of which we attain some knowledge, there dwells such an immensity of divine power, goodness, and wisdom, as absorbs all our senses.[65]

This sensuous language may sound surprising to people long accustomed to thinking of John Calvin as a killjoy, determined to suppress every inordinate desire he could find.[66] Max Engammare argues, however, that, for Calvin, "pleasure" referred far more often to "*le bon plaisir de Dieu*" (Phil. 2:16) than to "voluptuous lust" of any sort. Drinking a glass of good wine with friends, wearing tasteful clothes, living in a beautiful house, and taking delight in the playfulness of language are all commendable pleasures, like enjoying the beauty of a tree or the smell of flowers or the joy of fine music.[67] The pastor whose salary was supplemented by 350–700 liters of wine a year could happily reflect that "we have never been forbidden to laugh, or to be filled, or to join new possessions to old or ancestral ones, or to delight in musical harmony, or to drink wine."[68] He went on to say:

> [I]f we ponder to what end God created food, we shall find that he meant not only to provide for necessity but also for delight and good cheer. Thus the purpose of clothing, apart from necessity, was comeliness and decency. In grasses, trees, and fruits, apart from their various uses, there is beauty of appearance and pleasantness of odor.... Has the Lord clothed the flowers with the great beauty that greets our eyes, the sweetness of smell that is wafted upon our nostrils, and yet will it be unlawful for our eyes to be affected by that beauty, or our sense of smell by the sweetness of that odor?.... Did he not, in short, render many things attractive to us, apart from their necessary use? [69]

The Genevan Reformer certainly recognized the danger of twisted desire and undisciplined affection. *Cupiditatis*, he observed, is a matter of being "tickled" and incited to sin by a desire that contradicts the will of God. But he reflected far more often in the *Institutes* on the positive yearning of *affectus*, a term that appears most frequently in his section on prayer in book III. Prayer, he knew, is but an outpouring of intense longing for God. He delighted in Bernard of Clairvaux's summation of spiritual desire when he said, "The name of Jesus is not only light but also food ... honey in the mouth, melody in the ear, rejoicing in the heart."[70] For Calvin, pleasure was properly a spiritual virtue.

In one of his sermons, he spoke of the lack of "joyfulness and gladness of heart" as a *sin*, almost recalling Hildegard of Bingen's observation that Adam and Eve's original error was a failure to take delight in all the trees of the garden, focusing instead on only one. Calvin said:

God of his own nature is inclined to allure us to himself by gentle and loving means, as a father goes about to win his children, by laughing with them and giving them all they desire. If a father could always laugh with his children and fulfill their desires, all his delight would surely be in them. Such a one does God show himself to be toward us. [71]

FIGURE 2.1. John Calvin, 1509–1564. Engraving by Ary Scheffer and Carl Mayer (1863).

But if God's performance of desire (in the theater of this world) is intended to evoke desire in return, Calvin recognized that humans fall behind other creatures in responding appropriately. Human sin has damaged the capacity of men and women to comprehend the power of the world to delight or to instruct. The effects of the Fall are such "that human reason is grievously wounded by sin, and that the will is very much embarrassed by corrupt affections."[72] As a result, nature's book is not rightly read, nor the garden enjoyed with the delight it deserves.

> For it is true, that this world is like a theater, in which the Lord presents to us a clear manifestation of his glory, and yet, notwithstanding that we have such a spectacle placed before our eyes, we are stone-blind, not because the manifestation is furnished obscurely, but because we are alienated in mind . . . , we lack not merely inclination, but ability.[73]

Calvin recognized repentance and desire as the most appropriate human responses to the world as a theater of God's glory—repentance over what has been misused (or misread) and desire for what should be heartily enjoyed. He knew that nature both terrifies and allures the human audience. God's chief intention is to woo by the attractions of beauty those who have separated themselves from God's love, but God may have to "daunt us and tame us" in order to make that possible.[74] Calvin observed, for example, that this is what Job encountered as he met God in the wilderness. He imagined Yahweh saying to Job, "Gird up thy loins like a lusty stout fellow. . . . If one feather of a peacock is able to ravish us. . . . if wild beasts are able to stop men's minds. . . . what will God's infinite majesty do?"[75] Job is left speechless, Calvin said, by a world (and a God) he cannot comprehend. The *theatrum mundi* has a humbling effect on its viewers, reminding them of how little they know.[76]

The Genevan pastor, therefore, found little to support a "natural theology" based upon native human capacity to grasp the full significance of God's presence in the world.[77] While a vague longing for God remains intact, men and women lack the ability to choose what attracts them most.[78] Indeed, they contribute to the destruction of the very world that draws them by its loveliness. They lack the eyes of faith to see what is there before them.

> Correctly then is this world called the mirror of divinity; not that there is sufficient clearness for man to gain a full knowledge of God, by looking at the world,

> but . . . the faithful, to whom he has given eyes, see sparks of his glory, as it were, glittering in every created thing. The world was no doubt made, that it might be the theater of divine glory.[79]

What opens the eyes of faith, says Calvin, is what happens at the most telling moment in the performance—at that point of Aristotelian reversal on which everything turns in the play. To grasp the significance that Calvin attaches to this, we have to imagine an audience at a typical theatrical production. The playgoers are a mixed group. Some marvel at the set or gawk at the special effects of thunder and lightning. Others laugh in inappropriate places, missing the point of the dialogue. Yet a few are stirred to the depths of their being, breaking into song along with the performers on stage.

At the heart of the performance—near the end of the second act, perhaps—there is something easily misunderstood, if not missed altogether. What is set up to be the grandest display of God's glory in the whole production turns out to be the enigmatic entrance of a clown, a fool who dies on a cross. This scene provokes nervous laughter from some, a degree of pity from others, but for most of the audience a strange sense that the play has somehow gotten off track and lost its direction. Yet *this* is the point of dramatic reversal on which everything else hinges. In this moment, all masks are removed, all costumes taken off, and God's desire is revealed at last as naked and unbounded love.

> For in the cross of Christ, as in a splendid theater, the incomparable goodness of God is set before the whole world. The glory of God shines, indeed, in all creatures on high and below, but never more brightly than in the cross, in which there was a wonderful change of things (*admirabilis rerum conversio*) . . . in short, the whole world was renewed and all things restored to order.[80]

In this "wonderful change of things," this grand Aristotelian reversal, God focuses the attention (and concentrates the desire) of the audience on Jesus, the Creator-made-creature who immerses himself in the brokenness and futility of the world, even dying on the cross. Calvin realizes, of course, that sophisticated playgoers given to "neatness and elegance of expression, to ingenious speculations, . . . to eloquence and show," will react with disgust at this point—failing to see the beauty of God's intention in a display of unspeakable humility.[81] Bored critics will go home to write weary reviews after the lights have gone up. Only the few in the audience who have become like children are likely to respond, having seen God more fully revealed in the glory of the cross than anywhere else in the world.[82] As Calvin says,

> The Lord admits none into his school but little children. Hence those alone are capable of heavenly wisdom who, contenting themselves with the preaching of the cross, however contemptible it may be in appearance, feel no desire whatever to have Christ under a mask.

Only in this modest company does God's alluring performance find a response of perfect delight.

"The School of the Beasts": We All Are Creatures of Desire

All this points up the unparalleled importance of the other creatures, the supporting cast and their role in directing attention to the center of the action. Calvin says of them:

> It is evident that all creatures, from those in the heavens to those under the earth, are able to act as witnesses and messengers of God's glory. . . . For the little birds that sing, sing of God; the beasts clamor for him; the elements dread him, the mountains echo him, the fountains and flowing waters cast their glances at him [*luy iettoient oeillades*: they wink at him], and the grass and flowers laugh before him.[83]

These other creatures may lack human reason, but their vigorous consent to the grace of their own being constitutes the character of their praise.

Calvin admitted that it may "seem strange" to hear the Psalmist speak of pastures filled with flocks or valleys covered with corn as "rejoicing," "singing," and "shouting for joy."[84] Yet he recognized the importance of pushing the edges of language in the task of theological reflection:

> Although a figurative expression is less precise, it expresses with greater significance and elegance what, said simply and without figure, would have less force and address. Hence figures are called the eyes of speech . . . because they win attention by their propriety and arouse the mind by their luster, and by their lively similitude so represent what is said that it enters more effectively into the heart.[85]

He could speak enthusiastically of the stars as teachers of desire, for example. Delighting in the night sky above Lake Geneva, he saw God's glory in these flashes of light, "as if the stars themselves sang his praises with an audible voice." "Astronomy may justly be called the alphabet of theology," he added, knowing that the stars "contribute much towards exciting in the hearts of men a high reverence for God."[86]

This is not to say that Calvin's universe was not thoroughly anthropocentric. He perceived humans as the chief vocalists of God's praise, the "illustrious ornament and glory of the earth." His theological anthropology recognized creation as designed primarily for "man's" use, since God has "imprinted his image in us more than in all the rest." He proclaimed "man" to be a microcosm of the entire world, "because he is above all other creatures a proof of God's glory."[87] It is not in his anthropology, therefore, but in his theology of worship that we discover a Calvin who is much more species inclusive. The poet (and the liturgist) in him remained intrigued at the praise expressed by the more-than-human world.[88] He observed that:

> [T]he Psalmist calls upon the irrational things themselves, the trees, the earth, the seas, and the heavens, to join in the general joy. Nor are we to understand that by the heavens he means the angels, and by the earth men; for he calls even upon the dumb fishes of the deep to shout for joy. . . . As all the elements in the creation groan and travail together with us, according to Paul's declaration, (Rom. 8:22,) they may reasonably rejoice in the restoration of all things *according to their earnest desire.*[89]

God invites "the very beasts" ("even the minutest plants"), Calvin observed, "to a participation in the people's joy."[90] He thought that all creatures, as brought into being by God, are able to exercise a desire toward that for which they were created. Humans, in contrast, bring a distinctive consciousness to what they desire. They call attention to it, are able to focus it on God alone, and collate it with the rest of the praise-giving world.

In his commentary on Romans 8:19–23, Calvin pictured every part of creation as engrossed in longing.[91] "There is no element and no part of the world which, touched with the knowledge of its present misery, is not intent on the hope of the resurrection." The apostle Paul, he noticed, "ascribes hope to irrational creatures." The sun, moon, and stars in their courses, fruit-bearing plants in their fertile abundance, winds in their wandering and flowing streams in their search for the sea—all these, though "bound by great anxiety and held in suspense by a great longing, look for that day which will openly exhibit the glory of the sons of God."[92] A fragile cosmos, subject to ecological ruin by the effects of sin, strains forward in anticipation of a promised resurrection.

Calvin admitted that the biblical text was not so much affirming the intelligent response of the more-than-human creation, as putting human beings to shame for their own failure in taking delight. When the Psalmist describes the heavens as "witnesses and preachers of God's glory," Calvin explained that the writer was "attributing to the dumb creature a quality which, strictly speaking, does not belong to it, in order the more severely to upbraid men for their ingratitude." Nonetheless, God sends human beings to the "school of the beasts" to learn the duty and desire that these creatures are able to teach. The ox, at least, knows his master's stable, and the ass knows his crib. "Even irrational creatures give instruction," Calvin argued.[93]

In discussing what humans can learn from the "school of the beasts," Calvin disclosed a keen ecological sensitivity. He pointed, for example, to the intrinsic value of species diversity, recognizing every colorful creature as offering its own way of glimpsing God's glory. After the pattern of the hexaemeral works of Basil and Ambrose, with their long lists of fascinating creatures made in the six days of creation, he celebrated the "innumerable variety of things" in the natural world. He emphasized God's plan "for the preservation of each species until the Last Day. . . . ," seeing God as actively involved in the propagation of plant and animal life, "lest by their death the entire species perish."[94] What we describe as biodiversity was, for Calvin, an irreplaceable expression of God's glory. He acknowledged its importance even in the sixteenth century.

Another lesson taught by the "school of the beasts," said Calvin, had to do with the violence of human behavior in mistreating the earth. He warned, in a sermon on Deuteronomy 22:6–7, that to senselessly kill a mother bird tending its nest of fledglings is virtually to burn the book of nature that God has given humankind.

> If we burn the book which our Lord has shown us, wittingly undermining the order he has established in nature by playing the butcher in killing the defenseless bird with our own hands—if we thereby prevent the bird from discharging its fatherly or motherly duty, then what will become of us?[95]

He knew that human beings are accountable for their treatment of the other creatures with whom they share the responsibility of praise in the theater of God's glory.

Subjective and Objective Dimensions of Worship: The Constitutive Character of Praise

Given the importance of respecting all the creatures involved in the drama of the world as a theater of God's glory, how then does Calvin go on to understand the act of giving praise as generating the life it celebrates? Praise, for Calvin, is a performative utterance. It springs from an inner disposition of intense desire, influencing by its longing the object of its love. Hence, the act of praise has a double effect: It subjectively stirs desire in the one who celebrates and objectively makes present and efficacious that which is celebrated.

Carlos Eire, in his study of worship and idolatry in Calvin, analyzes these two aspects of Calvin's understanding of liturgy. The Genevan pastor's "war against idols" identified the potential for both good and harm that derives from the inner dynamics of worship as performance. There is a *subjective* aspect of worship that relates to what the person absorbed in praise is experiencing—what happens over time in the process of "becoming" what one desires.

But there is also an *objective* aspect of religious devotion, located in its projection of an ontological reality onto the object toward which it is directed. This objective attribution of ultimate value is "transferred" in every act of worship, says Calvin, even when directed toward an idol. "Each reverential act necessarily conveys an objective transaction of honor," as Eire explains.[96] Worship that should be aimed at the Source of all Being has the effect of reifying its object when directed at anything less than God. Honor that belongs to God is thus falsely (but effectively) transmitted to another.

Worship, for Calvin, therefore, is an exercise of great power. It accomplishes things, effecting internal changes and external results alike. From a ritual studies and performance theory perspective, Calvin's theology of worship involves both "celebrative" and "magical" processes.[97] Worship in Geneva is *celebrative* to the extent that its chief end is the praise of God's glory. It delights in nothing so much as in the object of its desire, absorbed in an exercise of ritualized play. Yet Calvin's conception of worship is also *magical* to the extent that the act of praise also contributes to the maintenance of the world. It participates in what Victor Turner calls a "social drama," involving the healing of a breach in the natural order, the transformation of a broken world.[98] It "reestablishes" a lost cosmic order.[99]

Still another way of comparing these subjective and objective dimensions in Calvin's theology of praise is to employ the distinction that anthropologist Richard Schnechner makes between "entertainment" and "efficacy" in describing the dynamics of ritual performance. A performance is *entertainment* when celebration is an end in itself, when it achieves the shared delight of performers and audience. But a performance becomes a matter of *efficacy* when the experience of theater steps forward into the magic of ritual. The performance then becomes a "transformance," creating a new world in which the participants now live.[100]

There is both entertainment and efficacy in Calvin's way of describing the subjective and objective characteristics of worship. Subjectively, Calvin sees the worshipper as being stirred to desire through the act of prayer. The most important reason for praying, he says, is "that our hearts may be fired with a zealous and burning desire ever to seek, love, and serve [God]. . . ." Prayer must be rooted in "ardor and eagerness."[101] This constitutes its celebrative or "entertainment" dimension—being absorbed wholly in delight.

Calvin stressed the importance of congregational singing, for example, in helping to realize this subjective experience of enjoying God. He knew that music stirs the sources of desire.[102] "We know by experience that singing has great power and vigor to move and inflame men's hearts to call upon and praise God with a more vehement and burning zeal."[103] People should sing lustily in church, he declared.

> [W]e are reminded to cry aloud in the present day with the greatest earnestness when we proclaim the praises of God, that we ourselves may be inflamed, and may excite others by our example to act in the same manner; for to be lukewarm, or to mutter, or to sing, as the saying is, to themselves and to the muses, is impossible for those who have actually tasted the grace of God.[104]

Encouraging the use of the metrical Psalms in worship, Calvin understood the singing of Psalms as a prime means of training the affections in the school of faith.[105] He perceived music in general as one of the "bright sparkling remnants of glory" to endure the Fall, urging that the enthusiastic voices of children take the lead in teaching adults to sing.[106] A visitor to Calvin's former congregation in Strasbourg exclaimed that, "No one could believe the joy which one experiences when one is singing the praises and wonders of the Lord in the mother tongue as one sings them here."[107] Music, for Calvin, was central in helping to accomplish the subjective realization of prayer.

When he turned to the *objective* dimension of worship, Calvin declared (as already mentioned) that the reverential act conveys a substantive transaction of honor. Praise is able to authenticate, valorize, and sustain that toward which it is directed. It realizes what it proclaims, even apart from the worshipper's intent. Thus idolatry was a concern for Calvin. To reverence idols is to "transfer the honor of God to others," granting fullness of being to something wholly undeserving of it.[108]

Calvin identified three objective "effects" in particular that derive from the performative act of true worship. The liturgy does more than cultivate a pious mood, he insisted. Its transformative action secures certain results as a natural consequence of the reverential act. These include the power of the preached word, the impact of music on the human will, and the effectiveness of praise in maintaining the fragile order of the world.

Preaching as Performative Utterance

Calvin's understanding of what happens in the preaching event was highly sacramental. If, in his Eucharistic theology, he understood the believer to be taken up into heaven to feed on the very flesh of Christ, he similarly understood the actual voice of God to be proclaimed in the words of the sermon. He introduced a prayer for illumination in the liturgy (before the reading of Scripture) that functioned as an act of *epiclesis*, calling on the Holy Spirit to guarantee Christ's real presence in the spoken Word.[109] Calvin possessed an almost magical sense of the power of speech in the performative event of preaching.[110]

Emphasizing with the Psalmist that creation is brought into being by "the Word of the Lord" and "the breath of his mouth," he underscored the creative capacity of "powerful and effective speech." For humanists like Calvin, language was power.[111] It was able to constitute what it declared. When God's Word is spoken in the performative setting of worship, it is *God* who acts and speaks. Calvin described the power of Haggai's preaching in this way:

> [T]here was no ocular view of God given; but the message of the prophet obtained as much power as though God descended from heaven, and had given manifest

> tokens of His presence. We may then conclude from these words, that the glory of God so shines in His Word, that we ought to be so much affected by it, whenever He speaks by His servants, as though He were nigh to us, face to face.[112]

The Genevan pastor had no hesitation in describing the Word preached as filled with the same power and presence as the Word spoken by God in Christ:

> The Word of God is not distinguished from the word of the prophet.
> God does not wish to be heard but by the voice of his ministers.
> Christ acts by them in such a manner that he wishes their mouth to be reckoned as his mouth, and their lips as his lips.[113]

To use the language of speech act theory, the Word preached in worship is, for Calvin, a "performative utterance." In contrast to "constative utterances" that simply offer a statement, these are acts of speech in which God performs what God speaks. To issue the utterance is to perform the action.[114] The language participates in (and creates) the reality. In a performance setting like that envisioned in Calvin's metaphor of the theater of God's glory, "it is not the case that words are one thing and the rite another. The uttering of the words itself is a ritual."[115] Moreover, the ritual act—performed "onstage," as it were—*achieves* its goal in a changed reality.

Music's Power to Create

Calvin recognized this same dynamic with respect to the power of music in worship. It not only exercises a subjective influence, he thought, but a powerfully objective one as well. The significance of the Psalms sung in prayer, for example, is that they "achieve" what they name through the mystery of words put to music. As Calvin expressed it, "When the melody is added [to a word], that word pierces the heart much more strongly and enters within. . . . Singing has great power and vigor to move and inflame men's hearts."[116]

He had learned from Plato that "there is scarcely anything in this world more capable of turning or bending hither and thither the customs of men." Music "has a secret power, almost unbelievable, to move morals in one way or another." Indeed, the Psalms virtually sing themselves in the mystery of performed utterance. "We are certain that God has put the words in our mouths as if they themselves sang in us to exalt his glory."[117]

Words that are sung have a way of bringing into being the glory of which they speak. When we sing, we pray twice, as Augustine said.

The Praise of the Church as World-Sustaining Act

One of the reasons that Calvin considered prayer to be so important was its ability to "confirm God's providence," to participate in the task of invoking God's providential care of the cosmos.[118] He saw the prayers of the faithful as contributing in some profound way to this earth-sustaining work. The Genevan pastor denounced those who "babble that God's providence, standing guard over all things, is vainly importuned with our entreaties."[119] God actually encourages the prayers of the faithful in the task of preserving the universe. Praise is not simply celebrative, but also *constitutive* of the world, maintaining its life and well-being.

> If on earth such praise of God does not come to pass, if God does not preserve His church to this end, then the whole order of nature will be thrown into confusion and creation will be annihilated when there is no people to call upon God.[120]

The church, as the "orchestra" in the theater of God's glory, has to assume a leading role in this work. Yet Calvin goes on to affirm the role of the rest of the cosmic order in offering world-changing praise as well. He observes, for example, that when Psalm 7:17 speaks of the clouds pouring out their waters in awe at Yahweh's presence, "the waters which were suspended in the clouds *yielded to God the honour to which he is entitled*, the air, by the concussion of the thunder, having poured forth copious showers."[121] This language of "yielding honor to God" is what Calvin described as the most dependable definition of authentic worship.[122] In other words, he boldly attributes the power of performative praise to rain clouds that respond in agitated wonder at God's glory.

All creatures are absorbed in sustaining the order of creation through the endless offering of praise. Thunderheads rising over distant mountains, East African black rhinoceroses with their tickbird companions, hundreds of species of iridescent scarab beetles, microscopic rhizobia bacteria helping roots process nitrogen in plants everywhere—all are part of the "critical mass" required for God's glory to be sufficiently honored. God's delight (and ours) is incomplete without these voices, said Calvin. The world itself fails without the power of this enjoyment.

Yet awe is intensified, he went on to say, as the multiplication of species expands, as praise is widened. "If we compare a hawk with the residue of the whole world, it is nothing," he wrote. "And yet if so small a portion of God's works ought to ravish us and amaze us, what ought *all* his works do when we come to the full numbering of them?"[123] Hawks and angels, all things visible and invisible, he exclaimed, are finally necessary in the universal celebration of the theater of God's glory.[124]

The Liturgical Implications of Calvin's Thought

"If ever there was a theologian who saw the universe sacramentally it was Calvin," writes Nicholas Wolterstorff. "For him, reality was drenched with sacrality. . . . Calvin's reforms meant a radical turn toward the world. But for him . . . the world to which one turns is a sacrament of God."[125] The practice of piety, in the Genevan Reformer's understanding, was far more than an anthropocentric rehearsal for heaven, lived out against a backdrop of temporary stage settings and bit players with no significance of their own. The earth itself shares in the longing of the faithful, hoping for the Sabbath rest of justice and peace toward which all creation aims. If the world, then, is indeed absorbed in a theatrical performance of stunning proportions, the liturgical implications of this are astounding. This is especially the case for churches today, where worship too often remains a vacuous and non-sacramental denial of the rest of creation.

To conceive of worship as an experience of "theater" is not to seek ways of "jazzing it up," enhancing its theatrical appeal as a matter of popular entertainment. It is to recover, instead, the subversive character of worship, honoring its role in the making and unmaking of worlds. Like the best experience of theater, liturgy forces its participants into multiple levels of encounter. It pleases, but it also profoundly disturbs, prompting at times a complete reversal of things previously held certain. It leads to conversion. The performance demands deep participation. This was how Calvin understood the significance of the Sabbath.

In blessing the seventh day, he said, God proclaimed "the proper business of the whole of life" to be the celebration of God's matchless glory "in this magnificent theater of heaven and earth." The Sabbath was for him "a symbol of sanctification," a ritual event participating in (and helping to create) the reality it signifies.[126] The Sabbath liturgy does more than celebrate God's creative work. It reenacts (and anticipates) the event of creation, declaring anew Yahweh as King. In the act of praise, the liturgy *effects* the very world it calls into being. It "opens creation for its true future," says Jürgen Moltmann.[127] This is the power of the cult to engender what it names, the capacity of ritual to summon what it celebrates. It is a mystery full of ecological as well as liturgical significance.[128]

The Genesis creation narrative concludes not on the sixth day with the making of human beings, but on the seventh day with the Sabbath rest of all creation. Human praise is incomplete without the inclusion of all these others. As Moltmann says:

> It is for this that human beings are created—for the feast of creation, which praises the eternal, inexhaustible God. . . . This song of praise was sung *before* the appearance of human beings, is sung *outside* the sphere of human beings, and will be sung even *after* human beings have—perhaps—disappeared from this planet. . . . The human being is not the meaning and purpose of the world.[129]

The inclusivity of Sabbath praise ultimately requires the rethinking of our liturgical practice. It invites us to a recovery of forgotten traditions in the church's life and suggests new ways of including the more-than-human world in how we worship. *The Apostolic Tradition* of Hippolytus (ca. 200 CE), for example, was an early manual of Christian life and discipline that encouraged believers to pray at midnight because "at this hour all creation . . . praises the Lord: stars and trees and waters stand still with one accord."[130] Other early Christian writers taught that the prayers of the creatures restored the world anew each night. *The Apocalypse of Peter* spoke of the second hour of the night as devoted to "the service of large fishes and of all animals that live in water." In the eighth hour, "the grass springs up from the earth" and "glorifies the One who caused it to grow."[131] The ancient church celebrated the fact that the world, from dark to dawn, continually sings glory. How can we worship *apart* from this larger community?

The assurance that we do not pray alone may drive us back to the inclusion of animals in worship, for example, as practiced in medieval cathedrals. This would involve more than the occasional blessing of animals—as on the feast day of St. Francis at New York's Cathedral of St. John the Divine or at Easter on Olvera Street in Los Angeles. It might include the consecration of "pastoral dogs" as recently practiced in some churches. These animals, as pastoral assistants, process and recess with the clergy, lie in the chancel during worship, and share as well in the pastoral care of the sick during the week.[132] Cats, of course, have always had the run of great churches and cloisters, from Westminster Abbey to Julian's cell in fourteenth-century Norwich. Calvin's theology may require our asking about the inclusion of other-than-human creatures in the church's life of prayer.

An awareness of nature's increased role in liturgical life also raises questions about church architecture. In using natural materials, church buildings have often had the effect of leading the faithful more deeply into nature rather than away from it. Ninth-century churches in Cappadocia, for example, were carved out of the soft volcanic rock found in the region. The medieval stave churches of Norway, built from locally grown Norwegian spruce, were filled with carvings of surrounding animals, birds, and vines. How might we echo this today in creating worship sites that are ecologically responsive, opening the senses onto the outside world? What have we to learn from wilderness retreats and gardens of prayer, outdoor labyrinths and community gardens built on vacant city lots (where fruits and vegetables are brought to the communion table on Sundays and shared with the poor)? What may be required of us in the work of liturgically reclaiming toxic waste sites and urban housing projects? These are important questions for today.

The church's liturgical life may even need to add a new Season of Creation to the church year, as prompted in recent years by Metropolitan Bartholomew, the "Green Patriarch" of the Eastern Orthodox Church. The four Sundays of September, leading up to the feast day of Francis of Assisi, are increasingly honored by a number of churches in this way. Lukas Vischer observes how striking it is that the first article of the creed—celebrating God as Creator—has no firm place in the liturgical calendar. Adding a Season of Creation to the seasons of Christmas, Easter, and Pentecost can better reflect the Trinitarian pattern of Christian praise.[133] Yet another possibility, along these lines, would involve retrieving the Celtic tradition of marking the seasons of nature themselves in celebrating St. Brigit at the winter lambing season, St. John at the summer solstice, and St. Michael at the fall equinox. The potential for inclusiveness is boundless.

These implications for liturgical practice derive from the notion of worship as a performative act involving the whole earth in praise. It is all about ravishment, as Calvin would say. There is a time in any deeply moving experience of theater, he realized, when the distance between audience and actors dissolves. The imaginary "fourth wall" disappears. Everyone is drawn onto the stage, as it were, caught up with the cast in the power of the performance. To use Paul's imagery, the participants strain together in reaching toward a grand and glorious conclusion (Phil. 3:13). This is what happens in worship, said Calvin, as a newly transfigured universe takes shape in the dynamic act of common praise.

Day after day, God brings the world to its feet in ecstatic applause as the curtain falls once again on God's dramatic performance of desire. Smitten by longing, we stand alongside the others in speechless awe, clapping our hands in hope of another encore, determined—if we can help it—that the performance never end. We cannot imagine a God as eager to perform as we are to enjoy. Held in that strange and awesome embrace, in the joyous meeting of God's desire and our own, we and the whole world with us are sustained by praise.

Can We Chant Psalms with All God's Creatures?

Beside the common song of praise, which all things have as they are creatures, every one of the creatures have their own proper parts in the Song: The Sun in his particular virtue and motion, the moon in hers, and the stars in theirs, every one by themselves, and these also jointly make up a sweet and harmonious melody to the praise of God.

—Puritan Divine David Dickson, *A Brief Explication of the . . . Psalms*[1]

I've pulled the canoe out of the water, stopping along the banks of the Eleven Points River to sit by a spring nearby. I've stopped for the night at Turner's Mill, the site of what used to be the village of Surprise, Missouri, flourishing here in the nineteenth century. All that's left today is a 26-foot iron waterwheel that once powered the mill. But the place still thrives. A pileated woodpecker works on the branch of an oak tree overhead. Watercress dances in the spring. Raccoons explore the overturned canoe, looking for food. An unlikely community converges. I sit with my Anglo-Genevan Psalter, imagining everything singing with the cadence of what Gregory of Nyssa called the *harmonia mundi*, a musical harmony to which all creation is tuned.

In languages of their own, the watercress, woodpecker, oak, and raccoons do a better job than I'm able to muster with the chanting of Psalm 104. But for a single moment at sunset we're all gathered by the river, at Turner's Mill in the Missouri Ozarks, sharing in the common work of praise at the end of a day. It's what the whole of creation lives for.

Brother Anthony, a thirteenth-century Franciscan, insisted that all creatures are able to respond to God. He lived in Rimini, a town east of Assisi, where he spoke one day to a group of prestigious scholars. They dismissed his teaching as naïve, so he walked down to the Marecchia River where it flows into the Adriatic Sea and began to talk to the fish. "Since scholars refuse the word of God," he said, "here I give it to you, my friends."

A huge throng of fishes gathered to listen: little ones lined up near the shore, middle-sized ones behind them, and larger ones in back, all holding their heads above the waves so as to attend to his words. Anthony reminded them that, during the flood, when all the animals outside the ark were perishing, God preserved them alone without loss. He recalled that it was they who paid the tribute money when Jesus had nothing for the tax due to the Roman authorities. It was they who were chosen as food for the Eternal King as Jesus ate his first meal with the disciples that morning on the shore of the Sea of Galilee after his resurrection.

Listening to the Word, the fish opened their mouths and nodded their heads, moving their fins to praise God in the best way they knew. When scholars back in the city heard of this, most of them still scoffed, but a few came running to sit at the feet of Brother Anthony to listen as attentively and joyfully as the fish had done.[2]

This story points to the necessity of including all species in the proclamation of praise. John Calvin urged that Psalms be sung not only in church, but in houses and fields as well, "lightening one's toil" as they are shared with the rest of creation.[3] He knew the worship of the Psalms to be profoundly communal, far broader than human practice alone. Humans are but a chorus adjoined to a vast orchestra containing trees rustling in the wind like a string section, wolves and coyotes sounding off in the horn section, whales breaching and elephants stampeding with the percussion players, and blackbirds and sparrows singing with the piccolos and flutes high above it all. This is the wider community of praise, joined by angels as well, that the multi-species character of Psalmic worship celebrates.

I rediscover it every time I venture alone into the wilderness of southern Missouri. The Psalms come alive in the presence of white-tailed deer, bald eagles, and bullfrogs singing to the brightness of the stars on a late fall evening. The Psalms were written, after all, in the early monarchy when the Yahwist material of the Pentateuch was taking shape. "The Yahwist Landscape," as Ted Hiebert reminds us, shaped the thinking of Israelite highland farmers who regularly found God in their tilling of the soil and longing for rain. Like Adam, the Psalm writers were closely linked to the *adama*, the rich arable soil that produced olives, grapes, wheat, and oak trees. Nature imagery naturally found its way into their poetry.[4]

The Psalms insist that we share with other creatures a common desire for God. We take part in a mutual performance of ritual life. We participate in a deeply embodied experience of communal praise. We even find ourselves joined together in reciprocal grief.[5] My forays into wilderness have involved all these experiences. I marvel at the insistent desire of red cedar trees growing out of the cracks in boulders along an Ozark creek bed. I join red-tailed hawks, tree frogs, and whippoorwills in their assorted ways of welcoming the setting sun. My body fits the curvature of the ground as I sleep at a site where falling water sings in the creek. On the way back home the next day, I hear the mournful sound of wind over the lifeless slope of mine tailings near Leadington, Missouri. In each of these I share the earth's offering of praise as desire, performance, embodiment, and lament. These four dimensions of Psalmic worship demonstrate the continuity of biblical praise as it crosses lines of species and language.

My purpose here is not to anthropomorphize the "intentionality" of other-than-human beings. Other species "offer praise," as humans do, by simply being what they are. They imitate God in being most perfectly the particular falcon or fern they were made to be. Psalmic language doesn't distinguish between praise that arises out of human consciousness and praise that other species offer in voices of their own. It assumes a continuity of responsiveness to God across the entire creation, something we as humans don't readily grasp. My goal, then, is not to "explain" the praise of other species, but simply to report the startling sense of shared responsiveness that the biblical hymns portray. Norman Habel's Earth Bible Project is an example of scholars beginning to take seriously this phenomenon. They interpret Scripture from an ecological perspective—giving voice to the earth in the biblical text in the same way as feminist and liberationist hermeneutics have sought to retrieve the voices of women and the poor.[6]

We Desire Together

Calvin spoke of the Psalms as offering an "anatomy of all the parts of the soul," covering the full range of emotions that we experience as creatures of earth.[7] The Psalms weave these assorted desires into grandly orchestrated praise. The Psalter is a book riddled with longing, continually bubbling up into exultation. Enjoying God is the goal of its worship. Hebrew words for "longing," "panting," and "delighting-in" permeate its language.

We see the extraordinary capacity of the Psalms to stir desire in the lines of an eleventh-century Celtic poet, Mael Isu Ua Brollchain. He wrote a love poem to the old, thumb-worn copy of the Psalter he had read as a child, confessing that *she* had been the occasion of his first falling in love with the Word. "Dear one," he addressed her:

> Lady of measured melody,
> Not young, but with modest maiden mind,
> Together once in Niall's northern land,
> We slept, we two, as man and womankind.
> You came and slept with me for that first time,
> Skilled wise Amazon annihilating fears,
> And I a fresh-faced boy, not bent as now,
> A gentle lad of seven melodious years.[8]

The Psalter's facility in arousing desire transcends all ages, embracing lovers of every kind.

The human and more-than-human world alike express longing in numerous Scriptural hymns. Cows returning the ark of the covenant from its captivity in the land of the Philistines "moo" for all they are worth as they return in delight to Beth-shemesh (I Samuel 6:12). Hills, meadows, and valleys in Psalm 65:8–13 sing together in response to God's blessing, even as "the gateways of the morning and evening shout for joy." Physical hunger and thirst (as biological experience *and* as a metaphor of longing for God) are shared across species. The hart's panting for the water brooks (Psalm 42:1), the Psalmist's flesh fainting for God, and the dry, weary land aching for water are part of a common longing (Psalm 63:1). Creatures look continually to God for their food, says Psalm 104:27–28. They are filled with good things when God's hand is opened, dismayed when God's face is hidden from them. Their longing is ever toward Yahweh.

God, in short, "satisfies the desire of every living thing" (Psalm 145:16). The yearning of an acacia tree sinking its roots a hundred feet into the sand of the Sinai communicates a restive wanting that points to God's luring of everything back to God's self. The Psalms understand this intimately. They identify unsatisfied desire as that which prompts the human and more-than-human response to God. Everything reaches toward what theologians in the early church described as the *apokatastasis panton*, the final restoration of all things. The whole of created reality longs to return to God in a great Sabbath rest, a reconstitution of its original created glory.

Paul echoes this image in the Psalmic hymn of Philippians 2:5–11. (Not all Psalms and hymns in the Bible are limited to the 150, of course.) Paul anticipates the day when every knee shall bow and every tongue confess that Christ is Lord. Every beak and fluttering wing, every dorsal fin and bank of clouds and swarm of bees—"*in* heaven and *on* earth and *under* the earth" (yes, earthworms as well!)—will someday chirp and splash and hum and squirm in declaring Christ as Lord, to the glory of God. Joyous desire is the first mark of worship in the Psalms.

From the lusty Psalm singing of Calvin's sixteenth-century Geneva to Isaac Watts's revitalization of congregational singing in eighteenth-century England, the songs of David's harp incited the ardor of the faithful. Even Queen Elizabeth acknowledged the jubilant quality of Reformed worship in a backhanded way, scoffing at the "Genevan jigs" (the metrical Psalms) so popular in Puritan worship.[9] David himself had urged that the Psalms be danced as well as sung.

We Perform Together

A second characteristic of Israel's praise is its notion that worship follows a structure, a pattern of performance in which the entire world community takes part. Praise does not depend on any single individual's (or species's) sustained experience of desire. The larger community of earth is borne along by the power of a common liturgical practice, as Psalms are "acted out" in ritual settings.

Psalm 104 offers a fine example of Psalmic praise as a world-embracing and world-transforming event. Written after the exile, recalling God's creative power through its agony, the Psalm is a liturgical reenactment of the Genesis creation story. Creation tales are always told in times of chaos, when things fall apart. They remind people of the power associated with their beginnings. They recreate the world in their midst.

This greatest of the nature Psalms is a stunning hymn sung by all the creatures. It is Genesis 1 put to song, a poem arranged in seven stanzas that ritually echo the seven days of creation. Each creature plays an appropriate role in its ritual reenactment of the earth's beginning. The world is reborn in every new performance of the hymn.

Psalm 104 is an enthronement Psalm, following the pattern of a hymn to Yahweh's glory. In his book *Israel's Praise*, Walter Brueggemann observes that Psalms like this were composed each year for the enthronement festival in Jerusalem at Rosh Hashanah (the New Year celebration). Yahweh was ritually inaugurated as sovereign once again for the coming year, even as the realm of Yahweh's creation was reinstituted. This was more than a "remembering" of what once had happened. It was the reconstitution of a new reality.

In the ritual moment of declaring God as King, a "new world" came into being. Israel's praise, says Brueggemann, not only recognizes who God is, but "calls into being the world God requires." The worship of the Psalms is not only responsive, but is also *constitutive*![10] It creates what it names. Liturgy in this sense is an experience of theater prompting such world-shaking awe that people in the audience may have to run to the restroom before they finish the first act. Witnessing such power, they can't help themselves.

Like the song and dance of Miriam at the crossing of the Red Sea in Exodus 15, the liturgy of re-creation comes down through the centuries to the people of God in ever new settings. Each time the story is told and the dance is danced, the Red Sea opens again, God delivers again, and pharaoh is defeated again. Brueggemann reminds us that the descendents of Miriam who dance this liturgy centuries later in the slave huts of Babylon must do it in whispers. The Babylonians know that liturgy is dangerous, so they disallow it. "But in the act of unpermitted dance, the world is transformed."[11] That is the power of liturgy.

It is why the Lakota Sioux often tied buckskin thongs to their children while listening to sacred stories around a campfire at night. They knew the children could be snatched away by animal spirits drawn to the telling of the powerful tales. Listening to stories—like participating in liturgy—can be dangerous. It occasions an overlapping of unanticipated worlds.

Central to the experience of Psalm 104 is the participation of the entire creation in its world-constituting liturgy. Its community of praise is highly bio-diversified, not at all human-centered. It tells a story of the earth remarkably similar to the universe story told by scientists today, a tale some five billion years old. If it were written in a ten-volume set of books (says Robert Overman), with 500 pages to a volume, each page would relate a narrative a million years long. Biological life wouldn't be mentioned until volume eight, with plants taking up most of that. Reptiles, birds, and animals would fill the remaining pages until humankind finally made its appearance on page 499 of the last volume.[12] Psalm 104 presents a similar sweep of creation's wonder, summoning all creatures into being as if for the first time, with men and women tagging along at the end, as it were. Humans are simply not the pivotal, indispensable part of the tale.

This mystery of Psalmic worship as performative act, re-creating the world in the process of re-naming its creatures, is later reflected in a Eucharistic prayer found in the fourth-century Apostolic Constitutions. It lists all the participants (human and otherwise) who sing God's praise in this crucial moment of the mass: a chorus of stars, a world full of sweet-smelling and healing herbs, the hissing of snakes (yes!) and chirping sounds of multicolored birds, even a stable of winds blowing at God's command. At the heart of the celebration, each of these have a role in offering thanksgiving and exalting the risen Lord, resubmitting the world to God's reign.[13]

We Are Embodied Together

A third characteristic of the worship modeled in the Psalms is its deeply embodied reality, performed in and through the body, intimately engaging all the senses. One finds more attention to the human body (and other bodies) in the Psalms than in any other biblical book (aside from the Song of Songs). Praise for the Psalmist is never a purely cerebral activity. In Psalms 38 and 51, for example, David pours himself out to God, repenting of his sins against Bathsheba and her husband. He prays with his lips, mouth, tongue, intestines, muscles, bones, skin, thighs, heart, lungs, eyes, ears, and throat, crying out in the intensity of his longing. He engages God with the whole of his body in a fervent act of prayer.

This is typical of Hebrew consciousness. One knows God in biblical religion, not through rational abstraction, but through the concrete, personal experience of one's physical self. H. Wheeler Robinson observed that the Hebrew Scriptures mention no less than 80 different parts of the human body. Curiously, the brain—the part of the human anatomy we would value most—is not one of them. In Hebrew thought, the seat of consciousness isn't located in the intellect (between the ears) but in the gut—the "bowels," the kidneys, the intestines. This is where God most powerfully meets the soul.[14]

Christianity at its best has always affirmed as much. Despite the Platonic dismissal of the cosmos as a dim shadow of the true world beyond it, despite a Gnostic-Manichaean tendency to reject the "flesh" as inimical to "spirit," and despite the Enlightenment's triumph of reason over emotion, incarnational faith celebrates the body as the locus of God's presence.

Julian of Norwich, for example, could even praise God for sphincter muscles controlling bowel movements. As she said in her *Showings of Divine Love*:

> A person walks upright and the food in his body is shut in as if in a well-made purse. When the time of his necessity comes, the purse is opened and then shut again, in most seemly fashion. And it is *God* who does this . . . For he does not despise what he has made, nor does he disdain to serve us in the simplest natural functions of our body.[15]

This solitary nun in fourteenth-century England was able to offer (to embody) praise with every inch of her being.

Worship in the Psalms similarly involves a meeting of bodies joined in community. Psalmic praise is a "contact sport," as it were. It's gotta be danced. It demands sensuous involvement in a performance that is inescapably communal, embracing the rest of creation not merely as stage background, but as full-scale participants.

Many Psalms recognize the more-than-human world as singing and praising God along with human beings, as well as the rest of the seen and unseen world. In Psalm 19, the heavens "tell" of God's glory. The sky "proclaims" God's handiwork. There's a "voice" spoken by the mysterious turning of night and day. Psalm 148 speaks of sun and moon, shining stars, clouds, fire, snow and wind, hills, trees, animals and birds all praising God's name. Humans do not give praise *for* these creatures in this Psalm. They offer their own praise. Similarly, in Psalm 96:11–12, we find that the skies are glad, the field exults, the trees of the wood sing for joy before the Lord, anticipating God's coming.

Our tendency is to dismiss all this as mere figures of speech. We are told we shouldn't be so naive as to attribute human emotions of joy or longing to an evening sunset or to corn growing in a field on a hot summer day. Literary critics and language analysts are quick to remind us of the function of anthropomorphism, personification, and metaphor in language. I understand their concern. But I also know that if literary critics and language analysts have never walked through a Georgia cornfield on a hot July day after a hard rain—hearing the crackling of plants thrusting themselves up through the earth—they may not know what they're talking about. They may never have experienced the wildly insistent speech of sentient, non-human beings.[16]

Barbara McClintock, the Nobel prize-winning biologist who worked on the cellular structure of corn plants, attributed the success of her work to listening carefully to the corn, talking to it, developing a "feeling for the organism." She knew it was alive—that it opened itself to her, as she opened herself in return. George Washington Carver said the same thing about his work with peanut plants: "If you love it enough, anything will talk with you," he said.[17]

When the hymn writer in Isaiah 42:10–12 speaks of the sea roaring, the desert lifting up its voice, and all their inhabitants shouting glory, do we have the right to dismiss this language as "mere metaphor" (a case of humans toying with words)? Dare we not recognize it as a call to a wider community of worship, inviting us beyond narrowly anthropocentric ways of thinking? The Psalms force us to entertain the idea that praise is more than a conscious act of intellection. It involves bodies that move and species that sing in languages beyond our comprehension.

We Lament Together

A final characteristic of worship in the Psalms is that it embraces the ambiguity and risk of a life lived in a broken world. The Psalms also weep, even rage, over the grinding dislocations that the earth and its creatures share with human life.

Biblical worship in the Psalms is never sugar-coated. It lacks the saccharine pleasantries that too often characterize our bankrupt liturgies. We imagine a God unwilling to listen were we to complain as the Psalmists sometimes do, were we to scream in agony out of the anguished mess we've made of our lives and the earth as well. Johannes Metz says that "the absence of suffering" in the official language of prayer signals an enormous impoverishment of our worship.[18]

The Psalms won't let us live in a naive and romantic world, stripped of pain. God is present in nature's power and beauty. But God is also there (and most reliably so) in the despair and hunger of children, in rivers that flow with toxic waste and sewage, in ancient redwood trees cut down by Pacific Lumber. God appears most clearly in the scandal and brokenness of the cross. A biblical theology of creation, therefore, must also be a theology of the cross. It will not shrink from including the tormented cries of Psalm 88, for example, a Psalm often left out of lectionary readings. A free translation of its Hebrew text might read: "Where the hell are you, God? Nobody seems to give a damn, including *you*!" Yet the Psalmist insists that if the only prayer we have to offer is one of bitter anguish, we pray it nonetheless. The poet knows that in the release of anger, intimacy is realized. God longs for whatever lies in the depths of the soul.

Psalms of lament make reference to the natural world in three different ways. Some bewail the threats that human beings experience from a world beyond their control. Psalm 58, for instance, grieves the unkindness of an earth filled with venomous serpents, lions with sharp fangs, and unrestrained evil in general. The Psalm goes on to observe, by the way, that humans who assume these characteristics are more threatening than anything in nature. Yet the Psalmist encourages a bold liturgical complaint regarding a world of tornadoes and earthquakes, cancer cells and the AIDS virus. It highlights Annie Dillard's tortured and persistent questions about a universe often filled with horror.

Another variety of lament Psalms summons the awful powers of nature in punishing those who are lawless and violent. Imprecatory Psalms like Psalm 83 call down the harshness of natural disasters on the heads of the wicked. "As fire consumes the forest, as the flame sets the mountains ablaze, so pursue them with your tempest and terrify them with your hurricane," the Psalmist cries. This is a strange, seemingly vicious sort of prayer. We may have to ask ourselves: Who are the ones who suffer at the hands of others to such an extent that they have no other prayer than this to offer? Does liturgically expressing their anguish in this way prevent them from having to act upon it? From a Jungian perspective, the Psalm may even invite our reflection on the shadow within us, seeing how we project onto others the violence we suppress in ourselves.

A third category of lament Psalms (and other biblical hymns like them) are those expressed not by humans, but by the more-than-human world itself, grieving over the pain inflicted on it by men and women.[19] These expressions of grief come from the land itself. A Psalmic hymn in Isaiah 24 declares that, "The earth dries up and withers, the world languishes . . . lying polluted under its inhabitants. Therefore, a curse devours the earth. The wine dries up, the vine shrivels . . . the gladness of the earth is banished." The ground itself virtually cries out, "How long, O Lord?" (vss. 4–7, 10–11).

Hosea 4:1–3 indicts Israel for the enormity of its sin and injustice, an indictment rich in ecological significance. "The land mourns, and all who live in it languish; together with the wild animals and the birds of the air, even the fish of the sea are perishing" because of the people's sin. The earth gives anguished expression to grief, again within a liturgical setting. Isaiah 12:10–11 similarly bemoans a land trampled down by sinners. "They have made it a desolation; desolate, it mourns to me," says Yahweh.[20] In Zechariah 11:2, the cypress tree and the oaks of Bashan wail over the destruction of their habitat.

A resonant power comes from this prayer of lament, the irrepressible grief voiced by Mother Earth herself. Clarissa Pinkola Estes, in her book *Women Who Run with the Wolves*, speaks of the earth as "bone woman," *La Huesera*, the one who stalks the Sonoran desert of southern New Mexico, gathering bones—wolf bones, coyote bones. When she has assembled an entire skeleton, she begins to sing. Out of the dark places of her grief, she sings the *canto hondo*, the "deep song" that brings flesh to the bones once again, allowing the wolf creature to breathe and rise to new life.[21]

This is where human beings begin the journey back to themselves, back to praise and to wholeness. The earth sings with us through all the changes rung by the Psalms in the various turnings of our lives. It shares desire, performs praise, embodies presence, and mourns suffering, as part of a vast community crossing lines of species as well as language. Every time I welcome a sunset at a Missouri campsite, I have to ask myself once again: Isn't this what the whole of creation lives for?

· 3 ·

Nature and Desire in Seventeenth-Century Puritanism

> I heard the merry grasshopper then sing.
> The black-clad cricket bear a second part;
> They kept one tune and played on the same string,
> Seeming to glory in their little art.
> Shall creatures abject thus their voices raise
> And in their kind resound their Maker's praise,
> Whilst I, as mute, can warble forth no higher lays?
>
> —Anne Bradstreet, "Contemplations"[1]

The Puritans were a people of passion as well as paradox. Despite their wordiness, their spiritual arrogance, and their reduction of the ways of God to a fixed logic, they plumbed the human experience of desire in every possible way. They saw the yearning that God had sewn into the fabric of creation as echoing God's own insistent longing for relationship. Sexual passion in marriage and the beauty of an English (or New England) countryside were particularly compelling to them, pointing to an even greater want in the human soul.

When John Milton pictured the nuptial passion of Adam and Eve at the beginning of *Paradise Lost*, he described the young groom as ecstatic in receiving the gift of his "other self" in an evening garden. Adam leads his gentle wife, blushing like the morn, into a bower under the trees, where the leaves themselves whisper happiness and nearby hills "give sign of gratulation." Joyous birds, whispering breezes, and welcoming stars all share in the couple's holy delight in each other and in God.[1] Nature and desire walk hand in hand.

Lewis Bayly's *The Practice of Piety*, another classic of seventeenth-century Puritan spirituality, similarly spoke of beauty as the chief longing of the Christian believer. "When we behold the admirable colours which are in Flowers, and Birds," he said, "and the lovely beauty of Women, let us say, how fair is that God, that made these fair!"[2] In joining the delight aroused by the loveliness of nature to the attraction of a husband to his spouse, Bayly—like Milton—indicates the two schools of desire that were most operative in the Augustinian spirituality of seventeenth-century Puritans.

Perry Miller identified the "Augustinian strain of piety" in early New England Puritanism as a fixation on divine sovereignty and human sin.[3] But he overlooked the "other" Augustinian emphasis on desire and delight that carries one from this world (with all its twisted longings) to a contemplation of the rapturous beauty of God's inherent splendor.[4] As Lewis Bayly put it, "When we taste things that are delicately sweet, let us say to ourselves, O how sweet is that God from whom all these creatures have received their sweetness!"[5] Puritan spiritual writings repeatedly emphasized themes of pleasure and desire, sweetness and felicity, in describing the means by which God lures God's people—exiled by sin—back to the Jerusalem of union with Divine Beauty.

Underneath the stern moral exactitude of Puritan public life lay a passion for union with Christ, the *unio mystica*—a vision of God transfixing their hearts and minds. This was a truth lost on generations of Puritan interpreters, from nineteenth-century English historian T. B. Macauley to twentieth-century American journalist H. L. Mencken. The former once quipped that "the Puritan hated bear baiting, not because it gave pain to the bear, but because it gave pleasure to the spectators." The latter sardonically defined Puritanism as "the haunting fear that someone, somewhere might be happy."[6] Only people unfamiliar with the positive role placed on desire by seventeenth-century Puritans could perceive them as a people somehow taking joy in "*dis*-pleasure."

The best expressions of Reformed piety, from the Puritans to Karl Barth, have never separated God's power from God's beauty. Barth saw the glory of God to be most clearly revealed as a "power of attraction." A sovereign God, he said, is "One who is pleasant, desirable, and full of enjoyment."[7] Seventeenth-century Puritans knew this as well.

The two schools of desire by which these early Calvinists were most trained in the contemplation of divine beauty were the wonders of the created world and the mystery of conjugal love, nature mysticism and bridal mysticism—the poet's delight in "the heavens telling the glory of God" and married couples' passion for their spouses. In these two spheres the Puritans revealed themselves as intensely a people of desire. Their espousal of passion, in fact, made necessary the severe cautions against misdirected longing that we have come to regard as characteristically Puritan. In a spirituality where temporal beauty was recognized as an unpolished mirror of Eternal Beauty, there was ever the danger of lingering at the enjoyment of the one without pressing on to ecstatic union with the other.

While this chapter attends to nature and marriage as Schools of Desire, the next chapter will look at another aspect of Puritan spirituality, focusing on its perception of nature as a School of Affliction. The Puritans employed nature imagery in these two different ways so as to elicit fervent desire, on the one hand, while also keeping it in check, on the other. Despite the dangers involved, Puritan devotional literature joined nature imagery with erotic language in describing the spiritual life, summoning human beings along with the rest of the natural world to a common longing for God.

A Puritan Theology of Desire

A firm tradition of "glorifying God and enjoying him forever" was well established in English Puritan thought by the time Anthony Tuckney put the final touches on the larger catechism of the Westminster Assembly. Thomas Watson spoke for the whole Reformed tradition when he commented on its first question about the chief end of human life:

> God is a *delicious* good. That which is the chief good must ravish the soul with pleasure: there must be in it rapturous delight and quintessence of joy. *In Deo quadam dulcedine delectatur anima immo rapitur*: The love of God drops such infinite suavity into the soul as is unspeakable and full of Glory.[8]

This theme of "desiring God" appeared so often in Puritan sermons that desire itself became a dominant way of articulating the knowledge of God. It served as the surest test of human character, a means of authenticating spiritual experience generally, and the underlying power of prayer itself. Sermons on the Song of Songs, like Richard Sibbes's "The Spouse, Her Earnest Desire after Christ," were echoed throughout New England as well, in the sermons of John Cotton and Thomas Shepard.[9]

In one of the most remarkable examples of this genre, Francis Rous preached a sermon on *Mystical Marriage*, taking as his text the words of the prophet Isaiah, "Fear not, for thy Maker is thine Husband" (Isa. 54:4–5).[10] Not only did he speak of "a chamber within us, and a bed of love in that chamber, wherein Christ meets and rests with the soul. . . ."[11] He went on to exhort his listeners to desire this husband with a language as vivid as anything found in the writings of Bernard of Clairvaux.

> Clear up thine eye, and fix it on him as upon the fairest of men, the perfection of spiritual beautie . . . , accordingly fasten on him, not thine eye only, but thy mightiest love, and hottest affection. Look on him so, that thou maist lust after him; for here it is a sin, not to look that thou maist lust, and not to lust having looked.[12]

The biblical warrants for this ardent fervor are readily apparent. This was a language drawn from the Song of Songs and the gospel parable of the ten virgins, as well as the Pauline image of the bride of Christ. The Puritans were quick to connect a passion for God with the pleasure of the biblical text.

The reading of Scripture as a pleasure-giving act had itself enjoyed a long history from Augustine to Calvin. For centuries, the love of learning (*biblical* learning) and the desire for God had been inseparable.[13] Writers in the Augustinian tradition pictured the reader of Scripture as one who thirsts after God—yearning for God's Word, feeding upon it, nursed by it like a child at her mother's breast, satisfied only as the Word enters most deeply into the heart of her being. Augustine's *Confessions* had explicitly connected the act of reading to desire. As a teacher of rhetoric, the Bishop of Hippo knew reading to be a richly oral process. It engages the moving of the lips, the projection of sound, and a careful attentiveness to one's breathing. "To read, for Augustine, was to ingest, swallow, digest and incorporate—to *eat* the text." It was inescapably an embodied act—sensual and pleasurable.[14]

Augustine also knew that "delight orders the soul." "Where the soul's delight is, there is its treasure," he declared.[15] His search for God inescapably carried him through the world of the senses. "What do I love when I love you?" he asked of God. Not light, nor the fragrance of flowers, nor the taste of honey, nor the gentle touch of a human body. None of these, he said, and yet at the same time . . . *all* of them! "I do love a kind of light, a certain fragrance, a food and an embrace, when I love my God."[16] Despite his discomfort with his own sexuality and his poverty of intimacy with women other than his mother, he knew that experiencing God was a matter of pleasure, beginning with the beauty of the senses.

> I said to all those things which stand about the gates to my senses: "Tell me about my God . . . tell me something about him." And they cried out in a loud voice: "He made us." My question was in my contemplation of them, and their answer was in their beauty.[17]

If the Puritan tradition of desire had its origin in an Augustinian reading of the Song of Songs, it came to seventeenth-century New England by way of Calvinist Geneva and the ferment of Puritan thought at Cambridge University.[18] Calvin himself had emphasized that it is not the craving of the mind, but the desire of the heart that is most pleasing to God. "We will never spontaneously and heartily sound forth his praises until he wins us by the sweetness of his goodness," Calvin argued.[19] While his finest expression of this truth is found in the emotional intensity and colorful imagery of his Psalms commentary, he speaks even in the *Institutes* of a deep "enjoying" (*fruor*) of God's benefits in the contemplation of nature, as well as union with Christ through the Eucharist.[20]

Michael Winship attributes the prevalence of the language of desire in Puritan discussions of marriage to the influence of Calvinist theology.

> The Calvinist conception of the justification of the believer, where an overpowering God imputes his grace to a fundamentally passive soul, lent itself to gendered imagery, as did the resulting affective nature of the indwelling of Christ in the soul of the believer.[21]

This early Puritan language of "the ravished soul" was, like Calvin's before it, extravagant in its use of metaphor. After the Restoration, later seventeenth-century Anglicans scoffed at the "Nonsensick Raptures" and "Fulsome, Amorous Discourses" of these naive Puritan preachers, preferring instead a more "reasoned" homiletic style purged of unsavory tropes.[22] The Puritan language of desire, as a result, largely disappeared by the coming of the eighteenth century. Its comparatively brief but stunning recovery of a theme stretching from Augustine to Bernard to Calvin raises interesting questions in the history of spirituality in the early modern period.

What makes this seventeenth-century Puritan fascination with desire important for today is the extent to which it spurred attentiveness to the natural world and the potential it had for affirming the equality of women and men in a joint thirst for God. The seeds of a deeper justice were sewn here, despite the failure of the Puritans to live out more fully the implications of the spirituality they espoused.

The Seventeenth-Century Roots of Puritan Desire

English Puritans drew on more than Scripture and the Augustinian tradition in finding sources to support a spirituality of desire. Their appreciation of the natural world grew out of an effort to relate their spiritual practice to a life lived close to the earth. It was spurred also by developments in the history of science in this period. Their approval of sexual pleasure in marriage emerged out of a new openness to sensory experience generally in seventeenth-century thought as well as debates with Roman Catholics over the nature of marital love.

Puritans made their livelihood as farmers, sea-faring fishermen, carpenters, smiths, and tanners—holding occupations that kept them in close contact with the natural world. A delight in creation came naturally to them. They viewed a meditative attentiveness to the heavens and the earth as an appropriate way of celebrating God as Creator. A flood of spiritual handbooks appeared in the seventeenth century, helping Puritan believers to draw spiritual truths from their life in the world. Richard Steele's *The Husbandman's Calling* offered devotional insights from the daily work of farmers.[23] John Collinges published *The Weavers Pocket-Book: or Weaving Spiritualized*. John Flavel was hugely successful with a pair of such handbooks—*Husbandry Spiritualized, or the Heavenly Use of Earthly Things* and *Navigation Spiritualized, or a New Compass for Seamen*.[24] In America, Cotton Mather almost single-handedly duplicated this English Puritan output with works of his own for fishermen, sailors, and agriculturalists.[25] Puritan spiritual experience was never far removed from the earth and the details of ordinary life.

Accordingly, they shared a keen interest in the seventeenth-century emergence of modern science. A fascination with natural philosophy led scientists of Puritan sympathies like Samuel Hartlib, Robert Boyle, John Wilkins, and others to assist in the founding of the Royal Society of London. Hartlib was a Prussian-born polymath who edited books on scientific farming and beekeeping. During the Commonwealth Era

(1650–1660) he led an influential circle of scientists who shared his Reformed convictions. Boyle, a chemist, defined his work as a discovery of "the true nature of the Works of God." After a conversion experience (in a thunderstorm, no less) while studying in Geneva, he embraced science as the best way of glorifying God. Jonathan Goddard, an army surgeon with the forces of Oliver Cromwell, did research in medicine. John Wallis, a secretary at the Westminster Assembly, was a mathematician and cryptographer. Lawrence Rooke, an astronomer, studied the moons of Jupiter.[26] A love of nature, as ordered by God, was clearly given spiritual sanction in Puritan intellectual life.

The Puritans could legitimate "desire" as a spiritual virtue in this period because of an increased emphasis on sensation and feeling as a ground of moral action. From Francis Bacon to John Locke, people in Stuart England learned to attend more carefully to the moral implications of their own sense experience. Sensitivity to feelings of anguish, ecstasy, and deep longing characterized Puritan conversion narratives as a natural expression of this impulse. In the emblematic literature (both Catholic and Protestant) that flourished in the seventeenth century, one continually finds "tears and sighs, outpourings of which that century was extravagantly fond," along with expressions of "voluptuous swoonings and sweet and subtle pains."[27] Apprehending the depths and heights of loss and joy—knowing the full range of sensory experience—became increasingly a measure of one's creaturehood before God.

Given this validation of desire, the Puritans were bold in defending the sanctity of sexual pleasure in marriage.[28] They reacted to Roman Catholic claims that the marital relations of husbands and wives can be justified only as a matter of "duty," not as a matter of "desire."[29] Puritan marriage manuals forthrightly defended "mutual dalliances for pleasure's sake" within the marriage covenant, urging "that husband and wife mutually delight each in the other," maintaining a "fervent love" in their regular yielding of that "'due benevolence' one to another which is warranted and sanctified by God's word."[30]

When Margaret Durham, wife of the celebrated Scots divine James Durham, wrote an epistle dedicatory for the posthumous publication of her husband's *Exposition of the Song of Solomon*, she spoke without embarrassment of the "love-faintings . . . , high delightings . . . , love-languishings . . . , and heart-ravishings" that characterize marital and mystical bliss alike. She delighted in "those bashful, but beautiful blushings [and] humble hidings . . . on the Bride's part, and those urgent callings and compellings . . . on the Bridegroom's part." The most impassioned bedroom imagery seemed to her a natural (and appropriate) expression of the human and divine love described in the Song of Songs.[31]

Within the wider constellation of seventeenth-century Puritan thought, yet another authorization of desire came from the writers and poets who made up the Cambridge Platonists. This philosophical movement arose out of the "cradle of Puritanism" at Emmanuel College, Cambridge. Benjamin Whichcote and his followers insisted that creation reflects the perfection of God's beauty.[32] The height of enjoyment, to which all beings are drawn, is to desire this perfect Simplicity, this ultimate Beauty from which every lesser thing emanates.

Accordingly, Whichcote declared that "Every creature is a line leading to God." Every blade of grass, every herb, every plant imparts something of the Divine.[33] His colleagues, Henry More and Ralph Cudworth, reacted to Descartes' view of animals as lacking any sort of intelligence or feeling, ridiculing his notion that "a saddled horse has no more sense than its harness." By contrast, they perceived the whole world as infused by spirit, drawn to the enjoyment of God's perfection.[34] The Cambridge Platonists deeply influenced Puritan thought, especially in later writers like Jonathan Edwards.

A final source of seventeenth-century Puritan desire was, oddly enough, the theology of the covenant itself. Covenant theology, as outlined by Calvin and developed in the writings of Reformed theologians like Bullinger and Ursinus, had been a way of underscoring a theology of grace, assuring believers of God's promise of faithfulness. They understood the covenant as the means by which an untamed God of holy majesty willingly "tamed" God's self, entering into loving, intimate relationship with those who had been estranged from God by sin. It was later referred to as federal theology, the Latin word for covenant being *foedus*.

To own the covenant, as the Puritans understood it, was to spur on a holy desire. "The church (and so every Christian) after this contract and taste of Christ's love, hath evermore springing up in them an insatiable desire for a further taste and assurance of his love," proclaimed Richard Sibbes.[35] One's deepest wants become discernible only from within an initial commitment to covenantal relationship. This was true in the covenant of marriage as well, they said. Desire may initially draw couples to each other, but covenant faithfulness releases a still greater affective response. The covenant, as they saw it, makes people better lovers.[36]

Connecting covenant theology to the affectionate bond of marriage was natural for the Puritans. They drew on a long history of marital imagery in the church's effort to understand the divine-human relationship. Medieval theologians had discussed God's covenant "promise" to God's people as a *sponsum*, that is, "a pledge or to contract for a marriage."[37] The dominant image of the two parties in a covenantal relationship was that of a bridegroom and bride. To covenant with God is to enter into a union of marriage with God. Puritans knew that Yahweh, in making a new covenant in Jeremiah 31:31–32, had reminded Israel that God was their "husband." Hence, the notion of covenant, along with these other influences, helped to shape the seventeenth-century Puritan enthrallment with desire.

Husbanding and Husbandry: Two Schools of Desire

This rhetoric of desire afforded the early Puritans a way of expressing an intensity of relationship with God that would not have been possible in a more rational, strictly bookish spirituality. "If thy meditation tends to fill thy note-book with notions and good sayings concerning God, and not thy heart with longings after him, and delight in him, for aught I know thy book is as much a Christian as thou," observed Richard Baxter, the Puritan author of *The Reformed Pastor*.[38] Desire was important to Baxter's understanding of the spiritual life because he recognized how central a role it plays in every aspect of human knowing.

> As the bodily senses have their proper aptitude and action, whereby they receive and enjoy their objects; so doth the soul in its own action enjoy its own object: by knowing, by thinking, and remembering, by loving and by delightful joying: this is the soul's enjoying.[39]

Desire, in Baxter's thinking, was fundamental to Puritan epistemology. "We shall never be capable of clearly knowing till we are capable of fully enjoying," he insisted.[40] Hence, he urged the Christian, forty years before Locke's *Essay concerning Human Understanding*, to "bring down thy conceivings to the reach of sense." One should learn to "compare the objects of sense with the objects of faith," desiring them both so as to embrace the beauty of the natural world in the larger exercise of desiring God.[41] "What a pleasure is it to dive into the secrets of nature," he proclaimed, knowing (with Augustine) that lesser delights—when properly used—become a preparatory school for greater delights. [42]

Baxter's emphasis on the illuminative role of desire and the importance of the bodily senses in biblical interpretation was remarkably akin to Ignatian spirituality at the time. In the final prelude to each meditation in his *Spiritual Exercises*, Ignatius Loyola had invited his retreatant to ask for "that which I want and desire." In the Constitutions of the Society of Jesus, he similarly spoke of the importance in the spiritual life of "the desire to *have* the desire," if nothing else.[43] Ignatius's highly personal, even sensory reading of scripture, employed the use of the five senses and the "reconstruction of place" in imagining one's participation in the vivid details of biblical narratives. In the same way, Baxter argued that "heavenly contemplation is assisted by sensible objects." He encouraged the reader of the book of Revelation to "suppose thyself a companion with John in his survey of the new Jerusalem, viewing the thrones, the majesty, and the heavenly hosts in the shining heavenly splendor which he saw."[44]

These early Puritans went on to identify desire as the surest test of human character, revealing the deepest propensities of the self. "Desires, I confess, are the best character to know a Christian, for works may be hypocritical, desires are natural," said Richard Sibbes. He maintained that "desires are the vent of the soul," providing clearer access even than one's deeds to the inclination of the human will.[45]

John Cotton of First Church, Boston, could even proclaim that sustained desire constituted the best test of spiritual experience generally. The insatiability of delight serves as the most dependable sign of the authenticity of grace. The best assurance of having truly acquired Christ is a continued longing for still more of his love. "It will inflame our hearts to kisse him again, if the kisse be from God," Cotton said in his exposition on the Song of Songs.[46] Similarly, John Bailey, in nearby Watertown, Connecticut, stoutly pronounced that "True Grace is not contented with Little Grace."[47]

By the time of the Westminster Assembly at mid-seventeenth century, therefore, desire had become—in all of these ways—the heart and blood of Puritan spirituality. Francis Rous spoke for many others in celebrating "the new Wine of the Kingdom of Heaven which makes the Soul drunken with high comforts, raptures, and extasies: which . . . fill up a man with an excess of Joy and Happiness, that he shal [sic] be even swallowed up, and over-ravished with joy."[48]

Nature and marriage became the principal "schools" by which Puritans were instructed in this earnest desire. Here they learned to appreciate two important covenantal relationships—the covenant of Noah between God and the created world and the renewal of that covenant in Hosea between God (as spouse) and Israel. The covenant with Noah in Genesis 9:9–11 had explicitly included every living creature in the covenant community. The reiteration of that covenant in Hosea 2:16–23 (including again the beasts of the field and birds of the air) made Yahweh the husband of Israel, betrothed to the people of God *and* to the heavens and the earth as well.[49] To be a covenant people, therefore, meant being joined in spiritual marriage to God through Christ and to be joined by a shared desire to all the rest of creation. Puritan sermons on nature and marriage were often intertwined.

Alongside seventeenth-century Puritan treatises like Robert Crofts's *The Lover: or, Nuptiall Love*, John Allin's *The Spouse of Christ . . . Leaning upon Her Beloved*, and Richard Sibbes's *The Bride's Longing for Her Bridegroom* were another genre of Puritan works like John Flavell's *Husbandry Spiritualized*, Ralph Austen's *The Spirituall Use of an Orchard*, and Thomas Taylor's *Meditations from the Creatures*.[50] All of these used rich imagery drawn from a delight in sensuous beauty to point the faithful toward intimate union with Christ. The arts of husbanding and husbandry were viewed as similar means for sharpening one's desire toward God.

Puritans, for example, understood the institution of marriage as a training ground in the learning of affection, one that led to Christ's even more-compelling beauty.[51] Thomas Hooker, the Puritan founder of the colony of Connecticut, used the intimacy of marriage to describe the saints' love of God.

> The man whose heart is endeared to the woman he loves, he dreams of her in the night, hath her in his eye & apprehension when he awakes, museth on her as he sits at table, walks with her when he travels and parlies with her in each place where he comes . . . the heart of the lover keeps company with the thing beloved.[52]

The joy that married couples like John and Margaret Winthrop, Edward and Elizabeth Taylor, or Simon and Anne Bradstreet took in each other was readily apparent in seventeenth-century America. "One of the most striking phenomena about the New England Puritans is that their greatest ministers and governors . . . loved their wives beyond measure," says Amanda Porterfield. They looked on them as "earthly representatives of God's beauty."[53]

John Cotton, in fact, had to caution husbands and wives who were "so transported with affection" that they ran the risk of aiming "at no higher end than marriage itself."[54] Puritan love letters between husbands and wives were always careful to remind each other that their "heavenly husband" should draw their deepest love. They were careful to observe an ordered pattern of affection, putting God first in their lives.[55]

Nature served a similar role in pointing the faithful to a beauty beyond itself. Nathanael Culverwel, a fellow of Emmanuel College, argued that "Every entity [is] sugared with some delight." He urged his readers to meditate on each of the "sensitive creatures" that school believers in a restless longing for God. "Have you not seen a Bee make a Trade of pleasure, and, like a little Epicure, faring deliciously every day; whilest it lies at the breast of a flower, drawing, and sucking out the purest sweetness?"[56] William Bates, a Puritan vicar in London, argued that "Our five senses are so many Doors whereby . . . External Objects are conveyed to us, and the Soul is to take notice of them." We hear God speaking in each of these. "From the Sun, to the Stone; from the Cedar, to the Violet; every creature hath a voice to teach us something of God. This whole World is a School of man. All the Creatures spell this to us. . . ."[57]

John Bailey of Connecticut spoke of everything in creation as constituting a part of "God's library," a vast resource from which people could "read their fill." From the beauty of open fields to the hard-working faithfulness of a good horse, the natural world provided entry to the mystery of God's glory. For the person of discerning spirit, the tiniest creature witnesses to the source of its amazing life in God's providential care. "When he tasts [sic] sweetness in any creature, . . . thinks he then how sweet is he that made it!" said Bailey. But don't stop with the creature, he said, go on to the source. "The Fountain must needs have more than the Stream."[58] In the same way, John Flavell of Dartmouth urged his congregation to "Make a ladder out of earthly materials," using matter—even cattle and corn fields—to ascend to God.[59] He described "the World below [as] a Glass to discover the World above; *Seculum est speculum*."[60]

Absence and the Enhancement of Desire

Nature and marriage imagery abounded in this vast literature of desire, among English as well as American Puritans, women as well as men. They came to understand that desire could be enhanced and even purified by the absence of its object, by a delay of satisfaction. Richard Baxter, for example, had always been drawn to nature's beauty. He was accustomed to following Isaac's example (from Genesis 24:63) of "walking forth to meditate in the field at eventide." During a dreadful experience in the English Civil War, however, he was kept from this spiritual practice. He later found refuge again in hiking the English Midlands of his parish at Kidderminster. A sense of God's absence in the horror of war had led him to appreciate even more the solace of an evening landscape.

> What an excellent book is the visible world for the daily study of a holy soul! . . . O wonderful wisdom, and goodness, and power which appeareth in every thing we see! in every tree, and plant, and flower; in every bird, and beast, and fish; in every worm, and fly, and creeping thing; in every part of the body of man or beast, much more in the admirable composure of the whole; in the sun, and moon, and stars, and meteors. . . .[61]

Baxter knew that desire for God is initially stirred by the senses. In fact, he found even more delight in God after falling in love with Margaret Charlton at the late age of forty-seven. He had previously advised ministers not to marry (because of the many demands on their time), but he was swept away by his love for Margaret, his senses once again taking the lead in carrying him ultimately to God. In more than one way he came to learn that desire flourishes on absence.

Edward Taylor—Massachusetts's finest example of a seventeenth-century metaphysical poet—was also smitten by his love for his wife Elizabeth. He spoke of their being inseparably knit together in a "True-Love Knot," like branches grafted into the stock of a fine fruit tree.[62] This was a frequent Puritan emblem drawn from nature and expressed, for example, in Ralph Austen's *Spiritual Use of an Orchard.* Austen was a Puritan horticulturist and keeper of the gardens at Oxford who found in the grafting of trees an image of the "firme and constant union between Christ, and every Believer."[63] In this knot lay the core of holy desire.

Taylor's funeral poem at the loss of his "ever endeared and tender wife" in 1689 was a testament to the intimacy of Puritan married love. After her death he attended more than ever to nature as a teacher of desire. Her absence (and the natural world's capacity for praise) gave greater focus to his longing for God.

> But shall the Bird sing forth thy Praise, and shall
> The little Bee present her thankfull Hum?
> But I who see thy shining Glory fall
> Before mine Eyes, stand Blockish, Dull, and Dumb? [64]

"Shall I court thee onely with dull tunes?" he asked of the One he had learned to love even more than he loved Elizabeth.[65] The fact that God desired him far more than he desired God was what amazed him most.

> Shall Mortall, and Immortall marry? nay,
> Man marry God? God be a Match for Mud?
> The King of Glory Wed a Worm? mere Clay?
> This is the Case. The Wonder too in Bliss.
> Thy Maker is thy Husband. Hearst thou this?[66]

The weaning of desire from an earthly love that cannot last to a wanting that has no end remained a poignant theme in the writings of Puritan women as well as men. When Elizabeth Rowe, a late-seventeenth-century English poet, lost her husband (and the dearest joy of her life), she spent the rest of her years in seclusion, writing poetry about the aching absence of a God she also loved but could not grasp.[67]

"Eros is that odd sprite that thrives on absence," writes Wendy Farley, reflecting on the provocative ideas of Emmanuel Levinas.[68] This twentieth-century Jewish philosopher's understanding of metaphysical desire is helpful in perceiving the way that seventeenth-century Puritans thrived on a desire they knew they could not satisfy. In seeking a God who was radically "Other," their training in the exercise of longing (and loss) prepared them for accepting the "desired" as something they never would fully realize. Yet, in the process, their attraction was only deepened.

Levinas distinguishes between physical need and metaphysical desire in a way that the Puritans might also have done:

> The "other" metaphysically desired is not "other" like the bread I eat, the land in which I dwell, the landscape I contemplate . . . I can "feed" on these realities and to a very great extent satisfy myself, as though I had simply been lacking them. . . . The metaphysical desire tends toward *something else entirely*, toward the *absolutely other.* [69]

Desire for what he calls the "Most-High" is keenly aroused by the joining of beauty with absence, by that which is inherently most desirable and yet at the same time most elusive. "[Desire] nourishes itself, one might say, with its hunger," says Levinas.[70] Sounding like Gregory of Nyssa, Bernard of Clairvaux, and many other classic writers on longing, Levinas insists that desire for the Other is necessarily "a desire without satisfaction."[71]

Hence Elizabeth Rowe can write, with anguished longing, in one of her poems on the Song of Songs:

> O! if you meet the object of my love,
> Tell him what torments for his sake I prove;
> Tell him that all my joys with him are gone,
> Tell him his presence makes my heav'n; and tell,
> O tell him, that his absence is my hell![72]

Yet paradoxically God's absence was for her the medium through which she most experienced desire. She had learned, like Bartholomew Ashwood, that "Absence of Lovers is sometimes the way to starve [and enhance] affections."[73] Also like Ashwood, she used nature imagery to express this aching sense of loss. In a period of spiritual dryness, she writes: "I listen, but I hear those gentle sounds no more; I pine and languish, but thou fleest me; still I wither in thy absence, as a drooping plant for the reviving sun."[74] Nature serves as a tantalizing veil, shading the glory of what she seeks most.

> I pine, I die for the sight of thy countenance: Oh! turn the veil aside . . . Let it interpose no longer between me and my perfect bliss. . . . I search thee in the flowery meadows, and listen for thee among the murmuring spring. . . .' 'Tis all in vain: nor fields, nor floods, nor clouds, nor stars, reveal thee.[75]

She knows that the natural world struggles with the same sense of absence that she herself feels. It echoes her passion and loss. She laments that, "I murmur to the winds and streams, and tell the solitary shades my grief. The groves are conscious of my complaints, and the moon and stars listen to my sighs."[76] Nature participates in her longing, yearning for its own redemption. They wait together in a common anguish of longing.

Anne Bradstreet of Andover, Massachusetts, was another Puritan poet who wrote of the absence of her loving husband as suggesting the absence of a still deeper love. The Psalmist's image of "the hart panting after the waterbrooks" became for her (and others like her) a language that thrived on deprivation. In a poem to her husband away on business, she writes:

> As loving hind that (hartless) wants her deer,
> Scuds through the woods and fern with hark'ning ear,
> Perplext, in every bush and nook doth pry,
> Her dearest deer, might answer ear or eye:
> So doth my anxious soul, which now doth miss
> A dearer dear (far dearer heart) than this.[77]

This is a richly porous language in which longings for nature, spouse, and God are constantly played against each other, reverberating in a mutual awareness that "the true life is [always] absent," as Emmanuel Levinas observes. Absence allowed Puritan couples to make sure that the ardor of their love for each other contributed to (instead of detracting from) the strength of their love for God.

The Transposition of Gender: Men Becoming Women

Puritans knew that this process of risking themselves to metaphysical, open-ended desire could lead potentially to the radical transformation of the human person.[78] One cannot give oneself to sustained reflection on God as spouse or God as revealed in natural beauty without breaking into a rash and poetic language, without being forced into a new identity shaped by the exercise of prolonged desire. Entry into the spousal and nature imagery of the wisdom tradition in Scripture led the Puritan imagination to a transposition of gender and of species that could be as provocative as it was creative.

Michael Winship speaks, for example, of a "gender polymorphousness" that characterized much of seventeenth-century Puritan spiritual writing.[79] As Puritan men wrestled with appropriating the bridal imagery of the Song of Songs, they were forced necessarily into a metaphorical change of gender. Thomas Shepard of Cambridge, Massachusetts, writes in his diary of the spiritual distance he felt between himself and God in the spring of 1641, grieving over "my widow-like separation and disunion from my Husband and my God."[80] Conceiving of himself as the "bride of Christ," as the text had demanded of him, he could do no other. The language of the Song forced upon him a new spiritual vulnerability—through a shift in gender—that potentially questioned the position of power he normally held within the community.

This "gender polymorphousness" was rooted in the Puritan conviction that the human soul (in men as well as in women) was essentially feminine. It had "wifely" traits and could be described as either barren or fecund, depending on its relationship to Christ, its divine husband.[81] Puritan males, therefore, were explicitly invited to recognize the *anima*, the feminine archetype of the soul, within themselves.

Joseph Bean, a Puritan in Boston, wrote out a marriage covenant between himself and God, vowing, "I do here with all my power accept the[e] and do take the[e] for my head husband for biter [sic] for worse for richer for poorer . . . ," going on to "love, honor, and obey" the Husband given to him in Christ. Spousal imagery offered him a way of defining his relationship to God while also rethinking his role as a man in Puritan society.[82] "As rulers and husbands on earth, and thus in some sense as imitators of divine sovereignty, men were precariously balanced between social authority and religious humility," Amanda Porterfield writes of seventeenth-century male Puritan experience.[83]

Marital imagery in Puritan spirituality thus threatened to undo the very order it had attempted to achieve through the gendered structuring of religious experience. As Porterfield again observes:

> The Puritan depiction of grace as an erotic struggle for submission to God [had] helped construct ideas, expectations, and experiences of marriage that sanctioned authoritarian behavior among husbands and also stressed the importance of willing consent among wives.[84]

But if at some point men "had to become women," through the invitation of the biblical text, then traditional patriarchal patterns might have to be reconsidered in a new light.[85]

Francis Rous, for instance, could speak in highly disparaging ways of the "husband" one had to leave behind in one's fuller entry into the experience of the bride. "No soul can marry with Christ Jesus, but a widow, for she must be freed from the law of her old husband by his death." He even contended that the soul must "give consent to the divorce and death of this usurping and bloody husband, without whose death there can be no marriage between her and happiness."[86] Men (and women) were thus summoned through the bridal imagery of the Song of Songs to a rethinking of their gendered identity in potentially revolutionary ways.

John Cotton of the early Massachusetts Bay colony offers an interesting case in point. Here was another Puritan whose marriage had provided him the clearest taste of God's love. He had experienced this so vividly at his own wedding that he would later celebrate "that day (as) a day of *double marriage* to me."[87] Being joined in matrimony to Elizabeth Horrocks, he knew himself simultaneously to be espoused to Christ. She represented the Beloved to him in such a way that she almost became bridegroom to his bride. In a similarly interesting shift in gender, Thomas Shepard confessed at the death of his wife Joanna in 1648 that he felt God "withdraw." It was as if his wife had functioned spiritually through the years in some way as "husband"—the one through whom he had most clearly seen God and known God's love.[88]

Perhaps more than any other Puritan preacher, John Cotton understood his self-identity as a minister to be molded by his role as Christ's bride. Repeatedly he employed wifely and maternal imagery in speaking of his office as minister of the Word. In his exposition of the Song of Songs he candidly described himself as the breasts of Christ from whom the faithful in his congregation were to suck the milk of the Word.[89] To receive the kiss of the Beloved's mouth, he added, is to hear with openness the revelation of Christ's love as this is offered through the pulpit. "The lips [of the sensual bride in Song 4:3] are instruments of speech . . . and so signify such as deliver . . . the doctrine of Christ to his Church in preaching."[90] Through all these connubial and oral images, full of sexual innuendo, Cotton presented himself as one through whom the congregation could intimately receive the grace of Christ. His *Spiritual Milk for Boston Babes in Either England: Drawn Out of the Breasts of Both Testaments for Their Souls Nourishment* became the earliest catechism printed in New England, extending still further this metaphor of motherly nurture he had found so definitive of his own experience.

While Cotton was more explicit than most in his use of spousal imagery as a rhetorical strategy, Puritan men in general were challenged by their piety to embrace a spiritual transposition of gender. They were urged to exclaim along with Edward Taylor, "I then shall be thy Bride Espousd by thee/And thou my Bridesgroom Deare Espousde shalt bee."[91] This inevitably suggested for them a rethinking of traditional roles, an exercise of desire that carried them potentially into a new construction of personal identity.

A feminist reading of these texts, however, could argue that spousal rhetoric in Puritan spiritual writing tended just as often to eclipse the significance of real women in Puritan society. As men employed feminine imagery to emphasize the emptiness and self-effacement they saw as prerequisite to being filled by God, they reinforced the image of women as essentially passive and receptive. Ivy Schweitzer urges that:

> Puritan doctrine was geared toward male saints, who were compelled by the logic of spiritual conversion—figured as a rape or ravishment, or, at the very least, an irresistible intrusion—to position themselves in relation to God and Christ as feminized, deauthorized, self-denying souls. . . .[92]

If the soul is invariably perceived as feminine, as the Puritans perceived it, then the use of the language of spiritual ravishment in describing the relinquishment of the soul to Christ could as readily suggest violence and domination as it could ecstasy and love. Transposition of gender for Puritan men, therefore, did not necessarily imply a deeper appreciation of the dignity of women in Puritan public life.

One has to be careful in presupposing any monolithic conception of male Puritan theology, however. Not all Puritan men followed William Ames and Thomas Hooker in emphasizing a God of sovereign power who "by a holy kind of violence . . . pluckes the soule from sinne."[93] Janice Knight argues persuasively that there were multiple orthodoxies in both Old and New England Puritanism. Alongside Amesian notions of divine domination and human abjection as central realities in the experience of conversion were Sibbesian notions of God's overflowing love melting the human heart instead of hammering it. Richard Sibbes and John Cotton stressed much more the tender mercy of God, looking to consummated union as the ultimate goal of conversion.[94] The suggestion of a transposition of gender in the spousal rhetoric of Puritan spirituality, therefore, had the potential for freeing both men and women from a God of domination and violence (and a social order justified by that conception of the divine) in their longing for ecstatic union with Christ.

The Transposition of Species: Humans Becoming Creatures

Something comparable occurred with respect to the application of nature imagery in the Puritan spirituality of desire. If the Song of Songs metaphorically invited Puritan men to regard themselves as women, passages from the Proverbs suggested a similar identification of humans with creatures of the earth. When Solomon ordered the spiritually torpid of ancient Israel to "Go to the ant, thou sluggard," the Puritans viewed this as a radical call to humility, a submission of the repentant to the teaching office of the least of God's creation. The Puritan premium placed on holy desire meant that sluggishness, "deadness of heart," and indifference were perennial causes for spiritual concern. The reproof of the tiniest creatures—the ant or coney, the locust or spider—therefore, became important means by which the faithless were summoned to renewed zeal (Proverbs 6:6; 30:25–28).

Joseph Caryl, the English Puritan Bible commentator, proclaimed that "All creatures have a teaching voyce, they read us divinity Lectures of Divine Providence." He taught that

> every particular beast, or every single creature is able to give instruction . . . the least as well as the greatest, the Mouse as well as the Elephant or the Lyon; the Shrimp as well as Leviathan; the Hysop on the wall, as well as the Cedar in Lebanon; the Grasse of the field, as well as the oaks of Bashan.[95]

John Flavell's reflections on "spiritual husbandry" resembled Francis of Assisi when he affirmed, "It's an excellent Art to discourse with Birds, Beasts and Fishes, about sublime and spiritual Subjects, and make them answer to our questions." "Believe me," he declared:

> thou shalt find more in the Woods than in a [library] corner; Stones and Trees will teach thee what thou shalt not hear from learned Doctors. By a skilful and industrious improvement of the creatures (saith Mr. Baxter excellently) we might have a fuller taste of Christ and Heaven in every bit of Bread that we eat, and in every draught of Beer that we drink, than most men have in the use of the Sacrament.[96]

This was more than a language of excess given to romantic flourishes; it was firmly rooted in a pragmatic Puritan empiricism. Flavell knew that "Notions are more easily conveyed to the understanding, by being first cloathed in some apt Similitude, and so represented to the sense."[97] Being instructed by the creatures of the earth in the arts of holy desire, therefore, meant putting oneself in their place, learning their own richly sensual language. As Ralph Austen put it:

> We must be content to stoope to their way and manner of teaching, as the Egyptians and others in former times, who were instructed by characters and Hyeroglyphiques, by somthing [*sic*] represented to the eye, Notions were conveyed to the understanding. Dumbe Creatures speake virtually and convincingly, to the mynde, and Conscience.[98]

When human beings view the world in this way, from the perspective of other creatures, they are further instructed in desire. Animals themselves "have a suitable will to take or refuse an object; to express their desires with sounds or notes or voice," even "to express their affections of love," claimed Nathanael Homes, an English Puritan writer at mid-century. We learn from their example. Arguing from symbiotic relationships found in the natural sphere, he could even say that "plants and trees and herbs have their passions or affections, their love appearing in their sympathy as . . . in the ivy and oak, etc.; their hatred in their antipathy, as in the vine and colewort."[99] All creatures participate in a mutual longing that is part of the covenant of creation.

When humans recognize this, they are forced to acknowledge their own creatureliness and to accept the duty of praise that is most properly theirs. Indeed, they are shamed into it by the animals and plants who spontaneously offer praise without even thinking about it. Caryl can go so far as to say:

> Things without life are expressed as putting forth acts of faith towards the living God. (Hos 2:21) The earth cryes to the heavens, and the corne, and the wine and the oyl cry to the earth; there is an intercrying from the lowest to the highest, till the cry come up to the most high God. The whole presents us with an elegant *prosopopeia*, all the creatures striving to do them good, to whom God had once betrothed himself in mercies and in loving kindness. . . .[100]

In this literary personification (or *prosopopeia*) of the more-than-human world, the biblical text invites—even requires—human beings to imitate what they are taught by other creatures.[101] Edward Taylor, therefore, could speak of the spiritual importance of "becoming" a tree, being fruitfully grafted onto the Tree of Life. "Make me thy Branch to bare thy Grapes," he prayed.[102] Such a transposition of species could summon the cold Puritan heart to a renewal of desire for God, in the same way that the green banks and shady bowers of Bernard's twelfth-century monastery had led him to delight in the Holy.[103] This process of mimetic identification also had the potential of significantly altering the ways that Puritans related to the natural world.

The Ethical Impact of Puritan Desire

We turn, then, to an analysis of how Puritan attitudes toward the dignity of women and the intrinsic worth of other-than-human creatures may have changed as a result of these transpositions in gender and species. If Puritan husbands were able to put themselves in the place of women, thinking of themselves as Christ's bride, did this have an effect on the way they treated their wives? And if Puritans carefully attended to the spiritual lessons of the creatures (from the "inside," as it were), did this lead to a more ethical treatment of animals? Having initially raised these questions in chapter 1, I want to take a step further in asking how Puritan practice measured up against Puritan spiritual ideals.

There is evidence that Puritan women in seventeenth-century New England did wield more power and enjoy a greater fluidity of role behavior than women in the Southern colonies or even later in the nineteenth century. William Secker, a seventeenth-century English Puritan widely read in the colonies, spoke of the marriage relationship as a matter of two instruments making music together, two streams flowing in a single current, a pair of oars rowing a boat to heaven. The husband and wife were like a pair of "milch kine" equally yoked in bearing the ark of the covenant. God had made Eve, he observed on reading Genesis 2:21, not from Adam's head, "to claim Superiority, but out of the side to be content with equality." Like Calvin, he recognized that Adam (before the gift of Eve) had been "imperfect," but was only now "rendered complete in his wife."[104]

Generally speaking, "the Puritan wife of New England occupied a relatively enviable position by comparison, say, with the wife of early Rome or of the Middle Ages or even of contemporary England."[105] Wives shared with their husbands a mutual responsibility for nurturing spiritual desire within the sanctity of family and social life. Moreover, says Laurel Thatcher Ulrich in her study of Puritan goodwives, they often served as "deputy husbands," empowered to act for their spouses on various financial and legal matters. They remained economically dependent, but were not exclusively locked into household roles. Puritan women worked alongside their husbands, were involved in community life, engaged in trade, transacted business, and exercised an influence on church affairs. Researchers in the early twentieth century went so far as to speak of a "Golden Age" for American women in the colonial New England experience. But the privileges that Puritan women enjoyed were still largely limited to a domestic setting. They were not based on any notion of individual rights, but on mutual responsibilities they shared with their husbands (in the covenantal relationship).[106]

Patriarchy remained firmly established in New England life, increasing in influence as the seventeenth century progressed. In some ways, in fact, the joining of nature and marriage as common themes in the colonial era contributed as much to the denigration of women as to their dignity. Carolyn Merchant reminds us of the long (and at times disturbing) tradition of identifying women with nature in the mythos of Western thought.[107] In patriarchal societies this often led to the social practice of regarding fields and wives as similar commodities for the use (or enjoyment) of men. I have mentioned Annette Kolodny's provocative book *The Lay of the Land*, documenting seventeenth-century descriptions of the landscape of the New World as a beautiful woman waiting to be taken by bold explorers.[108]

Puritans could be as prone as others to this objectification (even commodification) of land and wives, viewing both as empty spaces to be conquered.[109] Yet their theology suggested something better. Their emphasis on putting God—and the desire for God—at the center of their reflection on nature and marriage meant that the just demands of covenantal relationship should always assume priority over selfish use alone. God had established a covenant with the earth as well as a covenant of marriage. The purpose in each case was to draw the whole of creation into a community of mutual respect and love, giving common praise to God.

On the other hand, a more significant impact of Puritan theology on practice is seen in the way that Puritan farmers ascribed dignity to the creatures they employed in working the land. As previously noted, Puritans were at the forefront of the seventeenth-century movement to abolish animal cruelty. Since they perceived the whole of creation as absorbed in a desire for God, they attributed an uncommon degree of sensation, feeling, and thus worth to animal as well as human life. They called for the just treatment of farm animals, for example, on the basis that they too (as creatures of God) were subject to feelings of suffering and enjoyment. Even Calvin, they knew, had argued that God

> will not have us abuse the beasts beyond measure, but to nourish them and to have care of them. . . . If a man spare neither his horse nor his ox nor his ass, therein he betrayeth the wickedness of his nature. And if he say, "Tush, I care not, for it is but a brute beast," I answer again, "Yea, but it is a creature of God."[110]

Robert Bolton, rector of Broughton, Northamptonshire, considered it sinful to "take delight in the cruel tormenting of a dumb creature" or to revel in "the bleeding miseries of that poor harmless thing which in its kind is much more and far better serviceable to the Creator than thyself."[111] Elnathan Parr, revered commentator and rector at Thrandeston, Suffolk, said of the earth's creatures, "If the Lord would open their mouths [like Balaam's ass]: They would say, O sinfull man which complainest of us: Thy sinne hath made us unable to satisfie thy need. Complaine not of us, but of thy sinne, which excruciateth both thy selfe and us."[112] Presbyterian Thomas Edwards could go so far as to say, "God loves the creatures that creep on the ground as well as the best saints," adding that "there is no difference between the flesh of a man and the flesh of a toad."[113] All created life is sacred.

Puritan Sabbatarianism had included beasts in the Sabbath rest prescribed by Scripture, urging that animals be treated in the same way as other laborers.[114] Puritans opposed the unnecessary cruelty of animal games like dog-fighting and hunting for sport on the grounds that all of God's creatures were made "to enjoy themselves," thereby giving glory to God.[115] A concern for animals as well as the Sabbath led English Puritans to oppose the introduction of the Cotswold Games in 1612, for example. They denounced its blood sports, which pitted animals against each other and men armed with sharp pikes against wild bears and bulls. Drinking, gambling, and "wenching" were also common at these games, which were frequently held on Sundays. Puritans roundly criticized the practice and further denounced James I's proclamation of his "Book of Sports" in 1618, a tract supporting the games and urging people's participation on the Sabbath. Puritan opposition was not based on the rejection of "games" as such, but on their moral sensitivity to animal cruelty and the profanation of the Lord's Day.[116] The Puritans knew that God readily identified with the pain of abused animals, lame draft horses, and broken apple trees wracked by the storms of spring.

Jonathan Edwards later echoed this same Puritan sensitivity to animals when he offered his own critique of the meat markets of eighteenth-century New England.

> Some men would be moved with pity by seeing a brute-creature under extreme and long torments, who yet suffer no uneasiness in knowing that many thousands of them every day cease to live, and so have an end put to all their pleasure, at butchers' shambles in great cities.[117]

His sensitivity to the butchery of animals is telling, especially his recognition that the animals' capacity for "pleasure" was precluded by their death (and the manner of their dying). It even suggests a critique of "factory farming" practices today.

We have to be careful, however, not to overstate this Puritan emphasis on animal sensation and their call for human sensitivity to animal rights. Neither the Puritans nor Edwards can be read as proto-ecological advocates of an environmental ethic like Aldo Leopold proposed in the twentieth century. Yet if every creature is to be acknowledged as "a line leading to God," then it has to be seen as possessing an inherent worth of its own, not a purely instrumental value. While this perspective was not carried to its fullness in Puritan thought, it remained a thread awaiting later development in Reformed attitudes toward the natural world.[118]

Conclusion

Thomas Shepard epitomized the Puritan tradition of nature and marriage as twin schools of desire when he spoke of Christ as a lover who leads his bride to a beautiful garden. There water flows from the distant mountains of Lebanon and a south wind brings the fragrance of spring flowers (Song 4:15–16). There, as the Cambridge, Massachusetts, pastor told his parishioners, "he makes love to thee. . . .' 'Tis fervent, vehement, earnest love. . . . The Lord longs for this . . . pleads for this, . . . mourns when he has not this. . . . Take thy soul to the Bride-chamber, there to be with him forever and ever. . . ."[119] Such is quintessentially the Puritan language of desire.

Yet by the end of the seventeenth century this emphasis on passion had begun to fade as a dominant theme in Puritan/Evangelical spirituality.[120] Its bold expression of erotic language became something of an embarrassment as the Enlightenment gave rise to more carefully reasoned explications of the spiritual life. When Isaac Watts published Elizabeth Rowe's *Devout Exercises of the Heart* after her death in 1737, he felt obliged to apologize for her "language of rapture addressed to the Deity," explaining that "it was much the fashion, even among some divines of eminence, in former years, to express the fervour of devout love to our Savior, in the style of the Song of Solomon." [121] One is tempted to read his sense of chagrin as a failure of nerve on the part of subsequent Puritan writers. It was an unhappy loss, this pulling back from the passionate intensity of seventeenth-century piety.

Even today, in the renewed appreciation of Jonathan Edwards's recovery of the "religious affections" and in the ecological sensitivity of contemporary poets and farmers like Wendell Berry, we are reminded of the power of eros in our longing for the other.[122] A recommitment to the importance of embodiment, to the love of one's spouse, and to the cherishing of the land constitutes a return to God's covenant with all of creation.

The Puritans found no better text for the contemplation of these concerns than Isaiah 62:4–5, a passage that Calvin himself praised as a "highly beautiful" expression of the covenant linkage of land and marriage.

> You shall no more be termed Forsaken, and your land shall no more be termed Desolate, but you shall be called My-Delight-is-in-Her, and your land Married; for the Lord delights in you and your land shall be married. For as a young man marries a young woman, so shall your builder marry you, and as the bridegroom rejoices over the bride, so shall your God rejoice in you.[123]

In Reformed spirituality, simply delighting in beauty (whether the beauty of nature or the beauty of one's spouse) is not enough. It must lead to a delight in God's own matchless beauty *and* to the covenantal responsibility of safeguarding God's reflected beauty in the environment and in the mutual intimacy of married life. A Calvinist aesthetic remains restless until it expresses itself in moral action.

Yet desire will always be the starting point. Our enchantment with the world is prerequisite to the task of restoring and protecting its wild beauty. As evolutionary biologist Stephen Jay Gould has argued, "We will not fight to save what we do not love."[124] So long as we fail to recognize our "marriage" to God and to the land, we will be kept from honoring the covenant that joins us together as one.

Open the Kingdom for a Cottonwood Tree

A tree gives glory to God by being a tree. For in being what God means it to be it is obeying Him. It 'consents,' so to speak, to his creative love . . . Therefore a tree imitates God by being a tree . . . by spreading out its roots in the earth and raising its branches into the air and the light in a way that no other tree before or after it ever did or will do.

—Thomas Merton, *New Seeds of Contemplation*[1]

I call him Grandfather. This hundred-year-old cottonwood tree in the park near my house is one of my spiritual teachers. I stop to visit him on walks with the dog. I wander over on days when the winds are strong, especially in winter when ice has covered trees throughout the neighborhood. Grandfather knows the exhilaration (and the danger) of wind.

One dark spring morning, as thunderstorms racked St. Louis, I watched him flying a child's white nylon kite. It had gotten away from the child and its string had tangled in the cottonwood's upper limbs. There was something splendid about a kite soaring in the high wind, held aloft by a tree. But Grandfather was unable to release it as the winds continued to batter the kite, slowly tearing it to shreds. The tree's magical participation in flight dissolved into an inexorable embrace of death. Grandfather has known both the threat and the glory of wind. He is a sacred tree for me, despite the "pagan" connections long associated with such an idea.

The story of St. Boniface carrying his axe and the light of Christianity into the dark forests of eighth-century Germany is a sad but familiar one in the history of the West. He sets his blade to the great oak at Geismar, confronting the pagans who listen anxiously to a rushing sound in the treetops high above.

"A few more vigorous blows," says the legend of the saint, "and the great tree cracks and comes toppling down with its own weight, and splits into four huge pieces, leaving a great patch of light in the green leafy vault, through which the sun falls on the triumphant Christian prelate."[2] With this conflict of mythic opposites, the story proclaims the desacralization of nature in pre-Christian Gaul, securing once again the defeat of the natural world through the power of the cross.

This all-too-frequently repeated narrative distorts the actual importance of trees, and of nature generally, in the history of Christian spirituality. For every story about saints who cut down trees in an act of anti-pagan triumphalism, there are two stories of saints living in hollow oaks, singing the holy office along with their arboreal friends, even causing the trees to burst into leaf in deep midwinter. If St. Martin of Tours allowed himself to be bound to a stake in the path of a falling sacred pine (though on being cut, of course, it fell in the opposite direction), Saints Gerlach, Bavo, and Vulmar were all celebrated for living in hollowed-out trees, St. Victorinus for causing a dead tree to blossom at his death, and St. Hermeland for driving caterpillars from the forest she loved. In chapter 3, we witnessed the delight that Puritans like Ralph Austen took in trees and the loving work of aboriculture. The Puritans knew that even Yahweh was a tree: "I am like a verdant cypress—because of me you bear fruit (Hos. 14:8)."

Yet Manichean, dualistic strands of Western Christian thought have helped sustain the image of the tree as threatening and idolatrous.[3] They remind us that eating from the tree of the knowledge of good and evil caused Adam and Eve's fall. The tree thus became the serpent's abode, a sinister nature deity in its own right. Threatening to supplant the distinctive biblical emphases on history, transcendence, and redemption, the tree symbolized the foreign influence of numinous powers working through the rhythms and orders of nature. Only as the tree was objectified, turned into a lifeless unspirited being, could nature be "kept in its place" and biblical religion maintained in its universal, unearthly purity.

This pattern of interpretation has been radically critiqued in recent years, not only from the perspective of environmental ethics (in the work of writers like Sallie McFague and Baird Callicott), but from revisionist studies of biblical religion itself. Ted Hiebert's study of *The Yahwist's*

Landscape questions the history-versus-nature thesis that long dominated biblical interpretation. He shows how the J material in the Pentateuch describes Yahweh's people not simply as desert nomads following God into an open future, but as sedentary farmers working and honoring their land in the Canaanite hill country.[4]

At agricultural centers like Shechem, Hebron, and Beersheba, farmers set up altars to Yahweh alongside sacred oak trees, giving thanks for harvests of barley, grapes, and olives. The Hebrew word for "oak" (*elon*) is related to the word for God (*el*). Antagonism to nature was the furthest thing from the minds of these Israelite highland farmers. They were accustomed to finding God amid their tilling of the soil and harvesting of crops. To cut a tree, other than pruning it for its own good or using it to sustain life, would have made no sense to them.

This rediscovery of a deep sensitivity to nature in biblical religion, as well as our recognition of an ecological crisis, calls for a new appreciation of trees and other sentient beings. Condemning the sacred groves of Baal and Asherah has kept us too long from validating the fertile agrarian landscape—the world in which Yahweh also is revealed. The Psalmist (104:16) describes the Cedars of Lebanon as planted by a divine farmer whose delight in the land seems remarkably akin to Wendell Berry's.

A tree is more than "a rigid pillar in a flood of light," splashes of green that are reducible to measurements of photosynthesis and the hydrostatic pull of xylem tubes. Martin Buber spoke of a tree's thou-ness, of what happens, "if will and grace are joined" as tree and person enter into a relationship and the tree ceases to be an "it."[5] Phenomenologists like Edmund Husserl and Maurice Merleau-Ponty characterize our perception of the more-than-human world as dynamic, an exchange of intersubjectivities that is highly participatory. They can speak of a tree as "thinking itself within me," invoking in my body a sensual response that is more than my own perception. Magician and philosopher David Abram explores this mystery in his captivating book, *The Spell of the Sensuous*.[6]

Foresters are paying more attention to the responsive character of trees, noticing their high level of cooperation with other life forms, such as fungi. While they do not need each other biologically, trees and fungi are often astoundingly interdependent. Trees also show a remarkable ability to thrive in the most difficult circumstances, sometimes utterly contradicting mechanistic models for predicting tree growth. "Trees of the same species growing in the same soil, climate, and spacing conditions seem to respond individually to the same stimuli . . . suggesting that there is something else in trees—a selfhood, or subjectivity, or a factor 'x' contributing to their infinite variability."[7]

Trees are inexhaustibly unique, as Treebeard testified on behalf of the "tree-shepherds of the forest" in Tolkien's *Lord of the Rings*. Our ways of relating to trees are as varied as our ways of relating to people. Jungian psychologist Michael Perlman's ethnographic study of *The Power of Trees* reports on how people think and feel about particular trees, relating their accounts to fairy tale and myth. He shows, for example, how the loss (and recovery) of trees after the devastation of Hurricane Andrew gave people in south Florida a symbolic language of grief and hope in dealing with the disaster.[8] Trees are our long-term partners in an environmental relationship extending far back in our evolutionary history. "Less than two million years ago our australopithecine ancestors spent considerable time living in treetops," says an author of *Lessons of the Rainforest*. "Before we were human, we were intimate with trees."[9]

Buddhists have vigorously defended the responsiveness of trees and their inclusion in the community of the sacred. In rural Thailand, environmentally conscious monks have gone so far as to "ordain" particular trees in endangered forests, hoping villagers will refrain from harming stands of teak and mahogany that have been symbolically accepted into the Sangha, the Buddhist monastic order.

The Buddha nature of trees has long been recognized by Japanese Buddhist teachers like Ryogen and Chujin. In its own way, a tree naturally seeks enlightenment. It is always completely and utterly a tree, wrote Chujin in the twelfth century. It doesn't try to be anything else, but is perfectly accomplished at being itself. Stephanie Kaza's conversations with trees in her book *The Attentive Heart* have grown out of her own Zen practice of *shikantaza*—sitting in silence before sycamores along overgrown riverbanks or beside ancient bristlecone pines in California's high desert country.[10]

Other sources for honoring the importance of trees exist in the Christian tradition. Simon Schama, in his study of "the verdant cross," describes "a timber history of Christ—born in a wooden stable, mother married to a carpenter, crowned with thorns and crucified on the cross," all of this yielding an astonishing iconography of the sacred tree. Other expressions include recurring images of the Jesse tree in medieval art, Bonaventure's tree of life, and Hildegard of Bingen's tribute to the greenness of trees in the Rhine Valley. In Irish Christianity the Celtic tree alphabet, or Ogham, which used assorted species of trees for spiritual discernment, was carried over by St. Patrick from pagan nature cults.[11]

Yet Christians originally learned of the singing, speaking, and feeling power of trees from Scripture itself. Isaiah, like many of the prophets, spoke of trees clapping their hands for joy, while recognizing also the terror felt by exposed stands of cypress in a high Judean wind (Isa. 55:12; 7:2). Trees, we're told, have knowledge of Yahweh (Ezek. 17:24), they can grieve and be consoled (Ezek 31:15f), they readily sing in anticipation of the coming of the King (I Chron. 16:33). Trees speak, of course, in the same way that humans do, through a process of wind passing over cords or membranes like leaves. Anyone who has ever camped on a windy night under singing larches in Glacier National Park will never doubt the fact.

Nectarius, a recently canonized saint in the Orthodox tradition, taught an entire community of nuns on the island of Egina to recognize the differing songs of trees. One of his confreres could graft one sapling to another with amazing skill by carefully discerning the harmony of their songs. Anyone who listened with deliberate skill, he said, could hear the subtle vibrations of circulating sap.[12]

The recurring image of trees participating in the suffering of Christ on the cross is especially compelling in the history of Christian iconography. Blathmac, an eighth-century Irish poet, wrote that on Good Friday afternoon "a fierce stream of blood boiled until the bark of every tree was red; there was blood throughout the world in the tops of every great wood."[13] This identification with Christ's pain also appears in the image of the Green Man, covered with leaves, found in Europe's Gothic cathedrals. At the Munster of Freiburg-im-Breisgau, on the edge of the Black Forest, the faces of Green Men look down on a fourteenth-century stone carving of the dead Christ, their features contorted with suffering and grief. Julian of Norwich declared that "all creatures failed in their natural functions because of sorrow at the time of Christ's death." In each of these ways, trees are depicted as members of the Body of Christ, sharing in the groaning of creation, awaiting the redemption for which all of us long.

This forest tradition in Christian symbolism makes even more sense if one has personal experience with particular trees. I'm amazed at how many of my students are able to tell stories about their relationship with a given tree. It's not something they're accustomed to talking about at a university. One doesn't want to be labeled a druid or a pathetic tree-hugger in the erudite corridors of academe. (We forget that Plato's academy was itself in a grove near Athens.)

Many of the stories my students tell about "their trees" relate to a process of grieving and consoling at some period of crisis in their lives. That's been my own experience with Grandfather as well. For years I've had a close friendship with this tall Eastern Cottonwood in the park across the street from my home.[14] We met under peculiar circumstances when a fierce windstorm blew down one of the two great trunks growing out of his eight-foot bole. I was there when the Park Service workers cut into pieces the fallen half of that mammoth, wind-torn tree. Today there's a huge, gaping wound, over twelve-feet high and six-feet wide, on Grandfather's open side. I touch the scar tissue forming around it even as rot begins to set in from below.

What made our meeting providential was that I, too, was experiencing breakage at the time. My mother had Alzheimer's disease and was dying of cancer, forcing me, an only child, to wrestle with losses I'd been denying for a long time. We shared a lot together, Grandfather and I. He knew pain and relinquishment, and taught me much about relationship, about waiting and letting go, about the detachment that makes love possible.

I still go to him, sometimes with worries about the future or concerns over my children, and he tells me of all the catkins he produces each spring. They're carried away by the wind, mowed over by tractors, lost so he never has a guarantee of the future, of other trees to carry on what he's lived for. Through the years he has learned to wait—and to live in blind hope that the wind may have carried a single seed to a distant place where his life will go on. He tells me not to worry or rush around so much. "Everything you really need will come to you," he says. Only a creature that cannot move, who has to trust and wait, can say that with genuine persuasiveness.

It's hard for me to say how we communicate, though Merleau-Ponty comes close when he speaks of the tree seemingly "thinking itself in me." I lean my head against him, looking across the distant grass in the early evening light, and listen to the subtle changes that play on my imagination. We connect chiefly by way of metaphor, analogies that allow us to "cross over" (*meta-phora*) into each other's experience.

We make contact by way of bark, for instance. It is our only means of touching. Yet the bark of an old Cottonwood is rough and deeply furrowed. I have to lean into him carefully, the way porcupines approach each other, slowly and deliberately, from the proper angle. Rough-barked trees, like thick-skinned people, may often seem distant, abrasive, and uncaring. But the bark that serves as a protective wall is also a permeable membrane. There's a reserved, but deep and honest love underneath it. It isn't accidental that the English word "true" derives from the Old English *treow*, meaning "firm and dependable, like a tree."

Relating one's personal experience with trees to the longer tradition of biblical faith requires our rethinking how we define the limits of community. A case can be made for the inclusion of trees in the *Communio Sanctorum*, the communion of the faithful.[15] If Deuteronomy expresses concern that fruit trees not be harmed in the siege of a city (20:19), if the Psalmist speaks repeatedly of a tree "planted in the very house of the Lord" (Ps. 52:10; 92:14), if we're told that a tree grows in the heart of the New Jerusalem, its leaves meant for the healing of nations (Rev. 22:2), then why not recognize trees as participating in the company of the saints?

Theologians from Irenaeus and Isaac the Syrian to Paul Tillich and C. S. Lewis have argued for the inclusion of animals in heaven; I'd like to see the invitation extended to trees as well. It's more than a whimsical and heuristic proposal. The question of inclusion has occupied the moral center of the ecological movement from its beginnings. Half a century ago Aldo Leopold complained that "there is as yet no ethic dealing with [the human] relation to land and to the animals and plants which grow upon it."[16] He insisted that all life-forms have to be recognized as intimately interrelated. But how do we understand the character of that relationship, as well as the responsibilities required for maintaining it?

One way of assuring the maintenance of the biosphere is to speak of the legal "rights" of trees, as University of Southern California law professor Christopher Stone has done in his book *Should Trees Have Standing*? Similarly, Roderick Nash describes the Wilderness Act of 1964 and the Endangered Species Act of 1973 as logical developments in the Western liberal tradition of natural rights. Yet this language of "rights" may not be so helpful in creating the inclusiveness that allows us to live with trees in a fully shared community.[17]

Roger Gottlieb criticizes classical liberalism as being far too individualistic, too focused on personal identity and ownership, to assist us in confronting the environmental crisis. What is necessary is to see ourselves as intrinsically a part of that "nature" from which we so easily distance ourselves. We and the trees are bound together in a symbiotic relationship far deeper than we realize. As John Seed puts it, we aren't simply individuals defending the rainforest, but a "part of the rainforest defending itself." Gottlieb argues for an inclusivist ethic on the basis of ecological values.[18] I'd rather propose it theologically from within the framework of the communion of saints.

The article of the creed pertaining to the *Communio Sanctorum* traditionally speaks of a fellowship (or *koinonia*) among God's people—the ones who intercede for one another in prayer and deed. It includes those in heaven (the church triumphant) and those on earth (the church militant), and refers to a "communion in holy things." It focuses on the community of peoples gathered at table with the risen Lord. Theologians since Vatican II have asked how this communion extends beyond the church into the kingdom as a whole. The cosmic Christ of Colossians 1:15 summons all creation to a deeper unity. With leaves in his hair and seedlings in hand, he gathers great blue whales and whooping cranes, passenger pigeons and maidenhair ferns to join with human beings in a common song of praise to God.

The extension of fellowship to ginko trees and mountain ash seems harmless enough. But what are the ethical implications of this proposal for including trees in the communion of saints? I'm not arguing for a Sylvan Liberation Movement, abandoning all human uses of trees. That would deny the very interdependency that a common life demands. What I am suggesting is that the following corollaries flow naturally from the acceptance of a principle of inclusivity that welcomes trees into the community of the faithful.

We must recognize trees as sharing an intimate, even sacramental relation with us in the Body of Christ. Without the oxygen they exhale, we would have nothing to breathe. We need them as much as we need our own lungs. Metaphorically, and ecologically, they *are* our lungs. The tree-planting Eucharist adopted by the Association of African Earthkeeping Churches provides an important expression of this reality.[19]

We must extend justice to the creatures that sustain human life, using their products with gratitude and respect. Appreciation for these gifts requires an ethical appraisal of logging practices and reforestation plans, including the rejection of clear-cutting policies and "salvage logging." Particular respect must be given to trees in old-growth forests, where species diversity remains at high risk.

We must honor wood, whether cut or uncut. The spirit of Native American wood carvers who ask permission of the tree for the use of its roots or limbs is important to remember. Their ritual prayers to the tree's spirit may take on new meaning in light of the *Communio Sanctorum*. Shaker cabinetmakers who worked in such a way as to enable wood to respond to its "call" to become a chest or table or chair may model a way of honoring wood in our offices and homes.

We must attend, finally, to the distribution of gifts within the community of living beings, recognizing the unjust advantages enjoyed for so long by First-World humans. Nature must be acknowledged as "the new poor," to use Sallie McFague's powerful image.[20] Yet honoring the entire community means also that unemployed loggers and the families of Amazonian tree-tappers will concern us as much as owls and hardwood forests do. Love must be specific, and attentive to all those in need.

I weigh these thoughts as I walk across the street to the park. It's late afternoon and a light wind still blows in the tree tops. Grandfather is singing. The Plains Indians considered Cottonwoods sacred because their leaves move so readily in the wind—always praying, like their relatives, the poplars and aspens.

I think of St. Gudula, a young woman of prayer in eighth-century Brabant. She loved poplars, praying with them often. On the cold January day after she was buried, the people of the village of Hamme swore that a poplar tree at the foot of her grave suddenly burst into green leaf. It needed to sing, grieving for itself while also celebrating her passage into the church triumphant. It think I understand, having loved a poplar tree of my own.

I guess that's why I make this request. Open the kingdom for a cottonwood tree. Let the green creation sing at the banquet. Love alone demands it. Charles Péguy once told a story about God's welcoming faithful Christians into heaven. But on meeting them at the gate, God looked over their shoulder, anxiously asking, "Where are the others? You didn't leave them behind, did you?" The measure of the authenticity of the communion of Christ is the measurelessness of its power to include. For Christians, loving the natural world isn't any longer a matter of choice. It's required by the community in which they live.

· 4 ·

The Schooling of Desire

Nature's Purifying Role in Affliction

I can say in some measure, as David did, *It is good for me that I have been afflicted.* The Lord hath showed me the vanity of these outward things; that they are . . . but a shadow, a blast, a bubble, and things of no continuance; that we must rely on God himself, and our whole dependence must be upon him.

—*Narrative of the Captivity of Mrs. Mary Rowlandson* (1682)[1]

It was nearly a perfect storm that struck the ship *The Adventure* off the Grand Banks in late January of 1683. It had sailed out of Massachusetts Bay for England five weeks earlier with Richard Steere on board, a seventeenth-century Puritan merchant and poet. He was returning to London to attend to foreign trading concerns, following up on favorable prospects in the New World. The first five weeks of the journey had been uneventful. Steere spoke of sailing under "gentler winds" and "easie Breezes." The westerlies at their back hummed through the rigging, keeping the sails full in the morning sun. Fish were everywhere. Two centuries earlier, John Cabot said the huge numbers of swordfish in these waters had slowed his ship down.

Indeed, things were almost too comfortable for a people accustomed to living in covenant with a God whose grace became most apparent in times of trial. As Steere wrote in his poem, "A Monumental Memorial to Marine Mercy,"

> Had we continu'd thus upon the Deep
> We had bin Charm'd into a drowsie sleep
> Of calme Security, nor had we known
> The Excellence of PRESERVATION;
> We had been Dumb and silent to Express
> Affectedly the Voy'ges good success.[2]

Thus, as if to prevent their falling into a self-absorbed confidence, a huge nor'easter came blowing down on the fragile ship. It had been unwise to leave port as late as December that year anyway. The uncommonly pleasant weather had enticed them to take the risk. Seventeenth-century ships between England and America followed the route known today as the "Great Fishery," along the Grand Banks off the southeast coast of Newfoundland. But December and January is a dangerous time to negotiate such waters. They constitute one of the worst storm tracks in the world. Sebastian Junger, author of *The Perfect Storm*, says that waves of a hundred feet, some of the highest in the world, have been measured there, driven by Force-12 winds of 104 miles an hour or more.[3]

Richard Steere spoke of riding out the storm through a full week of horror, overwhelmed by "pondrous seas like Rowling Mountains." The waves constantly broke over the quarter-deck, even separating timbers in the hull. They stuffed bedding and blankets between the cracks. The pumps failed. At one point a rogue wave caught them, pushing the whole ship under "a prodigious Mountain of a sea." They "lay buri'd in the Oceans Womb," said Steere, having reached what marine architects call the zero-moment point, the point of no return, when a ship can no longer sustain bouyancy. But at that moment, Steere rejoiced, "the Great God did Snatch us from below. . . . Causing our buri'd Vessel to Ascend,/ And by degrees climb up the Mountain waves."[4] They survived, providing Richard Steere and other Puritans with yet another confirmation of God's reminder of unfailing grace and the importance of discipline.

Historian Donald Wharton says that, for seventeenth-century Puritans, "The sea experience, and particularly the storm . . . threw into question the possibility of establishing order out of chaos."[5] It raised doubt about the Creator's presence in a world seemingly run amuck. But it also occasioned an opportunity to see God's loving and disciplinary hand in the purifying trials of nature. Hardships would come, but their ultimate function was to strengthen relationship, not to question it. A covenant God utilized the threats of a disordered world to lead God's people beyond inordinate attachments and through adversity into a deeper faith. Times of affliction served as a purification (or schooling) of desire, reorienting the faithful to the highest object of their longing.

The Dangers of Desire and Nature's Purging Power

As much as the Puritans celebrated desire, they knew it was dangerous. They placed a high premium on the intense individual experience that spiritual longing evoked, but they were aware as well of the problems it posed. Desire for an immediate experience of God could be an explosive thing, potentially undermining the very order of society. As a result, for example, Puritan society in New England felt the need to purge itself of the evils of antinomianism. This was the idea that individual Christians (led by the Spirit) did not have to conform to the discipline of the elders as evidence of their salvation. They found another, equally hazardous threat in the excesses of the Quakers with their notion that God speaks to individuals through an Inner Light. And, of course, they attacked witchcraft as the epitome of idiosyncratic fanaticism, a satanic desire for individual power.

Fear of these excesses of desire led sadly, in the end, to the banishment of Anne Hutchinson, the hanging of Mary Dyer, and the death of reputed witches in Salem Village. Social control was perceived as absolutely crucial for a people enamored by a spirituality of longing. Kai Erikson, in his classic analysis of *Wayward Puritans: A Study in the Sociology of Deviance*, shows how important it was (in a society that valued fervent experience) to maintain social stability by identifying and excluding a deviant class of misfits.[6] Desire had to be controlled.

If this was thought to be the case on a societal level, it was no less so in the individual practice of the spiritual life. The faithful had to learn a personal discipline that kept desire aflame, while also keeping it strictly in check. The Puritans were a people of passion, but they were hardheaded Yankee realists as well. They understood the necessity for "a schooling of desire," a process of disciplinary correction able to order their affections. Hence, they interpreted the threats of storms at sea and the howling wilderness beyond their villages as signs of nature's adversity cleansing them of misdirected yearnings. The wild beauty of the world revealed God's glory, but it also taught them the sternness of God's love.

As a result, both sea and wilderness became prominent archetypes in Puritan mythic life, teaching them caution as well as delight. Each of these nature archetypes had a double meaning. The sea represented the ocean of God's love as well as the threat of God's anger (even the chaos of demonic power). The wilderness was a place of romance where Yahweh had led the children of Israel into a deeper intimacy (Hosea 2:14). But it was also a place of terror, full of serpents and scorpions, where Israel had failed God again and again. In each case, the archetype evoked a holy desire while simultaneously visualizing the frenzy of disordered longing.

The tossing waves and furious winds of the North Atlantic—the dense forest and frenzied dancing of dark figures in the wilderness of the interior—all these spoke of the dangers of uncontrolled desire, the wickedness of the human heart. A God of providential care thus found it necessary to use the afflictions occasioned by shipwreck, windstorm, and Indian attack to channel the reckless craving of the Puritans for less-than-holy things. In the winter of 1675, for example, Mary Rowlandson experienced this purging when she and her children were kidnapped by Indians and forced into the wilderness. She came to understand her captivity as a gift, however, teaching her "the more to acknowledge God's hand" in her life, directing her desire to God alone.

The double image of the wilderness archetype (as threat and promise) recurs repeatedly in the spiritual writings of colonial New England. John Cotton defined wilderness as a place of spiritual insight, yet recognized it also as a source of temptation. It was there that John of the Apocalypse had witnessed the chaste bride coming down from heaven, as well as the judgment of the great whore.[7] Wild terrain was potentially a garden of God's love *and* an abode of dark shadows. Roger Williams emphasized its consolations: "As the same Sun shines on the Wildernesse that doth on a Garden," he said, "so the same faithfull and all sufficient God, can comfort, feede and safely guide even through a desolate howling Wilderness."[8] Cotton Mather, however, stressed its dangers, seeing wilderness as the empire of Antichrist, "a squalid, horrid, American desart [*sic*]."[9] Wilderness served as a highly porous image.

In a similar fashion, the sea functioned mythically as a source of correction and a basis for hope in the Puritan imagination. Accounts of water blessing and water deliverance were frequent among Puritan writers in England and America. Water imagery was especially valued by a people whose livelihood was so closely connected to the sea. They found allusions to God's fullness in the flow of rivers emptying into the oceanic expanse of God's love. In their prayers during Atlantic storms, they trusted themselves to a God who "rulest the raging of the sea" (Psalm 89:9). Indeed, baptism by water signaled not only their entry into the covenant, but their deep participation in the sufferings of Christ as well as their thirst for intimate union with God. Water elicited both the terror of drowning and the promise of new life.

Through the use of such images, the Puritans were able to solve a major theological dilemma. They were aware that all was not well with themselves or with the natural world. A "horrible disorder" had cut through the fabric of creation because of the effects of human sin. Eden's peaceable kingdom had disappeared. As a result, "brute beasts, which ought to own men as their masters, [now] rage against them."[10] The Fall had altered the human ability to exercise desire appropriately and affected the phenomenal world as well, making it a threat to itself and to human existence. The Puritan dilemma, therefore, was twofold—knowing how to harness the energies of rampant desire, on the one hand, and how to perceive God as still present amid the dangers of a broken world, on the other. They found an answer to both questions in God's use of the distortions of a world in travail to restore God's people to wholeness. High winds at sea and fierce lightning storms were evidence of God's tough love at work, cleansing the soul like a refining fire.

I turn, then, in this chapter to the Puritan understanding of nature's role in the schooling of desire. It focuses first on the extremes of "sacred eroticism" found in the Puritan devotional literature of the early seventeenth century, pointing up the need for a stern discipline. As previously noted, this was a potentially hazardous spirituality of excess, employing highly-explicit sexual imagery. Its figures of speech were so vivid at times, heightening desire to such a pitch, that the purifying role of affliction had to be emphasized increasingly in Puritan piety.

The Song of Songs and the Problem of Desire

The Puritan emphasis on union with Christ meant that seventeenth-century Reformed spirituality was rampant with sermons on the Song of Songs and the intensity of bridal mysticism. Commentaries and books of sermons on the Song were read eagerly on both sides of the Atlantic.

George Gifford published his *Fifteen Sermons on the Song of Songs* in 1610, followed by Richard Sibbes's *Bowels Opened, or a Discovery of the Neere and Deere Love . . . betwixt Christ and the Church* in 1639. John Robotham's *Exposition of the Whole Book of Solomons Song* and Nathanael Homes's *Commentary on the Whole Book of Canticles* appeared in 1652. John Cotton's *Brief Exposition with Practical Observations upon the Whole Book of Canticles* came out in 1655, accompanied by William Guild's *Loves Entercourse between the Lamb and his Bride* in 1658 and James Durham's *Clavis Cantici: or an Exposition of the Song of Solomon* in 1668.

The most ambitious of all the Puritan commentaries on the Song was John Collinges's *Intercourse of Divine Love betwixt Christ and the Church* (1676). It took him two volumes of nearly 1,500 pages to get through the first two chapters of the biblical text alone. Edward Taylor's communion meditations on the Canticle were also composed in this period, but were never published in his lifetime. Such a list is far from comprehensive, excluding the dozens of published paraphrases of the Song that also appeared during these years. The Puritans, in short, were wildly enthusiastic about the Song of Songs.[11]

The language of desire had traditionally permeated Christian mystical writings, of course. Julian of Norwich had heard God say, "I am he who makes you to long; I am he, the endless fulfilling of all true desires."[12] Yet Puritan authors in the seventeenth century turned this passion up a notch, even as late medieval women mystics like Hildegard and Hadewijch had done.[13] Edward Polhill of Burghurst Manor in Sussex could argue in his commentary on the Song that Christ was "ravished, nay, excordiated" by the loving eye of faithful believers and, in turn, the believers themselves "ravished in him who is *totus desideria*, all or wholly desired."[14] Other Puritans scolded themselves for their coldness of heart, lamenting as Isaac Ambrose of Lancashire did:

> If there be such a thing as the passion of desire in this heart of mine, O that now it would break out! Oh that it would vent itself with mighty longings, and infinite aspirings. . . . Oh that my spark would flame! Lord I desire that I might desire; oh breathe it into me, and I will desire after thee.[15]

Obviously, such an impassioned arousal of longing—even when focused on union with Christ—was potentially problematic. When Bartholomew Ashwood wrote of the nuptial intimacy of the believer with God, he evoked the highly erotic imagery found in the popular (and sometimes scurrilous) literature of Elizabethan and Stuart England. His "bedroom language" was very explicit.

> The spouse of Christ . . . dwells in his presence, and lodges in his arms; she sees him within the veil uncloath'd of those coverings that stand between him and the eyes of strangers. . . . He puts aside his glorious Robe, and shews her his naked breast, and layes her hand upon his tender heart; she is much alone with him in his chambers, where he expresses intimacy with her, as Isaac did with Rebekah, and discloses the secrets of his heart, and the greatest unveilings of his love: He tells her what thoughts he had upon her from all eternity; when he was in his Father's Kingdom, his heart was working after her; and no sooner did he cast his eye upon her . . . but his heart did burn within him towards her; and it was the time of love. . . . [16]

There was nothing priggish about the Puritan exultation of divine love. Thomas Watson, in his "Mystic Union between Christ and the Saints," went so far as to brag about the many lovers that God draws to God's self. "Christ marries thousands," he said. "It is a holy and chaste polygamy. Multitudes of people do not defile this marriage bed."[17] With astoundingly explicit language, the Puritans "out-sang" the Song of Songs in their celebration of the conjugal union between Christ and believers in the marital bond of the covenant.

Managing the intensity of this desire was no easy task for the Puritans. Calvin himself had said, "The evil in our desire typically does not lie in what we want, but that we want it too much."[18] Passion is notoriously hard to control in human experience, and no less so in the spiritual life. The human ego broods over possessing the object of its desire, absorbed in its anxiousness to "have." But God is not an object one can ever "possess." Hence, the greatest danger, as Calvin observed, is the problem of transference. One all too easily transfers the desire that belongs to God alone to lesser persons or things. The dimly reflected beauty of an immediate object of desire distracts from the contemplation of God's definitive Beauty. This juxtaposition of multiple erotic impulses, therefore, gave Puritan spirituality its highly provocative edge.

Richard Rambuss, a scholar of early modern English literature, employs a psycho-sexual analysis in interpreting these seventeenth-century Puritan texts. Drawing on the work of French philosopher Georges Bataille, he suggests that the "sacred eroticism" of the Puritans thrived on its ability to pursue the highest reaches of devotion while traversing the very edge of transgression and the breaking of taboos.[19]

Bataille had insisted that eroticism "is in no respect foreign to the domain of religion." Indeed, it is "*primarily* a religious matter." Passion is a supreme virtue in the mystical traditions of all the great religions. "Even in the eyes of believers, the libertine is nearer to the saint than the man without desire."[20] As a result, he observed that the devotional and the lascivious are often strangely interrelated in religious experience. Kierkegaard, for instance, delighted in comparing the devoutly committed Christian to Don Juan, the profligate lover, and the religious pretender to his dispassionate sidekick, Leporello. The one ardently throws himself into passionate affairs of the heart, while the other objectively stands back with his notebook to keep track of the place, the date, and the woman.[21] Kierkegaard and the Puritans were alike in criticizing the cold objectivity of the state church of their day. In each case, they placed a higher premium on religious longing than on religious learning. Neither could imagine an exercise of faith without a fervency of desire.

The Puritans thus walked a perilous edge as they stressed the alluring character of Christ as bridegroom and lover. They borrowed the language of erotic fantasy that flourished in Elizabethan, Jacobean, and Stuart England. Their rhetoric drew its appeal from associations with the erotically transgressive. Their devotion was stimulated and heightened by its (inadvertent?) identification with contemporary images of sexual longing, trespassing traditional boundaries of morality in a variety of ways. As Rambuss observes, "Nothing heats the passions. . . . like the taboo."[22] When Francis Rous urged his devout readers to "stirre up thy spirituall concupiscence" in loving Christ (and "to lust mightily for him"), he was certainly stretching the holy imagination.[23] It was a bold rhetorical device, exhorting his readers to an intensity of spiritual devotion through a reckless language of sexual abandonment. Yet he could argue that the biblical canon had already done the same thing in its inclusion of the Song in holy writ.

Puritan Hedonism in its Seventeenth-Century Literary Context

It was no accident that this Puritan preoccupation with desire ran parallel to a literary celebration of pleasure extending from Rabelais's *Gargantua and Pantagruel* in the sixteenth century to Fielding's *Tom Jones* in the eighteenth century. These separate strains of "sacred" and "profane" passion might seem initially to have had nothing in common. On the surface, one can hardly imagine two more diverse movements in seventeenth-century England than the amorous spirituality of the ardent Puritans and the literary eroticism of the Cavalier poets.

Yet one is tempted to speak of a "Puritan bawdiness" in Stuart England, mirroring the excesses of secular poetry in its myriad sermons on the erotic imagery of the Song of Songs. What Puritan writer Richard Sibbes referred to as "Affectionate Theology" covered a wide spectrum of Puritan preachers from Richard Baxter to Francis Rous.[24] Their sermons made generous use of sexual language in stirring the souls of the faithful. While any direct literary dependence of Puritan authors on the Cavalier poets may have been minimal, a general fascination with the frank and high-spirited poetry of love was characteristic of the seventeenth century as a whole. It was in the air that everyone breathed.

Literary critic George Scheper argues that Puritan commentaries on the Song were less given to erotic imagery than Puritan sermons.[25] He points to Nathanael Homes, for example, who had warned of the dangers of lewd interpretations.

> Away, say we, with all carnal thoughts, whiles we have heavenly things presented us under the notion of Kisses, Lips, Breasts, Navel, Belly, Thighs, Leggs. Our minds must be above our selves, altogether minding heavenly meanings.[26]

Similarly, the Westminster Divines, in their *Annotations* on Holy Scripture, cautioned against being too explicit about drawing spiritual insights from highly erotic passages like Song 5:4, for example. There the bride speaks explicitly of sexual foreplay, saying "My beloved put his hand in the hole and my bowels were moved for him." "To an impure fancy," the Puritan fathers admonished, "this verse is more apt to foment lewd and base lusts, than to present holy and divine notions."[27] They also questioned the perceived excesses of Bernard of Clairvaux's Sermons on the Song of Songs. Not only had he mentioned sexual intercourse as a metaphor of mystical union; he extolled the bride's intoxicated passion as the reckless self-abandonment God expects of God's lovers.[28] Scheper suggests that the Puritans generally shied away from sexual interpretations of the Song, seeing it as extolling the domestic virtues of Christian marriage.

Yet the very fact that the Westminster Divines found it necessary to caution against the use of such imagery underscores the extent to which sensual metaphors had been widely incorporated in Puritan spiritual writing. Their commentators may have been more restrained in their careful explication of texts, but Puritan preachers were unrepentant in their eagerness to awaken desire through the Song's extravagant language of passion.

This license to explicitness is understandable, given the literary context within which these Puritan sermons emerged. In the first half of seventeenth-century England, metaphysical poets like John Donne and George Herbert (known for their lofty spiritual vision) were generally contrasted with the Cavalier poets (writers like Robert Herrick, Richard Lovelace, and Thomas Carew) who reflected the refined but often erotic court life of King Charles I. Donne was one who actually functioned within both camps. Known alternatively as "Jack the Rake" and "John the Divine," he was judged by many as "*the* poet of sexual desire" in the seventeenth century.[29] He equally celebrated the passion aroused by a woman undressing for bed and the desire for a God who created human passion out of God's own deep longing for relationship.[30]

While Francis Rous elicited an ardent lust for Christ in his reflections on the Song, courtly poet Thomas Carew (known for his profligate life) wrote poems about the raptures of physical love. "I will entwine/My sinowie thighes, my legs and armes with thine," he sings to his lover.[31] Yet Puritan poet Edward Taylor could match him just as readily with his own highly explicit sexual imagery. He wrote of his heart as a "featherbed . . . with gospel pillows, sheets, and sweet perfumes," prepared for Christ his lover. Taylor anticipated union with his Savior through an ecstatic encounter that he admitted might best be compared to the intimate sexual experience of penetration and orgasm. Asking God to grant the arousal of his spiritual "fancy," the Massachusetts poet prayed, "Yea, with thy holy oil make thou it slick till like a flash of lightning it grow quick." Shifting, then, from male to female sexual experience in his search for a language adequate to suggest the heights of rapture, he cried out to God, "O let thy lovely streams of love . . . spout their spirits pure/Into my viall, and my vessel fill/With liveliness."[32]

Such are the extremes to which a Puritan imagination could run in its effort to suggest the ardent joy of union with Christ. As vivid and explicit as this language may be, however, it remains closer in spirit to the ecstasy of Teresa of Avila than to the eroticism of D. H. Lawrence. Its excesses derive from the exuberance of divine worship, as well as Taylor's own loving and deeply fulfilling relationship with his wife Elizabeth.

Another similarity between Cavalier and Puritan conceptions of passion is the playful yet combative struggle that erotic (and divine) love could entail. Cavalier poet William Cartwright wrote of the insistent arts of seduction in his "Song of Dalliance." "Softer combat's nowhere found," he said, than in the persevering effort to lure a woman to one's bed. Yet he added (with a touch of male arrogance) that in this loving conflict, "[she] who loses, wins the prize."[33] This notion of the compulsive irresistibility of love finds its religious parallel in Richard Sibbe's contention that God's love "melts us" almost by force. "It constrains, it hath a kind of holy violence in it."[34] In a similar way, Donne had prayed, "Batter my heart, three-person'd God," in his longing to be "taken" by God in the ravages of love.[35] Samuel Rutherford similarly wrote:

> When Christ cannot obtaine and winne the content and good-liking of the sinner to his love, he ravisheth, and with strong hand drawes the sinner to himselfe; when invitation doe not the business, and he knocks, and we will not open, then a more powerfull work must follow.[36]

The wide range of erotic experience in the Cavalier poets thus finds an interesting parallel in the spectrum of spiritual eroticism expressed in Puritan writers.

Given this prevalence of sexual imagery in Puritan spirituality, it comes as no surprise that Seaborn Cotton, the son of John Cotton, copied many of the more explicit passages from the Cavalier poets in a notebook he kept as a student at Harvard in the 1640s. Later, as a pastor in New Hampshire, he continued to use the same notebook in jotting down ideas that came to him in church meetings.[37] He found no inconsistency in the joining of the two.

In summary, then, from Edmund Spenser's exquisite honoring of married love to Shakespeare's bawdy jests, Elizabethan and Early Stuart England was alive with desire. This expressed itself no less notably in the spiritual earthiness of the Puritan preachers. As one interpreter of English literature has claimed, "Puritanism was the hot-bed from which was to spring and blossom the sentimentalism and moving conflict between the conscience and the heart, of *Pamela* and *Clarissa* and *Jane Eyre* and of *The Mill on the Floss*, and other novels of the kind. . . ."[38] From Samuel Richardson to Charlotte Brontë and George Eliot, the Puritan fascination with desire-aroused and desire-thwarted continued to play itself out in popular romantic fiction.

Spiritual Affliction and the Management of Desire

Given, then, the pervasiveness of the language of desire in Puritan piety, what kind of spiritual discipline did the Puritans employ in keeping their passion in check? What theological principles did they bring to bear on the management of intense longing?[39] How did their awareness of God's providential hand at work in nature allow them to view loss and affliction as yet another way of experiencing union with Christ?

In Puritan thinking, the chastising experience of affliction aimed at loosening the soul's attachment to lesser things while binding it more closely to Christ alone. They considered hardships as occasioning a deeper intimacy with Christ, sharing in his suffering. Calvin had identified "bearing the cross" as a focal point of the Christian life. "Ingrafted into the death of Christ," he said, "we derive from it a secret energy, as the twig does from the root."[40] Adversity, for the Calvinist, was but another form of union with Christ.

Richard Sibbes, the English Puritan divine who carried "Affectionate Theology" to its rhetorical heights, contended that "The life of a Christian should be a meditation [on] how to unloose his affections from inferior things. He will easily die that is dead before in affection. . . ."[41] "Dying before one dies" thus became an essential dimension of Puritan spirituality. Anne Bradstreet emphasized the need for "weaning the affections," for example, comparing God's use of affliction to a mother's weaning her suckling infant by rubbing wormwood or mustard on her breast.

Bradstreet drew much of her imagery from the beauty of the Massachusetts countryside, even as she complained that her soul was "too much in love with the world." She knew how easy it is to be over-attached to earthly joys. "I have found by experience," she lamented, that "I can no more live without correction than without food."[42] She delighted in difficulties, finding God's sustaining love in the midst of every apparent catastrophe. "When I am in the cellar of affliction," said Samuel Rutherford, "I look for the Lord's choicest wines."[43]

Puritan spiritual discipline was thus rooted in a theology that focused on the management of desire. It instructed the faithful in three fundamental truths that kept them grounded in the proper channeling of their longing. These included: (1) a reminder that what they desired most they already had; (2) a promise that unsatisfied desire remained the highest form of spiritual passion; and (3) an assurance that purgative self-emptying was but a preparation for being filled with the love of Christ.

Spiritual Depression and the Assurance of a Grace Already Received

Reminding the faithful of the grace that was already theirs helped the Puritans deal with what I am tempted to call the bipolar quality of their spirituality. The emotional range of Puritan spiritual experience was extraordinarily wide (and often erratic). They knew the heights and the depths of all possible encounters with God. Puritan piety could be manic at times in its ecstatic apprehension of God's love and at other times deeply depressive in its agonizing sense of God's absence. What held it together, keeping the believer from emotional chaos, was its conviction that the believer already has (or already *is*) what he or she longs for most. This is a central theme underlying the peculiar dynamic of Puritan desire.

Gordon Wakefield observes that Puritan devotion starts from a very different premise than the classical Roman Catholic pattern of purgation, illumination, and union. It follows, instead, a cycle of justification, sanctification, and glorification. In the Calvinist scenario, union with Christ is secured at the very *beginning* of the Christian life rather than at its end. "It is not a result of a mystical technique, but of justification," of God's prior declarative act in Christ.[44] Consequently, the Puritan heart lives its way into a hidden reality (not yet fully apparent) to which it has already been intimately joined. In a legal and forensic manner, says Calvin, God has imputed Christ's righteousness to the believer, granting a deep participation in Christ's nature prior to anything the believer *does*. Hence, "all things [already] are ours and we have all things in him."[45] If the Catholic plods through the desert of self-renunciation in search of a beckoning Christ on its far side, the Puritan plods through the same desert in quest of the Lord who was within all along. The one "lives toward" an as-yet unrealized hope; the other "lives into" what has already been given. The distinction is an important one.[46]

Calvin, like Luther, had been careful to hold two principles in tension in understanding the process of sanctification in the Christian life. He recognized, on the one hand, that believers already are incorporated into Christ, made partakers of his nature, declared "bone of his bone and flesh of his flesh." By the free gift of justification, God "receives us into favor as if we were righteous." Yet he also knew that the faithful must be engaged in becoming what they already are. God, in Christ, "not only brings himself close to us by an undivided bond of fellowship, but by a wondrous communion grows with us daily more and more into one body until he becomes altogether one with us."[47] Calvin went considerably farther than Luther in urging a continued use of the law as a guide in living the Christian life, expressing concretely in one's behavior the union being realized.[48]

This notion that the mystery of *theosis* (becoming one with God) has already been "pronounced a reality" in Christian experience (though not yet wholly accomplished) was an electrifying truth in Puritan experience. [49] It required an enormous exercise in faith, a deep confidence in the power of God's declarative Word to make real what it speaks. The ritual performance of uttering (of reifying) a truth not yet visibly apparent was central in the Reformed liturgical experience of the assurance of pardon, the declaration of grace in preaching, and the Eucharistic reception of Christ's body. Living their way into the full meaning of what it meant to be "engrafted to Christ" was a lifelong task.

Only slowly did the Puritans come to realize that what they feared and desired most was already within them. What they yearned for with extraordinary intensity had been closer to them all along than they ever realized. Affliction, then, simply threw the soul back upon the resources it already possessed in Christ. It pointed the believer away from all misdirected desires to the heart's commitment to the indwelling Christ. Their longing, after all, was for something they already possessed—something they already "were." This took them out of themselves, and at the same time more deeply *into* themselves, so as to realize Calvin's truth that the knowledge of God and the knowledge of themselves were finally one. Their desire, at its most basic level, had already been satisfied in Christ.

Ecstasy Delayed in the Confidence of a Future Hope

Yet Puritans lived in the expectation of a mystical union with their Lord that went beyond what had been "declared" in their justification and "realized" in their sanctification, to what was also anticipated in their glorification. They remained thirsty for a still greater glory to come. Occupying that liminal space between what had been promised and what they still hoped for was not easy. It meant clinging to what they already had (by faith) while looking forward to a fulfillment that remained (for now) unsatisfied.

Hence they sought a spiritual discipline that exercised the soul in accepting the delay of the Beloved—seeing delay itself as a gift, sharpening their longing for what was yet to come. In such a way, unfulfilled desire suggested a deeper entry into participation with Christ. Frustrated longing became a sign of God's love. Disguised as adversity, the divine absence was but a "tease," luring them beyond anything they had yet tasted in the spiritual life.

Puritan love, as a result, learned to exult in tests of its faithfulness. Matthew Sylvester assured the believers that "God's dearest favourites" often have "the sharpest exercises and great darkness and disconsolateness on their spirits."[50] As Ramon Lull, the thirteenth-century Spanish mystic, had put it, there are two fires that nurture the lovers of God: one of pleasure and desires; the other of grief and tears. Oddly enough, he observed, it is hard to tell which brings the most joy.[51] Enduring loss, pining for one's beloved, waiting for what is yet to come can lift desire to its greatest pitch. The Puritans knew this well.

Given the tension, then, between the promise already given and a reality only partially realized, periods of depression were not uncommon in the Puritan practice of the spiritual life. They spoke of these times as the "dark night of the soul," the "soul's winter-time," or the experience of "desertions"—seasons of God's apparent withdrawal. They hesitated to identify them as signs of divine judgment, but rather viewed them as opportunities for being carried more deeply into grace.[52] An extensive literature was directed toward the theological and psychological understanding of these spiritual states of consciousness. Thomas Goodwin wrote *A Child of Light Walking in Darkness*. Joseph Symonds penned a book on *The Case and Cure of a Deserted Soul*. Other works included Christopher Love's *The Dejected Soul's Cure*, Richard Sibbes's *The Soul's Conflict*, and William Bridge's *A Lifting Up for the Downcast*.[53]

Learn to trust in "a withdrawing God," Thomas Manton of St. Paul's, Covent Garden, advised.[54] "By divine withdrawings, the soul is put upon hanging upon a naked God, a naked Christ, a naked promise," said Independent preacher Thomas Brooks, echoing the earlier *Cloud of Unknowing*.[55] Such desertions "are not the interruptions of God's love," said another Puritan divine, "but the acts of his love."[56] They constitute experiences of unrequited love, making the lover even more insistent in her longing. Faithful Puritans knew this was no exercise for the timid. Embracing a Divine Lover was a risky business. It demanded a tireless and stubborn trust.

The Puritans thus came to recognize affliction as one of the surest signs of union with Christ. Cambridge Puritan Edmund Calamy cautioned people against drawing unwarranted conclusions about the tragedies that they see others endure.

> Let us not pass rash censures upon persons under great afflictions. Say not, such a woman is a greater sinner than others, because more afflicted. . . . But when I see a godly woman afflicted, then I say, this is not so much for her sin, as for her tryal; this is not to hurt her, but to teach her to know God. . . . *For the best of Saints are subject to the worst afflictions*: This is the lot of all God's children, Christ himself not excepted. . . . [Hence] afflictions . . . are evidences that wee are in a blessed condition.[57]

One should never automatically assume adversity to be a sign of God's punishment, he argued.

In short, the enigma of God's sending "a sea of troubles" to heighten the longing of the faithful was a mystery that captivated the Puritan mind. Joseph Caryl, a member of the Westminster Assembly, published an enormous twelve-volume commentary on the book of Job, an effort that grew out of more than twenty-five years of continually preaching on this single biblical text.[58] I suspect that by the end of his tenure, his congregation was extraordinarily inured to affliction, having learned the patience of Job themselves in listening to so many sermons on God's presence in pain. But they expected this in a spirituality that thrived on desire delayed.

The Emptying of Self as Preparation for Union with Christ

Another dimension of Puritan spiritual discipline was the importance it placed on self-emptying as a condition for being filled with Christ's love. Puritans were fully aware of the impassioned soul's temptation to exalt itself, finding satisfaction in lesser attachments while awaiting its ultimate fulfillment in Christ. The unchecked play of desire within the human heart could be disastrous. Hence, they underscored Bernard of Clairvaux's emphasis on the proper order of the Wisdom books in the biblical canon. He had observed that one comes to the Song of Songs *only* after passing through the cautious discipline of the book of Proverbs and the disillusionment with earthly desires found in Ecclesiastes. Only then does one rightly comprehend the excesses of desire found in the Song.[59] The Puritans knew that a winnowing process of relinquishment was essential to the spiritual life.

The irony here is that Puritan spirituality simultaneously exalted the self while also finding it necessary to empty the self. A powerful sense of personal identity naturally derived from the experience of being chosen in Christ, but it could lead to illusions of grandeur as well. It gave the faithful a deep awareness of "Christic identity," joining them to God's larger mission in the world. Cotton Mather, for example, celebrated John Winthrop as a *Nehemias Americanus*, one of God's elect whose personal identity had merged with a lofty vision of national mission. Yet there was ever the danger of confusing priorities in the assumption of one's chosen role. Puritans, as a result, perennially found it necessary to question the designs of the self, to distinguish the nature of their true mission and remain wary of their call to greatness. Sacvan Bercovitch has traced the origins of the "American self," along with its problems, to this Puritan sense of extraordinary self-confidence.[60]

The emptying of the false self, therefore, became an important exercise in the life of the spirit. Calvin himself had spoken of the denial of self as "the sum of the Christian life," stressing that "we are not our own;" we belong to Christ. He knew that the "Old Man" (or false self) must be put to death so that the "New Man" (or true self) can be raised to new life. He was often relentless in his attacks on the false self's obsessive concerns for recognition and success. We need to "yield to [God] the desires of our hearts to be tamed and subjugated," he said. This "not only erases from our minds the yearning to possess, the desire for power, and the favor of men, but it also uproots ambition and all craving for human glory."[61]

Henry Scougal, a seventeenth-century Scots Calvinist, reiterated Calvin's teaching, when he said:

> Perfect love is a kind of self-dereliction, a wandering out of our selves, it's a kind of voluntary death, wherein the lover dies to himself, and all his own interests, not thinking of them, nor caring for them any more, and minding nothing but how he may please and gratifie the party whom he loves. . . .[62]

This relinquishment of self is prerequisite to mystical union with Christ. Only as the self is emptied—as God's love pours into a heart ravaged and exhausted by desire—is the believer restored to him or herself. Only then, says Scougal, does "he [begin] to mind his own concernments, not so much because they are his, as because the beloved is pleased to own an interest in them: he becomes dear to himself, because he is so unto the other."[63] Hence, the afflictions that come in one's life serve to weaken this inordinate dependence on the ego and turn the believer to God alone. Peter Sterry of St. Margaret's, Westminster, said the believer should pray like a child to its parent: "My God, thou art my Father; thou hast a greater share in me, than I have in myself. I was thine, before I was my own. . . . Thou art far nearer to me, than my Self to my Self."[64]

Resisting the superficial cravings of the ego so as to realize this deepest longing of the true self was the goal of Puritan devotion. They understood, paradoxically, that doing what one desires most requires an ascetic practice—an exercise in the abandonment of all lesser loves. This didn't happen unless God energized the will and they accepted the discipline. Hence, Baxter urged, "If thy heart draw back, force it to work: if it loiter, spur it on. . . ." The heart, he observed, was "an untamed colt not used to the hand."[65] Afflictions, therefore, constituted an important part of the taming process.

Divine Providence and the Healing Power of Nature

One of the primary means by which the Puritans discerned God's disciplinary hand at work in their lives was in the natural world around them. They perceived nature's wildness as bringing healing even in its corrective role. The doctrine of providence was thus an important part of their Calvinist theology, as witnessed in Richard Steere's narrative at the beginning of this chapter. They read the topsy-turvy events of earth and sky for continuing signs of God's providential direction, seeing the footprints of the divine in every detail. "The people of seventeenth-century New England lived in an enchanted universe," writes David Hall. "Theirs was a world of wonders."[66] They were fascinated (and terrified) by tales of comets, hailstorms, and sea-deliverances.

From Edward Johnson's *Wonder-Working Providence of Sion's Savior* (1653) to Increase Mather's *Essay for the Recording of Illustrious Providences* (1684), best-selling books pointed the faithful to God's hand at work in natural disasters. These were gripping stories of people adrift at sea for weeks at a time or surviving fire balls of lightning coming down their chimneys. Thomas Beard's *Theatre of God's Judgments* (1597) warned of the afflictions due to those most in need of discipline. In the wild excesses of an untamed world, the Puritans found a mirror of their own propensity to disorder. For them, nature was a vast textbook of spiritual correspondences.

Their notion of a distinct parallel between the natural phenomena of stormy seas and the spiritual state of being "temptest tossed" suggests an interesting conception of discipline and healing in the Puritan practice of pastoral care. The dominance of water metaphors in Puritan discourse accentuates the striking resemblance they noticed between natural occurrences and particular states of human consciousness. They employed the imagery of raging water and violent seas in what one might describe as a spiritual homeopathic remedy. They knew that bringing together like patterns has a meaningful effect. Connecting a believer's experience of inner chaos with the survival of North Atlantic squalls points the sufferer toward hope.[67] To confront the terror of an ocean storm is figuratively to pass through the Red Sea of one's spiritual turmoil. The horror of the one echoes (and releases) the dreadfulness of the other.

This principle of "like treating like" is an idea going back at least as far as Hippocrates. Samuel Hahnemann was the nineteenth-century German physician who developed the modern practice of homeopathic medicine, based on what he called the "law of similars." He argued that small dosages simulating the symptoms of a disease might strengthen the immune system, "mirroring" the very illness that the physician sought to cure.[68]

The Puritans recognized the spiritual equivalent of this in their enthrallment with windstorms, roiling ocean waves, and the raging of flooding rivers. The coincidence between spiritual conversion and thunderstorms in the history of Reformed spirituality is remarkable, for example. Puritans knew that the soul longs for equilibrium, finding its quiet center in Christ, filled with the "celestial liquor" of God's love.[69] But they recognized the sinful soul as hopelessly windblown and reckless, craving one new fulfillment after another.

Being "tempest tossed" was, therefore, a common metaphor in describing the movements of the Puritan spiritual life. Cotton Mather drove this home in a series of sermons he preached to Boston seamen at the turn of the eighteenth century. Speaking to shipowners, whalers sailing out of Nantucket, and Gloucester fishermen, he repeated the old proverb, "Would you teach a man to pray, send him to sea." One can find enough dangers there to drive any soul to his knees.[70] Spiritual practice, he recognized, is a matter of being "well-weathered" in faith.

Preaching to seafaring men about the discipline of the spiritual life, Mather spoke like one who had sailed before the mast himself. He vividly described weathering a storm at sea, comparing the experience to fierce tempests in the life of the soul. On sighting a squall on the horizon, sailors would hurry to settle the topsails, take in the spretsail, and furl tightly any loose sheets. When the storm finally hit and "the deep boils like a caldron," the commander "cannot have too much calmness and presence of mind." He had to know when and how to "hull the ship" (taking in sail) or to "spoon her" (running before a gale with reduced canvas or under bare poles), doing all this when simply turning the helm might require the strength of two or three men. In their experience at sea, Puritan sailors acquired a discipline that helped them weather their own inner storms, coming to terms with the raging desires within.[71]

The goal of this threatening experience at sea (whether metaphorical or real) was to turn its promise of watery harm into the wet and comforting solace of God's love. Water imagery in the Puritan mythos carried a double connotation of pleasure as well as peril, as we have seen.

It manifested the soul's inner turmoil and God's disciplinary hand in providence, but it also spoke of the oceanic experience of ecstasy found in the calm sea of union with the divine. In Puritan sermons there were rivers of paradise always running alongside the waters of affliction.[72]

Puritan preachers could lapse into rapturous descriptions of God as "an Immense Ocean of mercy and goodness." Edward Polhill asked his congregation, "What rapes and extasies of affection are due to him, who is all over beauty and amenity? . . . How vast an Ocean of grace is he!" Richard Baxter ended his account of *The Saints Everlasting Rest* by exhorting his reader to "Cast thy self in, and swim with the arms of thy love in this ocean of his love. . . . Is not the place a meeting of lovers?"[73]

While the route to this tranquil ocean of God's love inevitably passed through Jonah's experience of a storm-tossed sea, through the bitter waters of Marah and Meribah, the end was always assured. In Bunyan's *Pilgrim's Progress*, Christian and his companion Hopeful confront a deep river, the last obstacle in their quest for the Celestial City. Christian sinks into the depths as he starts across, entering "a great darkness and horror." But Hopeful calls out from further on, saying, "Be of good cheer, my brother. I feel the bottom, and it is good."[74] They make their way at last to their deepest desire, to the One for whom they had thirsted all along.

The Puritan journey was one that passed through a world of endless wonder and distracting beauty, full of temptations. Threatening storms revealed God's providential design in it all, serving as a curb on the very yearnings it awakened. Only through a life of affliction could the faithful learn to exercise temperance in their use of God's bountiful gifts. In looking back, they knew that their voyage over the sea of tumultuous desire led at last to a harbor where they found the love they had sought all along.

Richard Steere Redux: A Puritan Critique of Subsequent Reformed History

I conclude this chapter by returning to the Puritan merchant poet with which it began. Drawing from his experience, we may be able to assess the impact of Puritan/Reformed thought on later American life. Thirty years after his fateful voyage in 1683, Richard Steere (1643–1721) wrote a poem entitled "Earth's Felicities, Heaven's Allowances," looking back on his years as an ocean voyager, trader in ironware and English cloth, and religious poet. Having known wealth as well as poverty in his life, Steere had learned to appreciate and to hold lightly everything in the world around him. He urged "the true use and moderate enjoyance" of all earth's gifts.[75] I think he would have been scandalized, therefore, by the economic and environmental consequences of "Puritan desire" as it developed in subsequent American experience. He himself had learned at first hand the importance of affliction in the purging of desire.

Can we imagine Steere responding to the New England landscape (and American culture) if he were here today, viewing it from a three-centuries-later perspective? As a seventeenth-century Puritan, how might he react to the changes in commerce and international trade that have transpired since his days as a merchant in colonial Connecticut? How would he assess the impact of Reformed behavior on the ensuing problems of poverty and ecological deterioration?

As a trading agent working out of New London, Connecticut, Steere would have known all the shipping routes and trade connections between London, Barbados, and New England. Were he to reflect on the massive changes that have occurred since his day in light of that experience, I would imagine him expressing concern over worsening weather patterns in the North Atlantic. He might point to an increase in severe storms as a result of global warming, rising ocean temperatures, higher sea levels due to melting arctic ice, and more erratic weather patterns.

He might lament the demise of the North Atlantic cod fishery due to fishing trawlers scraping the ocean floor and ruining nesting areas. I suspect he would be appalled at rivers emptying industrial and agricultural wastes into the sea, the rise of mercury content in northern waters, and the extinction of various species of whales and seabirds—something unimaginable in the New London of his day. He would, in short, discover a world where nature itself was increasingly afflicted by the effects of human sin, by a failure to practice the "moderate enjoyance" expected of the people of God.

As a merchant, Steere would be astonished by today's worldwide expansion of trade and vast accumulation of wealth. These changes might initially enthrall his entrepreneurial vision. He could, after all, attribute them to the development of Calvinist principles. Calvin had perceived material goods as instruments of God's providence, money as a sign of the graciousness of God's Kingdom. He had allowed usury, encouraged economic development, and scorned idleness as contrary to nature. The Puritan theology of "calling" had gone on to emphasize a "worldly asceticism," as the mundane tasks of one's work in the world became a devotional practice. In all these ways, Calvinist values inadvertently contributed to the expansion of the capitalist spirit.[76]

But Steere's Puritan sensitivities might also balk at the extent to which uncontrolled desire had taken over the marketplace. He might well caution against the accumulation of wealth without a corresponding concern for the poor. Cotton Mather had lamented in his own day the trend toward materialism, saying that "Religion begat prosperity and the daughter devoured the mother."[77] Steere could echo Thomas Watson's warnings about affluence, saying that "Poverty [as a spiritual choice] works for good to God's children. It starves their lusts. It increases their graces."[78]

By contrast, today's consumer-driven economy would provoke his concern at the way it fosters a compulsive need to buy unnecessary goods. It engineers a continually heightened desire due to the fact that market stability no longer relies on traditional patterns of supply meeting demand. The system has to nurture a craving for ever new things if its promise of endless economic growth is be realized. The manufacture of "desire" thus emerges as the market's highest priority.

Steere would be amazed to learn the extent to which Reformed Christians in particular had contributed to this phenomenon, developing advertising practices that cultivated an acquisitive longing. Retail entrepreneur John Wanamaker, a prominent Philadelphia Presbyterian in the early twentieth century, was among the first to employ advertising campaigns that psychologically connected the human yearning for self-fulfillment to the purchase of desirable goods. Wanamaker celebrated America as a "Land of Desire," where everyone (not just the rich) could enjoy the never-ending benefits of consumption-driven desire.[79]

Steere would perceive the vast difference between rich and poor in the present economic climate as suggesting a radical breakdown in the social solidarity of a covenant community. He would be amazed, for example, to learn of the extent to which ministers of Puritan ancestry had nurtured the myth of the "self-made man" in nineteenth-century American life. Their celebration of prosperity (and a spirituality of desire) went beyond anything found in the Puritanism of his day. Henry Ward Beecher and Lyman Abbot, Congregationalist clergymen in New York, preached a gospel of wealth and wrote books on *How to Succeed* (1882). Matthew Smith, another Congregationalist minister and Wall Street journalist, published his reflections on *Twenty Years among the Bulls and Bears of Wall Street* (1870). Russell Conwell, a Baptist of Puritan heritage, wrote his *Acres of Diamonds* (1915), explaining how "it is your duty to get rich" while tracing poverty to the shortcomings of the poor. Horatio Alger, a Unitarian minister, popularized the "rags to riches" theme in dime novels like *Ragged Dick* (1867).[80] Reflecting on this in light of the Puritan concern for the taming of desire, Steere might be tempted to agree with Ivan Illich that a consumer society produces two kinds of slaves: prisoners of addiction and prisoners of envy.[81] The Puritan merchant and poet might well attribute these evils to an ultimate distortion of human longing.

Finally, I would imagine his being alarmed at the environmental impact of this nineteenth-century prosperity gospel on the New England landscape he had come to love. While a Yankee elite was amassing wealth in the Gilded Age, textile mills along the Connecticut River poured pollutants into the water from their bleaching and dyeing processes. More than 70 cotton, paper, and woolen mills pumped waste into the Nashua River Valley of New Hampshire. Tannery and wrought-iron factories contaminated the Concord and Merrimack Rivers in Massachusetts.[82] By the twentieth century, runoffs from these and other rivers resulted in massive dead areas in Long Island Sound and the loss of fisheries north of Massachusetts Bay. For a Puritan merchant sensitive to the "true use" of things—to just business practices along the waterways of New England—Richard Steere might well raise questions about the responsibility of Reformed Christians in light of this history. Given the prosperity that Puritanism eventually begat, he might fear (like Cotton Mather) that the daughter had truly devoured the mother.

This chapter has shown how nature functioned as a school of affliction in seventeenth-century Puritan consciousness, taming desire through the testing and reordering of misdirected longings. Ironically, today it is the earth itself that suffers from uncontrolled human desire. Afflicted by overdevelopment, the misuse and waste of its resources, environmental pollution, climate change, and habitat destruction, the world has become (says Thomas Berry) a collection of objects rather than a communion of subjects. Doubly disturbing is the fact that in New England and elsewhere we can trace these ecological consequences back to the very Puritans who first called attention to the volatile power and danger of desire.

The yearning of the soul for God is one of the most intense impulses in human experience. When properly ordered, as the Puritans were careful to observe, it celebrates God's matchless beauty, reflected in the world as a theater of divine glory. Jonathan Edwards, reflecting his love of the Connecticut River Valley, spoke of the spiritual life as an experience of being cast upon "the river of God's pleasure."[83] All other delights, he said, find their meaning and worth in God's delight. All other rivers acquire their dignity and deserve just treatment because of the way they mirror the flowing generosity of God's own care.

Pseudo-Dionysius observed that desire itself originates in a river flowing from beneath God's throne in heaven. The highest level of the nine orders of angels—the Seraphs—arise spontaneously from its flames, breaking into song as they exclaim "Holy, Holy, Holy." But their longing for God is so great, says Annie Dillard, that they can only utter the first "Holy" before their ecstasy dissolves them once again into flames and they return to the fiery river from which they came.[84]

Such is the desire that prompts the saints throughout the ages, the Puritans included. They were a people overwhelmed by their praise of a God more astounding and more loving than anything they could imagine. Their access to God's beauty derived in no small part from their delight in a world of crashing ocean waves, great white pines, and the sparkling waters of New England's rivers. Their spirituality of desire demanded even then (and especially now) the ultimate preservation of everything that serves God's glory.

Biodiversity and the Holy Trinity

The triunity of God is the secret of God's beauty. It is radiant and what it radiates is joy. It attracts and therefore it conquers. Once we deny God's threefoldness, we immediately are left with a lustreless and joyless (and also humourless!)—in short, an uncomely God.

—Karl Barth, *Church Dogmatics*[1]

Three times tonight I've heard the coyotes cry. Each time they seem to be getting closer. Their howling always fills me with a joy edged by fear. They're hungry tonight, tracking in the snow. Coyotes usually don't have to work so hard here in northern New Mexico, being near the top of the food chain. I've set up camp on Mesa del Yeso above Box Canyon behind Ghost Ranch. With ten inches of snow on the ground, I hadn't expected so much animal activity. But tracks of magpies, nuthatches, ground squirrels, and jack rabbits are scattered everywhere on the snow, like symbols on an Indian blanket. Even in winter, the New Mexican landscape offers the fourth highest native species richness of any state in the United States. It is alive with diversity. Ghost Ranch always astounds me by the excess of its beauty.

In contrast, a single tree grows on a wilderness hillside in northern California. Its name is *presidio manzanita*. Its world population is one. When I stood before a photograph of this tree in an exhibit of endangered species recently, I felt its enormous fragility. Should it die without reproducing itself, *presidio manzanita* will go the way of the dodo and the passenger pigeon.[2]

Scientists estimate that there are about 30 million species now existing in the world. We don't know for sure; there could be twice that many. So far we've only described and named about a million and a half. We've studied fewer than 100,000 of these in any detail. We know very little about the amazing heterogeneity of our world—its untold mysteries of being and unimagined combinations of DNA. We're like Job as God questions him about species after species; he is left speechless, confessing that he knows nothing about a world that utterly amazes him.

Scientists also tell us that we are now in a profoundly significant period of mass extinction. Species are dying off at a rate of one per day (many estimates are much higher), primarily because of human destruction of natural environments. We kill these species out of greed and overuse, or inadvertently by destroying their habitats.[3] The resultant spiraling loss is not only an ecological crisis, but also a failure of human beings to celebrate what God has made. It diminishes our capacity to show forth the luster of the Holy Trinity. The threat to biodiversity is a theological, even liturgical problem, reducing our potential as an interrelated family of species to give glory to God.

We log and burn rain forests to create more farmland for more cattle so that first-world people can buy cheap hamburgers at fast-food restaurants. Every year the rain forests of the world are reduced by an area nearly half the size of Florida. The runoff of fertilizers and pesticides from farms along the Mississippi River flows into the Gulf of Mexico, creating a dead zone the size of New Jersey. Huge algae blooms rob oxygen from the water and kill off the sea life.

No place is safe from humans. Marine biologist Carl Safina tells of observing one of the world's great colonies of albatrosses on Midway Atoll in the remote North Pacific Ocean.[4] These are huge, beautiful birds with a seven-foot wingspan. An albatross mother flies hundreds of miles on a single trip to gather food for her chicks. Safina watched as one returned. The chicks gathered around and waited for her to regurgitate what she had found. She arched her neck and threw up a supply of fish eggs and squid. But the young birds were still hungry so she tried again, struggling to get up something she had swallowed.

Safina watched in horror as a green plastic toothbrush began to emerge from her gullet. She tried several times to disgorge it, but couldn't, so she re-swallowed it and walked away with the toothbrush still caught inside. Things like this are happening in remote places all over the world.

In saltwater marshlands on Cumberland Island off the coast of Georgia, I've seen huge flocks of white ibises, wonderful birds with long, curved orange beaks that reach into the holes that fiddler crabs have dug in the sand. When first born, the baby ibises have not yet developed the salt-processing glands their parents have—openings above their beaks where salt water is drained out, extracted from the birds' systems by these glands. If this didn't happen, the salt from the fiddler crabs would poison them.

But the glands aren't developed in the babies until they are fourteen days old. So their parents have to fly inland fifteen to twenty miles to freshwater wetlands every day to catch crayfish to feed their young. Only after two weeks of travel do the adults know they can stop feeding the young birds freshwater food. The babies' glands are now working and they can eat fiddler crabs like the grown-ups. It's a compelling example of how important interconnecting ecosystems are to creatures like this. Freshwater and saltwater wetlands (in close proximity to each other) are absolutely necessary to the lives of white ibises. Habitat is crucial to the survival of species.

Species (and habitat) diversity sustains human beings, too. We have learned, for example, how dangerous the mono-cropping of plants can be. When we cut down ancient forests and reseed them with a single species of yellow pine (good for lumber), we find that a sudden disease comes along to which they are all susceptible, and they are wiped out. That's what happened with the potato famine in Ireland in the 1840s, and again in the 1970s when a corn blight taught American farmers how disastrous it can be to plant a single species lacking resistance to the new blight. Even genetically engineered corn with built-in resistance to all known disease and insects carries no guarantee against threats that may yet develop.[5]

Plant breeders often turn to "wild relatives," therefore, when looking for new genes that will be resistant to diseases or will be able to grow under severe weather conditions. These wild relatives, usually found in a remote rain forest, are essential to agriculture as we know it. Human beings feed on a very narrow range of life-forms. Biogeographer Chris Park tells us there are 75,000 edible plants in the world, but only twenty of them are used widely as a food source by humans. Only ten species of birds and wild animals provide the basic genetic material on which 98 percent of all livestock production in the world is based.[6] Maintaining species diversity and widening our use of resources are increasingly necessary for our survival.

Yet we assume that many species are worthless, even as we pay lip service to the doctrine of creation. Americans have an inordinate fear of insects, for example, and our excessive use of poisons to eradicate them is destroying all of us. E. O. Wilson at Harvard University insists that insects are the "cornerstone of life on Earth." We could lose wolves and bears and hawks and still survive, he says, but we wouldn't make it if we lost the insects. Yet we kill every bug we can because we've been taught to hate them by our parents and by almost every science fiction movie we've seen.

In *The Voice of the Infinite in the Small*, Joanne Lauck speaks of Americans' phobic reaction to cockroaches. The oldest insect in the world isn't nearly as dirty or disease-carrying as people think. Actually they do a lot of preening. Roaches are constantly cleaning themselves—especially after they've come into contact with humans. Yet we spend $240 million a year trying to kill them with poisons that pollute the whole environment.[7]

Or take maggots. During the Civil War, doctors learned that wounded soldiers who came in from battlefields with maggots in their open, decaying wounds often fared better than soldiers without them. The maggots ate only the decayed flesh and never harmed what was good, thus preventing gangrene. They even excreted substances that were later found to accelerate healing. The diversity of insect life that we find so horrifying in our mythic life actually contributes far more to our benefit than to our discomfort.

Utilitarian considerations alone make it to our advantage to learn to live with and preserve as many species as we can. None of them are worthless. Each one was created by the same God that made us. Yet we perceive God's apparent delight in the diversity of species as a matter of needless excess. If we require, as humans, only ten species of animals and twenty species of plants as our food source, why should we worry about losing a few superfluous species of beetles and bacteria? After all, entomologists have identified over 350,000 different species of beetles alone. What do we need them for?

Biologist J. B. S. Haldane, who devoted his life to the study of insects, was asked what a scientist like himself could infer about the Creator from the study of creation. He responded, a bit tongue in cheek, that God must have "an inordinate fondness for beetles." Why else would God populate the world with more of them than any other creature, since beetles make up two-thirds of the total number of insect species?[8]

What we respond to with indifference (if not fear and loathing), seeing the process of evolution as recklessly, even dangerously exuberant at times, may be viewed theologically as an example of God's own multiplicity of desire. We have to recognize diversity, not as something threatening, but as an opportunity for loving all that God loves. How, then, can we celebrate species diversity as a natural consequence of our perception of God as Trinity, an overflow of God's desire into ever-increasing possibilities for relationship?

Jürgen Moltmann observes that as the Father gives existence to created life, the Son "specifies and differentiates" creation, molding creatures into their distinctive shapes, while the Holy Spirit bestows a particular identity on each and every being, making it unique. When the Son calls forth flying beetles, for instance, the Spirit responds by multiplying thousands of variegated species, stunning in their colorful differences. Exuberant joy marks the entire process.[9]

Trinitarian theology has been at the forefront of theological research in recent years. Theologians influenced by liberation theology, feminist criticism, and ecological concerns have retrieved themes in the Christian tradition that stress the distinctive interrelationship of the three persons of the Trinity and the communion they share together.[10]

Recent Trinitarian thought speaks of God less in terms of divine *substance* (defining God's distinctive "essence") and more in terms of *relationship* (a reciprocal interconnectedness perceived as most characteristic of the divine). Talk about God, in fact, sounds increasingly similar to the language of quantum physics. In the foundation of matter at its subatomic level, we cannot "get at" the essence of things. The tiniest particles don't function in any predictable way. We know them only by their traces, by the impact they leave on other things. At its deepest level, the world is a matter of endless indeterminacy and interdependence. We grasp things only in their relation to everything else. Similarly, God's being can't be sought in any rudimentary divine "stuff," but rather in the hunger for relationship to which the doctrine of the Trinity witnesses.

Theologians like Leonardo Boff, Elizabeth Johnson, and Jürgen Moltmann reach beyond the static (and patriarchal) patterns to which

Trinitarian theology has often lent itself in the past.[11] They ask how the doctrine of the Trinity can maintain a creative tension between two principles: the validation of "difference" (honored in the separate integrity of the Trinity's members) and the realization of "interconnecting unity" (joining them in a love that binds them to each other and everything else). Johnson asserts, for example, that "at the heart of holy mystery is not monarchy but community, not an absolute ruler, but a threefold *koinonia*."[12] Learning to respect a diversity of species within the wholeness of a larger system, therefore, becomes a Trinitarian as well as an ecological exercise.

God is not self-absorbed in the solitude of a dominant, eternal One (cut off from relationship). Nor is God contained even in the narcissism of two figures ever facing each other (Father and Son, locked together in love, ignoring everything else). God is rather, as Boff suggests, the eternal spilling over into a *third* person, the Spirit who "forces the other two to turn their gaze from themselves in another direction," into an outpouring of love and relatedness that cannot be stopped.[13] God is a community of diversity bound together in unity. The Trinity continually seeks new webs of interconnectedness, while at the same time remaining separately and wholly itself. God is Wisdom/Sophia—creating, liberating, and gracing the world as Mother, Child, and Spirit.

All this has deep roots in the Reformed tradition. For Jonathan Edwards, the Father is an endless source of uncreated beauty. The Son images that beauty in a perfect reflection that expands it still further. Out of their shared love, Father and Son breathe forth the Holy Spirit as Beautifier, restlessly extending their beauty beyond themselves to everything in creation. The unity of the three is thus able to affirm difference, variety, and manifold relation. "Unless we grasp these [three persons]," Calvin warned, "only the bare and empty name of God flits about in our brains, to the exclusion of the true God." The dance of unity and difference within the divine being was, for Calvin and Edwards, the very nature of the Trinitarian mystery.[14]

Precise language about the nature of the Trinity is, of course, impossible. Who can presume to recount the inner workings of the divine being? Even Augustine had to admit, "I can experience far more than I can understand about the Trinity."[15] God's innermost being is not the solitary, unrelational, and distant entity that Arius wanted to affirm in the fourth century (when the Trinity was first defined), but is much more like a dance of desire. Hence the Eastern Church used the word *perichoresis* to describe the "interpenetration" of the members of the Trinity. God's deepest essence is a shared exchange of love (a *chore*-ography, a "dancing around") welling up from the center of God's hidden life, an expression of God's excess and exuberance of joy.[16] As Meister Eckhart put it, when the Father laughs to the Son, and the Son laughs back to the Father, that laughter gives pleasure, the pleasure gives joy, the joy gives love, and love gives itself forth in the Holy Spirit, ever finding new things to love.[17] An impulse to shared joy and mutual attractiveness springs naturally from the divine being. The more things there are to love, the happier God is. Diversity, exorbitance, and surplus of beauty are the natural creative expressions of a Trinitarian God.

Evolutionary biologist Adolf Portmann points to the ostentatious display of beauty in nature that does more than satisfy any functional need—more than what is required, for example, to attract a mate or astound an enemy. Ten miles deep in the ocean's abyss are blind creatures illuminated with some of the most lustrous colors imaginable. And for what purpose? They can't even see each other. It is almost as if their glory were created for its own sake. As if the universe had its own compulsion to celebrate, to make a spectacle of itself even when no one is watching. "Extravagance is beauty!" exulted William Blake.

Creation "struts its stuff" at every opportunity. Marvelous shades of color are found inside the shells of abalones. The feathers in the tail of a peacock display an incredible surplus of beauty, a "wanton exaggeration" (certainly more than is needed to arouse the interest of the average pea hen). It witnesses, says Alphonso Lingis, to the sheer overabundance of nature itself.[18]

If scientists recognize such excess of beauty as a mystery, theologians might ask, "What is this but an expression of God's endless and overwhelming exuberance?" The mysteries of creation, in their own outrageous way, give praise along with us to the wonder of God's glory. The Trinity delights in all its varied communications of itself, seeing its beauty replicated in every species. Each one turns God's beauty back onto its source, sharing in the dance of desire from which everything comes.

Alexander Rublev's fourteenth-century icon of the Holy Trinity expresses this dynamic exchange that emanates from the divine being (see figure 4.1). In his image the persons of the Trinity sit together around a low table. The heads of the Father and Son are intimately inclined toward each other, yet their bodies and hands reach at the same time toward the Holy Spirit. This visual torsion suggests an interdependency and relatedness among the three—an exchange of love that reaches out to engage the viewer as well. The lines of perspective in the furniture and floor plan at the bottom of the icon converge at the viewer's chest, completing the scene at the point of the viewer's heart as he or she stands before the icon at the chancel screen of an Orthodox church. Indeed, even the world of nature is absorbed in the act, as a distant tree and mountain in the background bend over in adoration of the God in which they too take delight.

All this summons us to the celebration of genetic diversity in a world that thrives (and a God that thrives) on dissimilarity and difference. If the world suffers at our hands, while yearning with us for a restored creation given to multiplied splendor, the doctrine of the Trinity demands an ethical practice that honors difference within the lively exchange of a loving community. It requires that we protect species diversity by preserving endangered habitats, by supporting free access to seed banks and the extension of the Endangered Species Act, and by questioning the sale of genetically modified and patented seeds that make farmers around the world dependent on huge agricultural conglomerates.[19]

The kind of passion we need in reverencing species diversity is exemplified in the seed martyrs of Leningrad during World War II. When the Germans invaded Russia in 1942, they put the city of Leningrad under siege. Over 600,000 people starved as enemy troops cut off supplies. Inside the city's Vavilov Institute, the best Russian biologists and geneticists had spent years collecting heirloom seeds from all over the world. They had preserved seeds from primitive varieties of wheat in Afghanistan and Ethiopia, bags of rice from species that had long ago died out in China. The Russian biologists stayed at the Institute throughout the siege, guarding the seeds from rats and destruction. Fourteen men died of starvation, surrounded by small bags of rice they could have eaten. These scientists felt an enormous responsibility to preserve their seeds for future

FIGURE 4.1X. *Russian Icons: The Trinity*. By Andrei Rublev. Wood, 1411. The Granger Collection, New York.

generations. Species diversity was a truth they died for, and because they did, we have strains of wheat and rice that can carry us into the new millennium.[20]

What do we honor in our efforts to maintain all the marvelous diversity possible? Can we see diversity as a longing deep within God's own heart? The world of God's design is rich in dissimilarity. Yet it functions as a vast homeostatic system, balanced and interlocking, a play of overlapping and unified fields (from quantum physics to biology). We inescapably live in a web of interconnectedness that mirrors the Trinitarian mystery.

The Iroquois, for example, speak of the "Three Sisters" (corn, beans, and squash) as a particular gift from the Great Spirit, providing for human needs and teaching mutuality throughout the natural order. When grown together, the corn stalks provide a trellis for the bean vines to grow on, even as the vines help to keep the corn stalks from being blown over by the wind. The beans, with the nitrogen-fixing quality of their roots, add nitrogen to the soil. The squash, in turn, provides shade with its large leaves, retarding the growth of weeds and maintaining moisture in the ground. The "sisters," moreover, provide a balanced nutrition for human beings as the corn supplies carbohydrates, the beans offer protein, and the squash yields abundant vitamins. This mutual interaction of the three (and the giving of themselves to others) expresses what Christians would identify as the unity in diversity that forms the core of the Trinity itself—mirrored in creation. How, then, do humans replicate this pattern of reciprocity in their relation to the rest of creation?

Australian ecologist Bill Mollison uses the word "permaculture" to describe the necessary integration of human life into the natural world. In urging a "permanent (eco-friendly) culture," he searches for human habitats and food production systems that mimic the patterns found in nature. If waste were handled with an eye to the operation of the entire system, he argues, the refuse of one part could become the food or habitat of another. This is how the biosphere itself recycles its materials without generating waste.[21]

An example is the Khanya model of community development found in South Africa today. It organizes village life around the overlapping of three intersecting circles that represent, respectively, the spheres of worship, agriculture, and animal life. One circle encloses a roofed church without walls, the second a garden, and the third a cattle corral. The altar stands at the center where the three converge. In this Trinitarian (trefoil) pattern, each sphere is intimately joined to the others. Cow manure fertil-izes the garden. Mulch feeds the cows. Rain water from the roof over the church fills a tank that supplies cattle, garden, and people alike with water for drinking, farming, and baptisms. Everything is symbolically—and literally—interconnected.

Even more impressive are examples of the same principle applied on an urban/industrial level. Ethicist Larry Rasmussen describes an experiment in Kalundborg, Denmark, on the North Sea, where a coal-fired power plant once emptied its spent steam into the bay nearby. But after a community-wide effort to determine how waste could be recycled, the steam heat is now redirected to an oil refinery nearby (to help with cleaning), to several greenhouses (to warm the plants), to a fish farm (where the fish grow more rapidly in warm water), and to 3,500 town residents who no longer have to run oil-burning heating systems. At every turn, what once was waste is now recycled in multiple ways.[22] In another example, a recent skyscraper in Philadelphia was built with a 90 percent recycling rate, incorporating materials from a previous building on the site, reusing construction waste, and employing discarded underground oil tanks for the storage of rainwater to be used in irrigation.[23]

These illustrations of ecological thinking follow the pattern of food webs in nature itself—interrelating everything, feeding waste and excess back into the health of the larger system. They model the dance, the *perichoresis,* of the Holy Trinity. If we survive as a family of species in this biosphere, the patterns of ecological behavior—the house rules by which we live together in the *oikos* (the home) of this world—will have to imitate the exchange of love and reciprocity that characterizes God's own innermost being. This is what the Holy Trinity can teach us best.

I recognize it once again in a northern New Mexican landscape where tracks in the snow reveal an immense diversity and interaction of species. In this amazing setting, where the Colorado Plateau, the Southern Rockies, and central shortgrass prairies all converge, I'm able to observe 368 extant native species of birds alone. Even in the desert, everything dances. On a cold winter night like this, I can hardly resist howling along with the coyotes at the reckless exuberance of it all.

· 5 ·

Jonathan Edwards on Beauty, Desire, and the Sensory World

> I am not ashamed to own that I believe that the whole universe, heaven and earth, air and seas, and the divine constitution and history of the holy Scriptures, be full of images of divine things, as full as a language is of words. . . .
>
> —Jonathan Edwards, "Types Notebook"[1]

Jonathan Edwards lived in a world that sang. He considered music to be "the best, most beautiful, and most perfect way that we have of expressing a sweet concord of mind." It joins heaven and earth in the harmony of the spheres, echoing a primeval beauty grander than anything we can imagine.[2] Hans Urs von Balthasar, another theologian entranced by beauty, declared in his book *Truth is Symphonic*, that "the world is like a vast orchestra tuning up."

> Each player plays to himself, while the audience take[s] their seats and the conductor has not yet arrived. All the same, someone has struck an A on the piano, and a certain unity of atmosphere is established around it: they are tuning up for some common endeavor.[3]

Each member of the orchestra, with eyes fixed on the Maestro, contributes to what finally becomes a grand celebration of the beauty and glory of God. In the endlessly alluring work of creation, Balthasar observed, "God performs a symphony and it is impossible to say which is richer: the seamless genius of his composition or the polyphonous orchestra of Creation that he has prepared to play it."[4]

Edwards would have delighted in such an image. Discerning God's harmony in the sights and sounds of his eighteenth-century Massachusetts landscape, he was a naturalist as well as a theologian. Metaphors of the world as a theater of God's glory, a school of desire, or a vast orchestral work suggest the manner in which he rooted theology in the concept of beauty. The world for him was alive with God's presence, witnessed in beech trees, the optical properties of sunlight, and even the balance of insect populations in southern New England. "The key to Edwards' thought," says George Marsden, "is that everything is related because everything is related to God."[5] A harmonious interrelation of parts is the core of divine beauty as Edwards understood it.

For him, the natural world is a communication of God's Trinitarian glory that prompts the human heart to a deeper longing. The conscious celebration of God's beauty is the end toward which the whole of creation is drawn. No other theme is more prevalent in his thought. Edward Farley goes so far as to say that in Jonathan Edwards's work, "beauty is more central and more pervasive than in any other text in the history of Christian theology."[6]

Humans, with their capacity to articulate wonder and to love, have a supremely prominent role in the task of giving God glory, but they do not perform it alone. They participate with the rest of the natural world in a reciprocal process by which the whole of creation is raised to a consciousness of its created splendor. This is the theme I want to develop in this chapter, focusing on Edwards's understanding of the new, aesthetic capacity to sense the sweetness of things that believers receive as one of the graces of salvation. This *sensus suavitatis* had been emphasized by Calvin and the Puritans before him, but Edwards developed it in a new way. In his thinking, it was a perception that illuminated the truths of Scripture and the magnificence of the natural world in a common apprehension of God's glory.

One of the difficult issues in the interpretation of Edwards's thought has been how this new "spiritual sense" should be understood. Some have viewed it as offering a virtual "sixth sense" by which the believer is equipped to perceive a spiritual reality altogether unavailable to non-believers. Others have understood it as providing a heightened and more integrated capacity to perceive reality through ordinary channels of sense experience. Actually both are involved, as Edwards tried to argue for two deeply held interests—the distinctively Christian experience of God as a graced reality *and* the importance of ordinary sense experience in grasping the way creation mirrors God's presence.[7]

The Northampton theologian continually sought to integrate mind and heart in an apprehension of God's beauty and the earth's wonder. In his understanding, God's "common grace" allows ordinary human beings to perceive something of the beauty and sweetness of God's presence in the world. But a "new spiritual sense" is required for seeing the world in all of its mystery. This new sense is a unique, God-given capacity to delight that incorporates and enhances natural modes of perception. Through its gift, the world of the senses can train one's perception still further in glimpsing God's grandeur. It opens the soul to the fullness of beauty.

For Jonathan Edwards, then, creation functions as a school of desire, training regenerate human beings in the intimate sensory apprehension of God's glory mirrored in the beauty of the world. Humans respond to creation by articulating its glory, bringing it to full consciousness, and by replicating God's own disposition to communicate beauty as they extend the act of beautifying to the world around them. The natural world, in other words, enlarges the human capacity to sense the fullness of God's beauty, and the appreciation of that beauty subsequently leads to ethical action. Nature teaches us God's beauty, and God's beauty drives us to its continual replication in space and time.

The implications of this for spirituality and the environment are many, suggesting that the chief purpose of human beings as a species is to cooperate with the rest of creation in mirroring God's glory. Hence, we dare not hinder the "great work" to which Thomas Berry says we all are called, the work of overcoming "the radical discontinuity between the human and the nonhuman."[8] Jonathan Edwards himself was never hesitant to mention sin, and here he would have us speak plainly: it is a sin to make ugly what God has created for the purpose of reflecting and sharing God's beauty.

Replicating the Beauty of the Holy Trinity

Edwards's theology begins and ends with God. It offers an extraordinary vision of the divine Beauty replicating itself in all of creation. Contrary to the still-popular stereotype of Edwards as a preacher of hellfire and damnation, he was far more concerned with God as a beauty to be enjoyed than with God as a power to be feared. He came to reflect, perhaps even self-critically, after his infamous Enfield sermon on "Sinners in the Hands of an Angry God": "'Tis beyond doubt that too much weight has been laid, by many persons of late, on discoveries of

God's greatness, awful majesty, and natural perfection . . . without a real view of the holy, lovely majesty of God."[9]

The God he sought most to realize, in both his preaching and writing, was a God filled with a restless longing for relationship. What had attracted him in his years at Yale to his future wife, Sarah Pierpont, was her familiarity with God and her extraordinary capacity for delight. In his late teens he had written in the front page of his Greek grammar, perhaps daydreaming in class one day:

> They say there is a young lady in [New Haven] who is beloved of that Great Being, who made and rules the world, and that there are certain seasons in which the Great Being . . . comes to her and fills her mind with exceeding sweet delight, and that she hardly cares for anything except to meditate on him. . . . She will sometimes go about from place to place, singing sweetly and seems to be always full of joy and pleasure; and no one knows for what. She loves to be alone, walking in the fields and groves, and seems to have someone invisible always conversing with her.[10]

Like Sarah, Edwards himself discovered this Great Being not so much in abstract metaphysics as in the delight he experienced in sweet communion with nature. He rarely spoke of God's essence in terms of a divine substance, using familiar patristic terms like *ousia* or *substantia*. He preferred to describe God more dynamically as a "disposition" to communicate love.[11] It is truer, he would have said, to think of God as a communicative "act" than as an existing "thing." God is not so much a self-contained and static entity as an impulsive beauty delighting more than anything else in sharing itself. Hence, a longing to extend love—a disposition to communicate—forms the dynamic core of the divine being.[12] God's essential nature, as it were, is God's will to act out of a longing that needs nothing whatever, but chooses longing itself as an expression of its deepest self-communication.

Edwards argued that God's ravishing beauty is the first and most important thing to be said of God. "God is God, and distinguished from all other beings, and exalted above'em, chiefly by his divine beauty."[13] To suggest that God enjoys being God is to recognize that the divine splendor is a fit subject for its own endless contemplation. Like Sophia in the wisdom literature, God thoroughly delights in her own loveliness. Understanding the theologian's vocation as a conscientious participation in this delight, Edwards anticipated the work of von Balthasar in saying that "[beauty] is what we are more concerned with than anything else."[14]

He was quick to add, however, that the divine beauty is never content with self-absorption, simply terminating in its own mirrored excellence. Its nature is to shine forth, manifest, and communicate itself. This is a beauty that insists on being shared. In the mystery of God's own being as Holy Trinity there is an eternal imaging forth of the Father's perfect beauty in his love of the Son, and (in turn) their mutual delight issuing still further in the fullness of the Holy Spirit. God's disposition as Trinity is to delight endlessly in the shared splendor of this intimate relationship.[15]

Hence the Trinity's celebration of a common joy cannot be contained within the divine being alone. God spontaneously seeks ever new ways of expressing love and replicating beauty, creating a world that occasions still further opportunities for self-communication and sharing. What is already complete in God (*ad intra*) nonetheless reaches out (*ad extra*) to extend itself in a continually greater celebration of mutual delight. God is a communicative being whose language is creation, reaching out with a love that is ever restless for more and more sensory expressions of beauty. God's grandeur never tires of being known and relished. "It will flame out, like shining from shook foil," as Gerard Manley Hopkins proclaimed.

For Edwards, this did not imply that God has to communicate God's self to others in order to complete something lacking in God's own being.[16] God's love, pleasure, and beauty are entirely perfect in themselves, requiring nothing to improve them. As a Reformed theologian, Edwards naturally affirmed the aseity of God—God's freedom to exist without being upheld by anything else. The Calvinist tradition insists that God would be free and glorious as God even if God had not decided to create the world. The divine self-communication, therefore, is a wholly "superfluous" action, in both senses of that term. It is wholly "unnecessary," required by nothing that is not already present in God's own being. And it naturally "overflows" in a vast superfluity from the wellsprings of an inexhaustible source, not unlike Bonaventure's image of the world flowing from the fecundity of God's own being.

In other words, the world's mirroring of the divine beauty does nothing to enlarge the divine nature. Nonetheless, as God's effulgence is repeated and extended in time and space, the perfection of God seems to become yet more perfect. "If the world had not been created," Edwards suggests, some of "[God's] attributes never would have had any exercise." God's glory would have been less apparent as a result. Self-contained beauty is never as lovely as a beauty in which others take delight. A perfection that elicits rejoicing is always superior to a perfection left to itself alone. Hence, says Edwards, "God looks on the communication of himself, and the emanation of the infinite glory and good that are in himself to belong to the fullness and completeness of himself, as though he were not in his most complete and glorious state without it."[17]

Edwards's God is discontent with being beautiful alone. Arrayed in her Shechinah glory, exploding all notions of gender and difference, this God longs to be recognized by others, to be part of a mutual celebration that extends beauty and happiness in every possible direction. "God is glorified not only by His glory's being seen, but by its being rejoiced in. When those that see it delight in it, God is more glorified than if they only see it." When this happens, Edwards implies, God almost becomes "more" than God had been, as if *delight* in Being adds something to Being itself. In creating the world and sharing the divine glory with it, God's happiness is "enlarged," God's pleasure made richer.[18]

Roland Delattre argues that Edwards was "a pioneer in the way he envisaged a lively universe created by God, not out of nothing or out of something, but out of the very fullness of God's own life overflowing into a world as a self-enlargement of the divine life."[19] This panentheistic conception of a world that is "other" than God even as it is "in" God offered a dynamic way of understanding creation. God's beauty within the world is infectious, Edwards knew. He sounds like Pseudo-Dionysius, the great sixth-century mystic who spoke of God creating the world out of the intensity of God's own desire. Dionysius had said:

> The beautiful, good abundance of [God's] benign yearning (*eros*) for all is carried outside of himself in the loving care he has for everything. . . . And he does so by virtue of his supernatural and ecstatic capacity to remain, nevertheless, within himself.[20]

Edwards sought to maintain this delicate balance between God's transcendent otherness and immanent presence, reaching always for what he could not put into words. He knew, as Denys Turner expresses so well, that "all language about God has to be stretched before it snaps."[21] How does anyone comprehend the mystery of God's intense desire for God's own beauty *and* God's astounding generosity in bestowing that beauty onto everything else?

Edwards realized that his emphasis on God's delight in God's own grandeur ran the risk of supposing that "God does everything from a selfish spirit," as if God were some kind of vain deity—anxiously needing applause, ever hungry for approval.[22] The Northampton preacher wanted to affirm that God "enjoys himself" immensely, finding nothing more captivating than God's own beauty. But God's joy remains restless until it completes itself in the delight of others. As Edwards put it, shared "happiness is the end of creation," the final purpose for which everything is made. "Creation," therefore, "had as good not be, as not rejoice in its being." Or to express it in another way, "God, in seeking our glory and happiness, [simply] seeks himself."[23]

Creation as a Communication of God's Glory

This irrepressible longing to extend the contemplation of God's beauty leads the divine being—in every lucid moment—to create a world that shows forth extraordinary wonder. Edwards's conception of *creatio ex nihilo* was a very dynamic one, insisting that God's task of continually bringing the world into being is, in every moment, an "immediate production out of nothing," that is, out of nothing outside of God's own infectious desire.[24] Everything emerges in each instant as something new, sensuous, and alive, overflowing from God's hand—calling attention to itself and what it mirrors of the divine longing. Reacting to the crass materialism of Thomas Hobbes, Edwards wanted to understand the entire world as dependent upon God. Nothing is self-reliant.

Edwards knew that God communicates God's glory most especially in the creation of human beings, those "capable of being proper images of his excellency." Their spiritual nature, by the gift of grace, is able to respond most fully to God's spiritual beauty. Edwards is unhesitatingly anthropocentric in declaring humans the "willing active subjects [most] capable of actively promoting God's glory."[25]

But God also communicates the divine glory through the rest of creation as well. Mountains, streams, and sunlight breaking through morning clouds operate as genuine "images" or "shadows" of God's restless desire to communicate. Edwards can go so far as to say that even though this is a less direct form of communication, in some respects it may be more reliable. Human beings, despite their spiritual nature, are often—on account of their sin—given to dissemblance. They can pretend to be what they are not. But the rest of nature is free from this artificiality. As Edwards explains, "Though beauty of face and sweet airs in man are not always the effect of the corresponding excellencies of mind, yet the beauties of nature are really emanations, or shadows, of the excellencies of the Son of God."[26]

Hence, natural phenomena are able truly to mirror God's disposition to pour herself out in reckless displays of beauty. Edwards can say that:

> when we are delighted with flowery meadows and gentle breezes of wind, we may consider that we only see the emanations of the sweet benevolence of Jesus Christ; when we behold the fragrant rose and lily, we see his love and purity. So the green trees and fields, and singing of birds, are emanations of his infinite joy and benignity; the easiness and naturalness of trees and vines [are] shadows of his infinite beauty and loveliness; the crystal rivers and murmuring streams have the footsteps of his sweet grace and bounty.[27]

In a brief essay that he wrote on the "Beauty of the World," Edwards observed that "the fields and woods seem to rejoice," noting "how joyful do the birds seem to be." Asking how this reflected beauty of God can so readily permeate creation at every angle, he offered an answer from his reading of Newton's optics.

> 'Tis very probable that that wonderful suitableness of green for the grass and plants, the blue of the sky, the white of the clouds, the colors of flowers, consists in a complicated proportion that these colors make one with another, either in the magnitude of the rays, the number of vibrations that are caused in the optic nerve, or some other way.[28]

The physical structure of the universe, as he understood it, mirrors and bodies forth the perfect proportions of the divine beauty, striking the human nervous system with a startling awakening of the senses, stirring delight at every turn.

In a paper on the scientific study of spiders, Edwards in his youth could celebrate the delight that spiders take in sailing through the air on wind-borne

FIGURE 5.1. Jonathan Edwards, 1703–1758. Engraving by S. S. Jocelyn and S. B. Munson (1829).

lengths of web. He saw their behavior as exemplifying "the exuberant goodness of the Creator in providing for the pleasure and recreation of all sorts of creatures, even the insects." Evidences of delight in nature are but a mirror of God's own pleasure in all that God has made. For Jonathan Edwards, the universe is an explosion of God's glory.[29]

But what for him was a blatant reality written across the cosmos was not so apparent to others walking through an eighteenth-century New England meadow surrounded by red maples in the fall. Edwards had to explain, then, how nature could serve as a reliable school of desire for some—leading them to God's beauty in Christ—while it remained opaque and indifferent to others. His way of accounting for this difference in perception was to posit the notion of a new spiritual sense given to believers by the Spirit of God at their conversion.

Coming to a "Sensory" Knowledge of God

For Edwards, like Calvin and the Puritans before him, nature functions as a school of desire, teaching humans how to perceive God's glory. He perceived the physical world, when appreciated with the new spiritual sense that regeneration brings, as offering direct training in the multidimensional way of knowing that is necessary for meeting God. This is a knowing that involves a tasting and delighting—not just an apprehension of the mind, but an intimate engagement of all the senses as well.

As an heir of John Locke, Edwards put a twist on the way that people in the eighteenth century ordinarily spoke of knowing God in comparison to how they knew the world around them. Most were accustomed to distinguishing between their knowledge of the physical world (by sensation) and their knowledge of an ethereal, non-sensory God (by faith and reason). Edwards argued, however, that God in the mystery of God's own being is far more "sensuous"—more full of infinite delights, more prone to the endless expansion of relationships, more astonishingly beautiful—than anything we can imagine in this stunningly sensuous world around us. In effect, he said, if you think *this* world is sensual and beautiful, you haven't seen anything yet! All this is but a dim, quasi-sensual reflection of God's still greater glory, overflowing spontaneously from the mystery of God's inner-Trinitarian life. That's where all desire and all connectedness find their birth.

Yet the sensory world, in its partial, "secondary" beauty available to us through the exercise of our senses, is what trains us in the polymorphous way of knowing that is required for encountering a super-sensory God of matchless glory. As Edwards put it, "The works of

God are . . . a kind of voice or language of God to *instruct* intelligent beings in things pertaining to Himself."[30]

One must be careful, of course, in speaking of God as a "sensuous" being. We have seen already that the core of God's being, for Edwards, is not primarily a divine "substance," certainly not anything available to sensory analysis. Yet the mutual delight that is shared within the exchange of the Trinity is something best suggested to us by a sensory analogy. If God's essence is a "disposition" to multiply the enjoyment of beauty, to reach out from Father to Son, and to Spirit, and subsequently to the whole of creation in a celebration of interconnected delight, then "one alone cannot be excellent."[31] God is ontologically hungry for relationship. Hence, the intimate interrelatedness of all things grows out of this divine propensity (God's own insatiable longing) for interconnectedness. Edwards, therefore, does not think of God as a "sensual being." God is rather what gives sensuality its meaning. Nothing is more truly "sensuous" than the delight in harmony, beauty, and connectedness that lies at the core of the Holy Trinity.

Accordingly, if we seek to practice the kind of knowing that is necessary for encountering such a God, we must look to nature as a school of desire in teaching us how to delight, how to savor and taste, how to desire the beauty to which it points. As our senses open us to harmonies of sound and delicacies of scent, as they teach us to delight in the play of light in a bubbling fountain of water, they offer a spiritual training in the knowledge of God. Edwards never tired of pointing out that to "know" God is also to enjoy God. The properly trained mind not only "speculates and beholds, but relishes and feels."[32] When it comes to matters of the divine, enjoyment is a precondition for any authentic knowing.

In speaking of nature as a school of desire, Edwards drew on a long tradition of the "colloquy with the creatures." This literary trope goes back to Job's injunction (in Job 12:7f) to "Ask the beasts, and they will teach you," and to Jesus's call to consider the lilies (in Matthew 6:28). The form became stylized in Augustine's *Confessions* when he "puts his questions to the earth," asking the creatures, the winds, and the sky to "tell him of God."[33] Their answer is that their beauty leads him to a Beauty beyond themselves in God. The pattern was later advanced by Bonaventure and the Victorines in the Middle Ages and given expression again by

John Calvin in his commentaries on the Psalms. The Puritan tradition extended it still further through Richard Baxter, the poetry of Edward Taylor, and the seventh book of *Paradise Lost.* Puritan "meditations on the creatures" became an instructive device in learning how the senses of the body lead us by delight to the contemplation of God.

When Puritan horticulturist Ralph Austen imagined an extended dialogue between a husbandman and his fruit trees, he was drawing on this time-honored motif. As he explained:

> When we seriously consider the nature, and properties of inanimate creatures; then we aske Questions of them; and they being thus Questioned, they return an answer unto men, when we clearly perceive that their wonderfull Natures, vertues, and properties, cannot be, but from the Power, and Wisdome of a superior Cause.[34]

Thomas Adam, esteemed as the "Shakespeare of the English Puritans" because of his exquisite use of language, similarly published a series of sermons on spiritual lessons to be learned from the herbs of an English garden, clarifying their various medicinal and devotional uses. These were writers who continued Bonaventure's desire to read the vestiges of God from the wonders of creation, who echoed Francis de Sales's insistence that colloquies (or "familiar talk") with "insensible creatures" can be instructive to the faithful.[35] The Calvinist pattern from which Edwards drew, therefore, was but one strain of a much wider Augustinian tradition.

In describing Edwards's own conception of nature as a school of desire, one has to admit that it is not always easy to characterize his understanding of the natural world. A reading of this eighteenth-century theologian, as viewed by current scholarship, would seem to suggest two very different Jonathan Edwardses, responding in diametrically opposite ways to the Western Massachusetts landscape of which he was a part.

There was Edwards the empiricist on the one hand and Edwards the idealist on the other. The careful observer of the natural world, avidly reading Locke and Newton, penning half a volume of scientific writings, finding God in the intricate beauty of the earth—*this* Edwards seems to stand in stark contrast to the philosopher of Neo-Platonic sympathies who viewed all objects of perception as no more than ideas of the perceiving mind, who spoke of the world as "less than nothing" from the perspective of eternity. Edwards as "empiricist" wanted to honor the world as a reliable and independent image of God's glory. Edwards as "idealist" wanted to recognize the world as upheld by the power of God alone.[36]

I would argue that these two dimensions of Edwards's thought come together most clearly in his emphasis on desire. The desire stirred by the beauty of the external world is one with the desire for the beauty of Being itself. The human heart and the rest of the created world share a reflected glory to which both are drawn. Each is shot through with a longing for intimate relationship. Each participates in and points to the attractiveness that holds all reality together. Words like pleasure and delight, relish and appetite, ravishment and enjoyment continually recur in Edwards's writings, like Calvin and the Puritans before him.

In a sermon on "Youth and the Pleasures of Piety," he scorned those who look down on "religion as a very dull, melancholy thing," arguing that far from hindering the "pleasure of outward enjoyments," the spiritual life actually promotes it. He referred to the highest pleasures of the soul and the highest pleasures of the sensory world in complementary ways. Edwards knew that "man [is] so unsatiable [for God] that nothing can be found in the world [that] will satisfy him."[37] Yet the earth serves to whet an appetite that it cannot fulfill. For those with an imagination awakened by the new sense, it teaches a savoring and tasting that is the deepest way of knowing God we are capable of having.

Edwards, even as a child, built huts for prayer in the woods of his father's central Connecticut farm. Throughout his life, his ideas always flowed best as he rode his horse or walked through the New England countryside, scratching thoughts on scraps of paper that he pinned to his waistcoat. On late August evenings in his youth he would lie on his back near the river, watching butterflies and moths flying toward the southeast. He loved to imagine himself "being alone in the mountains, or some solitary wilderness, far from all mankind, sweetly conversing with Christ, and wrapt and swallowed up in God."[38] The physical world never ceased to operate for him as a school of desire.

Like the Puritans before him, Edwards carried on the classical and medieval metaphor of nature as a "second book," another source—along with Scripture—for knowing God.[39] Neither he nor the Puritans understood this as a basis for establishing a "natural theology" as such. The created world does not offer any new "content" beyond what is found in the "first book" of Scripture. But it does offer an important exercise in epistemology, as it were. It gives us practice in a way of knowing that is far deeper and richer than the abstract speculation we usually exercise in understanding what we read.[40]

The Sensory World and the Sense of the Heart

The key to understanding the importance that Edwards attributed to the sensory world is found in his emphasis on the "new sense" that believers receive as part of the revivifying work of salvation. Doing more than allowing them to marvel at beauty in general, it turns the natural world into a training ground for discovering the affective receptivity that knowing God requires. It gives life to the analogical imagination, using beauty as a way of leading the soul to God. We can identify five different aspects of this new aesthetic sense that Edwards employed in giving expression to a spirituality of desire.

Basic to his thinking in understanding the operation of the new sense is his notion of a "sensible idea." This is the means by which we are able even to begin the task of knowing God. God can never be fully known as an object of intellection, he argued, but must be loved through a deeply visceral and participatory way of knowing. Edwards insisted that it is the impassioned mind, the *loving* mind, the mind made open to all of its senses that thinks most clearly.

He was indebted here to John Smith and other Cambridge Platonists in the seventeenth century who had contrasted the "thin, aiery knowledge that is got by meer speculation" with the "sweetness and deliciousness of divine truth" that has to be "tasted and relished" in order to be taken in. This happens when the regenerate soul is renewed by God's Spirit. "Reason is turned into sense." One receives a new capacity to embrace a "sensible idea"—to experience spiritual realities with all the vividness of a sense impression, whether visual, auditory, palatal, tactile, or olfactory.[41]

The Spirit-filled individual, for example, does not just "think" the idea of God's radiance as an exercise of the brain in rational understanding. The wholeness of the renewed person receives the idea as a "sensation" that awakens desire and delight.[42] Edwards described the spiritually enlightened individual's sense of God's excellency as follows:

> He does not merely rationally believe that God is glorious, but he has a sense of the gloriousness of God in his heart. There is not only a rational belief that God is holy, and that holiness is a good thing, but there is a sense of the loveliness of God's holiness. There is not only a speculatively judging that God is gracious, but a sense how amiable God is upon that account, or a sense of the beauty of this divine attribute.[43]

One perceives the idea of God's glory, in other words, with the same sort of indisputable immediacy as one glimpses sunlight passing through falling water. In Edwards's understanding, the mind is a sense organ, a mechanism of knowing that "feels ideas," that "senses concepts," that grasps with a totality of wonder what the unregenerate mind perceives (if at all) only as an abstraction.[44]

God is more "sensuous," more compelling, more engaging and alive than any parallel we can point to in all the luscious green splendor of earth. And yet it is the physical world that opens us to the senses, that actively participates itself in the process of replicating God's glory in time and space.[45] Edwards points to "an analogy, or consent, between the beauty of the skies, trees, fields, flowers, etc. and spiritual excellencies," even though he admits this connection is generally "more hid and requires a more discerning, *feeling mind* to perceive it. . . ." But if one exercises that "feeling mind," one suddenly discerns a "love and [delight] in flowers and bespangled meadows." One perceives "a rejoicing in the green trees and fields, [and] majesty in thunder." Through this new sense we recognize inanimate creatures—sharing in the same sensory world of God's making—as participating with us in a joint apprehension of God's beauty.[46]

Receiving a Spiritual Taste

A second aspect of Edwards's conception of the "new sense" is his conviction that this way of knowing comes primarily as a spiritual gift, offered by God as something more than simply the exercise of the other five senses. Its source is God's grace alone. While Edwards knew that God's ravishing beauty is the most important thing to be said of God, and that the natural world witnesses to this at every hand, he was also aware that the capacity to recognize God's glory is not immediately available to every man and woman. Sin has distorted the full sensory apparatus of the human person. Responding to God's self-communication in nature, therefore, requires the exercise of a particular sense of the heart, something received in the regenerative work of the Holy Spirit. This "new sense" goes beyond the ordinary "sense of the heart" that all human beings possess.[47]

Edwards, on the one hand, was able to affirm the "pleasant religious affections and apprehensions that natural men" possess, honoring their ability to discern beauty and even practice goodness. These are "common illuminations" available to everyone.[48] In saying this, he drew on the Reformed tradition's long-standing understanding of "common grace," as opposed to the "special grace" that comes through a work of God's Spirit in conversion. Calvin had emphasized a "universal grace which is spread over all the creatures." In his thinking, this explained how "natural men" like Plato could be so "sharp and penetrating in their investigations," and how secular human culture can often seek the common good (despite the inescapable reality of sin in human experience).[49]

What God's special grace does, on the other hand, is to transform this limited capacity that humans possess into a vibrant engagement of life in Christ. Edwards's goal was to see God's presence and power woven through all of human experience, infusing the ordinary with an entirely new spiritual vitality. He wanted to convey a deeper vision of God's work in *this* world, not simply an ethereal spiritual experience of an altogether different world. In his conceptions of the sense of the heart and a new spiritual sense, therefore, he was able to honor the mundane reality of sense experience while insisting on God's enlivening it with a power available only through the agency of God's Spirit.

Edwards developed this teaching out of the earlier Calvinist tradition, recasting it in terms of Locke's emphasis on sensory experience and his own experience in the Great Awakening.[50] Calvin had spoken of a capacity for discerning the "sweetness" (*suavitas*) of spiritual things that becomes part of the believer's way of grasping divine truth. As he had put it, "[M]an's understanding, thus beamed by the light of the Holy Spirit, then at last truly begins to taste [*gustare incipit*] those things which belong to the Kingdom of God, having formerly been quite foolish and dull in tasting them."[51]

As early as the spring of 1721, about the time of Edwards's own conversion, he began to speak of "a new sense of things," an "inward, sweet delight" that came to him from his walks in the woods of his father's farm, his reading of the Song of Songs, and his contemplation of God. Later, in the Northampton revival of 1734, he continued to develop this general sense of the heart as well as the notion of a new spiritual sense that allows the believer to go beyond all shallow and intellectual apprehensions of God's glory to a thoroughly sensual appreciation of its beauty. It is the difference, he could say, between rationally knowing that honey is sweet, and being able vividly to taste its sweetness. A dozen years later, in his treatise on the *Religious Affections*, he went on to make this new aesthetic sense one of the chief indicators of an authentic religious experience.[52]

What most distinguished the experience of those genuinely converted in the revival, he said, was not a dramatic display of religious feeling, but a new sensitivity to the world—an ability to discern beauty where it had not been apparent before. Edwards said of the people in Northampton after the awakening:

> The light and comfort which some of them enjoy, gives a new relish to their common blessings, and causes all things about 'em to appear as it were beautiful, sweet and pleasant to them: all things abroad, the sun, moon and stars, the clouds and sky, the heavens and earth, appear as it were with a cast of divine glory and sweetness upon them.[53]

This acquisition of an increased "spiritual appetite" was something that Edwards further understood to be sustained through communion with Christ in the Lord's Supper. While he mixed Zwinglian and Calvinist elements in his Eucharistic theology, he nonetheless emphasized that believers become "partakers of the divine nature" in receiving Christ through the sacrament. It causes "the soul to grow as food does the body," satisfying (and increasing) the appetite God had aroused. This emphasis led to his disagreeing with his grandfather Solomon Stoddard over the question of open communion and ultimately to his dismissal from the Northampton church in 1749. For him, the Eucharist was not just another means (like preaching) for converting the ungodly. It was a means of intimately binding believers in union with Christ, feeding their new sensory appetite for holy things.[54]

A Juxtaposition of Sensory Modes

A third dimension of Edwards's conception of this new spiritual sense was its necessary mixing of sensory modes in the exuberant effort to describe God's glory. Neuro-linguistic psychologists tell us that human beings seem to have a preferred sensory channel that influences the way they perceive and describe reality. It reveals itself subtly in the sensory metaphors of their language. For Edwards, like most people in the Enlightenment, it was seeing (and secondarily, hearing) that best conveyed the authenticity of what truly mattered.[55] Spiritual vision was central to his perception of truth, even though he thought music was the most beautiful and perfect way of expressing glory. He once described the new spiritual sense given to the Christian as a "recitified musical ear."[56]

But in talking about the new spiritual sense, he chose *taste* as the best way to characterize it, as Calvin and the Puritans had done before him. He knew that taste and flavor suggest "the immediate presence of a thing to the human palate."[57] In the other senses (like hearing, smelling, and seeing) there is a separating medium of air through which awareness is transferred, but not so with tasting. "Taste is an intimate sense," says Diane Ackerman. "We can't taste things at a distance."[58] Edwards's own exercise of a sense of taste was fairly moderate, by the way, due to his poor health and simplicity of life. He often preferred a supper of bread and milk. But he and his wife Sarah had a craving for chocolate that he would satisfy with packages brought back from his trips to Boston.

Throughout Edwards's writings, in all the imaginative analogies he employed, he drew on a wide range of the human sensorium. Auditory, visual, and kinesthetic metaphors recur constantly in his writings. After his conversion, for example, God's glory struck him most profoundly through the sound of thunder, the bright flash of lightning, and the charged atmosphere into which he loved to run at the coming of a storm. These had been the very things that frightened him most before his conversion. In his hand-sewn notebooks, full of reflections on "Images of Divine Things" gathered from his observations in the Connecticut River Valley, he wrote of songbirds, flowing water, and the intricate movement of stars. He spoke of *seeing* these things, strangely enough, as the *voice* of God, *glimpsing* what is *held* out to us by the divine hand.[59]

This is a muddled language, as if spoken words could be perceived by the eye or images of the mind touched by one's hand. Clyde Holbrook has criticized Edwards's mixing of sensory metaphors, seeing it as something that "jars the literary symmetry" of his writing.[60] But he misses the deeper concern that underlies Edwards's use of language here. Sensory imagery has to be recklessly multiplied if one hopes even to begin adequately to express the glory of God.

His wife Sarah similarly juxtaposed images of flowing water and dancing sunlight as she reflected on her own vivid religious experience of January 28, 1742. Her language shares in the same ambiguity one might find in a late twentieth-century physicist alternating between wave and particle images of light. Language, she knew, has to be twisted if it is to suggest a reality beyond normal human perception. This is how she recalled the experience:

> [T]here seemed to be a constant *flowing* and reflowing of heavenly and divine love, from Christ's heart to mine; and I appeared to myself to float or swim, in these bright, sweet *beams* of the love of Christ, like the *motes* swimming in the beams of the sun, or the *streams of light* which come in at the window.[61]

Edwards and his wife found the reality of God's presence most apparent at moments of sensory overload, when one perceives in this world a brief harmony of glimpses, sounds, tastes, scents, and tactile impressions.

This juxtaposition of sensory modes in Edwards's cognitive processing is similar to what psychologists associate with the phenomenon of synaesthesia. As an experience of "joint perception" (Greek, *syn-aesthesia*), this is a neurological condition where stimuli to one sense mode produces sensations in one or more additional modes. Certain individuals, for instance, can speak of "hearing colors" or "seeing sounds."[62] They associate numbers with particular scents or recognize musical notes as bearing distinct shades of color. While this may or may not have been the case neurologically for Edwards, his language is filled with overlapping sensory imagery of this sort. In speaking of the nature of the Trinity or the mystery of God's glory, he often juxtaposed images of sight and touch, picturing God simultaneously as light and water, "sun" and "fountain"[63]—as if the optimal image for contemplating God were "flowing light" or "resounding touch," a noisy, splashing waterfall through which the sun shines, making each drop of water a prism for reflecting still greater light. In short, multidimensional sensory awareness was crucial to Edwards's understanding of the nature of spiritual knowing.

The Sensory Perception of Types in Nature

Yet another aspect of Edwards's conception of the role that nature plays in the exercise of the new sense has to do with his understanding of typology. This was how he conceived the world of created things as actively "participating" in the beauty to which it points. Earlier Puritan practice had often drawn on "types" from the natural world to substantiate the claims of Scripture. Cotton Mather, for example, had written widely on meteorological matters—from thunder (in his *Brontologia sacra*) to storms at sea. But his practice, like others, had always been to move as quickly as possible from the natural phenomenon to the truth it allegorically represented. Edwards, in contrast, was able to linger with the text of nature itself because of the greater attentiveness that the "new sense" made possible. Nature, for him, never led simply to a reality wholly beyond itself. It participated in the very mystery it represented.[64]

Hence, he clearly affirmed the natural world as *itself* a communication of God's majesty, one that intimately joins with humans in achieving its own goal in God's end for creation. Flowing rivers like the Connecticut and Housatonic serve as more than mere stage settings for God's drama. They are more than empty "significations" of holy things in which they never participate—allegorical hints of the rivers of paradise, for example.[65] For Edwards, their splashing movement, the way their waters reflect light, the play of sun and shadows along their banks offer a direct apprehension of God's glory and majesty. They communicate this themselves as "images and shadows" that require the participation of human perception in bringing them to the completion of their divine purpose. Similarly, the attraction of gravity, the delight of bees in the sweet taste of pollen, the appetite of babies for breast milk, the intimate union of a branch grafted onto a fruit tree, even the sexual appeal of a wife to her husband—all these, he proclaimed, are teachers of desire drawing us to God.[66]

The nature imagery that Edwards found most persuasive—most able to trigger an experience of God's glory (with all the spiritual sensuality that involves)—were images that powerfully suggest a sense of reciprocal interaction. He exulted in images of effulgence and refulgence, the gleaming forth of light and its being reflected back again, as in the play of moonlight on the surface of a river. Dynamic images that highlight the relationships between bodies were the ones that intrigued him most. As he expressed it with poetic splendor:

> In the creature's knowing, esteeming, loving, rejoicing in, and praising God, the glory of God is both exhibited and acknowledged; his fullness is received and returned. Here is both an *emanation* and *remanation*. The refulgence shines upon and into the creature, and is reflected back to the luminary.[67]

This keen observer of the landscapes of desire in eighteenth-century New England knew that human language itself is deeply rooted in the sensory world. The communication skills available to us are derived from our human experience of embodiment. This is what equips us in speaking of God. Nothing is more suited for analogically suggesting the "supersensory" reality of God, Edwards thought, than the concrete specificity of human language and the physical world out of which it arises. In describing the genesis of language, he explained that,

> [T]he names of spiritual things, or most of them, [are] derived from the names of sensible or corporeal ones . . . because there was no other way of making others readily understand men's meaning when they first signified these things by sounds, than by giving of them the names of things sensible to which they had an analogy.[68]

He would have recognized generative words like "companion" and "supercilious," for example, as having their source in the bodily experience of eating bread with another or raising one's eyebrows in haughty arrogance. Anticipating Emerson's intimate dependence of human language on the physical world, Edwards knew that the human being—like God—is necessarily a communicative being whose language is creation, ambiguous and accommodated as that always may be.

The New Sense and the Beauty of the Cross

A fifth and final aspect of Edwards's understanding of the new spiritual sense as it relates to the natural world has to do with the role that nature plays in teaching us the way of the cross. The whole creation, in its groaning and travail as it awaits the promised glory, models the frustration of holy desire that human sinfulness has brought into the world. The earth suffers continually at the hands of human abuse. Edwards almost seems to speak with an ecological sensitivity when he deplores the "abusive improvement that man, who has the dominion over the creatures, puts the creatures to." He scorns this misuse as "a force upon the creature; for the creature is abused in it, perverted to far meaner purposes than those for which the author of its nature made it."[69] He grieves over humans killing brute creatures by the "thousands and millions" every day, making the earth a "meat shop of sin."[70]

One has to resist stylizing Jonathan Edwards as a proto-envirotheologian. While his thinking may be full of ecological implications when read from a contemporary perspective, he had no intention himself of providing an environmental ethic aimed at protecting the natural world. His concern was more with the tragedy of human sin than the destruction of the environment. Yet in an unpublished 1737 sermon on Romans 8:22, Edwards lamented the extent to which the created world is "debased below its nature" by human pollution. "No wonder the whole creation is represented as groning [*sic*] under such an abuse & in being held under such bondage," he exclaimed. He not only decried the number of animals that humans daily destroy "to satiate their vicious appetites," but warned that if dominion-sated human beings (the "cumberers of the ground") continue in their sin "the creation will surely spew you out. . . . The world will disburden it self of you & and you shall be cast forth as an abominable branch."[71]

He knew that God's most astonishing beauty lies hidden in the earth's suffering, because the anguish of nature points to the agony of the cross. For Edwards, the highest expression of God's glory revealed in creation is witnessed in the God-become-Creature who died on Golgotha. In the humiliation of Christ we find the greatest consent of the creation to its Maker. The Creator becomes in this moment the lowest of all creatures on earth. The power of consent, the unity of being, the persuasiveness of the senses, the centrality of embodiment to the apprehension of God's glory—all these are discovered here at the cross.

Edwards echoed Calvin and Augustine before him (anticipating von Balthasar after him) in affirming that God is beautiful, not only in the loveliness of the earth, but even "beautiful on the cross."[72] Obviously it is a long stretch, by any reach of the imagination, to discern beauty in the midst of pain. But once again it is the "new sense" imparted by God's spirit that makes this discernment possible. The new capacity for perceiving God's beauty makes one simultaneously more sensitive to deformity, more attentive to the distorting of God's mirrored loveliness. It breeds a resistance to the disfiguring of the world's beauty as well as an identification with that which is most disfigured.

Beauty requires this, for it is the nature of God's beauty never to be static. God continually reaches out to beautify, to embrace in love, to reclaim what is lost. In the strange beauty of the cross, we perceive the extent to which God goes in assuming the full brokenness of creation. Here we grasp most dramatically God's disposition to communicate with reckless longing. Edwards found Christ's highest beauty in "the greatest degree of his humiliation." "Never [more than at the cross] was his divine glory and majesty covered with so thick and dark a veil . . . yet never was his divine glory so manifested by any act of his, as in that act of yielding himself up to these sufferings."[73] Here, in the agony of the cross, the beauty of the Holy Trinity is finally discerned most perfectly—at least to eyes made able to see. Through the gift of the *sensus suavitas* one can know, even in the midst of despair, that the world is saved in the end by beauty. Long before Dostoyevsky and Berdyaev, Edwards recognized this truth.

But he went on to argue that this understanding of beauty requires the acceptance of an ethical imperative that goes along with it. The beauty of the cross demands not only an intellectual comprehension of radical abandonment, but a practice of it as well. This is what imitators of a Triune God have to risk for the sake of love. "True happiness, the crown of glory, is to be come at in no other way than by bearing Christ's cross, by a life of mortification, self-denial and labor." The new sense is brought to full exercise only as it expresses itself finally in a life of concrete, sensory identification with those who suffer.[74] The surest test of an authentic work of the Spirit, Edwards urged, is an eagerness to reclaim the hidden beauty of those who remain unloved. Necessarily, he said, "Grace tends to holy practice."[75]

Delighting in Beauty and Bestowing It

My concluding concern in this chapter is to identify more specifically the human responsibilities that derive from this distinctive aesthetic awareness made possible by the new sense. If, as Edwards argues, God's deepest inclination or disposition is to communicate beauty for the sake of love, and if we as humans are prime recipients of that beauty in the mystery of the cross, then how do we extend the act of beautifying to the rest of the creation around us? How do we continue to replicate God's glory in space and time?

For Jonathan Edwards, aesthetic sensitivity has to reach out to something beyond itself. Glory is instinctively communicative. Frank Burch Brown says that for all Augustinians, "the greater the art's beauty, the greater the sense of yearning that it evokes."[76] It inevitably makes one hungry for more than it is able to satisfy. Beauty never ends in itself, therefore. There is no "art for art's sake." Aesthetics and ethics are necessarily joined. Hence, even as God's own beauty is inherently disposed to the beautifying of others, so the new sense in Edwards must lead to the adorning work of love exercised as justice.

What astounded Edwards, like Calvin before him, was that God's beauty remains restless (and in some sense incomplete) until it communicates itself to all that God loves. The goal of the divine beauty is to join itself in the most intimate way with the whole of creation, starting with the church as a promise of God's larger vision of restored glory. Believers who experience union with Christ, then, become full "partakers of the divine nature" (II Peter 1:4), as God's beauty and fullness are bestowed upon them. Edwards did not hesitate to employ the language of deification in speaking of this union, using words like "participation," "indwelling," even the "emanation and remanation" of the divine refulgence as it is received from God and returned. He described the incorporation of believers into the divine life with a highly mystical language: "Elect creatures [are] brought home to him, united with him, centering most perfectly in him, and *as it were swallowed up in him*: so that his respect to them finally coincides and becomes one and the same with respect to himself."[77]

For Edwards, the purpose of this intimate union was not simply to bask in God's acquired beauty, celebrating one's individual experience of oneness. The saints, he knew, were expected to manifest this beauty in their lives, becoming "proportioned Christians" who express the beauty of proportioned affections in their relationships with others.[78]

The replication of God's beauty in human life, achieved through the mystery of divinization or *theosis*, is complete, then, only as the beauty is shared with others. Indeed, the entire creation awaits the return of its original resplendent glory.

Near the end of his life, as a missionary to the Housatonic Indians in western Massachusetts, Edwards wrote a pair of exquisite dissertations on the nature of beauty and its impact on the human soul. His *Dissertation concerning the End for Which God Created the World* focused on the magnificence of God's reflected beauty in creation, and his *Dissertation on the Nature of True Virtue* attended to the ethical implications of the contemplation of this beauty.

In the latter he defined true virtue as a process of being so transfixed by the beauty of God as Being-in-general that those who perceive such glory are able also to grasp the as-yet unrealized beauty of every being-in-particular. True virtue is a disposition (or habit of the heart) that recognizes and extends the beauty of God into continually new expressions of loveliness.[79] To exercise this virtue is to participate in God's own disposition to communicate glory, bringing what is still an indiscernible beauty into consent and union with God's own matchless grandeur. What we love in a given person or thing is the contingent fullness of God's own beauty, wanting to replicate itself still further in creation. God, after all, is "the foundation and fountain of all being and all beauty."[80]

Admittedly, love of "Being-in-general" sounds extremely vague, lacking any passion—a matter of loving everything in general and nothing in particular. But to put God's magnificence at the center of attention is to allow oneself to love not only what is already there in the person or thing, but also the mysterious potential of the other as one grasps more fully its relation to God. We perceive what is "greening" itself within, growing into a beauty that is yet incomplete, to use the language of Hildegard of Bingen.

To act ethically, then, is to act as if there truly are interrelated harmonies that exist among all beings as they cohere together in God. This is not only to perceive (and celebrate) the mirror of God's beauty in every single being, but to engage in "joyful, beautifying activity" of our own. Roland Delattre observes that, for Edwards, "beauty . . . is more fully exhibited in *bestowing* beauty than in receiving it."[81]

Two implications derive from this ethical impulse in his thinking. The first is that extraordinary attentiveness and moral passion are demanded of all the lovers of God, as they bring the world to a consciousness of God's glorious presence within it. The meticulous powers of observation and literary artistry of an Annie Dillard or Mary Oliver are invaluable aids to the theologian's craft, drawing lines of interconnectedness across the cosmos, inciting a wonder that necessitates action. The second is that the work of recognizing and bestowing beauty has to be sustained ultimately by an eschatological hope. It draws its strength from Gregory of Nyssa's contention that our longing for God's beauty is never finally satisfied, but presses on from glory to glory—stretching itself into eternity in its ever-expanding sensual capacity to appreciate (and extend) beauty everywhere.[82]

Bringing the World to a Consciousness of its Beauty in God

To contemplate the divine glory aright, according to Edwards, is to make the universe conscious of its own being. Humans function as "the consciousness of the creation," he argued.[83] Theirs is the responsibility of discerning and articulating the aesthetic/moral character of the cosmos as a mirror of God's glory. Theirs is the task of pursuing the scientific (and liturgical) work of identifying interrelationships within the universe at large. They show how God's beauty fills the earth in the exercise of the principles of attraction, cohesion, consent, and proportionality that characterize the dynamic life of the created world. Roland Delattre observes that:

> One of the most remarkable features of Edwards's vision of the universe at the dawn of modern science is how close it is to the universe as we are coming to know it today—an evolving, living system governed by more complex relationships than simply mechanical ones, a very lively and animated universe.[84]

Without this cognizance of the world's interconnectedness in God, the cosmos remains radically at risk. We mend its fragility by restoring the awareness of its coherence in God. "Except the world had such a consciousness of itself, it would be altogether in vain that it was," Edwards could say. Our task as a species, therefore, is to identify and honor the conjoining of all interlocking systems in the speechless splendor of creation, bringing everything to its fullness in the glory of God. To use the language of Thomas Berry and Brian Swimme, we are the earth's activity in being aware of its future. We are "the self-reflexion of the universe," allowing it "to know and feel itself."[85]

The role of human beings is not simply to contemplate God's beauty in the individual perfections of line and balance that we discern in the world around us, lovely as these may be. This is what Edwards referred to as "secondary beauty." It is what we commonly describe as the "beautiful," displaying qualities of harmony and proportion that appeal to the eye or ear. It forms the principal aesthetic measure, "the great theory of beauty," that has dominated Western thought since Pythagoras. By contrast, Edwards defined "primary beauty" as the celebration of Being itself. This is what God invites us to in naming and honoring the intrinsic value of the being of others, bringing it to self-awareness.[86] God's beauty, exercised through us, actively anticipates and elicits all the beautiful possibilities that are inherent in the world God loves.

Thus, while secondary beauty focuses on what immediately delights, primary beauty takes us out of ourselves into a contemplation of God's own beautifying life and how we contribute to its expansion in the world. The first concentrates on the experience of "enjoying" beauty; the second on the activity of "bestowing" beauty. As Delattre suggests, the one is often cosmetic, while the other is cosmic in its life-enhancing effects on the world around us.[87]

As an aesthetically sensitive theologian, Edwards was fascinated by eighteenth-century science and philosophy, delighting in its attention to the intricacies of the natural world, its grand celebration of symmetry and order. But he directed its conclusions toward far different ends from Deistic thinkers like John Toland and Matthew Tindal. They perceived the self-contained harmony of the universe as ruling out the personal involvement of the divine. Such intervention, as they perceived it, was derogatory to God's omnipotence and unchangeableness. Edwards, in contrast, saw the new science as revealing a God of intimate relationships hidden within the very structure of the universe. Symmetry and interlocking order are indicators of a warm, convivial affinity, not cold indifference. His quest, then, was to incorporate Enlightenment science into the service of mystical union with Christ, bringing together the empirical work of science and the aesthetical work of theology.

The way one thing relates to another continually occupied Edwards's mind, as scientist and theologian alike. "Reality is a matter of relationship for [him]," said Wilson Kimnach. "The higher the truth the greater the extent of relationships involved."[88] The Massachusetts pastor was overwhelmed by the interconnecting unities that make up the universe. "When we think of the sweet harmony of the parts of the corporeal world," he exclaimed, "it fills us with such astonishment that the soul is ready to break."[89] In today's language, the awareness of God's beauty inevitably drives us to ecological thinking, to the recognition of the mysteries of Gaia, to the maintenance of those bonds of interrelationship and recylings of energy that join all living beings in a great whole.

"It was, perhaps, the profoundest insight of the eighteenth century that a thing becomes meaningful when we discern its relation to something else," says another recent interpreter of Edwards's thought.[90] He was ever attentive to the "general agreeing and consenting together" of interrelated bodies in the operation of the universe. He remained spellbound by the "agreeablenesses" that one discerns "between the colors of the woods and flowers and the smell, and the singing of birds."[91] At times, he sounded like contemporary exponents of chaos theory who speak of the "butterfly effect," noting how the beating of a butterfly's wings in China can affect weather patterns in New York City. The complexity and unpredictable wonder of the world was, for him, an expression of God's holding all things in dynamic, ever-changing relationship to each other (and to God's self). Gravity, for example, was but an expression in the realm of physics of the "attraction, or the mutual tendencies of all bodies to each other." To respond to God's beauty, then, is to value and nurture these various interrelationships, being sensitive to all the ways that ecosystems and biotic processes operate together to sustain mutuality and homeostasis in the maintenance of life. This, in Edwards's thinking, is an expression of the finest exercise of God's glory. Accordingly, "it is requisite that the beauty and excellency of the world, as God has constituted it, should not be kept secret."[92]

Ecological Ethics and Eschatological Hope

If ethical practice is needed to preserve the world in its divinely-appointed task of evincing God's beauty in the joining of all things in love, the practice has to be anchored in hope. Only there can it find the power to sustain deliberate action. The task of continually recognizing and extending beauty is one that reaches ultimately into eternity. The earth itself yearns for the fullness of interelatedness that redemption will finally bring. Edwards says, "Though the creature is [now] subjected to vanity, yet it don't [*sic*] rest in this subject, but is constantly acting and exerting itself in order that the glorious liberty that God has appointed [might appear]. . . . all the creatures, in all their operations and motions, continually tend to this."[93]

Edwards's theology is unequivocally God centered and future oriented, reminding one at times of Teilhard de Chardin. He was a God-intoxicated thinker, seeing everything to cohere at last in the Holy Trinity. It may seem unusual to root an environmental ethic in a theology of profound transcendence. But Edwards would say that there is no foundation for the true worth of the world in anything less than God. In a boldly theocentric theology, anthropocentrism is radically judged. For Edwards, human beings realize their createdness most fully, not in their exercise of *dominion*, but in their ability to *delight*, to extol beauty and nurture relationship. One of his great insights was that, "God governs the world, not by the application of force or coercive determination, but by the creative and attractive power of God's own beauty."[94]

This practice of delight, however, is one that reaches with the rest of creation to a realization beyond the immediate limits of history. Edwards's keen expectation of the coming millennium included a confidence that natural phenomena will be understood yet more perfectly in the age to come. He concluded that: "[t]he late invention of telescopes . . . is a type and forerunner of the great increase in the knowledge of heavenly things that shall be in the approaching glorious times."[95]

Paula Cooey argues that "understanding Edwards' apocalypticism is essential to understanding his view of nature." Admittedly, at times he seems ambivalent about the continuity of the present world of nature in the age to come, twisted as it is by sin. He can speak of the "very material frame of the old heavens and old earth" as finally being "destroyed" so that a new heaven and earth can be created.[96] After all, once one has seen (in the beatific vision) the ultimate Beauty to which the physical world as a school of desire has pointed all along, there would seem to be no need any more for a teacher. On the other hand,

Edwards knew that one *never* stops learning, and longing, in the unending sensory process of knowing/delighting in God's beauty.

Thus, he declared that the heaven to which the saints are taken in the "new heavens and new earth" will still be a part of this universe, where the laws of nature continue to apply. It will be a "place of the habitation of bodies as well as souls, a place wherein their bodily sense shall be exercised" and even extended in remarkably astounding ways. "The beauty of the bodies of the saints in the new earth . . . shall not only consist in the most charming proportion of features and parts of their bodies, and their light and proportion of colors, but much in the manifestation of the excellencies of their mind. . . ."[97] All manner of sensory enhancements will accompany the embodiment of the saints in heaven. Edwards anticipated their range of hearing and seeing to be vastly improved, enabling them to perceive multiple ratios of resonance that make up a single harmony or to glimpse "the beauty of another's countenance" at a thousand miles distance.

> How ravishing [will be] the proportions of the reflections of rays of light, and the proportions of the vibrations of the air! And without doubt, God can contrive matter so that there shall be other sort of proportions, that may be quite of a different kind, and may raise another sort of pleasure in a sense, and in a manner to us inconceivable, that shall be vastly more ravishing and exquisite. . . . there shall be external beauties and harmonies altogether of another kind from what we perceive here.[98]

For Edwards, the spiritual life is inescapably a sensuous life. It carries with it the hope of a continual expansion of sensory delight in the splendor of God. Such is what finally gives this world and the next their enduring worth and importance. The ecological responsibility that humans share for the biosphere in which they live is intricately tied to the earth's role in reaching with them toward the endless expansion of God's beauty.

In conclusion, we find in Jonathan Edwards a theologian who understood the contemplation of the natural world as an exercise in prayer. The physical universe is, for him, a mirror of God's glory, participating in what it reflects. The world is not simply a thin veil through which we reach toward a God wholly beyond it. For Edwards, nature—in all of its sensory palpability—is itself taken up into the still more sensuous glory of God. In the process, it teaches us desire, opening its mysteries to all who have received a new sense for the perceiving and extending of beauty in their common life.

His richly sensual spirituality has many parallels to contemporary environmental concerns. If it is true that, as humans, we share with all other creatures a common capacity to delight in the sweet taste of life itself, if we are in some way "family"—joined by social ties that have their roots in the Trinitarian life of God—and if the future toward which we are growing involves a Sabbath rest embracing all of creation, then we simply cannot act any longer as if we were disconnected from a lifeless universe toward which we bear no responsibility. We must commit ourselves, at last, to honoring the web of life, with all of its intimate connections. The very beauty of God requires it of us.

On Pilgrimage with Jonathan Edwards

There is really an analogy, or consent, between the beauty of the skies, trees, fields, flowers, etc. and spiritual excellencies. . . . When we behold the light and brightness of the sun, the golden edges of an evening cloud, or the beauteous bow, we behold the adumbrations of [Christ's] glory and goodness. . . . There are also many things wherein we may behold his awful majesty: . . . . in comets, in thunder, in the towering thunder clouds, in ragged rocks and the brows of mountains.

—Jonathan Edwards, *Miscellanies*[1]

The interior of the Bieneke Rare Book and Manuscript Library on the campus of Yale University is bathed in translucent light. Sun shines through the slabs of Vermont marble that form its exterior walls, lending a soft warmth to the place where Jonathan Edwards's handwritten manuscripts are preserved today. Within this outer shell, a huge, climate-controlled glass cube contains six stories of ancient books and manuscripts. I sit near one of the original Gutenberg Bibles, not far from Edwards's hand-sewn notebooks of nature observations drawn from his walks in the Massachusetts woods. All this is a far cry from the few shelves of recent books from London that Edwards was charged with cataloguing as a tutor here in 1724.

The library building joins the world of abstract ideas with the sensuous world of nature beyond its walls. It connects me to Edwards himself and the glory he sought to capture in all of his work. Admittedly, the universe he occupied was preeminently one of the mind. He lived for ideas—intricate, beautiful, convoluted ideas. The multiple volumes of the Yale edition of his works are filled with dense philosophical insights. They're not easy reading, as graduate students will readily affirm. Yet, at the same time, Edwards's experience of God was very down to earth, embracing the religious affections of delight and joy, reverberating with the sensuous world around him. Meeting God regularly drove him beyond his otherworldly idealism into the concrete world of the senses. His highly philosophical, reserved temperament required the ravishing loveliness of a world eager to teach him the wild extravagance of praise.

As the 300th anniversary of Edwards's birth approached on October 5, 2003, I set out with my wife on a pilgrimage to experience the places that had occasioned the Northampton pastor's highly sensual understanding of the spiritual life. I was curious as to how actual contact with the physical world in which he lived might illuminate the texture of his thought.

Our long loop of a pilgrimage started in Princeton, New Jersey (where Edwards is buried) and took us up through New York City (where he briefly served a Presbyterian church after college). Taking the Connecticut Turnpike east toward New Haven (where he finished his studies at Yale in 1722), we then followed the Connecticut River Valley toward Northampton (where he preached for twenty-three years). Traveling west on the Mohawk Trail through northern Massachusetts, we finally turned down to the village of Stockbridge in the Berkshire Hills. There he served an Indian mission for seven years prior to his appointment (just before his death) as president of what would become Princeton University. During three weeks of hiking and exploring we covered most of the territory through which Edwards had moved in the fifty-five years of his life (1703–1758).

In every place that he lived, Edwards enjoyed being "much alone in solitary places," especially the forested enclaves of lush river valleys, from the Hudson to the Connecticut to the Houssatonic. The Connecticut River Valley constituted a particularly sacred landscape for him. From its source above Beecher Falls near the Quebec border, the river winds its way between the White and the Green Mountains, flowing through the Pioneer Valley of western Massachusetts and emptying into Long Island Sound near the village of Old Saybrook, Connecticut.[2] While his philosophical idealism made heaven more real to him than Mount Holyoke, the view of the river from that summit near Northampton offered him a sensory exercise in imagining a heaven more palpable than all of New England.

The notion that it's possible to know God through the wonders of the natural world has had a mixed history in Christian thought and the Reformed tradition in particular. Thomas Aquinas claimed we can know what God is like through an "analogy of being" (*analogia entis*). He perceived the world of existing things as disclosing certain dimensions of God's nature. Translucent light whispers glory. A Connecticut landscape conveys mystery. Yet Reformed theology has often been suspicious of the idea. Karl Barth vigorously rejected it. He feared that starting with the world as an analogy of God means never getting beyond the analogy itself to the God it images. It's too easy to confuse the two, he thought, lapsing into idolatry. Instead, he argued that we encounter God solely through an "analogy of faith" (*analogia fidei*), a prior relationship to the Creator that (only subsequently) allows us to make any sense of creation.[3]

Edwards provides a middle way between Aquinas and Barth, employing what we might call an "analogy of desire or delight" (*analogia delectationis*).[4] Of all the mysteries in the cosmos, it is the yearning of creation that most points us to God. He argued that echoes of God's glory are received and returned in the creature's knowing, loving, and delighting in a world that mirrors the divine. While he thought this occurred in its fullness only among those blessed with a new spiritual sense, the world evokes a definite—if imperfect—delight in God's beauty for all those created in God's image.

"Nothing on earth can entirely represent the glories of heaven," Edwards acknowledged. But "God condescends" to us, accommodating truth to our sensuous manner of perceiving it.[5] Knowing that humans are most susceptible to love, God uses the analogous world of physical experience to stir desire. As divine glory breaks through its mystery, something is sensed that the mind can't comprehend but the heart is able to love. For Edwards, the empirical world became a school of desire opening the heart to an apprehension of God's extraordinary beauty.

If he lived in a world of the mind, it was a world at least as sensuous and beautiful as anything he found around him. He regularly kept track of the dates in the spring when cherry, peach, plum, and apple trees first came into bloom. Glimpses of his world, therefore, convey something of what he experienced in awakening to the intensely sensory character of spiritual ideas. The following vignettes of significant places in Edwards's life suggest how the New England landscape may have influenced his conception of a more-than-sensuous God.

In mid-June, maple trees are in full leaf on the Old Campus of Yale University. Bicycles stand outside the heavy doors of Sterling Library, housing one of the finest collections of books in North America. I sit within its interior walls beside my wife on a wooden bench in Selin courtyard, a small quadrangle of grass open to the sky. I'm reading Edwards's "Dissertation on the End Toward Which God Created the World" while she sews quietly on a triple-rail rainbow quilt. White clouds pass overhead as the sun illuminates oak leaves and acorns carved in stone on the arched windows around us. The sound of water echoes from a fountain in the middle of the yard. Mountain laurel bushes are in bloom nearby.

Attending to the rhythmic sound of my wife's needle pulling thread through material stretched on a wooden hoop, I experience Edwards's realization that the world is a laboratory for practicing a sensory awareness of God's beauty. I listen to her series of small stitches followed by the long, cello-like draw of the thread through tightly stretched cloth. It's a repetitive sound that constitutes the sustained pattern of her own spiritual practice. It forms a musical cadence, singing to the texture of clouds overhead and the endless shelves of books beyond these walls. Everything in this exquisite moment mirrors God's own disposition to delight in the simplest, most exuberant, displays of quiet, ordered beauty.

What is it that allows Edwards's thought to come alive for me in this fleeting experience of God's splendor? How does the Yale theologian's "idea" of divine glory translate into my sensory awareness of its reality? Is it the ambience of the Yale library, the grandeur of a Connecticut summer day, the ritualized mystery of quilt-making? Or is it delight in my wife's absorption in her work? Edwards himself took joy in his wife Sarah's sewing, recognizing her needlework and his writing as similar exercises in a life of prayer. Letters survive that he sent to Boston, asking for knitting needles and yards of towcloth as well as multiple quires of good paper to provide for their respective passions.[6] Sitting beside my own Sarah with her handiwork, I marvel at the glory of a God so endlessly extravagant in beauty. Everything speaks of a palpable "analogy or consent" between what I see, hear, and feel and the mystery of God's being. In this moment I experience far more of Edwards's text than I'm able to understand.

Willows overhang the banks of the Connecticut River near East Windsor, Connecticut, where the preacher of the Great Awakening was born and spent his first twelve years. I'm watching water dance in rippled sunlight on the underside of dangling willow limbs. Shadows flicker on violets in the grass nearby. The subtle play of light on water entranced Edwards throughout his life, providing his favorite image of the universe as an explosion of God's glory.

"We find ourselves pleased in beholding the color of the violets," he said, "but we know not what secret regularity or harmony it is that creates that pleasure in our minds." The capacity of the human nervous system to recognize beauty never ceased to astonish him. He marveled at the subtle beauties of a universe where "mere light is pleasing to the mind." He observed that "each sort of *rays* play a distinct *tune* to the soul."[7] In this strange synaesthetic fashion, the dance of light on the lavender petals strikes a corresponding chord of inner harmony, awakening delight in the soul.

I'm looking here for swampland and spider webs along the east bank of the river. In thickets of oak, maple, and elm scattered between farmhouses and cornfields, I'm searching for a place that could have sparked Edwards's delight as a child.[8] Down the road from the marker that signifies his birthplace, I notice a small creek running through a culvert under the road. It's called Taylor Brook, and the heavy underbrush around it suggests a wilderness area where a ten-year-old boy might have built huts from dead branches. Rays of the late-afternoon sun illuminate all kinds of spider webs among its brambles and fallen trees.

I picture Edwards reflecting here on the web-spinning capacity of flying spiders, marveling at God's exuberance in providing for the pleasure of insects as well as human beings.[9] Even as a youth, he lived in an enchanted universe. In a place like this, his desire is contagious. The sun sets as I make my way back to the car, pants covered with burrs, trying to picture a bramble-covered teenager wandering home late for supper on another summer evening long ago.

A coral blue sky rises above the meeting house of the First Congregational Church in Enfield, Connecticut. Surrounded by scattered maple and dogwood trees, the building is typical of the colonial churches that mark the New England countryside. Its tall steeple and white clapboard exterior speak of stability and tradition. The present church stands a quarter of a mile north of the original site where Edwards preached his infamous sermon on the Wednesday evening of July 8, 1741.[10]

One might expect the residual smell of smoke and brimstone to linger in such a place. But on the afternoon we arrive, half a dozen ladies from the congregation are preparing fried chicken, mashed potatoes, and coleslaw for a church dinner that night. They remain oblivious, it would seem, to the divine wrath once evoked from their pulpit. One struggles to imagine the "great moaning and crying out" that filled the house that evening in response to Edwards's sermon on "Sinners in the Hands of an Angry God."

To understand Edwards's preaching on this occasion, we have to envision ourselves in a world where God is so real (so terrible in beauty) that only one thing is worth fearing—being separated from such a God, retreating instead into a hell of one's own making. For Edwards, God was more substantive than Sarah in his arms; and for his listeners, hell was a reality as easily mapped as China. He lived in a God-intoxicated world where a desire for union with Christ was matched by an absolute terror of living apart from God's presence.

"At the core of Edwards' outlook is a rigorously unsentimental view of love," says George Marsden in his biography of the New England theologian. There's nothing naively romantic about Edwards. He was no proto-Transcendentalist, seeking harmony with an idealized landscape. He lived in a world of "dazzling beauty set against appalling horrors."[11] If he could celebrate the playfulness of spiders, he also lamented the spiderlike capacity of human beings to destroy themselves in their own webs. His world was plagued with thunderstorms, flash floods, and the imminent threat of Indian attack. Spellbinding awe was an intrinsic part of his Connecticut landscape. Meeting God, therefore, involved a full range of sensory experience. It was as much like touching fire as it was like the laughter of women in a church kitchen. While I'm repulsed by his vengeful images of divine wrath, I exult in his apprehension of a God who remains wild in splendor as well as fierce in love.

Northampton, Massachusetts, stands on a hilltop overlooking the Connecticut River twenty-five miles north of Enfield. In the heyday of the Great Revival, beginning here in 1734, Edwards was convinced the millennium was about to dawn. The Christian church's centuries-long desire for Christ's return would soon bear fruit in the coming of a new world order. "This work will begin in America," he proclaimed in *Some Thoughts on the Present Revival of Religion* (1742).[12] Amid the rushing streams and tree-covered hilltops of New England, humans would learn to live in harmony with nature and each other, revealing an unparalleled glory. The Desire of the Ages was about to appear. Nature itself would be restored to all its original vitality.

Yet the place that sparked most keenly Edwards's anticipation of the fulfillment of his longing was also the place where people eventually soured on his ministry and voted overwhelmingly for his dismissal as pastor. To his disappointment, the dream was never realized. As the fervor of the revival waned, his congregation failed to appreciate his highly intellectualized message of God's astounding beauty. They also lacked much interest in "bestowing beauty" on each other, preferring instead to squabble over church pews and social status.

Main Street in Northampton today displays all the colorful idiosyncrasies of Tracy Kidder's "home town."[13] A community of 30,000 people, it offers a taste of staid New England life, but with teenagers wearing multiple nose rings and splashes of orange hair. Its contradictions and delights reflect what Edwards would have found here in the 1730s and 1740s.

The young people outside Harrell's Ice Cream Shop are not unlike the teenagers Edwards encountered when he first arrived. Prone to "company-keeping" and "frolicking" on Sabbath evenings, he won them over so well that they became important leaders of the Awakening in its early years. But they also contributed to his later removal from the pulpit, as the community reacted to his strict views on closed communion and adolescent moral behavior.

The original church where he preached no longer exists, but the "First Churches of Northampton," a union of Congregationalists and Baptists, stands on the corner of Center and Main—an old Victorian building of red sandstone. The only memory of the Awakening (and Edwards himself) is a small commemorative plaque on one of its walls.

For Edwards, Northampton was a place of desire awakened and desire disappointed. There he reached into the past, writing a "Personal Narrative" of his earlier conversion in the pasture of his father's farm and his continued habit of riding into the woods to be alone with God. There he reiterated Calvin's image of the world as a theater of God's glory, marveling at the work of divine providence in governing the "grand system of beings [that] the spacious theatre of nature contains."[14] Yet God's dramatic performance in the Northampton revival and in the hoped-for restoration of its surrounding landscape ultimately proved short-lived and premature.

I'm struck by Edwards's reference to Calvin as I pass the marquee of the old and shuttered Calvin Theatre and Performing Arts Center on King Street. It's only four blocks from the site where Edwards's home once stood. In another curious juxtaposition, a tiny Polish Catholic church stands on the property where Jonathan and Sarah raised their eleven children. A sign indicates that Father Soberka celebrates mass there every Saturday afternoon. A fleeting sense of "what might have been" seems to linger in Northampton. A lost glory, an unrealized desire, and yet at the same time an apprehension that something glorious had once been glimpsed here.

An enormous red maple tree stands on the bank of the Houssatonic River beside the Red Lion Inn in Stockbridge, Massachusetts. Great trees are the defining reality of the Berkshire forests in this western part of the state. Stockbridge today is a quiet village with a Norman Rockwell Museum, a Shrine of Divine Mercy (run by the Marians of the Immaculate Conception), and an inn famous for its menu of Yankee specialties. As a missionary to this remote site in the 1750s, Edwards continued to be absorbed by beauty. But he shifted his effort to awaken desire in others by focusing less on the art of preaching and more on the craft of writing. He wrote furiously, filled with ideas for ambitious projects of all sorts. Here Edwards wrote many of his greatest works, including his dissertation on the End of Creation. Tall white pines still witness to the resplendent glory he feverishly tried to express.

The house where he lived on Main Street is gone, but the 1739 home of his predecessor John Sergeant (and his wife Abigail, Edwards's cousin) has been faithfully restored. One imagines Edwards sitting at the kitchen table, set with treenware and pewter mugs. He chats with Sergeant as Abigail reaches out the window to pick mint leaves for flavoring a mutton stew. In a small upstairs room where Sergeant wrote his sermons, quill pens lie on the desk. It's easy to think of Edwards absorbed in his writing here.

But the basement of the Stockbridge Public Library on Main Street provides two objects that allow me even deeper access to the man I've been seeking. A letter penned in his own hand and a small wooden book rack connect me with the passion for writing that absorbed him so much in his closing years. More than anything else on this trip, they offer something of a kinesthetic feel for his exuberant longing to express glory. They symbolize Edwards's delight in the alchemical mystery of writing by which ideas are transformed into things and things into ideas. His greatest desire was to replicate beauty in words, to give abstract thoughts a sensuous life of their own.

The letter was written to his daughter Esther on November 20, 1757, just before his leaving for New Jersey. Edwards had no idea that he'd be dead in four months. He writes with a strong, flowing hand, complaining about the meager salary he'll be receiving in Princeton, reporting that her younger brother Timmy's health is better, asking Lucy (another daughter) to buy him a new staff. His focus on family, on the ordinary world of things in Stockbridge and beyond, are indicative of the man's attention to detail in everything.

The letter rests on an unusual, hexagonal-shaped book rack that Edwards employed in his academic writing. He arranged books or papers on its six sloping surfaces for ready access. Built on a swivel base, it can easily be turned by hand. I envision him sitting at his desk, reaching over to check a reference in the works of Hutcheson, Locke, or Hume, as he wrote the last great treatises of his life—*Freedom of the Will*, *Original Sin*, and his two dissertations on the End of Creation and the Nature of True Virtue. Touching the smooth, dark wood of the book rack, I sense how the wood and the handwritten page participate (even now) in the spiritual connections that Edwards made as he wrote.

How do the objects of Edwards's world convey (in their own peculiar way) the sensuous character of the truth he described? Dun Scotus taught that every created thing possesses a distinct quality that singles out its particularity, disclosing its participation in the life of the Creator. He used the term *haecceitas*, or "thisness," to speak of the remarkable specificity of being. *This* piece of paper constitutes a unique presence, proclaiming the mystery of existence through its distinctive texture and feel, its worn and yellowed quality. These were objects touched by a man who perceived the sensuous world around him as a mirror of God's sublime being. For the Stockbridge theologian, their sensory intensity offered a "taste" of God's super-sensuous beauty, something grander than anything the mind can bear.[15]

Jonathan Edwards, in short, was a man for whom God was a constant amazement, a man for whom angels were ultimately more real than carriage bolts. But he never dismissed the tactile world of carriage bolts and harnesses, quill pens and mint sprigs as unimportant. He simply knew that reality, at its deepest level, is more than mere "stuff." It's a matter of intimate relationships initiated by a communicative God. A purely material, non-relational world (like that of Thomas Hobbes) could never be "real" for him. Yet the closest he came to imagining God's ideal Beauty was by attending to the endless array of nature's interrelationships. He loved the world because of the access it offered him to God, but he loved it nonetheless.

Robinson Jeffers, in his poem "The Excesses of God," asks a question that's implicit in all of Edwards's work: "Is it not by his high superfluousness [that] we know our God?" In a universe where need could have been satisfied in so many unimaginative ways, God nevertheless "flings rainbows over the rain and beauty above the moon, and secret rainbows on the domes of deep sea-shells." God makes even "the necessary embrace of breeding/beautiful as fire."[16] Edwards expressed the same sense of wonder when he observed that God created the world to be a loving spouse on whom the Son could endlessly pour out his affection. "The mutual joys between this bride and bridegroom are the end of creation," he declared.[17] Such is the restless impulse of a God who lures everything back to the longing of God's own heart. It was a notion that filled the soul of Jonathan Edwards with an exquisite desire.

· 6 ·

Transformed by Beauty

Environmental Ethics and the Wildness of God

> Can we—when we behold the stately theatre of heaven and earth—conclude other, but that the finger, armes, and wisdome of God hath beene here, although we see not him that is invisible...? Every creature in heaven and earth is a loud preacher of this Truth.
>
> —Thomas Shepherd, *The Sincere Convert* (1647)[1]

As a kid growing up in central Florida, almost every Saturday morning in winter I participated in a formative ritual. Before dawn, the boys next door and I would climb into Frank Marion's 1946 Ford truck, carrying our BB guns and a sack of baloney sandwiches. We would drive to Merritt Island on the Atlantic coast, where his orange grove adjoined a neighboring cypress swamp. There we spent the morning picking bushels of navel oranges to be dropped off at the Indian River Fruit Company on the way home. But in the afternoon, while Frank worked contentedly with his bees, we boys would tromp through tall palmettos, build huts in the surrounding jungle, trap opossums, and stand in amazement at a world that triggered desire at every turn.

It was a boy's dream in the 1950s and a weekly ritual that shaped my Reformed vision of God as much as anything that happened in church on the following day. As dusk arrived on a typical Saturday night—after chasing armadillos and looking for moccasins in remote parts of the swamp—we would climb into the old truck for the long ride home. Exhausted, with the smell of dirt and dried orange juice on our faces, shoes caked with mud, and guns and knives in need of cleaning, we were happier than toads in a midnight pond. We brought back with us unsettling memories of a dead baby rabbit cut from the bulging side of a rattlesnake and the decayed carcass of a raccoon filled with maggots. But we had shrunk from nothing of what the world had shown us of its glories and its horrors. We'd spent the day in a mystery we had survived, though certainly not understood.

On the next morning when the preacher spoke of God's grandeur from the book of Psalms, I listened from that remembered place of swinging vines, deep underbrush, and the harsh cry of hawks screaming overhead. I knew myself to be part of a world incessantly alive, singing in registers far exceeding my understanding, calling me beyond childish things to a still deeper sense of wonder. Desire for God was born in me through that curious juxtaposition of cypress knees and Psalms. The Jesus whom I encountered there had a passion for all living things. No mere flannel-graph figure from Sunday School, he had Spanish moss tangled in his hair and the smell of swamp water on his feet. This was a God I could love.

But learning to "love well" came much more slowly. As a boy with a BB gun set loose on Florida swampland, I'd been impressed by my imagined prowess with a gun. The weapon allowed me to touch what was otherwise beyond my reach. Trying to grasp it all, I shot (as I've confessed) at everything. Wilderness was something to possess, an object of desire to claim as my own. I had no relationship to the land, no responsibility growing out of awe. It took me a long time to succumb to a mystery I'd at first tried to control. Only as I attended to Frank Marion's own deep love of the land—giving myself to swamp lore, studying the habits of armadillos and bees, noticing the loss of surrounding swampland to housing developments—only then did a transformed desire emerge out of a new sense of interdependence. Then I could know myself as an intimate part of a world that mirrored God's ravenous hunger for relationship. Then I could begin to know God as well.

But very little in my religious background had prepared me for encountering the God I met in the beauty of that Merritt Island wilderness. Nor had it warned me of the destructive potential of my own desire unleashed upon the land, as much as I'd been cautioned about the darkness of my sinful heart. The Reformed Christians I knew had not grasped the truth that I have encountered in the writing of this book. They had no awareness of the world as a theater of God's glory, no concern for ecological responsibility. They were content with God's otherworldly power and a revivalist individualism. Despite our occasionally singing hymns like "This Is My Father's World," my love of the earth had almost nothing to do with the church.

By contrast, what I have discovered in this work is Calvin's God of beauty, mirrored in creation, and Edwards's communicative God, eagerly seeking ways of multiplying relationships. This is a God extravagant in beauty, reckless in love, indifferent to many of the things I imagine important—in short, a God of cosmic wonder I'm not able to pin down and control. In the church where I grew up, any notion of God's wildness, glimpsed in the surrounding landscape, remained a forgotten part of the tradition.

Reformed theology has been more absorbed in multiplying words than in entertaining mystery. Despite its lip service to the notion of God's indescribable grandeur, the tradition talks and writes endlessly about what cannot be said. It aspires to an apophatic sense of awe, but retains a penchant for logical explanation. It pierces the mystery of the divine will through intricate efforts at reconciling God's foreknowledge and human destiny. It solves the conundrum of God's permission of evil by reducing the divine to tidy intellectual constructs. It emphasizes God's utter transcendence to the extent of trivializing the world that God has made. The result is a relentless proliferation of words and an utter failure of wonder.

In contrast, God's self-disclosure in creation (as emphasized in other parts of the tradition) would take us out of ourselves, opening our language to the energy of metaphor, challenging our presumptions about our place in the world, and questioning our arrogant claims to master the mysteries of the divine. It summons us to amazement—to the irrepressible energies of desire. Calvin himself urged that the goal of God's revelation in creation and Scripture alike is "that we may be ravished in love with our God (*d'estre ravis en l'amour de nostre dieu*) and inflamed with a right affection to obey him, and keep ourselves strictly in awe of him."[2] To know God, in his thinking, is to desire God, to be ravished by a beauty beyond understanding.

Calvin and Edwards grasped the truth that the sensuous body of the earth teaches us what our minds are unable to bear. For them, the spiritual life necessarily begins with longing. Intellectual questions are always secondary. Ours is a faith seeking understanding (*fides quaerens intellectum*). We understand only what we have first experienced through an arousal of desire. In the end, these two theologians have simply given me lively images for comprehending a desire first stirred in a Florida wilderness.

Ecological Implications of a Spirituality of Desire

The Calvinist reading of nature described in these pages explicitly locates the mystery of the Trinity in the intricacies of the natural world. It discerns God's arms and fingers everywhere in creation, as Thomas Shepherd affirmed in the epigram of this chapter. These are the lithe, smooth limbs of a New England sycamore, for example, reaching toward the sun. Their loveliness stirs an impulse to honor the tree itself—in its own particularity—as a sacrament of God's presence. Over time, however, the arms of the tree wither and die as they succumb to the impact of acid rain. Yet even here God's daring entry into the world's suffering is evident, coming in empathy and in judgment. God participates most deeply in the throes of creation through the beauty of another tree: the cross. Writhing in a death occasioned by human sin, both trees invite repentance over a lost beauty. They foster the weaning of the affections from all that harms the larger covenant community. Throughout the process, God is there in the ebb and flow of desire that the tree shares with the rest of creation.

This theological reading of nature, rooted in notions of beauty and desire, differs from the eco-critical rendering of the natural world expounded by environmental scientists. Their analysis of biological life understands desire as an instinctual, species-supporting drive in the process of evolutionary development. Science does not look for a world of harmonious beauty, revealing God at every turn. It simply describes the way things are—a tangle of competing desires in an amoral universe where homeostasis and conflict are in constant tension. Theoretical notions of theodicy and divine providence are not found in such a world. The cosmos, viewed biologically, is irrefutably wild. How wild, then, can our God be as well? How do we understand God's role in a universe continually driven (and twisted) by desire? This is a question that the Reformed tradition has to address in confronting hard ecological realities.

Any spirituality (or environmental ethic) rooted in desire must be grounded in critical insight as well as theological passion. We dare not rhapsodize too glibly over a world that takes universal delight in God's splendor. Doing so would mean too easily projecting human emotions onto inanimate creatures, forgetting the impact of human sin, boxing God into neat categories, and ignoring a world fraught with as much danger as delight. The earth's loveliness, after all, comes generously laced with terror. In Jeremiah's experience, to meet God in this world is to be seduced by a deity as dangerous as he is ravishing. Yet no other encounter makes one more fully alive. What does it mean, then, to affirm John Muir's insistence that "in God's wildness lies the hope of the world?"[3]

My goal in this chapter is to summarize the book's central themes in a way that is both theologically and ecologically credible, exploring the possibilities for an environmental ethic in the Reformed tradition. I want to ask how the tradition affirms the dignity of other-than-human creatures as well as how it perceives God's involvement in the travail of nature described in Romans 8. Doing this requires our wrestling with the question of how to reconcile God's beauty and God's wildness in a world torn by conflicting desires. My intention is first to sum up the book's conclusions, laying out an argument for an ecology (as well as a theology) of desire. Then I will ask how a Reformed theologian like Horace Bushnell was able to conceive of wildness itself as a dimension of God's glory.

This nineteenth-century New Englander reacted to naive conceptions of a divinely ordered cosmos, filled with concord and bliss. His God was not predictably tame, and was certainly not preoccupied with human comfort. God, from his perspective, boldly engaged the messiness of a world filled with dark things, bearing the whole of creation toward a final redemption. In this torturous way, God teaches resilience, humility, and a toughened love—even as God herself (a fiercely loving mother) assumes the birth pains of a suffering world. This is a God truly worthy of praise, luring an entire universe to a haunting beauty. Meeting this God requires a transformation of consciousness, a mystical encounter that, for Bushnell and others before him, was the goal of Reformed spirituality.

My first concern, then, is to summarize the themes of this book, showing how a spirituality of desire expresses itself not only in the human response to God's glory, but in the way the rest of the world participates in that mystery as well. This requires attending to the work of environmental ethicists who ponder the larger implications of a Reformed, Trinitarian theology for understanding a world of evolutionary complexity, moral ambiguity, and increasing fragility. Christopher Southgate, Holmes Rolston, and Jürgen Moltmann prove especially helpful in this regard. They ask how God is involved in healing a world that has been summoned to life, but also deeply wounded, by desire. Southgate, in his recent book on *The Groaning of Creation*, explores God's entry into the agonies of the evolutionary process. His is a God who dares to embrace the suffering of every creature in redeeming a world torn by conflicted desire.

We turn first, then, to a survey of seven themes gleaned from the work of John Calvin, the seventeenth-century Puritans, and Jonathan Edwards. These dimensions of a Reformed spirituality of longing are rich in ethical implications for understanding our relationship to the more-than-human world. They help us to outline an ecology of desire, asking how the earth itself shares in our common (but wild and tortured) quest for beauty.

Desire as a Response to Allurement

What strikes us first about the Reformed spirituality encountered in this work is that it portrays a universe caught up in deep yearning, grasping instinctively for God's loveliness, glimpsed in mirrored fragments of wonder. The world dances in wild abandon to an ultimate attraction that it is wholly unable to name. Calvin realized that God could have made a bland world in which necessities alone predominate, a mechanistic cosmos stripped of delight and enjoyment. God might have produced a universe with minimal interaction among all of its parts. But the desire of the Trinity required extravagance, resulting in a heaven and earth riddled with desire. Calvin's God hides in the earth's beauty, drawing others by allurement rather than by force.

Echoes of this desire reverberate through all of the created order. We see it in whatever drives the alewives each spring up the fish ladders at Damariscotta Mills on the Maine coast or the salmon to make their run up the Columbia River in Northern Oregon. From the attraction of gravity anchoring us to earth, to a eucalyptus tree's thirst for water on a summer day, to the electrical charges that connect sub-atomic particles—the universe thrives on the lure of the "other." We see it in the croaking of spadefoot toads calling for a mate in the desert after rain, in the African lion patiently stalking its prey, or in parents frantically searching for a missing child. Yearning for the other is a fundamental mystery of the world we inhabit. Jonathan Edwards spoke of a "universal attraction in the whole system of things from the beginning to the end."[4] Or as physicist Brian Swimme puts it, "The unity of the world rests on the pursuit of passion."[5]

We marvel at biologically rich transition zones, where one ecosystem is closely linked to another. These are places of converging desire attracting an immense diversity of life. Along the edge of a water hole in the Serengeti desert, for example, we find wildebeests and lions, grey herons and dung beetles, water striders and algae inexorably drawn to each other for feeding and mating. The whole world is strangely linked together in a vast mystery of attraction and interdependence.[6]

Conflicted Longings

But if desire (or attraction) characterizes the life of the natural world at every level, these longings are also deeply conflicted, operating often at cross purposes, even endangering the well-being of those who become objects of attraction. Desire has a volatile, risky character, ever teetering on the edge of disaster. The human response to God's longing for relationship is an imperfect, often twisted repetition of God's own desire. It is easily distracted and distorted, as we have seen in the course of Puritan history. Abandoning their deepest yearning for God, human beings seek out objects to dominate and use to their own advantage. The desire of the moment becomes more satisfying than the open-ended longing that is God's persistent lure of the hungry heart. Wonder and awe give way to a quest for immediate possession and use. The result is a world transformed into commodities of desire.

Timothy Dwight thus came to lament in his day the "increasing evil" of deforestation in New England, a product of inordinate desire that had left the land "naked and bleak." Puritan prophets like Samuel Danforth had years earlier rebuked the people of the covenant for the loss of their first love due to "inordinate worldly cares." Roger Williams had censured the colonists in Massachusetts for their insatiable hunger for Indian land and decimation of native settlements. He said he had found more of the spirit of Christ among the Narragansetts than the Puritans. [7] The tradition thus made clear, in its periodic pattern of the jeremiad, that unbounded desire leads to social and ecological as well as spiritual disaster. Yet Calvin's descendents remained remarkably slow in realizing the possibilities latent in his creation theology.

If desire is deeply conflicted in human relationships, as witnessed in Puritan experience, we discover an equally dark reality of unwanted attraction in the non-human sphere of biological life. The yearning that fills the universe, at every level of existence, is as destructive as it is life-giving. Desire everywhere is fraught with danger. The older and weaker members of a caribou herd certainly do not welcome the longing they arouse in a passing pack of arctic wolves. Yet an intensity of attraction is what orders life in a world of predators and prey.

This is not necessarily a result of the Fall or human sin. We have no reason to imagine that the wolves of Eden happily munched on straw. Death and predation are natural realities in the kind of world that was necessary for God to use in bringing the healing of desire to its fullness. Therefore, we cannot measure the morality of desire in the biological sphere in the same way as we might in the world of human relationships. Arctic wolves reveal God's glory by hunting well and providing for their young, not by expressing kindness to a weakened caribou calf. The universe is far wilder than our sensitivities might prefer.

Nature's ferocity unnerves us at times. We shudder at a preying mantis eating the head of her mate after he has fertilized the eggs of their young. We cringe at the ichneumon wasp's injecting its eggs into the living body of a caterpillar, where they eventually hatch and eat their way out. Darwin found this to be wholly irreconcilable with the idea of a beneficent and omnipotent deity.[8] Nor will Annie Dillard let us forget that the world God has made, with all of its desire, remains as insistently wild and terrible as it is lovely. It is impossible to affirm any "Bambi theology" that would deny the evolutionary reality of a world filled with predators and pain.[9] The God of nature is a deity full of disturbing wonder.

The Ethical Quandary of Frustrated Desire

The fact that others are frequently harmed (and even destroyed) by the exercise of God-given desire creates an ethical quandary in a world supposedly governed by divine providence. How do we discern God's justice in a universe where creatures made to extol God's glory, like the vulnerable caribou calf, are prevented from realizing the fullness of their created being? How do experiences of tragic loss serve the ends of love in a cosmos riddled with God's wild and fierce beauty?

From an ecological perspective, we understand the animal's death as a means by which a greater complexity and richness, more highly focused desires, are achieved in the earth's evolutionary development. Christopher Southgate argues that "an evolving creation [filled, as it is, with death, pain, predation, and self-assertion] was the only way in which God could give rise to the sort of beauty, diversity, sentience, and sophistication of creatures that the biosphere now contains."[10]

It is not that God callously preordains bloodshed and natural disasters as a way of enhancing life, but that God works within a broken system to bring wholeness out of chaos. Natural selection itself "suggests to us that suffering is a necessary driver of progressingly richer and more intense experience."[11] Without the struggle that affliction occasions in the process of evolution, says Holmes Rolston, there would be "no horns, no fleet-footed predators or prey, no fine-tuned eyesight and hearing, no quick neural capacity, no advanced brains."[12] In the evolutionary order of things, frustrated desire is a means toward growth.

Similarly, in the spiritual life—as the Puritans continually emphasized—affliction serves an important purpose in the winnowing of desire, the "weaning of the affections." It points toward the need for a higher longing in human experience. In their understanding, the unattainability of God's beauty was far more compelling than anything else they might desire. Fixing themselves on this ultimate longing allowed them to stand in awe at the irreducible mystery of every other thing. Only in this way could they avoid the ever-present danger of improperly using what was meant to be enjoyed.

But they knew that loosening their hold on the things they were tempted to grasp was not easy. At times it required an entry into the dark night of the soul, the aching loss of what they had thought so important. Hence, they came to recognize windstorms, house fires, even the death of their children as part of a painful winnowing process. Ultimately, they had to lose even God for the sake of God, letting go of their *concept* of an abstract deity in their quest for a deeper *love*. The absence of the one they desired most, but were unable to possess, became itself a tease, inviting a more persistent love and trust. In the dark, empty night they banked the embers of frustrated desire to a slow burn, reaching for a hope that came only with the long-awaited dawn. The intensity of anticipation was everything.

God's Entry into a World Torn by Desire

Yet the danger in this idea was the possibility of conceiving God to be a jealous, spiteful lover, coldly using affliction to force his reluctant children to himself. God could become heartless, if not vicious—manipulating praise for the enhancement of a self-centered glory. Such a deity, from a mechanistic perspective, might care nothing for a sickly caribou calf, seen as a mere speck within the longer, more important process of divine teleology or evolutionary change. But the Reformed tradition insists that God intimately participates in the world's suffering for the sake of a redeemed creation. Lest there be any doubt as to where God stands, the Trinity radically embraces (in the mystery of the divine vulnerability) the pain of an anguished world.

Calvin and Edwards speak of a "beauty" in suffering because of what they witness in the cross. There they discern most perfectly the theater of God's glory, discovering a foundational wildness at the core of God's being. They sit amazed, along with the rest of the audience, as a rough-hewn cross is thrown up on stage and they discover the extent to which God is willing to go for the sake of love. In the midst of the performance God acts out, shares, and embraces the world's immense suffering. God assumes it all (at deep personal expense) for the purpose of healing. The spectator is undone, as a result, says Hans Urs von Balthasar. He "is suddenly seized at a deeper level than he expected: he is no longer in charge of his own participation; he himself is called into question by his experience of the play; he is struck by it."[13]

God has embraced wildness for the sake of love, a beauty named compassion has been born, and nothing will be the same again. Because of this pivotal event at the heart of the performance, the redemption awaited by all of creation is assured at the conclusion of the final act. At Golgotha, monstrousness and magnificence thus merge in a profoundly disconcerting way.[14] Calvin, Edwards, and Balthasar can all speak of the "beauty of the cross" without being obscene, because they know God's goal for creation is the ultimate transformation of pain, not its transmission.

Hence, the Reformed tradition holds in tension God's power witnessed in a wild and wondrous world alongside God's utter vulnerability disclosed in the cross. It grapples with the paradox that God creates a world of terrifying splendor (where the timid tread lightly), while God simultaneously exposes God's self to its greatest threats, identifying with those at risk. It affirms a God of wild majesty working through the mystery of evolution to bring life and hope out of a system inescapably prone to suffering and death. God suffers in every painful part of the process. The giving and taking of life thus becomes a Eucharistic reality, understood only in God's remarkable choice of defenselessness in the Paschal mystery.

Holmes Rolston uses the language of a passion play to describe the age-long process of evolution. He observes that an experience of the *via dolorosa* appears long before humans even arrive. The biological world participates deeply in the "divine pathos."[15] Yet he says one can affirm God's justice and make sense of the suffering of non-human creatures to the extent that their pain enhances the adaptation of their species. Individuals may fail to thrive, but "they suffer through to something higher," as they contribute to the evolutionary development of their kind. A frail caribou calf may die before its time, but its death serves the ongoing process of species improvement.[16]

In the winter of 1981–1982, Rolston supported the decision of Rangers in Yellowstone National Park not to treat a number of bighorn sheep struck by a severe case of conjunctivitis, leading to partial blindness. As he explained:

> The Yellowstone ethicists knew that intrinsic pain is a bad thing in humans or in sheep, but pain in ecosystems is instrumental pain, through which the sheep are naturally selected for a more satisfactory adaptive fit. To have interfered in the interests of the blinded sheep would have weakened the species. Simply to ask whether they suffer is not enough. We must ask whether they suffer with a beneficial effect on the wild population. As a result of the park ethic, those sheep that were genetically more fit, able to cope with the disease, survived—and this coping is now coded in the survivors.

Other ethicists in the Reformed tradition would argue that it is not enough to perceive God's goodness simply in the long-range advancement of general classes of creatures. The Trinity's delight in nature's details, in the beauty of individuals as well as species, requires that God share in the frustrated desire of every sentient being kept from realizing its original intention in God's creation. Its pain ultimately has meaning only if God somehow participates in the plight of every caterpillar injected by an ichneumon wasp, in the loss of every dying caribou calf. The anguish that nature reflects at every level is the aching of God's own heart for the healing of a restored world. The dignity of creatures is thus rooted, not only in their mirroring of God's beauty, but also in God's sharing their pain when the mirror is tarnished or broken. God remains restless until the clear and distinct voice of every created being is added to the earth's final song of praise.

Desire Fulfilled in Eschatological Praise

We recognize God, therefore, as Creator of a world that talks back, a world made for relationship. The Reformed tradition affirms God's involvement with creation to be far broader than the divine-human encounter alone. The earth is a theater or symphony of God's glory. We are part of a larger, interdependent community sustained by God's pathos, each one possessing its own dignity, each responding to God in its own fashion as a unity of diverse beings. We are not alone. Praise is a multi-species activity, expressed in the peregrine falcon's graceful flight as well as a performance of Handel's *Messiah*. The larger covenant community shares, just as vigorously, in a common cry of lament, from urban lots filled with toxic waste to neighborhood children suffering from asthma. The whole of creation joins in an exultant, if often erratic, dance in response to the Trinity's desire for connectedness.

The capacity of every creature to offer praise (each in its own way) is the basis for affirming an environmental ethic in the Reformed tradition. This is why the Puritans, drawing on Calvin's exaltation of God's beauty in creation, could argue that the world be treated with appreciation and justice. They made such a claim, despite the fact that their own misplaced desire often led to a very different practice. Consistency was not one of their gifts. Nonetheless, their contribution to the history of animal rights, calling for an end of cruelty to non-human creatures, was vigorous and surprisingly effective in seventeenth-century England and America. They attacked the mistreatment of wild animals in popular sports and of domestic animals in the workplace. They knew God to have extended the covenant to include the whole of creation, not simply human life alone. If the world was indeed a theater of God's glory, they urged that it be treated as such.

They understood, however, that the ultimate realization of a world where every creature raises its voice in praise is something only God can bring. Restoring an appropriate dignity to every being that God has created is not finally the result of human engineering or evolutionary development. The "great work" to which Thomas Berry calls us is great because, in the end, it is *God's* work, one in which we simply share. The Reformed tradition, therefore, necessarily anchors its call for environmental justice in an eschatological hope, in God's own longing for a restored cosmos.

Calvin and Edwards, like Irenaeus before them, affirmed that the Christian hope lies in God's eventual recapitulation (or "summing up") of all things in Christ.[17] Their expectation was that everything which had fallen in the first Adam, even the garden itself, will be restored in the second. In Christ, all is finally renewed and reversed from its original lapse into indiscriminate chaos and pain.[18] This hope encourages Christians to affirm life in all of its diversity, to honor the world as a sensuous means of knowing God, and to opt for choices that favor interdependence. Justice arises out of a liturgical and aesthetic imagination, aroused to desire by God's beauty, and spurred to action by the expectation of a world made new.

The hope that sustains desire for a restored creation is grounded in God's own longing to recapitulate the world in all of its splendor. An expectation that the New Heavens and New Earth will include the entire range of human and nonhuman creatures lends increased value to species diversity in the world that God is presently bringing to eventual fulfillment. The eschatological realization of God's work may be slow in coming. It depends, to no little extent, on the community of those who accept as their own the task of implementing God's vision. Covenant theology emphasizes God's long-term investment in the risk of human responsibility. We, too, are the hands and feet of Christ, taking on the wounds of a broken world. The work of environmental justice commits the church to repairing the biological infrastructure of the Kingdom. It witnesses to God's universal love for the whole of creation, drawing energy and perseverance from its hope in the promise of what is to come.

The specific character of this future recapitulation remains unclear. Christian ethicists differ as to whether they anticipate creatures in the coming Kingdom to be recapitulated only in the memory of the Trinity, restored simply as representative species, or re-created as individual creatures enabled at last to fulfill the desire for which they were created. Calvin would have considered all of these questions as dangerously speculative. But Edwards (as we have seen) remained far more open to envisioning the particular dimensions of a future cosmos.[19]

Jürgen Moltmann, following in the vein of Edwards, anticipates an emerging world in which all creatures are finally restored to wholeness. He says there is "no meaningful hope for the future of creation unless 'the tears are wiped from every eye.'"[20] He joins other environmental ethicists, from Jay McDaniel to Christopher Southgate, in affirming the continuity and enlargement of the entire created order in God's vision of a renewed world. A dull homogeneity can be no more a part of God's vision for a new earth than it is a dimension of God's being as Trinity.

Hence, the inclusion of animals and a vast variety of other creatures in a transformed world has to be taken seriously. This is more than a matter of knowing what to say about the hope of heaven to a child whose favorite pet has died. It is a question about the extent of God's exuberant wildness. How far is God willing to go in making sure that nothing is lost of the Trinity's imaginative joy in the original creation of every single being?

Evelyn Underhill once scolded C. S. Lewis for having too narrow an assessment of biological life in the world to come. In his book, *The Problem of Pain*, he made a case for the inclusion of animals as pets in heaven. He thought that creatures who live in close attachment to their human masters acquire a sense of soulfulness by association. But Underhill, in a feisty letter to the Oxford don, rebuked him for granting his docile and domesticated cat entrance into paradise while excluding the feral grandeur of snow leopards and Himalayan condors. "I feel your concept of God would be improved by just a touch of wildness," she replied. As she saw it, God's joy in the roisterous world we now have requires the continuation, if not expansion, of wildness in the world that succeeds it.[21]

Desire as a Gift in Itself

Delight in anticipating a world made new becomes a fundamental incentive to action in a Reformed environmental ethic. Everything depends upon the power to enjoy and the ability to expect. As Reformed spirituality reiterates over and over again, unremitting desire is itself an incalculable gift. Edwards identified the capacity to delight as one of the most important signs of an authentic work of grace. In the peculiar alchemy of the spiritual life, "wanting" is strangely better than "having." Indeed, the wanting *is* the having. Indefatigable desire is one's earnest expectation of what is to come, as well as evidence that one possesses what had been sought all along. Rumi, the thirteenth-century Persian poet, once comforted an anguished man whose yearning for God had never received a response. "Ah, don't you see," he sighed, "the longing you express *is* the return message." God cries in the yearning itself.[22]

This is the sustaining hope of creation. The fervent wish for the restoration of the earth's beauty is itself God's down payment on the gift of a promised redemption. It becomes the driving force of environmental action. Our longing for a world set free from global warming, acid rain, and the loss of species diversity is nothing less than God's own deep longing within us. Desire may well have been the cause of our problems, but it is also the solution to them. Our inexplicable yearning is God's promise in keeping covenant with the whole of creation. It is proof that we already have what we long for most—the assurance of God's sustaining care in preserving everything that has been brought into being. Hence, the focus of environmental concern (and of the spiritual life) is not so much a matter of clutching and acquiring, but of relishing and savoring. It involves the honing of our ability to delight. We will not be able to save, after all, what we have not learned to love.

Our first task, then, is to cultivate an appreciation of the wonders and agonies of a world caught up in longing with us. The living earth invites us to heed that which stirs our deep-felt pleasure. Profound enjoyment is the life blood of environmental preservation.[23] Reformed spirituality has a long tradition of taking joy in reflecting on a world that is alive with God's glory. Calvin urged our attending "the school of the beasts," where "it behooves us to prove ourselves good scholars."[24] How, for example, can I gaze on the world once again with the astonishment of an eleven-year-old boy in a Florida wilderness? How do I recover my own practice of the "gathering art," as Richard Baxter described it, marveling at the fluid motion of blue herons in flight, of red-wing blackbirds darting through stands of cattails?

As a boy, I watched alligator eyes gliding through the water of a Southern swamp, pushed aside weeds to glimpse a nest of coral snakes writhing in rings of bright color, felt the winds of a hurricane lift the corner of the small frame house where we lived. I devoured field guides in identifying stars and gawked through a microscope at rotifers swimming in a drop of pond water. These were "spiritual disciplines" that I practiced inadvertently, never labeling them as such. My world was ablaze with a wonder close to terror, God's wildness filling it all. How do any of us recover that initial sense of astonishment that marked our childlike view of the world?

Thoreau once said he knew the woods of his native Concord so well that if he were to wake up from a long sleep (like Rip Van Winkle), he could pinpoint the date on the calendar (within a three-day margin) by observing the trees and plants. He was that familiar with the changing ecosystem of his eastern Massachusetts bioregion.[25] Local knowledge of this sort is highly integrating and redemptive, rare as it also may be. Jonathan Edwards rejoiced in every interrelated detail of nature in his Connecticut River Valley. "There is not one leaf of a tree, nor spire of grass, but what has effects all over the universe," he declared.[26] The Northampton pastor spied wonder (and connectedness) in everything he saw. Like Teilhard de Chardin he could testify that "God truly waits for us in things."[27] From a Reformed perspective, a passionate inquisitiveness about the natural world is as central to the spiritual life as it is to ecological justice.

The Humility of Desire: Beyond Anthropocentrism

God's exuberant desire for a world made whole will be, at last, extremely humbling to human beings tempted to overrate their importance in the larger scheme of the cosmos. In the light of God's aseity (God's inaccessible wildness), it becomes apparent that everything in the world is not about us. If the Trinity delights in the entirety of creation as a theater of God's glory, there are no grounds for an arrogant anthropocentrism. A God of wild freedom is not exclusively solicitous of human concerns. James Gustafson insists that a theocentric ethic in the Reformed tradition roundly challenges such thinking.

> If one's basic theological perception is of a Deity who rules all of creation, and one's basic perception of life in history and nature is one of patterns of interdependence, then the good that God values must be more inclusive than one's normal perceptions of what is good for me, what is good for my community, and even what is good for the human species.[28]

God's governance of nature will not always appear beneficent from a human perspective. It nurtures the larger interdependence of creatures that continually sustain and rely on each other. It struggles toward a wholeness not yet realized. God is guiding a broken creation to its torturous goal, says Moltmann, "not through supernatural interventions" on our behalf, but "through his passion, and the opening of possibilities out of his suffering."[29] We are brought to fulfillment, not independently, but only as part of the rest of creation.

Daniel Quinn's novel *Ishmael* reiterates the dangerous story that Mother Culture continually whispers in human ears, claiming that "man is the climax of the whole cosmic drama of creation."[30] We alone are the end product of fourteen billion years of evolution. The rest of the world exists exclusively for us. This is a story the Reformed tradition has to reject. Everything is *not* about us.

Even Karl Barth anticipated that humans, in the end, will stand humbly alongside other creatures at the Marriage Supper of the Lamb. They assume their place, not in a superior position of honor, but "*under* the table, in the company of publicans, in the company of beasts and plants and stones, accepting solidarity with them, being present simply as they are, as a creature of God."[31] This is the posture of deep humility, of loving kinship with the rest of creation that finally has to characterize Reformed thought. It does not deny the unique gift of consciousness that humans possess, but takes equal delight in the larger community of creation responding to the lure of God's glory. Humans are but the poets and narrators of all that is mimed, danced, and sung so irresistibly by an enormous cast of characters on the world's stage.

In summary, the awakening of desire and the subsequent difficulty in managing it are concerns that recur again and again in the history of Reformed spirituality. As a result, the tradition is in a unique position to offer a mirror for understanding the current ecological crisis. It shows us (from its mistakes) how we have gotten into the dilemma of unrestrained craving in using the earth's resources and (from its longings) what we must do in finding a way out. Reformed spirituality identifies our ecological problem as, at root, a theological problem—requiring a radical reorientation of desire.

What we need is an awareness of God's rejuvenating presence filling the world with an amazement wild enough to capture the human heart. Too often we have attributed all wildness and exuberance to *sin*, while turning *God* into a "Puritanical" schoolmaster, restraining every impulse to gaiety. We think of sin as being inherently wild and free, as if "sowing one's wild oats" were a liberated expression of one's deepest humanity. But even Calvin defined sin on occasion as a matter of "dullness," a lack of imaginative insight, a pathetic failure in taking delight. From this perspective, redemption means being delivered from the banality of sin and summoned to true wildness—to a high-spirited celebration of God's presence in an astonishing world. This is the God the Reformed tradition has to reclaim.

Incorporating Wildness as a Dimension of God's Glory

Horace Bushnell, a nineteenth-century Reformed theologian writing from his study in the old North Church in Hartford, Connecticut, asked himself how the God of Calvin and Edwards might still engage the human imagination. He worked at relating the older Calvinist theology to Samuel Taylor Coleridge's new Romantic conception of nature. His concern was to recover God's awe-inspiring immensity as the underlying principle of nature's organic life. He delighted in a world as endlessly challenging as the wild and glorious God it mirrors. Coleridge's ability to draw a "deep, heartfelt, inward joy" from nature's haunting mysteries resonated with his own quest for "an immediate experimental knowledge of God."[32] With

Horace Bushnell the Calvinist tradition continued its quest for a God of incomparable glory, able to match the intriguing world of nature that nineteenth-century science was exploring.

Bushnell's reflections on the natural world arose in reaction to two very different theologies of nature current in his day. On the one hand, he scorned as hopelessly naive William Paley's attempt to prove God's existence from nature's harmonious design. He argued that the book of nature can no more be used as a proof-text for establishing metaphysical certainties than an inerrant Bible can be used to guarantee precise language about God. He feared that Paley's argument from design reduced the Creator to a sappy sentimentalism, turning a blind eye to a world in disarray, "interlarded with agues and miasmas" of every sort.[33] It caricatured the universe as "the best of all possible worlds," with proofs of divinity hanging from every bush. The Hartford theologian dismissed such ideas as having no place either in sound theology or good science.

On the other hand, he reacted just as vigorously to the anti-supernaturalism of the Naturalists, what he perceived as "the new infidelity" spreading through Western thought in the nineteenth century. Naturalism viewed the world of nature as a closed mechanistic system, disallowing any possibility of dynamism and freedom. Bushnell said it reduced human beings to "mere wheels turned by natural causes" and perceived God as nothing more than the operation of the cold, material forces of the universe.[34] The movement had begun with the rationalist criticisms of David Strauss and Theodore Parker and led eventually to the dark depictions of a determined world found in the novels of Stephen Crane and Frank Norris. Bushnell challenged its pessimism by emphasizing God as the principle of freedom that opens nature to more than a dull, dead pattern of cause and effect. The supernatural invites nature to the wildness of its deepest possibilities, to the "about-to-be" character of its inner life in God.[35]

Resisting the "Paleyizing theologians" and the Naturalists alike, the Connecticut pastor opted for a much more resilient view of nature as an organic process actively sustained by God's Spirit. Redemption, he said, lifts the natural into the supernatural, restoring "a central, regulating, new-creating force in our disordered growth."[36] Hence, the world is neither an objective proof-text for divinity nor an endless repetition of cause-and-effect necessity. It is alive! The earth shares in the vital energy of God's own life, eliciting the involvement of human beings in its hope for "the glorious liberty of the children of God" (Rom. 8:21). It comes as no surprise that Bushnell was an avid outdoorsman who marveled at the giant redwoods in California and expressed outrage at their destruction. Nature's grandeur filled him with "a sense of the divine beauty and majesty."[37]

His view of God similarly evinced a "wildness" that incorporated inherited orthodoxy's "God of power and might" while re-appropriating its mystery in significantly different ways. Bushnell affirmed a God of wild splendor found in nature's dark side as well as its lightness and beauty. He rejected simplistic notions of God's sugary benevolence, while underscoring God's invitation to a vigorous engagement with life. His desire was not to retrieve a deity of harsh judgment, renewing fears of fire and brimstone. He wanted a God too wild to be contained in the dry, rationalistic formulas of either the Calvinists or the Unitarians. He wanted to see the biblical text explode into meaning as its words recover their roots in nature's powerful imagery, as the reader "experiences" its truth rather than simply "defining" it.[38] His was a God reckless in love, continually enticing the world to relationship. He reveled in a God boundless in freedom, motivating men and women to a bold exercise of the will in the face of a culture bound by nature's fixed laws. Bushnell's theology, in short, brought new life to nineteenth-century reflections on the natural world and its ability to awaken a desire for God.

In his book, *The Moral Uses of Dark Things* (1868), the Yale-trained theologian countered both Paley and the Naturalists by underscoring the discontinuities found in "the night side of creation." He argued that God incorporates the hazards of a threatening world in nurturing an enlivened and disciplined will. "Our God is not a summer God only, but a winter God," he declared, "ruling with stout emphasis, and caring visibly less for all mere comfort, than for the grand prerogatives and rigours of principle."[39] A God of wild beauty toughens our aesthetic sensitivities and empowers our will to persist in the work of restorative justice.

Bushnell knew that the first thing a child learns is that "nature goes her own way by herself, and does not consider or pity or spare." We might wish that the world "had been set on a footing of perfect, inviolable security," that we could be "dandled in the world-mother lap," but this would leave us utterly unprepared for a life of responsibility. It would also suggest a God of anxious over-protectiveness, unworthy of adoration. Only by steering through life's dangers do we learn to practice a "manly state of attention," he declared. Otherwise, we would "live in a low, mean key, and die of mediocrity and dullness."[40] Nor would we ever learn compassion.

Encountering God means facing head-on the unexplainable mysteries of a world filled with pain. This, in the end, is the way of the cross—living with impenetrable mystery, lingering in solidarity with a suffering we cannot change, anticipating a resurrection we are not yet able to see. This is what Christ models in his own vicarious sacrifice, says Bushnell. In the cross we see a world of suffering absorbed into the churning grief of God's own heart. This evokes an equally bold response of suffering love in return. To experience the cross is to be shocked by the depth and mystery of God's own wild compassion.[41]

Bushnell struggled with the moral difficulties posed by a world of "beaks and talons, fangs and stings." He marveled at God's having created a world of wild ferocity and then sharing in its own suffering. He concluded that:

> Whatever else may be true, God has created venom, and we must not scruple to say it. If we have any conception of goodness that forbids this kind of possibility in God, then our God plainly enough does not exist, or the God that does exist is not He. . . . And we need not scruple to confess a degree of satisfaction in this kind of discovery, showing that goodness is no such innocent, mawkishly insipid character, no such mollusc softness swimming in God's bosom as many affect to suppose. . . .[42]

The world's harshness, he knew, opens us to God's own tough and demanding love. Without it, "what we call [God's] goodness would only be a weak, emasculated virtue, which, if we should praise it, would not long keep our respect." Hence, says Bushnell, "It is better for us to be shocked sometimes than never to be impressed. . . . [D]angerous and fierce animals are wanted as the necessary furniture of our discipline."[43] They contribute to our moral training, even as they suggest the larger dimensions of God's own wild and undomesticated beauty.

Bushnell's goal was to inspire action in a world that despaired of human freedom. In his book *Nature and the Supernatural* (1858), he argued that the world still sings, even in its broken state—in the haunting notes of "a mysterious, transcendent hymn." The supernatural may seem to be squeezed out of the universe by the claims of a cold naturalism, but Bushnell insisted that God remains actively at work as a principle of integrating wholeness. The supernatural acts underneath "the chain of cause and effect" to renew the fallen natural order with the organic life of God in Christ.[44]

Sin may have weakened the vital energies that sustain natural life, impairing the will of the universe, as it were. But God's spirit infuses the created world (and especially human beings as they are restored in Christ) with a new, energized will, freeing them to choose the life that God continually brings into being. Nature and the supernatural are thus "cosubstantial and interfused," filling the world with miraculous possibilities.[45]

Bushnell's emphasis on nature's organic participation in the life of Christ has similarities to the work of his contemporary, another Reformed theologian, John Williamson Nevin. Nevin's Mercersburg theology understood creation's inmost life as having been incorporated, through Adam's fall, into an "organic ruin." In Christ, however, Adam's fallen humanity is exalted once again into a new divine life, a "life introduced into the very center of humanity itself." This new life revitalizes the entirety of creation. Hence, the incarnation is "the supernatural linking itself to the onward flow of the world's life, and becoming thenceforward itself the ground and principle of the entire organism, now poised at last on its true center."[46]

Bushnell and Nevin's dynamic conception of nature's true center in Christ gave nineteenth-century Reformed theology a way of appreciating the world as sacramentally grounded in God's own life. They spoke of a deity who permeates the "secret workings" of organic chemistry, a "mystical presence" encountered in the Eucharist, a process of change and development wholly infused by God's Spirit, a mysterious world that "gets us out of ourselves," pointing us to God's incomparable grandeur.[47] They urged, in short, a mystical consciousness that occasioned a new and richer way of perceiving the world around them.

Their work points to the non-dualistic consciousness that our culture needs today if we are to overcome the subject-object split that has long characterized Western approaches to God as well as the world. Without an incarnational theology that affirms God's presence in creation, we will continue to separate nature from the supernatural, the soul from the body, the hope of a future world from the pressing environmental concerns of the present one. The earth will not be healed so long as we persist in distinguishing ourselves so completely from it, imagining that God is not a part of its mystery.

Interbeing and the Reformed Mystical Tradition

What we need is an entirely new way of seeing—a new "mystical" consciousness that recognizes our unity with the rest of the phenomenal world. I would argue, in closing, that such a consciousness has significant roots even in Reformed Christianity. In putting Christ at the center of the cosmos, Bushnell and Nevin built theologically on an earlier tradition. Even Emerson and Muir, in leaving the Calvinist milieu behind, continued to speak of the need for a spiritual awareness of interdependence, discerning God's presence "in the blowing clover and the falling rain." They were still drawing, in part, from the wellsprings of a Reformed mysticism. Emerson's avowal of pantheism, after all, had sources not only in Hindu mythology, but in the excesses of a Reformed celebration of nature as well.

I realize that it may sound strange to speak of "mysticism," much less a *nature* mysticism, within the Calvinist spiritual heritage. Calvinism, we have been told, fosters a hardheaded piety. It sharply distinguishes a God of majesty from a sinful world, encourages rigorous analytical reflection, and actively contributes to the moral reconstruction of society. We typically characterize its spirituality as transcendent, heady, and highly practical.

Yet, as we have seen, Calvin's piety emphasized the centrality of mystical union with Christ, seventeenth-century Puritans embraced a bridal mysticism based on the Song of Songs, and Jonathan Edwards fostered a sensuous delight in nature as an exercise in knowing God. For each of these, the goal of the spiritual life was a consciousness transformed by beauty, not a mind informed by ideas. Their hearts were fixed on the importance of an immediate experience of God encountered through the biblical text, but "tasted" in the mystery of marital love and nature's astonishing beauty. The union they sought with God went beyond logic and language.

This suggests the deeper consciousness that Calvin had in mind when he dared to exclaim that "nature is God." He was using the playful language of metaphor, juxtaposing opposites in the search for a paradoxical truth. He wanted to affirm that God's glory pervades every dimension of created life. Nature is *not* God, he knew, but neither is it *other* than God. It remains filled with the divine presence in a way we cannot explain, but are able to experience. The Reformed tradition has remained understandably anxious to avoid a slide into pantheism, but its overreaction to this propensity—radically separating God from the world—can be just as dangerous. This is what Calvin meant to avoid. His spirituality, like Edwards's, was fundamentally incarnational, celebrating creation's role in stirring the soul to a thirst for God's beauty. He knew God to have placed desire at the very center of existence, luring everything in the universe to a relationship with the divine.

Bernard McGinn defines mysticism as "an attempt to express a direct consciousness of the presence of God." This is the persistent concern of the writings we have surveyed from Calvin to Edwards. McGinn observes that "of all the modes of speaking available to the mystic, erotic language is the most appropriate way of using speech to surpass itself." Yet language evoking nature's unfathomable mysteries is nearly as prevalent in the writings of Christian mysticism. Curiously, both ways of using language against language are evident in the Reformed tradition.[48]

Its apophatic strain serves an important role in reminding the tradition of its limits. Reformed mysticism is adamant in declaring that none of us ever grasps the unsayable wonder of God's glory. If the Cascade Mountains at sunset are scarcely able to do the job, what can we expect of Reformed theologians probing the inscrutability of the divine decrees? There were times when even Calvin and Edwards needed to listen more carefully to their own reminder of God's unknowable mystery.

The importance of the Reformed mystical tradition for today lies in its ability to challenge human presumptions, to illuminate a world intricately joined by webs of interconnectedness, and to excite us to action by its vision of God's enduring love for creation. Mysticism thrusts the soul into a contemplative stillness in the presence of mystery. It cultivates a new perception of reality, a studied awareness of the interrelatedness of everything to its "other." This is what Calvin urged in attending to the creatures' school of desire, what Baxter practiced in his "gathering art," what Edwards sought in combing the Massachusetts landscape for "images of divine things." A Reformed mystical consciousness refuses to consider any single thing as separate from its other or from God. Everything belongs, as Richard Rohr insists.[49]

Thich Nhat Hanh uses the concept of "interbeing" to describe this interrelatedness. The eye of the mystic, he says, links together all that we might previously have thought disconnected. With a playfulness of language, the Vietnamese Buddhist teacher shows how seemingly unrelated things "inter-are," how they deeply affect each other's existence. The piece of paper containing these words, for example, is attached to everything else in the world. If you are a poet, he laughs, you can see the tree standing here, the sunshine and rain that nurtured the tree's growth, even the logger who brought it to the mill where it was processed as paper. All are here, mingling on the page that joins me and you (the reader) in an interlocking mystery of communication wholly dependent upon the same piece of paper. Thich Nhat Hahn insists that everything is related.[50]

Moreover, this connectedness is inseparable from the divine mystery in which all the exchanges occur. Calvin and Edwards perceived God as the ultimate connector, weaving everything into an incorrigible longing for relationship. Desire runs the show, with God (the desire itself) as the featured act. To recognize this propensity toward unity, to apprehend how all things cohere, is to recover the impulse to praise found in Calvin's image of the world as a theater of God's glory or Edwards's notion of an infinitely connecting God.

It requires a return to "beginner's mind," seeing the world once again with the eyes of a child. Children naturally move through the cosmos on their hands and knees, tasting and handling all the rocks, pine cones, and feathers they can find. Their sensuous and non-dualistic consciousness constitutes what Gary Paul Nabhan calls the geography of childhood. They have a need for wild places, seeking out niches from which they can study at close hand the mysteries of a world that is but an extension of the mystery of themselves.[51]

This was the impulse that drove the young Jonathan Edwards to a hut deep in the brush. It was my experience in the Merritt Island wilderness I explored as a child. From my own hiding place of palmetto fronds on an

Atlantic Coast marshland, I marveled at the inscrutabilities of quicksand, walking sticks on the leg of my pants, and the smell of orange blossoms in the grove nearby. The "interbeing" of all these things gradually awakened my sense of responsibility to the world beyond the hut. When I cut my foot with a hatchet one day, carelessly chopping green saplings, I felt shame at having destroyed living trees, fear as my boot began to fill with blood, and horror as Frank Marion poured turpentine into the open wound. Near the same place on another day, the boys and I shot our first squirrel. Overcome by guilt, we crudely skinned the poor thing, cooked it on an open fire, and made ourselves eat what we regretted having killed. We learned accountability at the place where connections were made and also broken.

There, amid the wild places of my childhood, I encountered a vivid sense of desire, and with it the wounds of desire as well. I imagined a God beyond my understanding, embedded in a larger, cosmic community of praise, arousing longing for an unparalleled beauty. If the hope of the world lies in God's wildness (as John Muir affirmed) and if God is so extravagant in adorning the cosmos and longing for its wholeness, how, then, can I love the world any less? In the end, it drives us crazy with desire. It leads us to a love we had known all along. And it demands, ultimately, our commitment to the work of justice in restoring the earth's lost beauty.

Epilogue

Dead Creek, East Saint Louis

For as long as anyone can remember it's been called Dead Creek, this small stream running through East Saint Louis alongside the Mississippi River. It's part of another world. I can be there in ten minutes from my university office in mid-town Saint Louis, yet economically and ecologically it feels like a Third World country. Eastern Missouri and Central Illinois are known for their beautiful, spring-fed creeks. Dead Creek is a stunning exception. Over the last twenty-five years the EPA has documented higher concentrations of dioxins, PCBs, chlorobenzenes, and heavy-metal pollutants in this stream than almost anywhere in the Midwest.

It was designated as a major superfund site several years ago, but hope for Dead Creek has been slow in coming.[1] Local people say it used to smoke by day and glow with an eerie light on moonless nights. Kids often rode their bikes over the creek bed, the friction of their tires causing small explosions due to spontaneous combustion. An underground fire brought new attention to the place a few years back.

In connection with courses I teach on nature, ecology, and spirituality, I've made field trips with students over the years to the lead belt of southern Missouri. We learn about lead contamination, especially in relation to the Doe Run plant in nearby Herculaneum. But we've also been drawn to East Saint Louis. Jonathan Kozol's description of its hopelessly polluted creek in his book *Savage Inequalities: Children in America's Schools* first drew my attention to the place.[2]

Telling the story of Dead Creek is an appropriate way to conclude this book. It lifts up an important theme in Reformed Spirituality—its need to serve the ends of justice. The last question of the book is a practical one: How does one bestow beauty on a polluted stream that summarizes all the poverty and injustice of a town described by HUD a few years ago as the most distressed small city in America? If this book began with a landscape of desire, in the high desert country of western Wyoming, it ends in another landscape of longing, an urban desert not far from home, perennially fighting racism, environmental pollution, and yawning despair.

There's a danger that a book like this might be perceived as fostering a Romantic delight in idyllic landscapes—as if being "ravished by beauty" were an individualistic end in itself. This would simply constitute another (if subtler) form of anthropocentric colonization, "suggesting that nature exists to please as well as to serve us." That isn't my purpose at all. Ecocritical writers caution that "enjoying nature" can become yet another "integral part of the consumer society" in America.[3] Ecological aestheticism runs the risk of turning unspoiled landscapes into commodities available to the wealthy for exotic travel, adventure tours, and time-share developments. By contrast, a perception of the world honed by prophetic justice refuses to separate the aesthetic from the ethical. To entertain beauty in this way of thinking is necessarily to attend to the plight of the poor (whether human or other-than-human).

Marriage of Beauty and Justice

In the Reformed tradition I've come to re-appreciate though the writing of this book, desiring God is a more corporate, liturgical, and socially responsible enterprise than anything I'd known in the Reformed-tinged fundamentalism of my youth. Desire for God in its thinned-down Calvinism was a privatized, individualistic affair, largely withdrawn from the world. When I was growing up, we were told that evolution was wrong not only because it denied Scripture, but because it paid too much attention to an earth lacking any lasting worth in God's eternal plan.

The minister's wife assured our high school Sunday School class in the 1960s that the Apollo Space Program—a massive exercise in pride—would never make it to the moon. She quoted a passage from Isaiah as proof, saying that the circle of the earth is the limit of man's habitation. I'd left for college by the time Neil Armstrong set foot on the Sea of Tranquility in 1969. I never went back to ask what she made of the event, but I heard from others that she'd said it was done with mirrors. Her truncated

Calvinism was a far cry from the activist and culture-transforming impulse that H. Richard Niebuhr attributed to John Calvin.[4]

Yet early in my life I had a glimpse of the prophetic Calvinism I'd come to admire most in a man named Marv Pranger. He was a layman in our congregation who worked with migrant laborers brought to central Florida from the Caribbean to pick oranges every winter. He called attention to open sewage running through the camps, workers sprayed by crop dusters while picking in the fields, and prostitutes brought in on weekends to keep the workers pacified. A sublime anger flashed in his eyes when he spoke of injustice.

As a twelve-year-old kid, I went with Marv to lead services on Sunday mornings at the camps. He'd preach and I'd play the accordion. He was, for me, the quintessential Calvinist preacher, proclaiming the reign of a sovereign God. A fiery prophet and agent of social change, he was everything a skinny kid with glasses longed for most.

In a meeting at our church one night, the all-white congregation decided not to participate in a joint service that had been planned with the migrant laborers. Marv stood up with a holy anger to quote the words of Jesus from Mathew 23. He denounced the church members as hypocrites, whitewashed sepulchers, and a brood of vipers given to racism and deceit. It was a "cussing-out" the likes of which I'd never heard in church, yet it resonated with everything I knew about Jesus and the little I knew about John Calvin. I recognized even then what I most wanted to claim out of my roots in the Reformed tradition.

Any Calvinist spirituality worth its salt will make its way from aesthetics to ethics, from the celebration of God's beauty to the communication of that beauty to others. Making the world beautiful—and *just*—is part of the proper "work" (the *liturgia*) of giving glory to God. As Elaine Scarry observes, "Beauty prompts a copy of itself."[5] It thrives on replication. This is the root of Reformed spirituality's deep commitment to social justice.

"Calvin's piety can be characterized as intensely activist," argues Elsie Anne McKee, "a devotion to God lived out in the practical present daily world."[6] The Reformed tradition insists that beauty and justice are inseparable dimensions of a single truth. Beauty adds grace and largesse to the exercise of justice. It illuminates and restores the original goodness of God's creative work. A justice that aims at bestowing beauty does more than call for an end to indiscriminate strip mining, for example. It insists on restoring topsoil and reforesting dismembered mountaintops—trying to recover a lost beauty. It argues that making inner-city schools and housing projects beautiful may be as important as making them functional in the long-term work of building communal identity and respect. Beauty gives justice a face of compassion, an endearing touch of bountiful excess that enlarges life rather than merely preserving it.

Beauty cultivates an eye for the correction of abuses. But it looks even more for possibilities that create a lasting sense of refinement and shared pride. Calvin sought legislation that required balcony rails on houses in Geneva, guarding the safety of young children in the process of beautifying and improving homes. Among the refugees that he welcomed to Geneva were wool, cotton, and silk weavers, as well as printers, goldsmiths, and watchmakers—people who could provide jobs for the local economy while also enhancing its cultural life. Reformed Christianity, if true to its roots, concerns itself with beautifying the ugly realities of urban poverty and ecological contamination. It naturally turns its eyes to places like East Saint Louis, attending to the decreased capacity of Dead Creek to mirror God's glory.

Life on the East Side

To the south of this distressed city across the river from the Gateway Arch, Dead Creek runs through the small municipality of Sauget. It parallels the Mississippi River before emptying into the Big Muddy ten miles south of downtown Saint Louis. Sauget has a population of 249 people. Incorporated in 1926 as a tax shelter for the Monsanto chemical plants there, it was never meant to be lived in. For years these plants were the nation's largest producers of PCBs. Today they've been joined by other chemical companies like Big River Zinc, Cerro Copper, and Pfizer Chemical, as well as the American Bottoms Treatment Plant, a huge sewage treatment and waste incineration site. For a half mile Dead Creek runs underground, directly beneath these chemical plants.[7]

A recent article in the *Wall Street Journal* observes how the town of Sauget has thrived economically by welcoming companies that produce (and incinerate) toxic wastes of all sorts. Its "yes, in my backyard" ethic has made Sauget "a peculiar island of prosperity in the sea of urban economic blight across the Mississippi River from St. Louis."[8] The few people who live there are town officials, fire fighters, and policemen. Sauget is also known for cheap liquor at its local package store, its off-track betting site (with the largest lottery outlet in Illinois), and its infamous strip clubs—including venues like Penthouse, Oz, and PT's. With its tall smokestacks and chemical leaks, the fictitious municipality of Sauget contributes to the culture of the East Side a unique combination of pollution, liquor, sex, and gambling.

It's not a particularly friendly place. People who ask questions about Dead Creek are particularly unwelcome at the chemical plants in town. Information offices generally seem to be closed. Calls aren't returned. My students find it a relief when we cross the river again. Sauget is an uninviting world of tangled refinery pipes, abandoned tanker cars, gaudy billboards, and deep suspicion.

East Saint Louis itself has long been an example of urban blight, despite its pride in the high school football team and the memory of hometown jazz musician Miles Davis. The town of 32,000 people is 97 percent African American, with a median family income of $21,000. A third of the population lives below the poverty line. For years the infrastructure of the city was practically nil, with no regular trash collection and very little police or fire protection. Raw sewage backed up in the homes due to collapsed pipes and dysfunctional pumping stations. Its city hall was auctioned off a few years ago to pay for a lawsuit against the municipal government.

East Saint Louis has been one of the most crime-ridden cities in the nation. Street gangs, copied after the former War Lords, Black Egyptians, and 29th Street Stompers, add volatility to its night life. The city has one of the highest rates of childhood asthma in the country. Lead poisoning is common. Hazardous waste dumps are everywhere.

East Saint Louis is another world. It serves as a poster child for the effects of environmental racism. Where the earth hurts most, the poor hurt with it, says Leonardo Boff. The cry of the earth *is* the cry of the poor. Older people there remember the 1917 race riots that left as many as a hundred African Americans dead and 6,000 driven from their homes. White mobs, resenting blacks who had been recruited to work during the war years at the Aluminum Ore and American Steel Companies, ransacked homes and lynched people from telephone poles while the National Guard did nothing.[9] There is beauty in East Saint Louis, but it isn't always easy to find.

Locating the original name of what people have long called "Dead Creek" proved no simple task, for example. Few people know it by any other name. Back in 1770, when East Saint Louis was founded, a Canadian entrepreneur built a grist mill and several log cabins on the banks of what was then known as Cahokia Creek. It was named after one of the five tribes of the Illini confederation, whose ancestors had built the famous Cahokia Mounds a few miles to the northeast. These are the largest and oldest sacred mounds in North America, remnants of a great civilization and a proud people, thriving in this region some 800 years ago. In years past, the creek connected the City of the Mounds to the Great River. It was a sacred waterway, a source of life. The Native American word *cahokia* means "the place where the wild geese fly."

But the wild geese avoid it today. In the year 2000, the EPA placed a 3.5-mile length of the stream on the National Priority List. A chain-link fence was built around it and Monsanto was ordered to remove 50,000 tons of sediment from the creek bed. When I was at the site with a few students a while ago, workers were installing a half-inch high-density polyethylene liner on a half-mile section of the creek bed. Its purpose is to keep polluted ground water from rising to the surface. The Army Corps of Engineers has a long-range plan "to restore Cahokia Creek and its adjacent forested floodplain to presettlement (ca. 1800) conditions." But plans are more easily made than executed.[10]

About 143,000 people live within a four-mile radius of the culverts where the stream runs out from under the chemical and waste treatment plants. Despite the improvements already made (or planned), their health may be affected for years to come by the poisons saturated in the ground.[11] Nonetheless, the creek looks better than it has in years. At the place where it flows alongside Holy Family Church in Cahokia (founded in 1699), it passes a stretch of green grass and sheltering trees. Frogs jump in the algae along its banks, and they don't even appear to be mutated species. One might never suspect the poisons still lying upstream. The earth has an amazing ability to renew itself, even with minimal help.

A Metrolink light-rail system now connects the East Side with Saint Louis across the river, gambling casinos attract people and money (along with other problems) to the riverfront, and a number of urban renewal projects are underway. Yet long-term healing for East Saint Louis will take years. Part of the problem is the willingness of people to accept the ugliness of urban poverty and pollution as inevitable realities. St. Louisans distance themselves from the squalor of the East Side. Older people pass by hurriedly on the interstate highway. Younger people are attracted to the risky edge of its nightlife. Yet few people consider it a place they'd want to live.

"It might not be the most beautiful place in the world, but there are more important things than beauty," says Yvonne McDaniel, the wife of a retired police officer who has lived comfortably in Sauget for 55 years.[12] I can sympathize with what she's saying, though I would put a higher value on beauty, viewing it as an intrinsic part of the larger concerns of justice. "Abandoned of beauty, *being* loses something of its essence," Plotinus wrote in the third century.[13] Beauty is the luster that gives every existent reality its deepest attraction. Edwards defined it as the final touch of the Spirit that God places on what the Father and Son have joyously brought into being. "The beauty of the world" he declared, "is a communication of God's beauty."[14]

How, then, might the Spirit move again over the waters of Dead Creek, transforming it into the image of its original beauty as Cahokia, the place where the wild geese fly? God works through the native, healing capabilities of the earth itself, as well as through human hands and hearts. The gifts of decisive action and conscious awareness (a deep "sense of the heart," as Edwards would say) are what humans bring to the process of healing. Ours is the task of telling the story, inviting repentance, and initiating change. This is our way of honoring beauty and giving glory to God. To shrink from this "Great Work" is to betray our calling.

Karl Barth acknowledged the earth as reflecting the super-abundance of God's glory. "Even the smallest creatures do it," he said. "They do it along with us or without us. They do it also against us to shame us and instruct us. They do it because they cannot help doing it." He observed that the human being, in contrast, is often "a late-comer slipping shamefacedly into creation's choir in heaven and earth, . . . [one] who refuses to co-operate in the jubilation which surrounds him."[15]

Hence, I'm put to shame by a polluted stream across the river from me that longs to sing. If Dead Creek is stripped of its natural ability to reflect God's glory by my inadvertent support of chemical companies contaminating its waters—if its voice of praise is squelched by my silence in speaking out for justice—I become a hindrance to the jubilation that surrounds me. Failing to exercise the consciousness I possess, I too fail to give praise.

The Call of the Wild

As I near the conclusion of this book, I realize that I've been wrestling all along with a tradition that had lost any life for me. But having recaptured something of its unexpected power, everything now changes in the way I think about the world. Henry David Thoreau once spoke of the church as an empty warehouse where munitions had long been stored. It may reek of dust and a forgotten danger, he said, but if a light were brought in, enough gunpowder remains in the walls that it might still blow up in an instant.[16] I've experienced such an explosion myself in discovering the intense longing for God and passionate love of the earth hidden in the dusty tomes of a Calvinist past. I can't relate to God or to the world in the same way any more as a result.

This book has been more than a journey into a retrievable past, allowing me to affirm a tradition I thought had failed me. It's a springboard into something new as well. It crosses all confessional boundaries in summoning the human community to a concern for places like Dead Creek. It declares with all sacred traditions that the earth is holy and one. There are, after all, no Presbyterian trees, no distinctively Catholic rivers or Buddhist mountains. The earth's beauty (as a mirror of divine glory) transcends every religious label and crosses every cultural frontier.[17] It pulls me out of the nurturing (and sometimes restrictive) depths of my Reformed heritage into an ever-widening universal vision.

Every religious tradition has to assume this task in our day. We all are responsible for the work of recovering an earth-related theology. A tradition, by definition, functions as a weight or ballast that grounds a community in its history. For a tradition to remain alive, however, it has to be a weight in *motion*, a pendulum that swings back into the past to recover its roots and forward into the future to accomplish something genuinely new. Only in doing both does the tradition serve its true purpose. It often takes a thousand-year running head start to create an entirely new way of thinking. And a new way of perceiving the world is what the earth now demands of us.

While the Reformed tradition likes to define itself as "Reformed, and continually being reformed" (*ecclesia reformata, semper reformanda*), it hasn't always been faithful to that vision, as we have seen. But today's challenge of responding to polluted creeks robbed of their beauty forces Reformed Christians to join with all others in restoring a glory that longs to fill the earth. Sharing in God's own passion for beauty, we are astounded by what none of us are able to name, but all of us are able to love.

Let us work, then, for the day when rivers and creeks filled with toxic waste may yet again run free. Despite all the reasons to despair, there is hope even for situations as formidable as Dead Creek. Stories told of the mud-mothers in the African American tradition would insist upon it. Sharon Welch reminds us that the mud-mothers are the ones anchored in the depths of their people's longing and pain. In the work of regenerating life, these are the women who *begin* when everyone else is ready to quit.[18] They refuse to give up. Their insistence on hope is glimpsed, for example, in the tale of another once-polluted waterway in central Illinois, the Illinois River. Sandra Steingraber spoke on its behalf in her 1998 book *Living Downstream*, a courageous work written out of the darkness of the river's pain as well as her own.[19]

The Illinois River flows south from Chicago and empties into the Mississippi a few miles north of East Saint Louis. It is something of a success story now, but for years it was filled with wastewater from upstream, including runoffs from chemical companies, aluminum foundries, and hazardous waste sites. The overflow of pesticides from adjoining corn and soybean fields added to its contamination. Wildlife in and along the river began to disappear.

Steingraber grew up along this waterway in a small town near Peoria. In her early twenties, she was diagnosed with cancer, like an uncommon number of others in her hometown. As a research biologist (and cancer survivor), she went on to correlate data regarding toxic releases into the Illinois River with the incidence of cancer cases along its banks. Her book argues that 90 percent of all forms of cancer may be attributable to specific environmental factors. Some have compared it to Rachel Carson's *Silent Spring*. It's done much to encourage the cleanup of the river, showing that polluted streams can indeed be healed. It suggests hope for Dead Creek as well.

Who will speak for the once beautiful Cahokia Creek, and places like it around the world? Dare we fail to resurrect its voice in proclaiming the beauty of holiness? The glory of the Lord longs, after all, to make everything "fair," in both senses of that word: fair as in being lovely and "treated fairly" as in being granted the dignity it deserves.[20] The aesthetic and the ethical have to be one. Both contribute to the fullness of praise.

The Holy Spirit, like the flight of the wild goose in Celtic lore, longs to sweep over the waters yet again. It cries high above the place where the wild geese once soared—over Dead Creek in East Saint Louis—summoning the earth to a beauty forgotten, but not lost. In the haunting sound of that cry, says Mary Oliver, we fret at the mess that we've made of things. We embrace a harsh repentance, a new awareness, and a readiness to act. Meanwhile the world continues in its wild and glorious determination to sing, with or without us.

> Meanwhile the wild geese, high in the clean blue air,
> are heading home again.
> Whoever you are, no matter how lonely,
> The world offers itself to your imagination,
> calls to you like the wild geese, harsh and exciting—
> over and over announcing your place
> in the family of things.[21]

Accepting our place in the family of things means doing everything necessary to assure our mutual delight and well-being. It comes ultimately as a gift, a shared longing, a consciousness that we all are one. We recognize it, at last, in the desire of the geese for exuberant song, the desire of the creek to flow unrestrainedly toward the sea, and the desire of human beings to join in God's own deep longing for beauty. May it be so.

Notes

Prologue

1. See Craig Childs, *The Secret Knowledge of Water: Discovering the Essence of the American Desert* (Boston: Little, Brown and Company, 2000), xii, xvi.

2. The terms "Calvinist" and "Reformed" are not generally distinguished in this book. Strictly speaking, the latter is the more general term, referring to Protestant Christians who trace their roots to the sixteenth-century Reformation in Switzerland, initiated by Ulrich Zwingli and John Calvin. Today these include Presbyterian, Congregationalist, Reformed, and, to some extent, Anglican and Baptist Church bodies. The term "Calvinist" refers more particularly to those who look to Calvin's work in Geneva as most formative of their thought. These include French Reformed Christians, English and Scots Presbyterians, Dutch Reformed believers, and a wide variety of Puritans in seventeenth-century England and America.

3. Leon Kellner, *American Literature*, trans., Julia Franklin (Garden City, NY: Doubleday, 1915), 40–41.

4. For a description of Reformed spiritualities, see the author's entries on "Calvinist Spirituality" and "Puritan Spirituality" in *The New Westminster Dictionary of Christian Spirituality*, ed. Philip Sheldrake (Louisville: Westminster John Knox Press, 2005), 162–164, 518–520.

5. Matthew Sylvester, "How May a Gracious Person, from Whom God Hides His Face, Trust in the Lord as His God," Sermon XXIX in *Puritan Sermons, 1659–1689, Being the Morning Exercises at Cripplegate, St. Giles in the Fields, and in Southwork* (Wheaton, IL: Richard Own Roberts, Publishers, 1981), originally published in 1690, vol. 4, 81–92.

6. Joseph Symonds, *The Case and Cure of a Deserted Soul, or a Treatise concerning the Nature, Kinds, Degrees, Symptomes, Causes, Cure of, and Mistakes about Spirituall* [yes!] *Desertions* (London: Luke Fawne, 1658), 10.

7. Ibid., 18.

8. Ibid., 74, 434.

9. Karl Barth (1886–1968) was the most important Reformed theologian of the twentieth century. He challenged the reigning modernist theology of Germany with his Romans commentary in 1919, and became a leading exponent of Neo-Orthodox Protestant theology. His 13-volume *Church Dogmatics* developed a highly Christocentric theology. The Reformed Baptists that I knew, indebted to preachers like Charles Haddon Spurgeon, would have found Barth's theology too liberal in its rejection of biblical inerrancy and its openness to a universal salvation.

10. Barth could discern a "creaturely correspondence" to God's transcendent reality only in human beings. "The glory of other creatures lies in the concealment of their being with God, no less than ours in its disclosure." *Church Dogmatics*, II/2, 138. For a discussion of Barth's theology in this regard, see Anna Case-Winters, "Does Reformed Tradition Have a Theology of Nature?" *Memphis Theological Seminary Journal* 41 (2005), 67–88.

11. *Church Dogmatics*, I/1:x.

12. Calvin argued that the image of God is still discernible in fallen humanity. "Should any one object, that the divine image has been obliterated, the solution is easy; first, there yet exists some remnant of it, so that man is possessed of no small dignity; and secondly, the Celestial Creator himself, however corrupted man may be, still keeps in view the end of his original creation." Comm. Genesis 9:6. CO 23:147, CTS I:295–296. Cf. *Inst.* I.xv.4. See also B. A. Gerrish, "The Mirror of God's Goodness: Man in the Theology of Calvin," *Concordia Theological Quarterly* 45:3 (July 1981), 211–222.

13. I owe this distinction to a conversation with J. Phillip Newell, former warden of Iona Abbey and author of *Listening to the Heartbeat of God: A Celtic Christianity* (New York: Paulist Press, 1997).

14. Having addressed his *Institutes of the Christian Religion* to King Francis I of France, Calvin focused on the kingly, as well as prophetic and priestly offices, of Christ in that work. He assured the faithful, for example, of Christ's readiness to lift them up into a participation of his own grandeur: "Such is the nature of his rule, that he shares with us all that he has received from the Father. Now he arms and equips us with his power, adorns us with his beauty and magnificence, enriches us with his wealth." *Inst.* II.xv.4.

15. Responding to Lucy's question about' the potential dangerousness of Aslan the lion, Mr. Beaver replied, "Who said anything about safe? 'Course he isn't safe. But he's good." C. S. Lewis, *The Lion, the Witch, and the Wardrobe* (Hammondsworth, UK: Penguin Books, 1959), 75.

16. These five articles of faith were first affirmed by the Synod of Dort, an assembly of the Dutch Reformed Church meeting at Dordrecht in 1618–1619.

17. Karl Barth would give me a new appreciation of the doctrine of double predestination, as he emphasized the Christological focus of this austere truth. In Christ, the True Human Being, all of humanity is chosen and in Christ, the Bearer of Sin, all of humanity is also reprobate. What Christ does, then, in his death and resurrection, is to pass on the gift of election to everyone else and to apply the rejection entirely to himself. This results in a triumph of God's grace in which it is hard to imagine anyone rejecting the free gift offered to them in Christ. Barth shied away from a confidence in universal salvation, however, affirming the "impossible possibility" that one might choose to reject what is already theirs in Christ. See his *Church Dogmatics*, trans. G. W. Bromiley and T. F. Torrance (Edinburgh: T. & T. Clark, 1957), II/2, 161–194, 306–506.

18. Cotton Mather, in his *Magnalia Christi Americana* (Cambridge, MA: Belknap Press, 1977), I:51, celebrated the 1619 epidemic that had wiped out 90 percent of the "pernicious creatures" who had occupied the Massachusetts colony before the arrival of the Puritans. Historian Francis Jennings, in his study of *The Invasion of America: Indians, Colonialism, and the Cant of Conquest* (Chapel Hill: University of North Carolina Press, 1975), describes the "First Puritan Conquest" in the Pequot War of 1637 as "one long atrocity" 226.

19. See Patrick Fuery, *Theories of Desire* (Carlton, Victory: Melbourne University Press, 1995); Margaret Miles, *Desire and Delight: A New Reading of Augustine's Confessions* (New York: Crossroad, 1992); Elizabeth Dreyer, *Passionate Spirituality: Hildegard of Bingen*

and Hadewijch of Brabant (New York: Paulist Press, 2005); and Mary Farrell Bednarowski, "Women, Spirituality, and History: Beyond Paralyzing Polarities," *Journal of Women's History* 17:2 (2005), 184–192; Hans Urs von Balthasar, *The Glory of the Lord: A Theological Aesthetics* (San Francisco Ignatian Press, 1983–1991); Frank Burch Brown, *Religious Aesthetics: A Theological Study of Making and Meaning* (Princeton, NJ: Princeton University Press, 1989); Richard Viladesau, *Theological Aesthetics: God in Imagination, Beauty, and Art* (New York: Oxford University Press, 1999); and Gesa Elsbeth Thiessen, ed., *Theological Aesthetics: A Reader* (Grand Rapids, MI: Eerdmans, 2004.

20. See Susan Schreiner, *The Theater of His Glory: Nature and the Natural Order in the Thought of John Calvin* (Durham, NC: Labyrinth Press, 1991); Janice Knight, *Orthodoxies in Massachusetts: Rereading American Puritanism* (Cambridge, MA.: Harvard University Press, 1994); William A. Dyrness, *Reformed Theology and Visual Culture: The Protestant Imagination from Calvin to Edwards* (Cambridge: Cambridge University Press, 2004); Amanda Porterfield, "Bridal Passion and New England Puritanism" in *Feminine Spirituality in America* (Philadelphia: Temple University Press, 1980), 19–50; and Roland Delattre, *Beauty and Sensibility in the Thought of Jonathan Edwards* (New Haven: Yale University Press, 1968.

21. Peter Gay, "Jonathan Edwards: An American Tragedy," in *Jonathan Edwards: A Profile*, ed. David Levin (New York: Hill & Wang, 1969), 231–251.

Chapter 1

1. Elizabeth Singer Rowe, *Devout Exercises of the Heart*, ed., Isaac Watts (Dedham: Nathaniel and Benjamin Heaton, 1796), 71, 104.

2. See "The Altus Prosator of Columcille (Columba)," in *Celtic Spirituality*, trans. Oliver Davies (New York: Paulist Press, 1999), 407, and George MacLeod, *The Whole Earth Shall Cry Glory: Iona Prayers* (Iona: Wild Goose Publications, 1985), 14.

3. Calvin, Sermon 96 on Job, CO 34:439, and Commentary on Hebrews 11:3, CO 55:144–146; CTS XXII:264–266. Calvin argues that Scripture and nature (where "the imprint of God's knowledge shines in his creatures") both share the same goal—"inviting us first to fear God, then to trust him." *Institutes* I.x.2.

4. Presbyterians for Restoring Creation is now known as Presbyterians for Earth Care. Caring for Creation, with the Reformed Church in America, is a similar organization, like the Eco-Justice Ministries of the United Church of Christ. See Robert Booth Fowler, *The Greening of Protestant Thought* (Chapel Hill: Univeristy of North Carolina Press, 1995), 15.

5. *The Book of Confessions: Study Edition* (Louisville, KY: Westminster John Knox Press, 1999), 193.

6. Joseph Sittler, *The Care of the Earth and Other University Sermons* (Philadelphia: Fortress, 1964), 88–98. For a fuller development of the environmental application of Augustine's distinction, see Francisco Benzoni, "An Augustinian Undxerstanding of Love in an Ecological Context," *Quodlibet: Online Journal of Christian Theology and Philosophy* 6:3 (July—September 2004), 1–8.

7. Richard Baxter, *The Saints Everlasting Rest* (1650), (London: Epworth Press, 1962), 110–111, 168–169. Richard Baxter (1615–1691) was Puritan pastor of the church at Kidderminster near Birmingham and a moderate noncomformist who sought unity among Presbyterians, Episcopalians, and Independents.

8. Thomas Taylor, *A Man in Christ, or: A New Creature. To Which Is Added a Treatise, Containing Meditations from the Creatures* (London: I. Bartlet, 1628), 5–8. Thomas Taylor

(1576–1632), one of William Perkins's disciples at Cambridge, was lecturer and curate at St. Mary Aldermanbury, London. The Belgic Confession, Article 2, said the "universe is before our eyes like a beautiful book in which all creatures, great and small, are as letters to make us ponder the invisible things of God." Written in the southern Lowlands by Guido de Bres in 1618, this is one of the earliest Reformed statements of faith.

9. Calvin, Commentary on Isaiah 57:1, CO 37:305, CTS VIII:194.

10. *Inst.* I.xiv.21.

11. Calvin, Commentary on Genesis, Argumentum. CO 22.8d, CTS I:57, 60. Emphasis added.

12. Alister E. McGrath, *A Life of John Calvin* (Oxford: Blackwell, 1990), 254–257. Calvin's understanding of the accommodated character of biblical language, viewing the Genesis story of creation, for example, as written for relatively simple and unsophisticated people, allowed him to reconcile scientific observations with biblical texts. See his commentary on Genesis 1:15–16, CO 23:22, CTS I:85–87.

13. "If the Lord has willed that we be helped in physics, dialectic, mathematics, and other like disciplines, by the work and ministry of the ungodly, let us use this assistance." *Inst.* II.ii.16.

14. Robert K. Merton's *Science, Technology, and Society in 17th Century England* (Atlantic Highlands, NJ: Humanities Press, 1978) argued that English Calvinism provided a context of social values that increased the attractiveness of science as a vocation. The "Merton thesis" has been debated by historians, yet it is generally accepted that there were important connections between the Reformed tradition and the rise of the new science. See Gary B. Deason, "Reformation Theology and the Mechanistic Conception of Nature," in David C. Lindberg and Ronald L. Numbers, eds., *God and Nature: Historical Essays on the Encounter between Christianity and Science* (Berkeley: University of California Press, 1986), 171–172.

15. Perry Miller and Thomas H. Johnson, *The Puritans* (New York: American Book Company, 1938), 286.

16. See Bonaventure, *The Journey of the Soul to God*, Chapters 1–2; his *Breviloquium*, II.12.1; and his *Commentary on the Sentences of Peter Lombard*, Distinction III, part 1, chapter 1, quoted widely by Calvin in his *Institutes*.

17. Calvin, Commentary on John 9:5, CO 47:220, CNTC 4:240.

18. Calvin speaks of the universe as a mirror (*Inst.* I.v.1), school (*Inst.* II.vi.1), theater (Commentary on Psalm 104:31), painting (*Inst.* I.v.10), God's clothing (Commentary on Genesis, Argumentum, 60), a "book of the unlearned"(Sermon 34 on Job, CO 33:428) and an imprint of God's lustrous glory (*Inst.* I.x.2).

19. Martin Bucer, in his *Treatise Declaring and Showing That Images Are Not to Be Suffered in* Churches (1535), argued that artistic images are unnecessary in that we have the whole frame of the world as "a monument and token to put us in remembrance of God." Quoted in William A. Dyrness, *Reformed Theology and Visual Culture: The Protestant Imagination from Calvin to Edwards* (Cambridge: Cambridge University Press, 2004), 92. Jonathan Edwards declared that "We can conceive of nothing more beautiful of an external kind than the beauties of nature. . . . Therefore, the highest beauties of art consist in imitation of them." *Miscellanies*, 1296, YE 23:238.

20. Richard Bernard, *Contemplative Pictures with Wholesome Precepts* (London: William Hall, 1610), 5. Richard Bernard (1568–1641) was vicar of Worksop, Nottinghamshire, and author of *The Faithful Shepheard* (1607), a handbook for Puritan ministers.

21. Dyrness, *Reformed Theology*, 74. See also Carlos Eire, *War against the Idols: The Reformation of Worship from Erasmus to Calvin* (Cambridge: Cambridge University Press, 1986).

22. *Inst.* I.xi.12 (1545 French edition). See Wayne Franits, ed., *Looking at Seventeenth-Century Dutch Art: Realism Reconsidered* (Cambridge: Cambridge University Press, 1997) and Reindert L. Falkenburg, "Calvinism and the Emergence of Dutch Seventeenth-Century Landscape Art: A Critical Evaluation," in Paul C. Finney, ed., *Seeing Beyond the Word: Visual Arts and the Calvinist Tradition* (Grand Rapids, MI: Eerdmans, 1999), 343–368.

23. *Inst.* III.xi.10 and III.i.3. See J. Todd Billings, *Calvin, Participation, and the Gift: The Activity of Believers in Union with Christ* (New York: Oxford University Press, 2007).

24. *Inst.* I.v.5.

25. Perry Miller, *The New England Mind: The Seventeenth Century* (Boston: Beacon Press, 1954), 15.

26. Panentheism seeks to affirm a God who is not simply "out there," but also "in here"—filling the world with God's glory even as God remains far "more" than the world itself. In this, it differs immensely from pantheism, with its entire identification of God and creation. See Jürgen Moltmann, *God in Creation* (Minneapolis: Fortress Press, 1993), 102–103.

27. *Inst* I.xiii.1. A better way of expressing this, and truer to Calvin, would be to say that God is present in the finite world to the extent that God has consented to be met in that way ("*finitum capax divinitatis per accommodationem*"). I am indebted to Dr. David Field of Transkei University, South Africa, for this formula. See David Willis, "Rhetoric and Responsibility in Calvin's Theology," in *The Context of Contemporary Theology: Essays in Honor of Paul Lehman*, ed. Alexander McKelway and David Willis (Atlanta: John Knox Press, 1974), 43–63; and Heiko Oberman, "The 'Extra' Dimension in the Theology of Calvin," *Journal of Ecclesiastical History* 21 (1970), 60–62.

28. Their spirituality would be caricatured by later American writers from Nathaniel Hawthorne to Mark Twain as a dour and moralistic practice of cheerless obedience. Literary critic William Shurr summarizes this kind of "rugged Calvinism, with all its gloom and glory" as constituting "a national mythology" in eighteenth- and nineteenth-century American life. It functioned, he claims, as an "infinite monstrousness that haunts the American mind." See William Shurr, *Rappaccini's Children: American Writers in a Calvinist World* (Lexington: University Press of Kentucky, 1981), 16, 25.

29. Calvin, *Catechism* (1537), trans. Ford Lewis Battles (Pittsburgh, PA: Pittsburgh Theological Seminary, 1972), 2; Sermon on Deuteronomy 28:46–50, in CO 28.441.

30. Janice Knight urges that "the early history of New England must be rewritten in terms of a continuing contest between . . . two orthodoxies." She contrasts the austere and warm-hearted strains in the American Puritan experience, distinguishing them as "Intellectual Fathers" and "Spiritual Brethren." Janice Knight, *Orthodoxies in Massachusetts: Rereading American Puritanism* (Cambridge, MA.: Harvard University Press, 1994), 11.

31. James M. Gustafson, *Ethics from a Theocentric Perspective: Theology and Ethics* (Chicago: University of Chicago Press, 1981), 190.

32. For a comparison of Calvin and Turretin, see Carl R. Trueman, "Calvin and Calvinism," in *The Cambridge Companion to John Calvin*, ed. Donald K. McKim (Cambridge University Press, 2004), 225–244. Francis Turretin (1623–1687) held the chair in philosophy (and later theology) at the Geneva Academy. The three volumes of his *Institutio Theologiae Electicae* were published in 1679, 1682, and 1685.

33. Calvin introduces this *duplex cognitio* (the two ways we know God) in his *Inst.* I.ii.1. He describes Scripture as the "spectacles" employed to read the book of creation in I.xiv.1.

34. "Nearly all the wisdom we possess, that is to say, true and sound wisdom, consists of two parts: the knowledge of God and of ourselves. But as these are connected by many ties, it is not easy to determine which of the two precedes and produces the other." *Inst.* I.i.1. See Edward A. Dowey, *The Knowledge of God in Calvin's Theology* (New York: Columbia University Press, 1965), 18–24.

35. Calvin says, "Indeed, the knowledge of God set forth for us in Scripture is destined for the very same goal as the knowledge whose imprint shines in his creatures, in that it invites us first to fear God, then to trust him." *Inst.* I.x.2. He adds in his Commentary on Acts 17:27, "Every man will find [God] in himself, if only he is willing to pay attention. . . . Above all other creatures he is proof of the glory of God, full of countless miracles as he is." CO 48:415–416; CNTC 7:119.

36. *Inst.* I.i.1–3 and I.v.8. Calvin acknowledges that few people are open to the wonders of the natural world: "scarcely one man in a hundred is a true spectator of it."

37. Commentary on Genesis, Argumentum, CO 23:11; CTS 1:64. Calvin says, "For Christ is that image in which God presents to our view, not only his heart, but also his hands and his feet. I give the name of his *heart* to that secret love with which he embraces us in Christ: by his *hands* and *feet* I understand those works of his which are displayed before our eyes." Emphasis added.

38. Peter Wyatt, *Jesus Christ and Creation in the Theology of John Calvin* (Allison Park, PA: Pickwick, 1996), 91.

39. Sermon 119 on Deuteronomy 20:16–20, in John Calvin, *Sermons on Deuteronomy* (London, Henry Middleton for John Harison, 1583), 734–735. Emphasis added. For a discussion of Calvin's contributions to ecological ethics, see Edward Dommen, "Calvin and the Environment," in *John Calvin Rediscovered*, eds. Edward Dommen and James D. Bratt (Louisville: Westminster John Knox Press, 2007), 53–66. This quote from Calvin is Dommen's translation.

40. Francis Turretin, *Institutes of Elenctic Theology*, ed. James T. Dennison (Phillipsburg, NJ: P & R Publishing, 1992), I:431.

41. Turretin's reflections on the created world are much more speculative and incidental than Calvin's. He attends, for example, to questions about the eternity of the world (which he rejects), about the instantaneous character of creation on each of the six days, and even about the season of the year in which the world was created (in autumn as opposed to spring). Ibid., I:436–446.

42. See William Ames, *The Marrow of Theology*, trans. John D. Eusden (Boston: Pilgrim Press, 1968), 100, and William Perkins, *A Golden Chaine, or the Description of Theologie: Containing the Order of the Causes of Salvation and Damnation* (London: John Legatte, 1612), 34–37.

43. Calvin, Commentary on Genesis, Argumentum. *Calvin's Commentaries*, CO 23:7; CTS I:60. See also the *Inst.* I.v.9.

44. Luther had distinguished a *theologia crucis* from a *theologia gloriae* in the Heidelberg Disputation of 1519. The latter imagines that one can approach God directly, through the power of reason; the former meets God in the foolishness of the cross, in a salvation found entirely outside of us (*extra nos*). See Gerhard O. Forde, *On Being a Theologian of the Cross: Reflections on Luther's Heidelberg Disputation, 1518* (Grand Rapids, MI: Eerdmans, 1997).

45. Calvin, Sermon 126 on Deuteronomy 22:5–8; CO 28:22–25. *Sermons of M. John Calvin upon the Fifth Books of Moses Called Deuteronomie*, trans. Arthur Golding (London: Henry Middleton for George Bishop, 1583), 774. Cock-fighting and bear-baiting, by the way, were reintroduced after the Restoration and the end of Puritan rule in 1660.

46. Philip Stubbes, *Anatomy of Abuses in England*, ed. Frederick J. Furnivall (New Shakspere Society, 1877–1879), 177–178. Emphasis added. Philip Stubbes (1555–1610) was a Cambridge-trained pamphleteer who sought a radical "reformation of maners and amendement of lyfe" in this work, published in 1583.

47. *The Works, Moral and Religious, of Sir Matthew Hale*, ed. T. Thirlwall (London: Symonds, 1805), I:273.

48. Historical Manuscript Commission, xvii.108. Quoted in Thomas, *Man and the Natural World*, 162.

49. George Hughes, *An Analytical Exposition of the Whole First Book of Moses* (London, 1672), 10. George Hughes (1603–1667) was a fellow of Pembroke College, Oxford, who was ejected in 1660 from the Plymouth pulpit because of his Puritan convictions.

50. "Massachusetts Body of Liberties of 1641," sections 92–93. The latter section stated that "If any man shall have occasion to leade or drive Cattel from place to place that is far of, so that they be weary, or hungry, or fall sick, or lambe, It shall be lawful to rest or refresh them, for a competent time, in any open place that is not Corne, meadow, or inclosed for some peculiar use." See Emily Stewart Leavitt, *Animals and Their Legal Rights: A Survey of American Laws from 1641 to 1978* (New York: Animal Welfare Institute, 1978). Nathaniel Ward (1578–1652), a graduate of Emmanuel College, Cambridge, had been trained as a lawyer before entering the ministry and coming to Massachusetts in 1634.

51. Thomas Wentworth (1593–1641) was a Yorkshire baronet, married to the daughter of a prominent Yorkshire Puritan. Serving in Ireland under Charles I, he was firmly Puritan in piety, if not in politics. See C. V. Wedgwood, *Thomas Wentworth: First Earl of Strafford: A Reevaluation* (New York: Macmillan, 1962).

52. Ralph Austen, *A Treatise of Fruit Trees* (Oxford: Henry Hall for Thomas Robinson, 1657), 8. Ralph Austen (1612–1672) was a Puritan radical who perceived his work in propagating seventy-five varieties of fruit trees and sowing thousands of timber trees as helping to establish a millennial kingdom on earth.

53. See James Turner, "Ralph Austen, Oxford Horticulturist of the Seventeenth Century," *Garden History* 6:2 (Summer 1978), 39–45. "Plants were the first animate bodies that God created," said Austen, "And fruit of Trees was the first seed that was given to man, his food appointed by God." Treatise, 12.

54. Ralph Austen, *A Dialogue (or Familiar Discourse) and Conference betweene the Husbandman and Fruit Trees* (Oxford: Hen. Hall for Thomas Bowman, 1676), 4–5, 76.

55. Ibid., 13–14, 73.

56. William Lawson, *A New Orchard and Garden, or, the Best way for Planting, Grafting, and to Make Any Ground Good for a Rich Orchard* (London: Printed for George Sawbridge, 1676).

57. Robert Wolcott, "Husbandry in Colonial New England," *New England Quarterly* IX (1936), 225, 252.

58. Cecelia Tichi, *New World, New Earth: Environmental Reform in American Literature from the Puritans through Whitman* (New Haven: Yale University Press, 1979), 15.

59. Edward Johnson, *Wonder-Working Providence of Sions Saviour in New England*, 1653 (New York: Barnes & Noble, 1959), 209–210, 120.

60. Northrup Frye, *The Stubborn Structure: Essays on Criticism and Society* (Ithaca, NY: Cornell University Press, 1970), 139.

61. See Steven George Salaita, *The Holy Land in Transit: Colonialism and the Quest for Canaan* (Syracuse, NY: Syracuse University Press, 2006), 24.

62. Annette Kolodny, The *Lay of the Land: Metaphor as Experience and History in American Life and Letters* (Chapel Hill: University of North Carolina Press, 1975), 10–25. Cf. Carolyn Merchant, *Ecological Revolutions: Nature, Gender, and Science in New England* (Chapel Hill: University of North Carolina Press, 1989), 101. In 1616, Captain John Smith described the New England seacoast as a virginal garden, "her treasures hauing yet neuer been opened, nor her originalls wasted, consumed, nor abused" (11–12).

63. John Putnam was a farmer in Salem Village whose property was cut off from outside markets by the surrounding land of John Porter, a wealthy Puritan in Salem Town. The families had been at odds since the dam on Porter's land had broken, flooding the Putnam farms nearby. When a new pastor, Samuel Parris, came to the village, the Putnams gave him land to settle on, currying favor but stirring additional resentment. One of the Putnam daughters and the daughter of Rev. Parris were found with the pastor's family slave Tituba, conjuring evil spirits one night in February 1692. In the turmoil that ensued, the Putnams and other villagers blamed the outbreak of evil on the insidious influence of "outsiders." It is interesting that 82 percent of those accused of witchcraft lived in the town, not in the village. See Paul Boyer and Stephen Nissenbaum, *Salem Possessed: The Social Origins of Witchcraft* (Cambridge: Harvard University Press, 1974), 90–91, 110–132.

64. See Carol F. Karlsen, *The Devil in the Shape of a Woman: Witchcraft in Colonial New England* (New York: W. W. Norton, 1987), 223–224.

65. Elizabeth Reis, *Damned Women: Sinners and Witches in Puritan New England* (Ithaca, NY: Cornell University Press, 1999), 100–107.

66. See Sharon Block, *Rape and Sexual Power in Early America* (Chapel Hill: University of North Carolina Press, 2006), 227 and Gordon Sayre, "Native American Sexuality in the Eyes of the Beholders, 1535–1710," in *Sex and Sexuality in Early America*, ed. Merril D. Smith (New York: New York University Press, 1998), 35–54.

67. See Peter Carroll, *Puritanism and the Wilderness: The Intellectual Significance of the New England Frontier* (New York: Columbia University Press, 1969).

68. In 1738, a Connecticut court overruled the claims of the Mohegans to their traditional lands on the grounds that the English families who settled it had "subdued the country from a wild wilderness to a fruitful field." Right of ownership, in Puritan thinking, was based on "improvement of the land." By contrast, the native peoples "enclosed no land" and had no "tame cattle to improve it." See Merchant, *Ecological Revolutions*, 95–112.

69. William Bradford, *Of Plymouth Plantation*, ed. Charles Deane (Boston: Privately Printed, 1856), 114; John Underhill, *Newes from America* (London: F.D. for Peter Cole, 1638), 39–40.

70. William Cronon, *Changes in the Land: Indians, Colonists and the Ecology of New England* (New York: Hill and Wang, 2003), 19–33, 83–126.

71. Timothy Dwight, *Travels in New England and New York*, ed. Barbara Miller Solomon (Cambridge, MA: Belknap Press of Harvard University Press, 1969), II:138–139, I:74.

72. Merchant, *Ecological Revolutions*, 69–111. She observes that "'civilizing' the Indians meant converting their female-dominated shifting horticultural production into male-dominated settled farming" (92).

73. See Rene Girard, *Violence and the Sacred*, trans. Patrick Gregory (Baltimore: Johns Hopkins University Press, 1979) and Gil Bailie, *Violence Unveiled: Humanity at the Crossroads* (New York: Crossroad, 1995).

74. See Emmanuel Levinas, *Totality and Infinity*, trans. Alphonso Lingis (Pittsburgh: Duquesne University Press, 1969), 33; and Wendy Farley, *Eros for the Other* (University Park: Pennsylvania State University Press, 1996), 77.

75. The Puritans delighted in images that mirrored God's presence, savoring creation's beauty and exulting in sexual desire within the covenant of marriage. These were ways of knowing God *kata-phasis*, "according to the image." But the image could quickly become idolatrous if it failed also to carry the soul away from itself (*apo-phasis*, "apart from the image"), pointing to a God beyond all analogies. Kataphatic attachment always required apophatic relinquishment.

76. For the impact of religious thought on American naturalist writers, see Thomas R. Dunlap, *Faith in Nature: Environmentalism as Religious Quest* (Seattle: University of Washington Press, 2004) and Mark Stoll, *Protestantism, Capitalism, and Nature in America* (Albuquerque: University of New Mexico Press, 1997).

77. From the author's notebook, quoted in Lucy Beckett, *Wallace Stevens* (Cambridge: Cambridge University Press, 1974), 172.

78. See A. Hunter Dupree, *Asa Gray, 1810–1888* (Cambridge, MA: Belknap Press of Harvard University Press, 1959), 45.

79. Perry Miller, "From Edwards to Emerson," in *Errand into the Wilderness* (New York: Harper & Row, 1956), 194, 185. Conrad Cherry similarly affirms that "there was, from early Puritanism to Edwards to Emerson, a persistent effort in New England to confront images of God within the physical universe." *Nature and Religious Imagination: From Edwards to Bushnell* (Philadelphia: Fortress Press, 1980), 2.

80. John Burroughs (1837–1921) was raised in a strict Calvinist (Old School Baptist) family. His rejection of orthodox theology is recounted in his *Accepting the Universe* (1920). Joanna Macy charts her own journey from being a Presbyterian youth minister to a Buddhist teacher and Deep Ecologist in her book. *Widening Circles: A Memoir* (Gabriola Island, B.C.: New Society Publishers, 2000).

81. Annie Dillard (1945–) is author of the Pulitzer Prize-winning *Pilgrim at Tinker Creek* (1974) and *Holy the Firm* (1977). Raised as a Presbyterian in Pittsburgh, Pennsylvania, she later converted to the Roman Catholic Church. Kathleen Norris (1947–), author of *Dakota: A Spiritual Geography* (New York: Tichnor & Fields, 1993) became a Benedictine oblate in 1986, while maintaining her membership in the Presbyterian Church in Lemmon, South Dakota. In her case, it wasn't a question of choosing one or the other, but of seeing the two traditions as mutually supportive.

82. "The American nature movement began with failed Protestants," says Dunlap, *Faith in Nature*, 48.

83. Samuel Hopkins (1721–1803) and Joseph Bellamy (1719–1790) were prominent theologians within the New Divinity movement in eighteenth-century New England. Graduates of Yale and students of Edwards, they were Congregationalist pastors in Newport, Rhode Island, and Bethlehem, Connecticut, respectively. Hopkins authored *Sin, through Divine Interposition, an Advantage to the Universe* (1758) and Bellamy a similar work, entitled *The Wisdom of God in the Permission of Sin* (1759). Nathaniel Emmons (1745–1840) was the most radical of these New Divinity men, concluding that God must be the proximate cause of human sinfulness.

84. Joseph Haroutunian, *Piety versus Moralism: The Passing of the New England Theology* (Hamden, CT: Archon Books, 1964), xxii—xxiii, 87–96.

85. John Muir, "Wild Wool," *Overland Monthly* 14 (1875), 361. See Roderick Nash, *Wilderness and the American Mind*, 127. John Muir (1838–1914), activist and writer, organized the Sierra Club in 1892 and lobbied for the federal protection of what became Yosemite National Park. His books include *The Mountains of California* (1894) and *My First Summer in the Sierra* (1911).

86. Letter from Daniel Muir to his son John in 1874, quoted in Richard Cartwright Austin, *Baptized into Wilderness: A Christian Perspective on John Muir* (Atlanta: John Knox Press, 1987), 23. The elder Muir was increasingly drawn to the restoration movement led by Scots immigrant Alexander Campbell on the American frontier.

87. See Thomas Dick, *The Christian Philosopher or, the Connection of Science and Philosophy with Religion* (Brookfield, MA: E. & G. Merriam, 1830), vii.

88. Muir's journals, quoted in Michael P. Cohen, *The Pathless Way: John Muir and American Wilderness* (Madison: University of Wisconsin Press, 1984), 95.

89. John Muir, *John of the Mountains: The Unpublished Journals of John Muir*, ed. Linnie Marsh Wolfe (Madison: University of Wisconsin Press, 1979), 319.

90. Quoted in Austin, *Baptized into Wilderness*, 90.

91. Cohen, *The Pathless Way*, 149.

92. Donald Worster, *The Wealth of Nature: Environmental History and the Ecological Imagination* (New York: Oxford University Press, 1993), 196–200. See Jürgen Moltmann, *God in Creation*, op. cit.; George S. Hendry, *Theology of Nature* (Philadelphia: Westminster Press, 1980); Holmes Rolston, *Environmental Ethics* (Philadelphia: Temple University Press, 1988); Richard Cartwright Austin, *Reclaiming America: Restoring Nature to Culture* (Abingdon, VA: Creekside Press, 1990); Calvin B. DeWitt, *Caring for Creation: Responsible Stewardship of God's Handiwork* (Grand Rapids, MI: Bake Books, 1998); Steven Bouma-Prediger, *For the Beauty of the Earth* (Grand Rapids, MI: Baker Academic, 2001); and Sallie McFague, *The Body of God: An Ecological Theology* (Minneapolis: Fortress Press, 1993).

Chapter 1X: The Whole World Singing: A Journey to Iona and Taizé

1. *Iona Abbey Worship Book* (Glasgow: Wild Goose Publications, 2001), 51.

2. Francis De Sales was born three years after Calvin's death in 1564. De Sales, later the Catholic bishop of Geneva, did meet with an aging Theodore Beza (Calvin's successor) when he was a young priest in the great lake city, but as men of utterly different temperament they had little in common. Things might have been different had Francis and Calvin met.

3. For de Sales's interest in nature, see Michel Tournade, "La nature dans l'oeuvre de François de Sales," an unpublished doctoral dissertation at Université de Metz, France, 1986–1987, 9–29.

4. Ron Ferguson, *Chasing the Wild Goose: The Iona Community* (London: Collins, 1988), 64.

5. Frère Roger Schütz-Marsauche (1915–2005) was tragically stabbed to death during the evening prayer service in Taizé on August 16, 2005, by a thirty-six-year-old schizophrenic woman from Romania.

6. See Cecil M. Jividen, "Taizé and Iona Worship with a Global Perspective," *Reformed Liturgy and Music* 25 (Fall 1991), 171–173.

7. Louis Bouyer, *Orthodox Spirituality and Protestant and Anglican Spirituality*, vol. III of his *History of Christian Spirituality* (London: Burnes & Oates, 1965), 87–94.

8. Ibid., 93.

9. Kathryn Spink, *A Universal Heart: The Life and Vision of Brother Roger of Taizé* (London: SPCK, 1986), 93–94.

10. Rahner spoke of the church of the future as a "little flock" thrust into diaspora. "It will be dependent in everything on faith and on the holy power of the heart, for it will no longer be able to draw any strength at all, or very little, from what is purely institutional." See his *The Christian of the Future* (New York: Herder & Herder, 1967), 80.

Chapter 2

1. John Calvin, *Institutes of the Christian Religion* (1539 edition), I.11. CO 1:286C.

2. Comm. Isaiah 42:14. CO 65:69–70, CTS VIII:302. For Calvin on God as mother see B. A. Gerrish, *Grace and Gratitude*, 38–41.

3. See Bernard Cottret, *Calvin: A Biography*, trans. M. Wallace McDonald (Grand Rapids, MI: W. B. Eerdmans, 2000), 265–287.

4. Comm. Romans 1:19. CO 49:23. Translation by William Bouwsma in *John Calvin: A Sixteenth-Century Portrait* (New York: Oxford University Press, 1988), 103.

5. John Calvin, *Inst.* I.v.1.

6. Calvin mentioned "the proclaiming of [God's] glory on the earth being the very end of our existence." Comm. Ps. 115:17, CO 32:192, CTS XI:358. Leon Wencelius writes about Calvin's conception of beauty, identifying it as very different from that of the Greeks. "For Calvin beauty is not something in itself, living its own life. It is an aspect of God, a reflection of his attributes, the splendor of his activity." *Ubi Deus, ibi pulchritude*, he adds in summarizing Calvin's view. Where God is, there is beauty. See *L'Esthetique de Calvin* (Paris: Société d'édition, 1937), 92.

7. See Susan Schreiner, *The Theater of His Glory: Nature and the Natural Order in the Thought of John Calvin* (Durham, NC: Labyrinth Press, 1991).

8. Lynda G. Christian, *Theatrum Mundi: The History of an Idea* (New York: Garland Publishing, 1987).

9. Brian A. Gerrish, "Calvin's Eucharistic Piety," in *Calvin Studies Society Papers, 1995, 1997: "Calvin and Spirituality," Papers Presented at the 10th Colloquium of the Calvin Studies Society*, May 18–20, 1995, Calvin Theological Seminary (Grand Rapids, MI: CRC Product Services, 1998), 56.

10. Ford Lewis Battles, "God Was Accommodating Himself to Human Capacity," *Interpretation* 31 (1977), 2–3.

11. Elsie Anne McKee urges "a fresh appreciation of the place of worship at the heart of Calvin's theology" in her "Contexts, Contours, Contents: Towards a Description of Calvin's Understanding of Worship," *Calvin Studies Society Papers, 1995, 1997*, 91, 72.

12. *Inst.* Introduction, xxxiii, OS 1:19.

13. "This skillful ordering of the universe is for us a sort of mirror in which we can contemplate God, who is otherwise invisible," Calvin writes in the *Inst.* I.v.1. Cf. I.v.6.

14. *Inst.* I.v.1–12; *Inst.* I.xiv.20; John Calvin, Sermon on Job 9:7–15, CO 33:428; *Inst.* I.vi.4. Diana Butler categorizes the various nature metaphors used by Calvin in "God's Visible Glory: The Beauty of Nature in the Thought of John Calvin and Jonathan Edwards,"

Westminster Theological Journal 52:1 (Spring 1990), 16–19. See also Michael Basse, "*Schöpfungsglaube und Naturerfahrung in Calvins Genesispredigten*," *Theologische Zeitschrift* 60:2 (2004), 145–164.

15. Comm. Rom. 8:20, CO 49:152–153, CNTC 8:173.

16. The word *spectaculum* ("show" or "spectacle") appears 23 times in the *Institutes* and the word *histrio/histrionicus* ("actor"/"acting") another 6 times. See *A Concordance to Calvin's Institutio 1559: Based on the Critical Text of Petrus Barth and Guilelmus Niesel*, ed. Richard F. Wevers (Grand Rapids, MI: Digamma, 1992).

17. Letter of Nov. 28, 1552, CO 14:415. Translation from Bouwsma, *John Calvin*, 178; Letter to Melanchthon, Aug. 23, 1555, CO 15:738.

18. See Ann Blair, *The Theater of Nature: Jean Bodin and Renaissance Science* (Princeton, NJ: Princeton University Press, 1997), 155. Basse, in his article on "*Calvins Genesispredigten*," 148, notes the influence of Erasmus and Budé on Calvin's conception of the *welttheater*.

19. See "Medieval Liturgy as Theater: The Props," in Diana Wood, ed., *The Church and the Arts*, Studies in Church History, vol. 28 (Oxford: Blackwell, 1992), 239–253.

20. Aristotle, *Poetics*, 1452a.

21. E. K. Chambers, *The Medieval Stage* (Oxford: Clarendon Press, 1903), 9–17; and O. B. Hardison, Jr., *Christian Rite and Christian Drama in the Middle Ages* (Baltimore: Johns Hopkins Press, 1965), 178. Miriam Usher Chrisman speaks of "a strong and flourishing popular theater in Strasbourg, Colmar, Marmontier, and other Alsatian towns" in the 1550s. *Lay Culture, Learned Culture: Books and Social Change in Strasbourg, 1480–1599* (New Haven: Yale University Press, 1982), 213.

22. Comm. Daniel 3:3–7, CO 40:620; CTS XII:206. The idea of pretending to be what one is not, being the essence of hypocrisy, was what particularly concerned him about theatrical companies. Sermon on Job 31:24–28, CO 34:686–687.

23. Minutes of the Council of 24 (May 24 and June 15, 1546) and Calvin's letter of July 4, 1546, to William Farel, in CR XI, col. 355 and XXI, cols. 381–383.

24. E. William Monter, *Calvin's Geneva* (New York: John Wiley and Sons, 1967), 109.

25. Martin Bucer, *De honestis ludis*, a section of his book *De Regno Christi* (Basil: Per Ioannem Oporinum, 1557). Bucer encouraged, as a training in classical languages, the performance of Greek and Latin plays, including the comedies of Aristophanes, Plautus, and Terence, as well as the tragedies of Sophocles, Plautus, and Seneca. But he also allowed plays in the vernacular "both for the exercise of youth, and for the honest and not unprofitable delectation of the public." Chambers, *The Elizabethan Stage*, I:240.

26. Randall C. Zachman provides an excellent study of the metaphors Calvin employed in his presentation of the universe as a living image of God. He traces the development of the reformer's images of the world as "theater" and "school" through his writings between 1535 and 1559. See his *Image and Word in the Theology of John Calvin* (Notre Dame, IN: University of Notre Dame Press, 2007), 25–101.

27. He begins with these words: "Nearly all the wisdom we possess . . . consists of two parts: the knowledge of God and of ourselves. . . . No one can look upon himself without immediately turning his thoughts to the contemplation of God, in whom he 'lives and moves.'" *Inst.* I.i.1.

28. *Inst.* I.xiv.20.

29. Jürgen Moltmann, *The Trinity and the Kingdom: The Doctrine of God* (San Francisco: Harper & Row, 1981), 106. While Calvin does not himself use the term

perichoresis, he employs similar terminology in his discussion of the Trinity's inner life. See Philip Butin, "Reformed Ecclesiology: Trinitarian Grace According to Calvin," *Studies in Reformed Theology and History* 2:1 (Winter 1994), 5–8; and Thomas F. Torrance, "Calvin's Doctrine of the Trinity," *Calvin Theological Journal* 25:2 (November 1990), 165–193.

30. *Inst.* I.xiii.18.

31. *Inst.* I.xiii.14. For this insight, I am indebted to David N. Field's doctoral dissertation on "Reformed Theology, Modernity and the Environmental Crisis," from the University of Cape Town, South Africa, 1996.

32. "In a word nothing is certain," he warned, "all things are in a state of disorder. We throw heaven and earth into disorder by our sins." Comm. Jeremiah 5:25. CO 37:635, CTS IX:301. See Peter Wyatt, *Jesus Christ and Creation in the Theology of John Calvin* (Allison Park, PA: Pickwick Publications, 1996), 55–85.

33. See Comm. Psalm 33:7, CO 31:328; CTS IV:543–544 and *Inst.* I.xiv.21.

34. Calvin speaks of sin as a matter of "dullness and ingratitude" in *Inst.* II.vi.1. He adds in *Inst.* III.ii.33, that "our mind . . . has such a dullness that it is always blind to the light of God's truth."

35. *Inst.* I.xvi.1 and I.xiv.17. See Schreiner, *The Theater of His Glory*, 7.

36. Calvin emphasizes the importance of "bearing the cross" (learning self-denial through affliction) in chapter 8 of book III in the *Institutes.*

37. Comm. John 13:31 (CO 47:317; CNTC 5:68), Acts 3:21 (CO 48:72–73; CTS XVIII:153), and Colossians 1:18 (CO 52:86–87; CTS XXI:153–155). Commenting on Paul's insistence that Christ has reconciled all things to himself (in heaven and in earth), Calvin acknowledges that this need not be limited to rational creatures alone. "There were, it is true, no absurdity in extending it to all [creatures] without exception."

38. Comm. Genesis 3:14, CO 23:69; CTS I:167. See also Comm. Isaiah 65:25, where Calvins insists that "Everything shall be fully restored. . . . All that is disordered or confused shall be restored to its proper order." CO 37:433–434; CTS VIII:406.

39. *Inst.* III.ix.5. Emphasis added.

40. Comm. Romans 8:21, CO 49:153; CNTC 8:174.

41. "Nothing in the world is stable except in as far as it is sustained by the hand of God." Comm. Psalm 104:5, CO 32:86; CTS VI:149.

42. Schreiner, *The Theater of His Glory*, 22–30. Schreiner notes that medieval commentators from William of Auvergne to Thomas Aquinas had understood the precarity of the natural world in this way.

43. Sermon on Job 38:8, CO 35:373; Comm. Jeremiah 5:22, CO 37:631–632; CTS IX: 294–295; and Jeremiah 31:35–36, CO 38:698–699; CTS X:143; *Inst.* I.v.6.

44. Comm. Psalm 145:1, CO 32:414; CTS VI:273. See William Bouwsma, "The Spirituality of John Calvin," in Jill Raitt, ed., *Christian Spirituality: High Middle Ages and Reformation* (New York: Crossroad, 1989), 323–324.

45. See Bouwsma, *John Calvin*, 32–48. Richard A. Muller questions this assessment in *The Unaccommodated Calvin: Studies in the Foundation of a Theological Tradition* (New York: Oxford University Press, 2000), 10, 79–98.

46. See William Bouwsma, *John Calvin*; Alister E. McGrath, *A Life of John Calvin: A Study in the Shaping of Western Culture* (Oxford: Basil Blackwell, 1990); and T. H. L. Parker, *John Calvin: A Biography* (London: Dent, 1975).

47. Author's Preface to the Psalms Commentary, CO 31:15–16; CTS IV:xxxvii–xl.

48. Commentary on Psalm 104:5 (CO 32:86; CTS VI:148), Psalm 96:10 (CO 32:41; CTS, VI:57), and Genesis 2:2 (CO 23:32; CTS, I:103–104). Calvin says in his commentary on Eph. 1:8, "Paul wants to teach us that outside Christ all things were upset, but through him they have been reduced to order. . . . The proper state of creatures is to cleave to God. Such an *anakephalaiosis* (restoration of another head) as would bring us back to regular order . . . has been made in Christ. . . . But without Christ, the whole world is as it were a shapeless chaos and frightful confusion." CO 51:283–284; CNTC 11:129.

49. Comm. Psalm 104:31, CO 32:97; CTS VI:170.

50. "*Si vero Dominus spiritum subtrahat, omnia in nihilum rediguntur.*" Comm. Isa. 40:7; CO 37:11. See Werner Krusche, *Das Wirken des Heiligen Geistes nach Calvin* (Göttingen: Vandenhoeck and Ruprecht, 1957), 15. Elsewhere Calvin says, "The earth would be swallowed up every moment were it not preserved by the secret power of God. . . . If the providence of God did not restrain the waters, would they not immediately rush forth to overwhelm the whole earth?" Comm. Ps. 104:5–6, CO 32:87; CTS VI:149–150. He adds in his commentary on Nahum 1:5 that "the mountains cannot continue in their own strength, but as far as they are sustained by the favor of God." CO 43:442–443; CTS XIV:426.

51. Comm. Psalm 104:33, CO 32:97; CTS VI:170.

52. "*Nisi Deus ecclesiam conservet, inversum iri totum naturae ordinem: quia irrita erit mundi creatio, nisi sit aliquis populus qui Deum invocet.*" Comm. Psalm 115:17, CO 32:192. Wilhelm Niesel's translation, in *The Theology of Calvin*, trans., Harold Knight (Philadelphia: Westminster Press, 1956), 64. Emphasis added. Calvin's full statement takes the form of a chiasm, using parallel clauses to emphasize the need to balance the earth's vulnerability with the church's worship. Hence, Christopher Evans at Saint Louis University translates it as follows:

> "If God does not preserve his church,
> the whole order of nature will be dissolved,
> because the creation of the world will be in vain,
> If no people exist to call upon God."

53. *Inst.* III.xx.43.

54. Comm. Isaiah 40:5, CO 37:9; CTS VIII:206.

55. "Not that [God] needs our praise, but it is profitable for ourselves," Calvin argued in Comm. Isa. 12:1, CO 36:250; CTS VII:397. Catherine La Cugna, *God for Us* (San Francisco: Harper, 1973), 338–339. Emphasis added.

56. Pattiann Rogers, "Supposition," in *Fire-Keeper: New and Selected Poems* (Minneapolis: Milkweed Editions, 1994), 35. Pattiann Rogers (1940–) is a prize-winning poet and author of *Firekeeper: New and Selected Poems* (1994), *Song of the World Becoming: New and Collected Poems, 1981–2001* (2001), *Generations* (Penguin, 2004). From a Presbyterian background in Missouri, she joins the careful eye of a naturalist with an intense mystical insight.

57. *Inst.* I.v.5. Emphasis added. John T. McNeill says this statement reflects Lactantius's reference to Seneca as the best of the Stoics, one who "saw nature to be nothing else than God." *Inst.* I.v.5, n. 22. In Calvin's commentary on Psalm 82:6 (where the psalmist says, "You are gods, sons of the Most High, all of you"), he explains that it was "common for the Hebrews to adorn with the title of *God* whatever is rare and excellent," i.e., whatever God has chosen to receive "special marks of his glory." He clearly uses the word "God" in this way in his unusual passage in the *Institutes*.

58. Calvin taught that while the divine nature was uniquely present in Christ's humanity, it is also present and active outside of his body in the universe at large. "Here is

something marvelous: the Son of God descended from heaven in such a way that, without leaving heaven, he willed to be borne in the virgin's womb, to go about the earth, and to hang upon the cross; yet he continuously filled the world even as he had done from the beginning." *Inst.* II.xiii.4. This notion came to be referred to as the "*extra Calvinisticum*," and was used to argue against the Lutheran Eucharistic idea that Christ's divinity could be wholly contained in the local presence of his humanity. Calvinists insisted that since Christ's finite human nature is not capable of containing his infinite divine nature, there is—since the incarnation—an "extra" infinite deity of Christ that is wider than his human nature. This fills the earth with his presence. See chapter 1, notes 40 and 47, and E. David Willis, *Calvin's Catholic Christology: The Function of the So-Called Extra Calvinisticum in Calvin's Theology* (London: Brill, 1966).

59. See Comm. Genesis, Argumentum, CO 23:7–8; CTS 1:59–60. In his Commentary on II Peter 1:4, Calvin says that believers, in partaking of the divine nature, do not share in God's "essence," but in God's "quality." CO 55:446–447; CTS XXII:371. See also Kallistos Ware, "God Hidden and Revealed: The Apophatic Way and the Essence-Energies Distinction," *Eastern Churches Review* VII:2 (1975), 125–136.

60. "The end for which we are created is that the divine name may be celebrated by us on the earth. . . . It is true that there is nothing more acceptable to God, nor any thing of which he more approves, than the publication of his praises. . . ." Comm. Psalm 104:33, CO 32:97; CTS VI:170.

61. Sermon on II Samuel 6. See John Calvin, *Sermons on 2 Samuel, Chapters 1–13*, trans. Douglas Kelly (Carlisle, PA: Banner of Truth Trust, 1992), 267–268.

62. Comm. Psalm 104:1, CO 32:85, CTS VI:145; Comm. I Timothy 4:8, CO 52:300, CNTC 10:244; Comm. Psalm 19:1, CO 31:195, CTS IV:309. Emphasis added.

63. See Margaret Miles, *Desire and Delight: A New Reading of Augustine's Confessions* (New York: Crossroad, 1992), 10f.

64. Comm. Gen. 2:3, CO 23:33; CTS I:106. See Randall Zachman, "The Universe as Living Image of God: Calvin's Doctrine of Creation Reconsidered," *Concordia Theological Quarterly* 61:4 (October, 1997), 299–312.

65. Comm. Gen., Argumentum, CO 23:5–6; CTS I:57.

66. Cornelius Van der Kooi observes that "the image of Calvin held by modern Protestantism has no room for this unrestrained enjoyment." He goes on to note that "Calvin is impressed at the way in which in his experience the presence of God and the sparks of his glory can be perceived by the external senses. . . . All our pores are open, so to speak, and all our senses participate in our encounter with God." *As in a Mirror: John Calvin and Karl Barth on Knowing God* (Leiden: Brill, 2005), 75–76.

67. Max Engammare, "*Plaisir des mets, plaisirs de mots: Irdische Freude bei Calvin*," in Wilhelm H. Neuser and Brian G. Armstrong, eds., *Calvinus Sincerioris Religionis Vindex: Calvin as Protector of the Purer Religion*, Vol. XXVI, Sixteenth Century Essays & Studies (Kirksville, MO: Sixteenth Century Journal Publishers, 1997), 189–208.

68. *Inst.* III.xix.9

69. *Inst.* III.x.2.

70. *Inst.* III.iii.10 and II.iii.12.

71. Sermon on Deuteronomy 28:46–50, CO 28:441. In vision 1 of book II of the *Scivias*, Hildegard saw the blazing fire of God's hand offering to Adam the white flower of the natural world. "Its scent came to the human's nostrils, but he did not taste it with his mouth or touch it with his hands, and thus he turned away and fell into the thickest darkness. . . ."

Columba Hart and Jane Bishop, trans., *Hildegard of Bingen: Scivias* (New York: Paulist Press, 1990), 149.

72. *Inst.* II.ii.4.

73. Comm. I Corinthians 1:21, CO 49:326; CTS XX:85.

74. Sermon on Job 40:20–41:25, CO 35:469. John Calvin, *Sermons on Job*, trans. Arthur Golding (London: George Bishop, 1574), 734. Calvin adds in the same context: "He calls and allures us to him, to the intent that we should find all joyfulness there, but yet we cannot come at him, till we have been utterly beaten down."

75. Sermons on Job 39:8–40:6, Golding Translation, 725, 716, 734. CO 35:415–450.

76. *Inst.* I.v.8.

77. "It appears that if men were taught only by nature, they would hold to nothing certain or solid or clear-cut, but would be so tied to confused principles as to worship an unknown god." *Inst.* I.v.12. See David C. Steinmetz, "Calvin and the Natural Knowledge of God," in his book *Calvin in Context* (New York: Oxford University Press, 1995), 23–32.

78. *Inst.* II.ii.26. Moreover, the sense of pleasure that humans were granted in their creation tends to degenerate into an inordinate desire and lust for lesser things. Ibid., I xv.8 and I.2ii.2.

79. Comm. Hebrews 11:3, CO 33:146; CTS XXII:266.

80. Comm. John 13:31, CO 47:317; CNTC 5:68.

81. Comm. 1 Corinthians 1:17, CO 49:320; CTS XX:73–74.

82. Comm. I Corinthians 1:17, CO 49:321; CTS XX:76.

83. John Calvin, "*A tous amateurs de Iesus Christ et de son evangile, salut*" (preface to the French translation of the New Testament by his cousin, Pierre Robert Olivetan, 1534). CO 9:795. Joseph Haroutunian's translation, in *Calvin: Commentaries* (Philadelphia: Westminster Press, 1958), 60.

84. Comm. Psalm 65:11, CO 31:609; CTS V:465.

85. John Calvin, *Dilucida explicatio . . . de vera participatione carnis et sanguinis Christi . . .* (1561), CO 9:457–524; *The Clear Explanation of Sound Doctrine concerning the True Partaking of the Flesh and Blood of Christ in the Holy Supper* in *Calvin: Theological Treatises*, ed. J. K. S. Reid (London: SCM, 1954), 319.

86. Comm. Psalm 148:3, CO 32:433; CTS VI:304–305; Comm. Jeremiah 10:1–2, CO 38:59; CTS IX:8.

87. Comm. Ps. 24:1, CO 31:244; CTS IV:402; Calvin, *Congregation sur la divinité de Jésus Christ*, CO 47:480–481; cited in Schreiner, 80; Comm. Acts 17:27, CTS XIX:167.

88. See Peter A. Huff, "Calvin and the Beasts: Animals in John Calvin's Theological Discourse," *Journal of the Evangelical Theology Society* 42:1 (March 1999), 67–75.

89. Comm. Psalm 96:11, CO 32:42; CTS VI:58.

90. Comm. Joel 2:22, CO 42:559; CTS XIV:81; Comm. Psalm 19:1, CO 35:437, CTS IV:309.

91. Jürgen Moltmann observes that the word *apokaradokía* ("longing" or "yearning") used by Paul in this passage is said to be exercised by believers (8:23), by the rest of creation (8:19), and by the Holy Spirit as well (8:26). *God in Creation: A New Theology of Creation and the Spirit of God* (Minneapolis: Fortress Press, 1993), 101.

92. Comm. Romans 8:19–20, CO 49:151–152; CNTC 8:172–173.

93. Comm. Isaiah 1:3, CO 36:30; CTS VII:41. See also Susan Schreiner, *Where Shall Wisdom Be Found? Calvin's Exegesis of Job from Medieval and Modern Perspectives* (Chicago: University of Chicago Press, 1994), 121–146; *Inst.* I.v.15.

94. *Inst.* I.v.15. Pointing to Jesus's concern for sparrows, for example, he rejected "the opinion of those who imagine a universal providence of God which does not stoop to the especial care of any particular creature." *Inst.* I.xvii.6.

95. Sermon on Deuteronomy 22:5–8, CO 28:24.

96. Carlos M. M. Eire, *War against the Idols: The Reformation of Worship from Erasmus to Calvin* (Cambridge: Cambridge University Press, 1986), 213–214. See *Inst.* I.xii.3.

97. "Every religion has both magical (achievement-oriented) and celebrative (expressive or *ludic*) processes deeply imbedded in its ritual system." Ronald L. Grimes, *Beginnings in Ritual Studies* (Washington, D.C.: University Press of America, 1982), 48.

98. See Victor Turner's books, *The Ritual Process: Structure and Anti-Structure* (Chicago: Aldine Pub. Co., 1969) and *Anthropology of Performance* (New York: PAJ Publications, 1986).

99. "The reinforcement, if not the actual creation, of social order is perhaps the most obvious of ritual's functions," says Tom F. Driver, in *The Magic of Ritual* (San Francisco: Harper, 1991), 132.

100. Richard Schnechner, *Essays in Performance Theory, 1970–1976* (New York: Drama Book Specialists, 1977), 75–79.

101. *Inst.* III.xx.3–6. In his Genevan Catechism, Calvin said that, ". . . when the faithful feel themselves cold and sluggish or somewhat indisposed to pray, they should forthwith flee to God and demand that they be inflamed with the fiery darts of his Spirit, so as to be rendered fit for prayer." *Catechismus ecclesiae Genevensis* (1542), OS 2:115. See J. K. S. Reid, ed., *Calvin: Theological Treatises*, 121.

102. By contrast, Ulrich Zwingli wrote in 1523 that, "As soon as it can be done, this barbarous mumbling [music in the mass] should be dispatched from the churches." Music was thus banned from Zurich between 1525 and 1598. Cited in Jeffrey T. VanderWilt, "John Calvin's Theology of Liturgical Song," *Christian Scholar's Review* XXV:1 (1995), 72.

103. John Calvin, *La forme des prieres et chantz ecclesiastiques* (1542), OS 2:15–16. Translation by Ford Lewis Battles, in "John Calvin: The Form of Prayers and Songs of the Church, 1542, Letter to the Reader," *Calvin Theological Journal* 15:2 (November 1980), 163. Hereafter referred to as Letter to the Reader.

104. Comm. Isaiah 42:12, CO 37:68; CTS VIII:300.

105. See "John Calvin and Choral Music," in Richard C. Gamble, ed., *Calvin's Early Writings and Ministry* (New York: Garland Publishing, 1992), 188. Calvin's first Psalter had been published for use in his Strasbourg congregation in 1539, but by 1549 the entire Psalter could be sung through (every seventeen weeks) in the churches of Geneva. See Witvliet, "The Spirituality of the Psalter: Metrical Psalms in Liturgy and Life in Calvin's Geneva," *Calvin Theological Journal* 32:2 (November 1997), 287; and VanderWilt, "John Calvin's Theology of Liturgical Song," 63.

106. Comm. Genesis 4:20, CO 23:100; translation from VanderWilt, 70. With respect to Calvin's recommendation that children lead in music, see his *Articles of 1537*, OS 1:275. Cited in Witvliet, "Spirituality of the Psalter," 280.

107. Cited in Witvliet, "The Spirituality of the Psalter," 276.

108. Calvin, *Inventoire de reliques*, CO 6:411. Eire, *War against the Idols*, 215. Eire states: "Calvin emphasized God's loss of honor so much that at times he even seems to refer to a gross transference of glory, almost as if he were speaking of an accounting ledger where the debts due to God are instead paid to the fictitious divinities dreamed up by man" (214).

109. See Ronald S. Wallace, *Calvin's Doctrine of the Word and Sacrament* (Edinburgh: Oliver and Boyd, 1953), 199–210; and B. A. Gerrish, *Grace and Gratitude: The Eucharistic Theology of John Calvin* (Minneapolis: Fortress Press, 1993).

110. See Belden C. Lane, "The Oral Tradition and its Implications for Contemporary Preaching," *Journal for Preachers* VII:3 (Spring 1984), 17–25.

111. Comm. Psalm 33:6, CO 31:327; CTS IV:543; Bouwsma, *John Calvin*, 114. Philip W. Butin says, "Calvin assumed that speech has the power to enact all the other necessary elements of true worship." See "John Calvin's Humanist Image of Popular Late-Medieval Piety and its Contribution to Reformed Worship," *Calvin Theological Journal* 29:2 (November 1994), 429.

112. Comm. Haggai 1:12, CO 44:95; CTS XV:343.

113. Comm. Haggai 1:12, CO 44:94, CTS XV:341; Comm. Isaiah 50:10, CO 37:224, CTS VIII:61; Comm. Isaiah 11:4, CO 36:240, CTS VII:381.

114. See John Langshaw Austin, "Performative-Constative," in John R. Searle, ed., *The Philosophy of Language* (London: Oxford University Press, 1971), 13–22. Philosopher of language J. L. Austin argues in his book *How to Do Things with Words* (Oxford: Clarendon Press, 1962) that there are cases (as in liturgical acts) when "to *say* something is to *do* something" (6–12).

115. Edmund Leach, quoted in S. J. Tambiah, "The Magical Power of Words," *Man: The Journal of the Royal Anthropological Institute* 3:2 New Series (June, 1968), 175.

116. John Calvin, Letter to the Reader, 163–164, OS 2:16. See VanderWilt, "John Calvin's Theology of Liturgical Song," 70–71.

117. See Plato, *Republic* 3:12, 401B; and Witvliet, "The Spirituality of the Psalter," 283. Letter to the Reader, 164, OS 2:17.

118. By calling on the Father's name, "we invoke the presence both of his providence . . . and of his power . . . We call him to reveal himself as wholly present to us." *Inst.* III.xx.2.

119. *Inst.* III.xx.3.

120. Comm. Psalm 115:17, CO 32:192.

121. Comm. Psalm 77:17, CO 31:719; CTS V:222. Emphasis added.

122. Eire, *War against the Idols*, 212–228.

123. Sermon on Job 39:22–35, CO 35:432.

124. Calvin says that for the angels the church is "a theater in which they marvel at the varied and manifold wisdom of God." *Inst.* III.xx.23.

125. Nicholas Wolterstorff, *Until Justice and Peace Embrace: The Kuyper Lectures for 1981 Delivered at the Free University of Amsterdam* (Grand Rapids, MI: Eerdmans, 1983), 160.

126. Comm. Gen 2:3, CO 23:33; CTS 1:105–106.

127. Moltmann, *God in Creation*, 276.

128. Tom Driver argues "that the life-threatening pollution of the earth's oceans, streams, and atmosphere is partly due to the neglect and decline of rituals that once regulated people's relation to their habitat." Tom F. Driver, *The Magic of Ritual* (San Francisco: Harper, 1991), 32.

129. Moltmann, *God in Creation*, 197.

130. Burton Scott Easton, trans., *The Apostolic Tradition of Hippolytus* (Cambridge: Cambridge University Press, 1934), 56.

131. *Apocalypse of Peter*, in A. Mingana, *Woodbrooke Studies* (Cambridge: W. Heffer & Sons, 1931), III, 114–115.

132. See Laura Hobgood-Oster, *Holy Dogs and Asses: Animals in the Christian Tradition* (Urbana: University of Illinois Press, 2008); and Andrew Linzey, *Animals and Christianity* (New York: Crossroad, 1988).

133. Lukas Vischer, "A Time of Creation," *Ecumenical Review* 51:4 (October 1999), 394–400.

Chapter 2X: Can We Chant Psalms with All God's Creatures?

1. David Dickson, *A Brief Explication of the Last Fifty Psalms from Ps. 100 to the End* (London: T. R. & E. M. for Thos. Johnson, 1654), 368.

2. Raphael Brown, trans., *The Little Flowers of St. Francis* (Garden City, NY: Hanover House, 1958), 131–133.

3. Calvin, "Letter to the Reader," in *The Form of Prayers*, OS 2:15–17. See Charles Garside, *The Origins of Calvin's Theology of Music, 1536–1543* (Philadelphia: American Philosophical Society, 1979), 32–34.

4. Theodore Hiebert, *The Yahwist's Landscape: Nature and Religion in Early Israel* (New York: Oxford University Press, 1996).

5. For studies of nature in the Psalms, see Terence E. Fretheim, "Nature's Praise of God in the Psalms," *Ex Auditu* III (1987), 16–30; Daniel Grossberg, "The Literary Treatment of Nature in Psalms," in Meir Lubetski, Claire Gottlieb, and Sharon Keller, eds., *Boundaries of the Ancient Near Eastern World* (Sheffield: Sheffield Academic Press, 1998), 69–87; Benedict Janecko, "Ecology, Nature, Psalms," in *The Psalms and Other Studies on the Old Testament*, eds., Jack C. Knight and Lawrence A. Sinclair (Nashotah, WI: Nashotah House Seminary, 1990), 96–108; R. J. Raja, "Eco-Spirituality in the Psalms," *Vidyajyoti Journal of Theological Reflection* LIII:12 (December 1989), 637–650; and Stacy R. Obenhaus, "The Creation Faith of the Psalmists," *Trinity Journal* 21:2 (2000), 131–142.

6. The Earth Bible Project was initiated by scholars in Adelaide, South Australia, who began "reading the Bible from the perspective of the earth"—viewing the earth as "a living entity capable of raising its voice in celebration and against injustice." See, for example, Norman C. Habel, ed., *The Earth Story in the Psalms and the Prophets* (Sheffield, UK: Sheffield Academic Press, 2001).

7. Calvin, Comm. Psalms, Author's Preface, CTS IV:xxxvii. See also Herman J. Selderhuis, *Calvin's Theology of the Psalms* (Grand Rapids, MI: Baker Academic, 2007), 61–87, and Allan M. Harman, "The Psalms and Reformed Spirituality," *Reformed Theological Review* 53:2 (April—July 1994), 53–62.

8. Esther de Waal, *The Celtic Way of Prayer* (London: Hodder & Stoughton, 1996), 180–181.

9. W. Stanford Reid, "The Battle Hymns of the Lord: Calvinist Psalmody in the Sixteenth Century," *Sixteenth Century Essays and Studies* 2 (1971), 52.

10. Walter Brueggemann, *Israel's Praise: Doxology against Idolatry and Ideology* (Philadelphia: Fortress Press, 1988), 4–38. See also Brueggemann's article on "The Psalms as Prayer" in *Reformed Liturgy and Music* XXIII:1 (Winter 1989), 13–26.

11. Brueggemann, *Israel's Praise*, 42.

12. See Larry Rasmussen, *Earth Community, Earth Ethics* (Maryknoll, NY: Orbis Books, 1998), 27.

13. R. C. D. Jasper and G. J. Cuming, trans., *Prayers of the Eucharist: Early and Reformed* (New York: Pueblo Publishing, 1987), 104–106.

14. H. Wheeler Robinson, *The Christian Doctrine of Man* (Edinburgh: T. & T. Clark, 1952), 12–13.

15. Edmund Colledge and James Walsh, trans., *Julian of Norwich: Showings* (New York: Paulist Press, 1978), 186.

16. For reflections on the sensitivity and intelligence of more-than-human creatures, see David Abram, *The Spell of the Sensuous* (New York: Vintage Books, 1997); Karl von Frisch, *The Dance, Langague, and Orientation of Bees* (Cambridge: Harvard University Press, 1967); Cleve Backster and Flora Powers, *Primary Perception: The Evidence of Sentience in Plants, Living Foods, and Human Cells* (Ana, CA: White Rose Millennium Press, 2003); Peter Tompkins and Christopher Bird, *The Secret Life of Plants* (New York: Harper Collins, 1989); Donald Griffin, *Animal Minds* (Chicago: University of Chicago Press, 1992); and Derrick Jensen, *A Langauge Older than Words* (New York: Context Books, 2000).

17. See Evelyn Fox Keller, *A Feeling for the Organism: The Life and Work of Barbara McClintock* (New York: W. H. Freeman, 1983), and L. O. McMurry, *George Washington Carver: Scientist and Symbol* (New York: Oxford University Press, 1981).

18. Johannes Baptist Metz, "Suffering from God: Theology as Theodicy," *Pacifica* 5 (1992), 284–285.

19. See Katherine M. Hayes, *"The Earth Mourns": Prophetic Metaphor and Oral Aesthetic* (Atlanta: Society of Biblical Literature, 2002).

20. Calvin, in his commentary on Micah 6:1–2, notes that the prophet is summoned to plead his case against his people before the mountains and hills. He says the very rocks will attend with "more attention and docility" than God's hard-hearted people. "There is not one of the elements which is not to bear witness respecting the obstinacy of this people; for the voice of God will penetrate to the farthest roots of the earth . . . ," adds Calvin. CO 43:385–386; CTS XIV:328–329. Cf. Jeremiah 2:12–13 where the heavens are said to be appalled and shocked at the wickedness of men and women.

21. Clarissa Pinkola Estes, *Women Who Run with the Wolves* (New York: Ballantine Books, 1995), 23–24.

Chapter 3

1. John Milton, *Paradise Lost* (1667), 8.510–520. Milton (1608–1674) was a graduate of Christ's College, Cambridge, and the greatest of the Puritan poets.

2. Lewis Bayly, *The Practice of Piety*, 1611, (London: Hamilton, Adams, 1842), 66.

3. Perry Miller, *The New England Mind: The Seventeenth Century* (Boston: Beacon Press, 1939), 3–34.

4. Margaret Miles, *Desire and Delight: A New Reading of Augustine's Confessions* (New York: Crossroad, 1992), 20–37.

5. Bayly, *The Practice of Piety*, 66.

6. Thomas B. Macaulay, *The History of England from the Accession of James II* (Philadelphia: Porter & Coates, 1882), 109.

7. Karl Barth, *Church Dogmatics*, eds. G. W. Bromiley and T. F. Torrance (Edinburgh: T. T. Clark, 1936), II/1, 650–651.

8. Thomas Watson, *A Body of Divinity, contained in Sermons upon the Assembly's Catechism* (1692), ed. George Rogers (London: Passmore and Alabaster, 1898), 17. Thomas

Watson (1620–1686) was Puritan vicar of St. Stephen's, Walbrook. Anthony Tuckney (1599–1670) was Regis Professor of Divinity at Cambridge, having earlier chaired the committee of the Westminster Assembly.

9. Spousal imagery appeared in all four types of Puritan piety, as Jerald C. Brauer has defined them. Nomistic, evangelical, rationalist, and mystical strains of Puritan spirituality, he argued, can be identified in Thomas Cartwright, Richard Sibbes, John Milton, and Francis Rous, respectively. See "Types of Puritan Piety," *Church History* 56 (March, 1987), 38–58.

10. Sir Francis Rous (1579–1659) was a member of Parliament and Puritan divine educated at Pembroke College, Oxford. As a Presbyterian, he participated in the Westminster Assembly, but in 1649 he went over to the Independents. His works include *The Art of Happiness* (1619), *Academia Coelestics: The Heavenly University: or, The Highest School Where Alone Is That Highest Teaching, the Teaching of the Heart* (1639), and an edition of the Psalms in English meter.

11. Francis Rous, *The Mysticall Marriage, or Experimental Discoveries of the Heavenly Marriage betweene a Soul and Her Savior* (London: William Iones, 1631), "A Reason of this Worke," A4.

12. Ibid., 13.

13. See Jean Leclercq, *The Love of Learning and Desire for God*, trans., Catharine Misrahi (New York: New American Library, 1961).

14. Margaret Miles, "On Reading Augustine and on Augustine's Reading," *The Christian Century* 114:17 (May 21–28, 1997), 511.

15. Augustine, *De Musica*, 6.11.29. Quoted in Miles, *Desire and Delight*, 100.

16. Augustine, *Confessions*, 10.8, trans., Maria Boulding (New York: Vintage Books, 1998), 202.

17. Ibid., 10.9. Quoted in Miles, *Desire and Delight*, 56.

18. Emmanuel, Pembroke, Christ's, and St. John's Colleges at Cambridge were particularly known as hotbeds of Puritanism in this period, training such prominent English divines as Thomas Cartwright, William Perkins, William Ames, and John Milton, as well as American Puritans like John Cotton and John Winthrop.

19. Quoted in William J. Bouwsma, "The Spirituality of John Calvin," *Christian Spirituality: High Middle Ages and Reformation*, ed. Jill Raitt (New York: Crossroad, 1989), 320–324.

20. See, for example, John Calvin's *Institutes* III.iii.1; IV.xvii.9, 12. A study of Calvin's use of the words for "enjoying" (*fruor*) and "taking delight" (*delecto*) suggests an interesting appropriation of Augustinian language. See Richard F. Wevers's *Concordance to Calvin's Institutio, 1559* (Grand Rapids, MI: Digamma Publishers, 1992). *Institutes* III.x.2, with its stunning celebration of natural beauty, is especially suggestive in its contrast of *frui* and *uti*, the enjoyment of creation's loveliness as contrasted with its necessary use.

21. Michael P. Winship, "Behold the Bridegroom Cometh! Marital Imagery in Massachusetts Preaching, 1630–1730," *Early American Literature* 27:3 (1992), 175.

22. Ibid., 176.

23. Drawing on the trope of nature as a "second book," Steele said that the farmer "hath an advantage herein above most other callings, in that his business lies among trees, and flowers, and grass, and cattle, and even all the creatures of God. And God's creatures are a book in Folio, each creature is a word, and each part of it a letter, out of which an holy heart may spell exceeding much of God. . . ." Steele, *The Husbandman's*

Calling: Shewing the Excellencies, Temptations, Graces, Duties, &c of the Christian Husbandman (London: George Calvert and Ralph Simpson, 1681), 33. Richard Steele (1629–1692) was the son of a farmer who became a non-conformist minister and chaplain of Corpus Christi College, Oxford.

24. Bartholomew Ashwood, *The Heavenly Trade, or the Best Merchandizing: The Only Way to Live Well in Impoverishing Times* (London: Samuel Lee, 1679); John Collinges, *The Weavers Pocket-Book: or Weaving Spiritualized* (London: A. Maxwell, 1675); John Flavell, *Husbandry Spiritualized: or, the Heavenly Use of Earthly Things* (London: Robert Boulter, 1669); and John Flavell, *Navigation Spiritualized, or, a New Compass for Seaman* (London: Thomas Fabian, 1682).

25. Cotton Mather, *The Religious Marriner: A Brief Discourse* (Boston: Green & Allen, 1700); *The Fisher-man's Calling, a Brief Essay* (Boston: T. Green, 1712); and *Agricola, or the Religious Husbandman* (Boston: D. Henchman, 1727).

26. Robert K. Merton, echoing the earlier work of Dorothy Stimson, notes that Puritans made up 62 percent of the initial membership of the Royal Society. See his *Science, Technology, and Society in Seventeenth-Century England* (New York: Harper, 1970), 114.

27. See Mario Praz, *Studies in Seventeenth-Century Imagery* (Rome: Edizioni Di Storia E Litteratura, 1964), p. 145.

28. They reversed the order of the three ends of marriage listed in the Anglican Prayer Book, for example. Procreation, the restraint of sin, and mutual comfort had been the traditional order, but the Puritans made the last first, declaring mutual help and enjoyment ("a remedy for loneliness") to be the chief end of Christian marriage. As Puritan divine Alexander Niccholes told his parishioners, "In thy Marriage, the very name whereof should portend to thee Merry-age, thou not only unitest unto thy selfe a friend, and comfort for society, but also a companion for pleasure. . . ." See his *Discourse of Marriage and Wiving* (London: N.O., 1615), 5.

29. Thomas Aquinas, in his *Summa Theologica*, part 3 (supplement), qu. 41, art. 4, had said that "If the motive for the marriage act be. . . . that [the husband and wife] may beget children for the worship of God, it is meritorious. But if the motive be lust . . . it is a venial sin."

30. William Whately, *A Bride Bush, or a Direction for Married Persons* (London, 1616), pp. 18–20; and William Gouge, *Of Domestical Duties* (London: J. Haviland, 1622), 221. See also Anthony Fletcher, "The Protestant Idea of Marriage in Early Modern England," in Anthony Fletcher and Peter Roberts, eds., *Religion, Culture and Society in Early Modern Britian: Essays in Honor of Patrick Collinson* (Cambridge: Cambridge University Press, 1994), 161–181; Roland Frye, "The Teachings of Classical Puritanism on Conjugal Love," *Studies in the Renaissance* 2 (1955), 155–156; Edmund Leites, "The Duty to Desire: Love, Friendship and Sexuality in Some Puritan Theories of Marriage," *Comparative Civilizations Review* 3 (1979), 40–82; and Daniel Doriani, "The Puritans, Sex, and Pleasure," *Westminster Theological Journal* 53 (Spring 1991), 125–143.

31. James Durham, *An Exposition of the Song of Solomon* (1668; reprint, Edinburgh: Banner of Truth Trust, 1840), 13–14. James Durham (1622–1658) served as a captain in the Scottish army in the English Civil War and was later appointed professor of Divinity at Glasgow University. He was best known for his *Key to the Canticles*, a volume of 460 pages.

32. Benjamin Whichcote (1609–1683) was himself a graduate of Emmanuel College, later serving as provost of King's College, Cambridge. Other Cambridge Platonists included prominent figures like Ralph Cudworth, Henry More, and John Smith, all of

Puritan background. See Daniel W. Howe, "The Cambridge Platonists of Old England and the Cambridge Platonists of New England," *Church History* 57 (1988), 470–485.

33. *The Works of the Learned Benjamin Whichcote* (Aberdeen: J. Chalmers, 1751), 3:176, 190.

34. See Charles E. Raven, *Natural Religion and Christian Theology:* The Gifford Lectures, 1951, First Series, Science and Religion (Cambridge: Cambridge University Press, 1953), 109.

35. Richard Sibbes, "The Spouse, Her Earnest Desire after Christ," published in *Two Sermons* (London: T. Cotes, 1638), reprinted in *The Works of Richard Sibbes*, 2:203–204. Richard Sibbes (1577–1635) was a graduate of St. John's, Cambridge, later becoming a lecturer at Holy Trinity, Cambridge. Sibbes was a friend of Abp. James Usher, and his book *The Bruised Reede and Smoaking Flax* (1630) exercised a profound influence on Richard Baxter.

36. Puritan marriage manuals regularly spoke of the importance of choosing one's love and then loving one's choice. While they knew that desire initially draws lovers to each other, they expected covenant faithfulness subsequently to release a still greater affective response. See William and Malleville Haller, "The Puritan Art of Love," 262.

37. See Derk Visser's article on "Covenant" in the *Oxford Encyclopedia of the Reformation*, ed. Hans J. Hillerbrand (New York: Oxford University Press, 1996), vol. I, 442–443. Thomas Doolittle of Pembroke College wrote a personal covenant in 1693, expressing his own experience of grace by declaring, "I do solemnly here join my self in marriage-covenant to [Christ, my head and husband], that he may be mine, and I may be his." From the unpaged "Memoir" at the beginning of his book, *A Complete Body of Practical Divinity* (London, 1723).

38. Richard Baxter, *The Saints Everlasting Rest* (London: Epworth Press, 1962), 143.

39. Ibid., 42.

40. Ibid., 40.

41. Ibid., 167–168.

42. Baxter, *The Christian Directory*, published in *The Practical Works of the Rev. Richard Baxter* (London: James Duncan, 1830), 353.

43. Ignatius Loyola, *Spiritual Exercises*, 48. Constitutions of the Society of Jesus, 102. On the importance of desire in Ignatian spirituality, see Edward Kinerk, S.J., "Eliciting Great Desires," *Studies in the Spirituality of the Jesuits* 16 (November, 1984), 1–29.

44. Baxter, *Saints Everlasting Rest*, 42, 387.

45. Richard Sibbes, "Balaam's Wish" (London: E. Purslow, 1639), reprinted in *Works of Richard Sibbes*, ed. Alexander B. Grosart (Carlisle, PA: Banner of Truth Trust, 1983), 7:11–12.

46. John Cotton, *A Brief Exposition with Practical Observations upon the Whole Book of Canticles* (London: T.R. & E.M., 1655), 3. John Cotton (1584–1652) was another Puritan divine from Trinity College, Cambridge, who served as minister in Boston, England, before immigrating to Boston, Massachusetts, in 1633.

47. John Bailey, *Man's Chief End to Glorifie God; or Some Brief Sermon-notes on I Cor. 10:21* (Boston: Samuel Green, 1689), 148. John Bailey (1643–1697) was from Blackburn, Lancashire, where he had been ordained a Congregationalist minister in 1670. Subsequently imprisoned for his nonconformity, he moved to Ireland and then on to New England in 1683.

48. Francis Rous, "The Art of Happiness," published in *Treatises and Meditations*, 91.

49. Referring to Hosea 2:21, Joseph Caryl spoke of God as having "betrothed himself in mercies and loving kindness" to all the creatures of earth. Joseph Caryl, *An Exposition*

with Practical Observations: Continued upon the Eleventh, Twelfth, Thirteenth, and Fourteenth Chapters of the Book of Job (London: J. Macock, 1652), 207. James Turner Johnson discusses "The Covenant Idea and the Puritan Doctrine of Marriage" in the first chapter of his *A Society Ordained by God: English Puritan Marriage Doctrine in the First Half of the Seventeenth Century* (Nashville: Abingdon, 1970), 19–49.

50. Robert Crofts, *The Lover, or Nuptiall Love* (London, 1638); John Allin, *The Spouse of Christ Coming out of Affliction, Leaning upon Her Beloved* (Cambridge: Samuel Green, 1672); Richard Sibbes, *The Bride's Longing for Her Bridegroom's Second Coming* (1638); John Flavell, *Husbandry Spiritualized: or, the Heavenly Use of Earthly Things* (London: Robert Boulter, 1669); Ralph Austen, *The Spirituall Use of an Orchard* (Oxford: L. Lichfield, 1653); and Thomas Taylor, *Meditations from the Creatures* (London: J. Bartlet, 1635).

51. Marital and horticultural images were regularly combined in Puritan spiritual writing, especially in connection with the rhetoric of the garden in the Song of Songs. Edward Taylor spoke of "Christ's Curious Garden fenced in/With Solid Walls of Discipline/Well wed, and watered, and made full trim." In language such as this the "wedding of the land" became intimately joined to the physical and spiritual union of husbands and wives. See Taylor's poem, "The Soule Seeking Church-Fellowship," from *Gods Determinations*, in *The Poems of Edward Taylor*, ed. Donald S. Stanford (New Haven: Yale University Press, 1960), 454.

52. Thomas Hooker, *The Application of Redemption* (London: P. Cole, 1659), 37. See Edmund S. Morgan, *The Puritan Family: Religion and Domestic Relations in Seventeenth-Century New England* (New York: Harper & Row, 1966), 61–62. Thomas Hooker (1586–1647) had been educated at Emmanuel College, Cambridge. He emigrated to Boston in 1633, thereafter moving to the Connecticut valley where Hartford was founded in 1636. His *Survey of the Sum of Church Discipline* (1648) helped to define the character of American Congregationalism.

53. Amanda Porterfield, *Feminine Spirituality in America* (Philadelphia: Temple University Press, 1980), 49. See also her book *Female Piety in Puritan New England* (New York: Oxford University Press, 1992). Cf. Morgan, *The Puritan Family*, 29–64.

54. John Cotton, *A Practical Commentary, or: An Exposition with Observations, Reasons and Uses upon the First Epistle Generall of John* (London: R.I. and E.C., 1656), 126.

55. See also Elizabeth Maddock Dillon's "Nursing Fathers and Brides of Christ," in Janet Moore Lindman and Michele Lise Tarter, eds., *A Centre of Wonders: The Body in Early America* (Ithaca, NY: Cornell University Press, 2001).

56. Nathanael Culverwel, *An Elegant and Learned Discourse of the Light of Nature, with Severall Other Treatises* (Oxford: Tho. Williams, 1669), 149. Nathanael Culverwel (1619–1651) moved in the circle of Cambridge Platonists and was best known for his book *An Elegant and Learned Discourse of the Light of Nature* (1652).

57. William Bates, *A Discourse of Divine Meditation*, in Wallace, *Spirituality of the Later English Puritans*, 102–103. William Bates (1625–1699), vicar of St. Dunstan-in-the-West, was ejected from his pulpit in 1661 for refusing to use the Book of Common Prayer.

58. John Bailey, *Man's Chief End to Glorifie God* (Boston: Samuel Green, 1689), 9–10.

59. John Flavell, *Husbandry Spiritualized*, Epistle Dedicatory, 3. John Flavell (1630–1691) was a Presbyterian divine trained at Oxford who was ejected from his Dartmouth pulpit by the Act of Uniformity. He wrote a companion volume to this work entitled *Navigation Spiritualized* (1671), based in part on his own experiences at sea.

60. Ibid., Epistle Dedicatory, 1.

61. Baxter, *The Christian Directory*, 2:377. Cf. His evocation of the delights of nature in *The Saints' Everlasting Rest*, 168ff.

62. See Taylor's poem "Upon Wedlock, and Death of Children," in *Early New England Meditative Poetry: Anne Bradstreet and Edward Taylor*, ed. Charles E. Hambrick-Stowe (New York: Paulist Press, 1988), 133. Edward Taylor (1644?–1729) was an English-born minister and physician who lived in Boston and later Westfield, Massachusetts.

63. Ralph Austen, *A Treatise of Fruittrees . . . Together with The Spirituall Use of an Orchard* (Oxford: L. Lichfield, 1653), 27.

64. Edward Taylor, Meditation 22, First Series, on Phil. 2:9, "God Hath Highly Exalted Him," in *Early New England Meditative Poetry*, 189.

65. Meditation 120, Second Series, on Song 5:14, "Hi Cheeks Are as a Bed of Spices," in *Early New England Meditative Poetry*, 258.

66. Taylor's Meditation 23, First Series, on Song 4:8, "My Spouse," in *Early New England Meditative Poetry*, 190–191.

67. Elizabeth Singer (1674–1737) was already a published poet by the time she married Thomas Rowe, another poet, in 1710. They were only married a few years before his death by consumption in 1715. The Puritan hymn-writer Isaac Watts published her *Devout Exercises of the Heart* after her death in 1737.

68. Wendy Farley, *Eros for the Other: Retaining Truth in a Pluralistic World* (University Park: Pennsylvania State University Press, 1996), 69.

69. Emmanuel Levinas, *Totality and Infinity: An Essay on Exteriority*, trans. Alphonso Lingis (Pittsburgh, PA: Duquesne University Press, 1969), p. 33. It is important to notice that, for Levinas, the "other" does not necessarily refer to God. Levinas (1906–1995) was born in Lithuania, but lived most of his life in France, teaching philosophy at the University of Poitiers.

70. Ibid., 34.

71. Gregory of Nyssa had said, "This truly is the vision of God: never to be satisfied in the desire to see him. But one must always, by looking at what he can see, rekindle his desire to see more." *The Life of Moses*, 2:239.

72. Elizabeth Rowe, "CANT. Chap. V.," in *The Poetry of Elizabeth Singer Rowe (1674–1737)*, ed. Madeleine F. Marshall (Lewiston, NY: Edwin Mellon Press, 1987), 205.

73. Ashwood, *Heavenly Trade*, 330.

74. Elizabeth Rowe, *Devout Exercises of the Heart*, ed. Isaac Watts (Dedham: Nathaniel & Benjamin Heaton, 1796), 65.

75. Ibid., 72, 97.

76. Ibid., 76.

77. Anne Bradstreet, "Another (Letter to Her Husband, Absent upon Public Employment)," *The Works of Anne Bradstreet*, ed. Jeannine Hensley (Cambridge, MA: Belknap Press of Harvard University Press, 1967), 229. Anne Dudley Bradstreet (1612?–1672) came to Massachusetts Bay with her new husband Simon on board the *Arbella* with John Winthrop in 1630. They settled eventually in Andover, where, as a writer of public and private poetic works, she was best known for her "Contemplations" and other poems.

78. On Puritan psychology and the dynamics of spiritual growth, see Charles Lloyd Cohen, *God's Caress: The Psychology of Puritan Religious Experience* (New York: Oxford University Press, 1986); David Leverenz, *The Language of Puritan Feeling: An Exploration in Literature, Psychology, and Social History* (New Brunswick: Rutgers University Press,

1980); and Sacvan Bercovitch, *The Puritan Origins of the American Self* (New Haven, CT: Yale University Press, 1975).

79. Michael Winship, "Behold the Bridegroom Cometh!," 172. David Leverenz offers a psychoanalytical study of male Puritan experience in his book, *The Language of Puritan Feeling* (New Brunswick, NJ: Rutgers University Press, 1980), 105–106. Puritan men, he says, "dreamed of being changed into women and babies and of finding in the Great Father a mothering protector."

80. Thomas Shepard, diary entry for May 5, 1641, in *God's Plot: Puritan Spirituality in Thomas Shepard's Cambridge*, ed., Michael McGiffert (Amherst: University of Massachusetts Press, 1994), 92.

81. See Elizabeth Reis, *Damned Women: Sinners and Witches in Puritan New England* (Ithaca, NY: Cornell University Press, 1999), 100–105.

82. See Philip Greven, *The Protestant Temperament: Patterns of Child-Rearing, Religious Experience, and the Self in Early America* (New York: A. A. Knopf, 1977), 126; and Ivy Schweitzer, *The Work of Self-Representation: Lyric Poetry in Colonial New England* (Chapel Hill: University of North Carolina Press, 1991), 26. In Joseph Bean's case, the struggle to deal with his own homosexuality underlay the language and imagery to which he was drawn. For a discussion of homoeroticism in seventeenth-century England, see Richard Rambuss, *Closet Devotions* (Durham, NC: Duke University Press, 1998), 11–71.

83. Porterfield, *Feminine Spirituality*, 27.

84. Porterfield, *Female Piety*, 14.

85. This shift in gendered identity played itself out in the social experience of Puritan men like John Milton. As a student at Christ's College, Cambridge, he was known as "the Lady of Christ's" because of his elegant appearance and his sensitivities in tastes and morals. The curious phenomenon of "men becoming women" in Puritan piety poses an interesting counterpoint to the pattern more common in Christian history of "women becoming men." The *Gospel of Thomas*, for instance, was an early Gnostic Christian text that spoke of women making themselves male in order to enter the kingdom of heaven (Saying 114).

86. Rous, *Mystical Marriage*, 688, 690.

87. Quoted in Cotton Mather, *Magnalia Christi Americana* (Hartford: Silas Andrus, 1820), 1.3.237. Cotton Mather (1663–1728) was pastor of the Old North Church in Boston and author of more than 450 books and pamphlets, ranging from scientific studies to theological reflections.

88. Shepard, *God's Plot*, 70–71.

89. Commenting on the breasts of the bride in Song 4:5, Cotton said: "Brests are the parts and vessels that give milk to the babes of the Church, which resemble the Ministers of this Church of the Jews." *A Brief Exposition.upon the Whole Book of Canticles*, 198.

90. Ibid., 3–4, 83. "All right preachers" have to be "wooers" of the faithful, claimed Puritan poet John Horne in his book, *The Divine Wooer*. Richard Sibbes similarly described devout preachers as *paranymphi*, "friends of the bridegroom that are to procure the marriage between Christ and his Church." Edward Taylor spoke of the souls of the faithful in his congregation who at "my Mammularies suck," as he preached and prayed for spiritual effectiveness in his ministry. See John Horne, *The Divine Wooer; or a Poem Setting Forth the Love and Loveliness of the Lord Jesus* (London: R. Taylor and T. Sawbridge, 1673), opening apology to the reader. Richard Sibbes, *Works*, V, 505–506. Edward Taylor, "Preparatory Meditations," in Donald E. Stanford, ed., *The Poems of Edward Taylor* (New Haven: Yale University Press, 1960), 354.

91. Meditation 23, First Series, on Song 4:8, "My Spouse," in *Early New England Meditative Poetry*, 191.

92. Schweitzer, *The Work of Self-Representation*, 87.

93. This image is from Thomas Hooker's *The Soules Exaltation* (London, 1638), 30–31.

94. Janice Knight, *Orthodoxies in Massachusetts: Rereading American Puritanism* (Cambridge, MA: Harvard University Press, 1994), 72–87.

95. Caryl, *An Exposition upon . . . the Book of Job*, 206, 211. Like Augustine and Calvin before him, he emphasized the smallest animals as often the most effective teachers. See Peter Huff, "From Dragons to Worms: Animals and the Subversion of Hierarchy in Augustine's Theology," *Melita Theologica* 43 (1992), 39–40.

96. Flavell, *Husbandry Spiritualized*, Epistle Dedicatory, 2–3.

97. Ibid.

98. Austen, *The Spirituall Use of an Orchard*, 4. Flavell urged that "irrational and inanimate, as well as rational creatures have a Language; and though not by Articulate speech, yet in a Metaphorical sense, they preach unto man the Wisdom, Power, and Goodness of God." *Husbandry Spiritualized*, Epistle Dedicatory, 1.

99. Nathanael Homes, *The Resurrection-Revealed Raised above Doubts and Difficulties* (London: Printed for the Author, 1661), 244. Quoted in Thomas, *Man and the Natural World*, 127, 179. Reflecting typically Puritan interests, Nathanael Homes (1599–1678) published a commentary on the whole Song of Songs (London, 1652) in which he wrote of the "ravishing love raptures between Christ and his church."

100. Caryl, *Exposition upon . . . the Book of Job*, 207.

101. This Puritan identification with creatures remained largely emblematic and anthropocentric. When Thomas Taylor urged his readers to "put thy selfe in mind to become a tree," he meant a "tree of righteousness, the planting of the Lord." Hence, he explained, "Thou seest the Tree stand firme upon his rootes against windes and tempests: see thou be firmely rooted on Christ, lest the blast of persecution shake thee." *Meditations from the Creatures*, 93–94.

102. Edward Taylor, Meditation 37, First Series, on 1 Co. 3:23, "You are Christ's," in *Early New England Meditative Poetry*, 211.

103. Flavell, *Husbandry Spiritualized*, 12.

104. William Secker, *A Wedding Ring Fit for the Finger* (London: Thomas Parkhurst, 1658), quoted in Ulrich, *Good Wives*, 8, 107. See Calvin, Comm. Genesis 2:18–21. CTS I:133. CO 23:49. . . . Jane Dempsey Douglass suggests that Calvin, in his view of women, was a "theoretical egalitarian," but a "functional subordinationist." *Women, Freedom, and Calvin* (Philadelphia: Westminster Press, 1985), 10.

105. Morgan, *The Puritan Family*, 45.

106. Laurel Thatcher Ulrich, *Good Wives: Image and Reality in the Lives of Women in Northern New England, 1650–1750* (New York: Knopf, 1982), 35–50. Elisabeth Anthony Dexter had fostered a "Golden Age" theory of Puritan women in her study of *Colonial Women of Affairs* (Boston: Houghton Mifflin, 1924). Mary Beth Norton challenged the idea, while admitting the extent to which Puritan women were incorporated into religious and civil society. See her study of *Founding Mothers and Fathers* (New York: Knopf, 1996).

107. Carolyn Merchant, *The Death of Nature: Women, Ecology and the Scientific Revolution* (San Francisco: Harper & Row, 1980).

108. Annette Kolodny, *The Lay of the Land: Metaphor as Experience and History in American Life and Letters* (Chapel Hill: University of North Carolina Press, 1975).

109. Cecelia Tichi shows, for example, how early New England Puritans justified their "right" to the land around Massachusetts Bay because of their ability to "use" it well, making a visible impress on the natural landscape. The Puritan "legitimates his claim to America by manifestly improving it." *New World, New Earth: Environmental Reform in American Literature from the Puritans through Whitman* (New Haven: Yale University Press, 1979), 9–10.

110. Calvin's Sermons on Deuteronomy, quoted in Keith Thomas, *Man and the Natural World: Changing Attitudes in England, 1500–1800* (New York: Oxford University Press, 1983), 154.

111. Robert Bolton, *Some Generall Directions for a Comfortable Walking with God* (London: Felix Kyngston, 1625), 155–157.

112. Elnathan Parr, *A Plaine Exposition upon the Whole 8. 9. 10. 11. Chapters of the Epistle of Saint Paul to the Romans* (London: George Purslowe, 1618), 87.

113. Thomas Edwards, *Gangraena* (London: Ralph Smith,1646), I:20. Thomas Edwards (1599–1648) was lecturer at St. Botolph, Aldgate, in London and author of a three-volume study of heretical sects during the tumultuous days of the English Revolution. Augustus Toplady, an eighteenth-century Calvinist deeply influenced by the Puritan tradition (and author of the hymn "Rock of Ages") similarly affirmed, "I firmly believe that beasts have souls; souls truly and properly so-called." *The Works of Augustus Toplady* (Los Angeles: The Bookshelf, 1980, 1837), III:465–466.

114. In James Usher's analysis of the fourth commandment, he asked, "Why is there mention of allowing rest to the beasts?" His answer: "First, that we may shew mercy, even to the beast. Prov. 12.10. Secondly, to represent after a sort of everlasting Sabbath, wherin all creatures shall be delivered from the bondage of corruption. Rom. 8.20, 21." *A Body of Divinitie, or the Summe and Substance of Christian Religion* (London: Thomas Downes & Geo. Badger, 1653), 248.

115. See Thomas, *Man and the Natural World*, 154–166.

116. See Bruce C. Daniels, "Early Modern Olympians: Puritan Sportsmen in Seventeenth-Century England and America," *Canadian Journal of History* 43:2 (Autumn, 2008), 253–263.

117. Jonathan Edwards, *Dissertation on the Nature of True Virtue*, YE 8:606.

118. See John Gatta, *Making Nature Sacred: Literature, Religion, and Environment in America from the Puritans to the Present* (New York: Oxford University Press, 2004), 56–69.

119. Thomas Shepard, *The Parable of the Ten Virgins Opened and Applied* (Charlestown: Jonathan Mitchell, 1695), 22–25. Edward Pearse similarly wrote of Christ's sweetly wooing sinners to himself in his sermon, *The Best Match: or the Souls Espousal to Christ* (London: Jonathan Robinson, 1673), 134. Edward Pearse (1633–1674) was a nonconformist divine and Oxford graduate who was preacher at St. Margaret's, Westminster.

120. Michael Winship notes that "marital imagery largely disappeared from discourse after the turn of the eighteenth century." "Behold the Bridegroom Cometh!," 173.

121. Isaac Watts, preface to Rowe, *Devout Exercises*, iv.

122. Writing on subsistence farming and ecological concerns from the farm where he lives in Kentucky, Berry speaks continually of desire, covenant, the care of the earth, and the love of his wife Tanya. See his poem, "A Marriage, an Elegy," in *The Country of Marriage* (New York: Harcourt Brace Jovanovich, 1973), 18.

123. See Calvin, Comm. Isaiah 62:4–5, CO 37:384–385; CTS VIII:325.

124. Stephen Jay Gould, "Unenchanted Evening," *Natural History* (September, 1991), 14.

Chapter 3X: Open the Kingdom for a Cottonwood Tree

1. Thomas Merton, *New Seeds of Contemplation* (New York: New Directions, 1961), 29.
2. *Butler's Lives of the Saints*, ed. David H. Farmer (New York: Continuum, 2000), vol. 6 (June), 42.
3. Robert Pogue Harrison traces the Western impulse for cutting down trees back as far as the Gilgamesh epic in his book *Forests: The Shadow of Civilization* (Chicago: University of Chicago Press, 1992).
4. Theodore Hiebert, *The Yahwist's Landscape: Nature and Religion in Early Israel* (New York: Oxford University Press, 1996).
5. Martin Buber, *I and Thou* (New York: Scribner's, 1970), 57–58.
6. David Abram, *The Spell of the Sensuous: Perception and Language in a More-Than-Human World* (New York: Pantheon Books, 1996), 31–72.
7. Brian J. Walsh, Marianne B. Karsh, and Nik Ansell, "Trees, Forestry, and the Responsiveness of Creation," *Cross Currents* 44:2 (Summer 1994), 149–162.
8. Michael Perlman, *The Power of Trees* (Dallas, TX: Spring Publications, 1994). 22–27.
9. Suzanne Head and Robert Heinzman, *Lessons of the Rainforest* (San Francisco: Sierra Club Books, 1990), 247.
10. Stephanie Kaza, *The Attentive Heart: Conversations with Trees* (New York: Fawcett Columbine, 1993).
11. Simon Schama, *Landscape and Memory* (New York: A. A. Knopf, 1995), 214–226. See also Nathaniel Altman, *Sacred Trees* (San Francisco: Sierra Club Books, 1994).
12. Donald Nicholl, *Holiness* (New York: Seabury, 1981), 17.
13. Caitlin Matthews and John Matthews, *The Encyclopedia of Celtic Wisdom* (Shaftesbury, Dorset: Element Books, 1989), 97.
14. Grandfather is a male cottonwood, dropping red catkins in the spring, as opposed to the females with their green catkins nearby—the mothering trees that shed their "cotton" in the air in early summer.
15. See Elizabeth Johnson, *Friends of God and Prophets: A Feminist Theological Reading of the Communion of Saints* (New York: Continuum, 1998), 240–243.
16. Aldo Leopold, *A Sand County Almanac* (New York: Oxford University Press, 1949), 203.
17. Christopher Stone, *Should Trees Have Standing?* (Los Altos, CA: William Kaufmann, 1974). Roderick Nash, *The Rights of Nature: A History of Environmental Ethics* (Madison: University of Wisconsin Press, 1989).
18. Roger S. Gottlieb, "Spiritual Deep Ecology and the Left: An Attempt at Reconciliation," in *This Sacred Earth* (New York: Routledge, 1996), 516–531.
19. See David Hallman, *Ecotheology: Voices from South and North* (Maryknoll, NY: Orbis Books, 1994).
20. Sallie McFague, *The Body of God* (Minneapolis, MN: Fortress Press, 1993), 165, 200–201.

Chapter 4

1. Mary Rowlandson, *The Narrative of the Captivity and Restoration of Mrs. Mary Rowlandson* (Boston: Houghton Mifflin, 1930), 79.

2. Richard Steere, "A Monumental Memorial of Marine Mercy &c," in *Seventeenth-Century American Poetry*, ed. Harrison T. Meserole (Garden City, NY: Anchor Books, 1968), 246.

3. Sebastian Junger, *The Perfect Storm* (New York: HarperTorch, 2000), 133.

4. Steere, "A Monumental Memorial," 249.

5. Donald P. Wharton, "The Colonial Era," in *American and the Sea: A Literary History*, ed. Haskell Springer (Athens: University of Georgia Press, 1995), 32. See also Roger B. Stein, "Seascape and the American Imagination: The Puritan Seventeenth Century," *Early American Literature* 7:1 (1972), 17–37.

6. Kai Erikson, *Wayward Puritans: A Study in the Sociology of Deviance* (New York: John Wiley & Sons, 1966), 197.

7. John Cotton, Foreword to John Norton's *The Answer to the Whole Set of Questions of the Celebrated Mr. William Appolonius* [1648], (Cambridge, MA: Belknap Press of Harvard University Press, 1958), 14.

8. Roger Williams, *A Key into the Language of America* (London: Gregory Dexter, 1643), 103.

9. At the same time, Mather knew that the Reformed church had fled into the wilderness as a refuge, where God had claimed "the utmost parts of the earth for his possession." Cotton Mather, *The Wonders of the Invisible World* (Boston: Benjamin Harris, 1693), quoted in George H. Williams, *Wilderness and Paradise in Christian Thought* (New York: Harper, 1962), 108.

10. Calvin, Comm. Hosea 2:18, CO 42:247; CTS XIII:110.

11. See Noam Flinker, *The Song of Songs in English Renaissance Literature* (Woodbridge, Sufflolk, UK: D. S. Brewer, 2000), and Timothy Hessel-Robinson, "'Be Thou My Onely Well Belov'd': Exegesis and the Spirituality of Desire in Edward Taylor's Preparatory Meditations on the Song of Songs," Ph.D. dissertation, Graduate Theological Union, 2006.

12. Julian of Norwich, *Showings*, trans. Edmund Colledge (New York: Paulist Press, 1978), 296.

13. See Elizabeth A. Dreyer, *Passionate Spirituality: Hildegard of Bingen and Hadewijch of Brabant* (New York: Paulist Press, 2005).

14. Edward Polhil, *Christus in Corde: or, the Mystical Union between Christ and Believers Considered* (London: Thomas Cockerill, 1680), 60. Edward Polhil (1622–1693) remained a conforming member of the Church of England, but was widely respected by non-conformists.

15. Isaac Ambrose, *Looking unto Jesus, A View of the Everlasting Gospel, or the Souls Eyeing of Jesus*, in *The Compleat Works of Isaac Ambrose* (London: Rowland Reynolds, 1674), 555–557. Isaac Ambrose (1604–1664) was one of the "king's four preachers" in Lancashire in 1632, influential in establishing Presbyterianism there.

16. Bartholomew Ashwood, *The Heavenly Trade, or the Best Merchandizing: The Only Way to Live Well in Impoverishing Times* (London: Samuel Lee, 1679), 157.

17. Thomas Watson, "Mystic Union between Christ and the Saints," in *The Godly Man's Picture: Drawn with a Scripture-Pensil* (London: Thomas Parkhurst, 1666), 346.

18. The quote has been attributed to Calvin's Sermon on Job 1:2–5, but I have not been able to confirm this. See also *Inst.* II.viii.50.

19. Philosopher and novelist Georges Bataille (1897–1962) is known for his essays on Nietzsche and interior experience, as well as his erotic novel *The Story of the Eye* (1928).

He had studied for the priesthood as a young man, attending a Catholic seminary, but later rejected Christian faith, saying that he considered the brothels of Paris his true churches.

20. Georges Bataille, *Death and Sensuality: A Study of Eroticism and the Taboo* (New York: Walker and Company, 1962), 31–32, 122. Emphasis added.

21. Søren Kierkegaard, *Either/Or*, trans. David F. Swenson and Lillian Marvin Swenson (Garden City, NY: Doubleday, 1959), I:74–102.

22. Rambuss, *Closet Devotions*, 5. As Bataille observed, "The simple taboo created eroticism in the first place . . . pleasure was bound up with transgression" (*Death and Sensuality*, 127).

23. Rous, *Mysticall Marriage*, 288–289.

24. See Mark Dever, *Richard Sibbes: Puritanism and Calvinism in Late Elizabethan and Early Stuart England* (Macon, GA: Mercer University Press, 2000), 135–160.

25. George L. Scheper, "Reformation Attitudes toward Allegory and the Song of Songs," *PMLA (Publications of the Modern Language Association of America)* 89:3 (May 1974), 551–562.

26. Nathanael Homes, *A Commentary Literal or Historical, and Mystical or Spiritual on the Whole Booke of Canticles*, bound in *The Works of Dr. Nathanael Homes* (London: J. Legate, 1652), 469. Nathanael Homes (1599–1678) was rector of St. Mary Staining in London. John Cotton admitted the problem of lewd interpretations in his own commentary on the Song, but argued that "the amourousness of the dittie will not stir up wantonnesse . . . if the words be well understood." If holy desire is "inflamed with heavenly love," it "will draw out and burne up all earthly and carnall lust." John Cotton, *A Brief Exposition of the Whole Book of Canticles* (London: Philip Nevil, 1642), 8.

27. *Annotations upon All the Books of the Old and New Testament* (London, 1657), sig. 712r. For an excellent (and very explicit) discussion of sexuality and spirituality in the Canticle itself, see Carey Ellen Walsh, *Exquisite Desire: Religion, the Erotic, and the Song of Songs* (Minneapolis: Fortress Press, 2000). She suggests that "The Song is concerned with the provocative question of whether the exquisite sensation of wanting another could surpass in any realistic sense the pleasure of sexual consummation. The surprising claim that it can does seem to be the premise of the Song, which stays focused on the experience of yearning, not its relief" (122).

28. See *Saint Bernard's Sermons on the Canticle of Canticles*, trans. a priest of Mount Melleray (Dublin, 1920), vol. I, 50–51 (sermon 7). On medieval interpretations of the Canticle generally, see E. Ann Matter, *The Voice of My Beloved: Song of Songs in Western Medieval Christianity* (Philadelphia: University of Pennsylvania Press, 1990).

29. See Helen Wilcox, Richard Todd, and Alasdair MacDonald, eds., *Sacred and Profane: Secular and Devotional Interplay in Early Modern British Literature* (Amsterdam: VU University Press, 1996), 130, 163.

30. See Elegy XIX, "Going to Bed," in John Donne, *Poems of Love* (Westerham, UK: Folio Society, 1958), 129–130. See also Henry L. Carrigan, ed., *Religious Poetry and Prose of John Donne* (Brewster, MA: Paraclete Press, 1999), 38–39.

31. "Rapture," in Rhodes Dunlap, ed., *The Poems of Thomas Carew* (Oxford: Clarendon Press, 1964), 51.

32. Edward Taylor, "Preparatory Meditations," in *The Poems of Edward Taylor*, 228, 362–363, 258, 142. Taylor wrote over two hundred "Preparatory Meditations" for communion, seventy-six of which were based on passages from the Song of Songs. See also Richard

Godbeer, "'Love Raptures': Marital, Romantic, and Erotic Images of Jesus Christ in Puritan New England, 1670–1730," *New England Quarterly* LXVIII:3 (September 1995), 368.

33. R. Cullis Goffin, ed., *The Life and Poems of William Cartwright* (Cambridge: Cambridge University Press, 1918), 34. His poem closes with the lines, "Let me use my force tonight,/The next conquest shall be thine."

34. Richard Sibbes, "The Excellency of the Gospel above the Law," in *Works*, 4:271 (Cf. Dever, *Richard Sibbes*, 150).

35. See Dunne's Holy Sonnet, "Batter my heart, three-person'd God," in John Booty, ed., *John Donne: Selections from Divine Poems, Sermons, Devotions and Prayers* (New York: Paulist Press, 1990), 81–82.

36. Samuel Rutherford, *Christ Dying and Drawing Sinners to Himself* (London: J. D. for Andrew Crooke, 1647), 282. Christopher Love could speak of *The Zealous Christian Taking Heaven by Holy Violence* (London: John Rothwell, 1654), urging the Christian to "strive to an agony" in the wrestling of importunate prayer.

37. Edmund S. Morgan, *The Puritan Family: Religion and Domestic Relations in Seventeenth-Century New England* (New York: Harper & Row, 1966), 63.

38. H. J. C. Grierson, *Cross Currents of Literature in the XVIIth Century* (London: Chatto and Windus, 1929), 155.

39. On the ordering of Puritan desire, see Kathleen Verduin, "'Our Cursed Natures': Sexuality and the Puritan Conscience," *New England Quarterly* 56 (1983), 220–237.

40. Calvin, Comm. Galatians 2:20, CO 50:443; CTS XXI:74.

41. Richard Sibbes, "The Soul's Conflict with Itself," in *Works* I:164.

42. Anne Bradstreet, "Meditations Divine and Moral," 38, and diary entry for Sept. 30, 1657, in *The Works of Anne Bradstreet*, ed. Jeannine Hensley (Cambridge, MA: Belknap Press of Harvard University Press, 1967), 279, 257. Robert Daly observes that, "Like her fellow Puritans, Bradstreet had to steer a middle course between two sinful extremes: loving the creatures too little was an affront to God, who had created them and commanded man to love them; loving them too much, without subordinating that love to the love of their Maker, was idolatry." See *God's Altar: The World and the Flesh in Puritan Poetry* (Berkeley: University of California Press, 1978), 127.

43. Samuel Rutherford, quoted in *The Golden Treasury of Puritan Quotations*, ed. I. D. E. Thomas (Chicago: Moody Press, 1975), 17. Samuel Rutherford (1600–1661) was a Church of Scotland minister in Anwoth and a Scottish commissioner to the Westminster Assembly.

44. Gordon Wakefield, *Puritan Devotion* (London: Epworth Press, 1957), 160. The Westminster Assembly's Larger Catechism (Question 66) described the union of the elect with Christ as the work of God's grace," which is done in their effectual calling," something prior to justification, adoption, and sanctification.

45. *Inst.* II.vii.14 (1536). See Michael J. Christensen and Jeffery A. Wittung, eds., *Partakers of the Divine Nature: The History and Development of Deification in the Christian Tradition* (Grand Rapids, MI: Baker Academic, 2007), 209.

46. See R. Tudor Jones, "Union with Christ: The Existential Nerve of Puritan Piety," *Tyndale Bulletin* 41:2 (November 1990), 186–208.

47. *Inst.* III.i.3, III.xi.12, and III.ii.24.

48. Luther had agreed with Calvin in urging the first two uses of the law—as a general guide in civic life and as a "harsh schoolmaster" convincing believers of their inability to obey God's commands, thus driving them to faith in Christ. Luther, however, rejected any third use of the law as a guide in the Christian life, lest it turn the believer away from justification by

faith and back to a confidence in works righteousness. See Edward A. Dowey, "Law in Luther and Calvin," *Theology Today* 41:2 (July, 1984), 146–153.

49. Scots Divine Henry Scougal urged his people to see "the image of the Almighty shining in the soul of man. . . . It is a beam of the eternal light, a drop of that infinite ocean of goodness; and they who are endued with it may be said to have *God dwelling in their souls and Christ formed within them.*" *The Life of God in the Soul of Man* (London: T. Dring and F. Weld, 1691), 9. Henry Scougal (1650–1678) was a Church of Scotland minister and lecturer at King's College, Aberdeen.

50. Matthew Sylvester, "How May a Gracious Person from Whom God Hides His Face Trust in the Lord as His God?" in James Nichols, Samuel Annesley, et al., eds., *Puritan Sermons, 1659–1689: Being the Morning Exercises at Cripplegate, St. Giles in the Fields, and in Southwark*, originally published in 1844 (Wheaton, IL: R. O. Roberts, 1981), 4:106.

51. Ramon Lull, *The Book of the Lover and the Beloved*, 45, in Ramon Lull, *Romancing God: Contemplating the Beloved*, ed., Henry L. Carrigan (Brewster, MA: Paraclete Press, 1999), 11.

52. See Peter Lewis, *The Genius of Puritanism* (Haywards Heath, Sussex: Carey Publications, 1975), 66ff.

53. Thomas Goodwin, *Certain Select Cases Resolved . . . the Case of Desertion, or Walking in Darkness* (London: R. Dawlman, 1647); Joseph Symonds, *The Case and Cure of a Deserted Soul* (Edinburgh: Robert Bryson, 1642); Christopher Love's *The Dejected Soul's Cure* (London: John Rothwell, 1657); Richard Sibbes's *The Soul's Conflict with Itself and Victory over Itself by Faith* (London: R. Edwards, 1808); and William Bridge's *A Lifting Up for the Downcast* [1649] (Edinburgh: Banner of Truth Trust, 1995).

54. Thomas Manton, *Works* (Nisbet Edition, 1681), VI:81.

55. Thomas Brooks, *The Mute Christian under the Smarting Rod* (1659) in *The Complete Works of Thomas Brooks* (Edinburgh: J. Nichol, 1866–67), I:378. Thomas Brooks (1608–1680) was minister of St. Margaret's, New Fish Street Hill, and a radical supporter of Independency.

56. Symonds, *The Case and Cure of a Deserted Soul*, 12.

57. Edmund Calamy, *The Godly Man's Ark* (1657), in Dewey D. Wallace, *The Spirituality of the Later English Puritans* (Macon, GA: Mercer University Press, 1987), 163, 165 (Emphasis added). He subsequently urged, "Therefore whensoever God brings us into the School of Affliction, let us labour to bee good Schollars in it" (169). Edmund Calamy (1671–1732) was minister at Tothill Street, Westminster, and an active defender of non-conformity.

58. Joseph Caryl, *An Exposition with Practical Observations upon Chapters of the Book of* Job, originally published in 1644 (Grand Rapids, MI: Dust & Ashes Publications, 2001).

59. Bernard spoke of these three biblical books as loaves of tasty bread, with the third as the best of all. See his first sermon on the Song of Songs, in *Bernard of Clairvaux: Selected Works*, trans. G. R. Evans (New York: Paulist Press, 1987), 210–211.

60. See Sacvan Bercovitch, *The Puritan Origins of the American Self* (New Haven: Yale University Press, 1975).

61. *Inst.* III.vii.1; III.vii.8; and III.vii.2.

62. Scougal, *Life of God in the Soul of Man*, 34–35. Cf. Richard Sibbes, *The Soules Conflict with It Selfe* (London: R. D., 1651).

63. Scougal, *Life of God in the Soul of Man*, 35. As Sacvan Bercovitch observed, "The Puritan's dilemma was that the way from self necessarily led through the self." See his book, *The Puritan Origins of the American Self* (New Haven: Yale University Press, 1975), 165.

64. Peter Sterry, *The Rise, Race, and Royalty of the Kingdom of God in the Soul of Man* (London: Thomas Cockerill, 1683), 73. Peter Sterry (1613–1672) was one of the leading Independents in London, nominated to the Westminster Assembly of Divines in 1643 and later prominent in Cromwell's inner circle.

65. Richard Baxter, *The Saints Everlasting Rest*, originally published in 1650 (London: Epworth Press, 1962), 180, 147.

66. David D. Hall, *Worlds of Wonder, Days of Judgment: Popular Religious Belief in Early New England* (New York: A. A. Knopf, 1989), 71.

67. Michel Foucault calls attention to the "ships of fools" on which mentally disturbed people were placed in the Renaissance era. The hope was that the choppy seas of their psychic landscape might find an echo—and resolution—in the peaks and vales of the ocean waves. See Michel Foucault, *Madness and Civilization: A History of Insanity in the Age of Reason*, trans. Richard Howard (New York: Vintage Books, 1988), vi.

68. Samuel Hahnemann (1755–1843) taught at the University of Leipzig and published his *Organan of the Healing Art* in 1810. He had been fascinated by the South American use of Peruvian bark (quinine) in treating malaria by duplicating its symptoms and experimented with the practice himself.

69. Nathanael Culverwel, *An Elegant and Learned Discourse of the Light of Nature* (London: T. R. and E. M. for John Rothwell, 1652), 73–76.

70. Cotton Mather, *The Sailours Companion and Counsellor. An Offer of Considerations for the Tribe of Zebulun; Awakening the Mariner* (Boston: B. Green, 1709), 43.

71. Mather, *The Sailours Companion*, 54–55. "The World is the Sea," Mather proclaimed. "The Church is the Ship. Our souls are the passengers. Christ is our Pilot. The Word is our compass. Faith is our Helm. . . . perseverance is our ballast." Ibid., x.

72. Peter Sterry could say, "If a man know not the way to the Sea, let him follow the course of a River. Every stream of Sweetness flows from our Savior, and runs into him." See his *Rise, Race, and Royalty*, 212.

73. Polhil, *Christus in corde*, unpaged introduction and conclusion; Baxter, *Saints Everlasting Rest*, 184.

74. John Bunyan, *The Pilgrim's Progress*, originally published in 1678 (New York: New American Library, 1964), 142–144.

75. Steere's ecological sensitivity is seen in his admonishment that we "let virtue guide us then in Earth's Enjoyments,/Let *Temp'rance* teach us how to measure all . . . without abuse." Quoted in Donald Wharton, *Richard Steere: Colonial Merchant Poet* (University Park: Pennsylvania State University Press, 1979), 56–57.

76. See Max Weber *The Protestant Ethic and the Spirit of Capitalism* (New York: Scribner, 1930) and R. H. Tawney, *Religion and the Rise of Capitalism* (New York: Harcourt, Brace, 1926), as well as Edward Dommen and James D. Bratt, eds., *John Calvin Rediscovered: The Impact of His Social and Economic Thought* (Louisville: Westminster John Knox Press, 2007).

77. Cotton Mather, *Magnalia Christi Americana* (London: Thomas Parkhurst, 1702), quoted in Stephen Foster, *Their Solitary Way: The Puritan Social Ethic in the First Century of Settlement in New England* (New Haven: Yale University Press, 1971), 121.

78. Thomas Watson, *The Beatitudes: or a Discourse upon . . . Christ's Famous Sermon on the Mount* (London: Ralph Smith, 1660), quoted in Leland Ryken, *Worldly Saints: The Puritans as They Really Were* (Grand Rapids, MI: Academic Books, 1986), 61. Steere would recall Puritan prayers like those of Samuel Hieron: "Oh, let not mine eyes be dazzled, nor

my heart bewitched with the glory and sweetness of these worldly pleasures." See Samuel Hieron, "A Prayer Fit for One Whom God Hath Enriched with Outward Things," quoted in Ryken, *Worldly Saints*, 69. Even Calvin had reminded the believers that "each man is to provide for the needy according to the extent of his means so that no one has too much and no one has too little." See Calvin, Comm. II Corinthians 8:13ff, quoted in Andre Biéler, *The Social Humanism of Calvin*, trans. P. T. Fuhrmann (Richmond: John Knox Press, 1964), 33.

79. See William Leach, *Land of Desire: Merchants, Power, and the Rise of a New American Culture* (New York: Vintage Books, 1993). John Wanamaker (1838–1922) was the "king of merchants" in Philadelphia and superintendent of the Bethany Presbyterian Sunday School.

80. Irvin G. Wyllie observes that the leading proponents of the American cult of the self-made man were clergymen from a Puritan and Reformed background. See *The Self-Made Man in America: The Myth of Rags to Riches* (New York: Free Press, 1966), 56–60.

81. Ivan Illich, *Tools for Conviviality* (New York: Harper & Row, 1973), 46.

82. See Theodore Steinberg, *Nature Incorporated: Industrialization and the Waters of New England* (Cambridge: Cambridge University Press, 1991), 205ff.

83. Edwards, "Discourse on the Trinity," YE 21:137.

84. Annie Dillard, *Holy the Firm* (San Francisco: Harper, 1977), 45.

Chapter 4X: Biodiversity and the Holy Trinity

1. Karl Barth, *Church Dogmatics*, II/1:651. Translation from Hans Urs von Balthasar, *The Glory of the Lord* (San Francisco: Ignatius Press, 1983), I:55.

2. Found only in California, this species (catalogued as *Arctostaphylos Hookeri var. ravenii*) is a shrub with a rarity level of 3.

3. See E. O. Wilson and Dan L. Perlman, *Conserving Earth's Biodiversity* (Washington, DC: Island Press, 2000).

4. Carl Safina, *Song for the Blue Ocean* (New York: Henry Holt, 1998).

5. Cary Fowler and Pat Mooney, *Shattering: Food, Politics, and the Loss of Genetic Diverstiy* (Tucson: Univ. of Arizona Press, 1990), chap. 3: "Value of Diversity."

6. Chris Park, *The Environment: Principles and Applications* (London: Routledge, 1997).

7. Joanne Elizabeth Lauck, *The Voice of the Infinite in the Small: Revisioning the Insect-Human Connection* (Mill Spring, NC: Swan Raven, 1998), 22.

8. Lauck, 121. See also Arthur Evans and Charles Bellamy, *An Inordinate Fondness for Beetles* (New York: Henry Holt, 1996).

9. Jürgen Moltmann, *God in Creation* (Minneapolis: Fortress Press, 1993), 100.

10. See Anne Hunt, *What Are They Saying about the Trinity?* (New York: Paulist Press, 1998), and Denis Edwards, *The Wisdom of God: An Ecological Theology* (Homebush, New South Wales, Australia: St. Paul's, 1995).

11. See Leonardo Boff, *Trinity and Society*, trans. Paul Burns (Maryknoll, NY: Orbis Books, 1988), 133–148, 220–231; Elizabeth Johnson, *She Who Is: The Mystery of God in Feminist Theological Discourse* (New York: Crossroad, 1992), chap. 10; and Jürgen Moltmann, *The Trinity and the Kingdom: The Doctrine of God* (San Francisco: Harper & Row, 1981), 105–114.

12. Johnson, *She Who Is*, 216. See also Patricia A. Fox, "God's Shattering Otherness: The Trinity and Earth's Healing," in *Earth Revealing—Earth Healing: Ecology and*

Christian Theology, ed. Denis Edwards (Collegeville, MN: Liturgical Press, 2001), 85–103.

13. Leonardo Boff, *Cry of the Earth, Cry of the Poor*, trans. Phillip Berryman (Maryknoll, NY: Orbis Books, 1997), 155.

14. Jonathan Edwards, "An Essay on the Trinity," in *Treatise on Grace and Other Posthumously Published Writings*, ed. Paul Helm (Cambridge: James Clarke, 1971), 100–111. John Calvin, *Inst.* I.xiii.2, 17. See also T. F. Torrance, "Calvin's Doctrine of the Trinity," *Calvin Theological Journal* 25:2 (November 1970), 165–193.

15. *Confessions*, XIII: 11, 12.

16. *Perichoresis* has been a term used in the Greek tradition to speak of the interpenetrating relationship of the persons in the Trinity, of the interpenetrating relationship of the divine and human natures in Jesus Christ, and of the interpenetrating relationship of the Trinity and creation. For a discussion of the latter, see Boff, *Trinity and Society*, 6, 134–136; and Verna Harrison, "Perichoresis in the Greek Fathers," *St. Vladimir's Theological Quarterly* 35:1 (1991), 53–65.

17. Adapted from R. Blakney, ed., *Meister Eckhart: A Modern Translation* (New York: Harper, 1941), 245.

18. Alphonso Lingis, *Excesses: Eros and Culture* (Albany: SUNY Press, 1983), 9. William Blake quoted in Robert Bly in *The Rag and Bone Shop of the Heart* (New York: Harper Collins, 1992), 16.

19. See Claire Hope Cummings, *Uncertain Peril: Genetic Engineering and the Future of Seeds* (Boston: Beacon Press, 2008).

20. Fowler and Mooney, *Shattering*, 220–222.

21. See Bill Mollison and Reny Mia Slay, *Introduction to Permaculture* (Tyalgum, New South Wales, Australia: Tagari Publishers, 1991).

22. See Larry L. Rasmussen, *Earth Community, Earth Ethics* (Maryknoll, NY: Orbis Books, 1996), 322–323.

23. The 58-story Comcast Center, completed in 2008, is the tallest LEED building in the United States.

Chapter 5

1. Edwards, "Types Notebook," 152, as quoted in Mason I. Lowance, "Introduction," YE 11:179.

2. *Miscellanies*, 186–188, YE 13:330–331. Edwards saw the Holy Spirit as expressing the harmony of music in the work of creation. "It was made especially the Holy Spirit's work to bring the world to its beauty and perfection out of the chaos; for the beauty of the world is a communication of God's beauty." See *Miscellanies*, 293, YE 13:384.

3. Hans Urs von Balthasar (1905–1988) was a Swiss Jesuit theologian whose two multivolume works explore the aesthetic and theatrical dimensions of the divine drama of salvation. See *The Glory of the Lord: A Theological Aesthetics* (San Francisco: Ignatius Press, 1983–91), 7 vols., and *Theo-Drama: Theological Dramatic Theory* (San Francisco: Ignatius Press, 1988–98), 5 vols.

4. Von Balthasar, *Truth Is Symphonic: Aspects of Christian Pluralism* (San Francisco: Ignatius Press, l987), 7–8.

5. George M. Marsden, *Jonathan Edwards: A Life* (New Haven: Yale University Press, 2003), 460.

6. Edward Farley, *Faith and Beauty: A Theological Aesthetic* (Burlington, VT: Ashgate, 2001), 43.

7. Michael J. McClymond, "Spiritual Perception in Jonathan Edwards," *Journal of Religion* 77:2 (April 1997), 214. See also his *Encounters with God: An Approach to the Theology of Jonathan Edwards* (New York: Oxford University Press, 1998), 9–22.

8. Thomas Berry, *The Great Work: Our Way into the Future* (New York: Crown Publishing, 1999), 80.

9. *Religious Affections*, YE 2:265.

10. "On Sarah Pierpont," YE 16:789–790.

11. In his essay on "The Mind," Edwards spoke of God as the "substance" of all bodies (see YE 6.344) and in his essay "On Being," he referred to God as "space," a kind of incorporeal substance existent in itself (see YE 6:203). Yet these are exceptions that must be understood in light of his more prevalent dynamic thinking. Sang Hyun Lee analyzes his dispositional ontology in *The Philosophical Theology of Jonathan Edwards* (Princeton: Princeton University Press, 1988), 4–6.

12. Indeed, Edwards can turn the older metaphysics of divine substance on its head, saying that "the *delight* of God is properly substance, yea an infinitely perfect substance, even the essence of God." Emphasis added. See *Miscellanies*, 94, YE 13:261.

13. *Religious Affections*, YE 2:298. Edwards adds that God delights "with true and great pleasure in beholding that beauty which is an image and communication of his own beauty." *Dissertation concerning the End for Which God Created the World*, YE 8:446. Hereafter referred to as *End of Creation*.

14. "The Mind," 1, YE 6:332. On the centrality of beauty in Edwards's theology, see Roland Delattre, *Beauty and Sensibility in the Thought of Jonathan Edwards* (New Haven: Yale University Press, 1968. On the importance of desire in Edwards's thought, see Paula M. Cooey, "Eros and Intimacy in Edwards," *Journal of Religion* 69:4 (October, 1989), 484–501.

15. Edwards begins his "Discourse on the Trinity" by speaking of the infinite happiness that God shares in the enjoyment of himself. YE 21:113f.

16. "God stands in no need of creatures, and is not profited by them; neither can his happiness be said to be added to by the creature. But yet God has . . . a real delight in his own loveliness, and he also has a real delight in the shining forth or glorifying of it." *Miscellanies*, 679, YE 18:237–238.

17. *End of Creation*, YE 8:429, 439. Cf. 432.

18. *Miscellanies*, 448, YE 13:495; and *End of Creation*, YE 8:461.

19. Roland A. Delattre, "Aesthetics and Ethics: Jonathan Edwards and the Recovery of Aesthetics for Religious Ethics," *Journal of Religious Ethics* 31:2 (2003), 277.

20. Pseudo-Dionysius the Areopagite, *The Divine Names*, 712A–712-B, in *Pseudo-Dionysius: The Complete Works*, trans. Colm Luibheid (New York: Paulist Press, 1987), 82.

21. Turner, *Eros and Allegory*, 53.

22. *Miscellanies*, 1151, YE 8:450 n2.

23. Ibid., 3, YE 13:199; *End of Creation*, YE 8:459.

24. *Original Sin*, YE 3:402. "It [is] most agreeable to the Scripture to suppose creation to be performed every moment. The Scripture speaks of it as a present, remaining, continual act." *Miscellanies*, 346, YE 13:418.

25. *Miscellanies*, 108, YE 13:279; and *Miscellanies*, 1218, in Harvey G. Townsend, ed., *The Philosophy of Jonathan Edwards from His Private Notebooks* (Eugene: University of Oregon Press, 1955), 152. Hereafter referred to as Townsend.

26. *Miscellanies*, 108, YE 13:279.

27. *Miscellanies*, 1296, YE 23:238. Edwards often used the word "emanation" in speaking of nature as a reflection of God's glory. He did not mean this in a purely Neo-Platonic sense of the universe flowing out of the very essence of God. An emanation, for him, referred to a spiritual power flowing forth from sensory images that suggest a taste of something larger than themselves. See Mason I. Lowance, "Jonathan Edwards and the Platonists: Edwardsean Epistemology and the Influence of Malebranche and Norris," *Studies in Puritan American Spirituality* 2 (January 1992), 129–152. See also John Navone's comparison of Edwards and Thomas Aquinas in his *Enjoying God's Beauty* (Collegeville, MN: Liturgical Press, 1999), 99–110.

28. "Beauty of the World," YE 6:306.

29. "The Spider Letter," October 31, 1723, in YE 6:163–169; Marsden, *Jonathan Edwards*, 463.

30. *Images of Divine Things*, 57, YE 11:67. Emphasis added.

31. "The Mind," 1, YE 6:337.

32. *Religious Affections*, YE 2:272.

33. Augustine, *Confessions*, X.9.

34. Ralph Austen, *Dialogue betweene the Husbandman and Fruit-Trees* (Oxford: Thomas Bowman, 1676), quoted in Kitty W. Scoular, *Natural Magic: Studies in the Presentation of Nature in English Poetry from Spenser to Marvell* (Oxford: Clarendon Press, 1965), 20 n.1.

35. Thomas Adam, *A Divine Herball, Together with a Forrest of Thornes* (London: George Purslowe, 1616); Bonaventure, *Itinerarium mentis in Deum*, 2.1–13; and Francis de Sales, *An Introduction to a Devoute Life*, trans. John Yakesley (Rouen: Cardin Hamillon, 1614), 139.

36. See Clyde A. Holbrook, *Jonathan Edwards, the Valley and Nature: An Interpretative Essay* (Lewisburg, PA: Bucknell University Press, 1987), 71–72, 88–93; Sang Hyun Lee, "Edwards on God and Nature: Resources for Contemporary Theology," in Sang Hyun Lee and Allen C. Guelzo, eds., *Edwards in Our Time: Jonathan Edwards and the Shaping of American Religion* (Grand Rapids, MI: Eerdmans, 1999), 15–44; Paula M. Cooey, *Jonathan Edwards on Nature and Destiny: A Systematic Analysis* (Lewiston, NY: Edwin Mellen, 1985), 13–64; and Avihu Zakai, "Jonathan Edwards and the Language of Nature: The Re-Enchantment of the World in the Age of Scientific Reasoning," *Journal of Religious History* 26:1 (February 2002), 15–41.

37. Sermon on "Youth and the Pleasures of Piety" (1734), YE 19:89, 85; and Sermon on "Nothing upon Earth Can Represent the Glories of Heaven" (1724), YE 14:152.

38. "Personal Narrative," YE 16:791–793.

39. Edwards argued, "As the system of nature and the system of revelation are both divine works, so both are in different senses a divine word, both are the voice of God to intelligent creatures, a manifestation and declaration of Himself to mankind." *Miscellanies*, 1340, Townsend, 233.

40. Nathanael Culverwel, a seventeenth-century Puritan divine and one of the Cambridge Platonists who influenced Edwards's thought, spoke of the way the book of nature prepares for the reception of the truth of Scripture. "This way of beholding him breeds rather admiration than begets knowledge . . . and admiration is at best but *semen scientia*. . . . This rather sets the soul a longing, than gives it any true satisfaction." See Nathanael Culverwell, *Spiritual Opticks: Or a Glasse, Discovering the Weaknesse and Imperfection of a Christian's Knowledge in This Life* (Oxford: H. Hall, 1668), 182.

41. John Smith, *Select Discourses* (London: F. Flesher, 1660), 4, 9, 16.

42. *Miscellanies*, 489, YE 13:533.

43. Sermon on "A Divine and Supernatural Light" (1733), YE 17:413.

44. "The Mind," 16, YE 6:345.

45. See Sang Hyun Lee, "Jonathan Edwards on Nature," in *Faithful Imagining: Essays in Honor of Richard R. Niebuhr*, eds. Albert Blackwell, Sang Hyun Lee, and Wayne Proudfoot (Atlanta: Scholars Press, 1995), 39–59.

46. *Miscellanies*, 108, YE 13:278–279. Emphasis added.

47. James Hoopes has emphasized the Edwardsean distinction between the "sense of the heart" and the "new sense." In the early 1730s, Edwards began to emphasize the former, with its natural inclination to wonder and adoration, as a basis for appealing to the unconverted. He expressed this developing preparationist tendency very clearly in Miscellany #539. See James Hoopes, "Jonathan Edwards's Religious Psychology," *Journal of American History* 69 (1983), 857–858 and YE 18.85–87.

48. Edwards, *Miscellanies*, 732 YE 18.357–359.

49. Calvin, Comm. Isaiah 44:3, CO 37:106; CTS VIII:360; and *Inst.* II.ii.15. Edwards himself had no illusions about the diminishing influence of sin in human culture. He referred to the common grace of creation as a "restraining grace." In restraining the worst of human behavior, it allows the unconverted to become "tolerable members of society," so that "the earth could bear them." See his "True Grace Distinguished from the Experience of Devils" (1752), YE 25:611.

50. See Terrence Erdt, *Jonathan Edwards, Art, and the Sense of the Heart* (Amherst: University of Massachusetts Press, 1980), 2–23.

51. John Calvin, *Inst.* III.2.34.

52. "A Divine and Supernatural Light," YE 17:414; and *Religious Affections*, YE 2:30–33, 270–283.

53. "A Faithful Narrative of the Surprising Work of God" (1737), YE 4:151, 174–175, 183.

54. Sermon on I Cor. 1:9 (before 1733) and Sermon on Luke 14:16 (before 1733), as cited in William J. Danaher, "By Sensible Signs Represented: Jonathan Edwards' Sermons on the Lord's Supper," *Pro Ecclesia* VII:3 (Summer 1998), 261–287.

55. Edwards said, in his 1724 sermon on "Nothing upon Earth Can Represent the Glories of Heaven," "Now nothing is so pleasing naturally to the sight as light, and nothing that is the object of our senses that is so glorious." YE 14:142.

56. *Miscellanies*, 141, YE 13:297–298.

57. Miklos Veto, "Spiritual Knowledge according to Jonathan Edwards," *Calvin Theological Journal* 31:1 (April 1996), 171.

58. Diane Ackerman, *A Natural History of the Senses* (New York: Random House, 1990), 128.

59. *Images of Divine Things*, 70, YE 11:74. Emphasis added.

60. Holbrook, *Jonathan Edwards, the Valley and Nature*, 81.

61. *The Works of President Edwards, with a Memoir by Sereno E. Dwight*, ed. Edward Hickman, originally published in 1834 (Edinburgh: Banner of Truth Trust, 1974), I:lxv. Emphasis added.

62. See Kevin T. Dann, *Bright Colors Falsely Seen: Synaesthesia and the Search for Transcendent Knowledge* (New Haven: Yale University Press, 1998).

63. See *End of Creation*, YE 8:530–531 and "Essay on the Trinity," 125–126. There are similarities between Edwards and Bernard of Clairvaux with respect to this overlapping of

sensory imagery. Bernard McGinn observes that, "Bernard's employment of the spiritual senses as modes of understanding the experience of the divine presence tends to be synaesthetic in nature, appealing to a wide range of sense images and sometimes deliberately mingling diverse sensory perceptions." *The Growth of Mysticism*, Vol. 2 of *The Presence of God: A History of Western Christian Mysticism* (New York: Crossroad, 1994), 187.

64. See Mason I. Lowance, Jr., "'Images or Shadows of Divine Things' in the Thought of Jonathan Edwards," in *Typology and Early American Literature*, ed. Sacvan Bercovitch (Amherst: University of Massachusetts Press, 1972), 235–238; and Janice Knight, "Learning the Language of God: Jonathan Edwards and the Typology of Nature," *William and Mary Quarterly* Third Series XLVIII:4 (October, 1991), 531–551.

65. See Conrad Cherry, *Nature and the Religious Imagination: From Edwards to Bushnell* (Philadelphia: Fortress, 1980), 31.

66. *Images of Divine Things*, YE 11:81, 124, 93, 109, 59. Perry Miller said that Edwards, in this work, offered "nothing less than an assertion of the absolute validity of the sensuous." Perry Miller, ed., *Images or Shadows of Divine Things by Jonathan Edwards* (New Haven: Yale University Press, 1948), 36.

67. *End of Creation*, YE 8:531.

68. "The Mind," 23, YE 6:349.

69. "An Humble Attempt," YE 5:345. In a 1731 sermon titled "East of Eden," Edwards said of the earth that "God had put his own beauty upon it; it shone with the communication of his glory." But as a result of human sin, "the earth lost its beauty and pleasantness . . . That bloom and beauty and joy that all nature seemed to [be] clothed with was gone." YE 17:334.

70. Unpublished manuscript sermon on Romans 8:22, "The whole creation does as it were groan under the sins of wicked man" (1737), Beinecke Rare Book and Manuscript Library, Yale University, 17.

71. Ibid., 17, 25, 29.

72. See Carol Harrison, *Beauty and Revelation in the Thought of Saint Augustine* (Oxford: Oxford University Press, 1992), 97–139. Hans Urs von Balthasar similarly points "through the ghastliness of the crucified, the seeming absence of all beauty [to] the breakthrough of the flaming mystery of the glory of love: *fulget crucis mysterium*." "Earthly Beauty and Divine glory, "*Communio* X:3 (Fall 1983), 206.

73. Sermon on "The Excellency of Christ" (1736), YE 19:576.

74. *Images of Divine Things*, 3, YE 11:52.

75. Tenth sermon in *Charity and Its Fruits*, YE 8:293. See also Gerald R. McDermott, *One Holy and Happy Society: The Public Theology of Jonathan Edwards* (University Park: Pennsylvania State University Press, 1992), 108–109.

76. Frank Burch Brown, *Good Taste, Bad Taste, and Christian Taste: Aesthetics in Religious Life* (New York: Oxford University Press, 2000), 122.

77. Edwards, *End of Creation*, YE 8:443. For an analysis of deification in Edwards's thought, see Michael J. McClymond, "Salvation as Divinization: Jonathan Edwards, Gregory Palamas and the Theological Uses of Neoplatonism," in *Jonathan Edwards: Philosophical Theologian*, eds. Paul Helm and Oliver D. Crisp (Aldershot, UK: Ashgate, 2003).

78. See Louis Joseph Mitchell, "The Experience of Beauty in the Thought of Jonathan Edwards," unpublished Th.D dissertation at Harvard University, 1995, 243.

79. *Nature of True Virtue*, YE 8:544, 542.

80. Ibid., YE 8:551.

81. Roland A. Delattre, "Religious Ethics Today: Jonathan Edwards, H. Richard Niebuhr, and Beyond," in Sang Hyun Lee and Allen C. Guelzo, eds., *Edwards in Our Time: Jonathan Edwards and the Shaping of American Religion* (Grand Rapids: Eerdmans, 1999), 70–71. Emphasis added.

82. Paul Ramsey compares Edwards's thought to Gregory of Nyssa's in YE 8:727–729. See also Patricia Wilson-Kastner, "God's Infinity and His Relationship to Creation in the Theologies of Gregory of Nyssa and Jonathan Edwards," *Foundations* XXI:4 (Oct.–Dec. 1978), 305–321.

83. Edwards, *Miscellanies*, 1, YE 13:197

84. Delattre, "Aesthetics and Ethics," 278.

85. Edwards, *Miscellanies*, 1, YE 13:197; Thomas Berry, *The Dream of the Earth* (San Francisco: Sierra Club Books, 1988), 18–22; and Brian Swimme, *The Universe is a Green Dragon* (Santa Fe: Bear, 1984), 58.

86. Jonathan Edwards, "The Nature of True Virtue," YE 8:540–549. For a discussion of the Great Theory of Beauty and Edwards's aesthetics, see Edward Farley, *Faith and Beauty: A Theological Aesthetic* (Burlington, VT: Ashgate, 2001), 15–50.

87. See Roland A. Delattre, "Aesthetics and Ethics: Jonathan Edwards and the Recovering of Aesthetics for Religious Ethics," *Journal of Religious Ethics* 31:2 (2003), 277–297.

88. Wilson Kimnach, "Jonathan Edwards's Pursuit of reality," in *Jonathan Edwards and the American Experience*, eds. Nathan O. Hatch and Harry S. Stout (New York: Oxford University Press, 1988), 106.

89. *Miscellanies*, 42, YE 13:224.

90. Leon Chai, *Jonathan Edwards and the Limits of Enlightenment Philosophy* (New York: Oxford University Press, 1998), 35.

91. "The Mind," 62, YE 11:380; and "The Beauty of the World," YE 6:305.

92. *Images of Divine Things*, 79, YE 11:81.

93. "An Humble Attempt," YE 5.345.

94. Delattre, "Aesthetics and Ethics," 281.

95. *Images of Divine Things*, 146, YE 11:101.

96. Cooey, *Jonathan Edwards on Nature and Destiny*, 7; Edwards, *History of Redemption*, YE 9:509.

97. *Miscellanies*, 743, YE 18:379–383; and "Apocalypse Series," 41, in YE 5:141; *Miscellanies*, 149, YE 13:301.

98. Ibid, 182, YE 13:328–329. See also *Miscellanies*, 188, YE 13:331.

Chapter 5X: On Pilgrimage with Jonathan Edwards

1. Edwards, Miscellanies 108, YE 13:278–279.

2. See Clyde Holbrook, *Jonathan Edwards, Nature and the Valley: An Interpretative Essay* (Lewisburg, PA: Bucknell University Press, 1987). Joseph A. Conforti offers a discussion and analysis of many of the landmarks of Edwards's life in *Jonathan Edwards, Religious Tradition, and American Culture* (Chapel Hill: University of North Carolina Press, 1995), 145–185.

3. In the first volume of his *Church Dogmatics*, Barth went so far to say that "I regard the *analogia entis* as the invention of Antichrist," adding that such a belief prevents one from being a Roman Catholic. *Church Dogmatics*, I/1: x. See also I/1: 279f.

4. David Bentley Hart speaks of the *analogia delectationis* in his book *The Beauty of the Infinite: The Aesthetics of Christian Truth* (Grand Rapids, MI: 2003), 250–253. He says that "the delightfulness of created things expresses the delightfulness of God's infinite distance. For Christian thought, then, delight is the premise of any sound epistemology: it is delight that constitutes creation, and so only delight can comprehend it" (253).

5. Edwards, "Nothing upon Earth Can Represent the Glories of Heaven," YE 14:139–140.

6. Elisabeth D. Dodds, *Marriage to a Difficult Man: The "Uncommon Union" of Jonathan and Sarah Edwards* (Philadelphia: Westminster Press, 1972), 173.

7. Edwards, "The Beauty of the World" (1725), YE 6:307. Emphasis added.

8. On East Windsor in Edwards's youth, see Ola Elizabeth Winslow, *Jonathan Edwards, 1703–1758: A Biography* (New York: Macmillan, 1940), 32–35.

9. Edwards's "Spider Letter" (October 31, 1723) can be found in YE 6:163–169. His description of his youthful retreats to the woods near his home appears in his "Personal Narrative" (1740) in YE 16:790–804.

10. See "Sinners in the Hands of an Angry God," in *A Jonathan Edwards Reader*, eds. John E. Smith, Harry S. Stout, and Kenneth P. Minkema (New Haven: Yale University Press, 1995), 89–105.

11. George M. Marsden, *Jonathan Edwards: A Life* (New Haven: Yale University Press, 2003), 136–137.

12. Edwards, "Some Thoughts on the Present Revival of Religion," YE 4:353.

13. See Tracy Kidder, *Home Town* (New York: Random House, 1999).

14. Miscellany 1184, YE 23:106.

15. See his *Ordinatio* II, d. 3, pars 1, qq. 1–6. John Duns Scotus (1266–1308) was a Franciscan theologian from Scotland who wrote and taught at Cambridge, Oxford, and Paris.

16. Robinson Jeffers, "The Excesses of God," in *Robinson Jeffers: Selected Poems* (New York: Vintage, 1965), 72.

17. Miscellany 271, YE 13:374.

Chapter 6

1. Thomas Shepherd, *The Sincere Convert* (Edinburgh: Gideon Lithgow, 1647), 2–3.

2. Sermon 20 on Ephesians, CO 51:496A, quoted in Randall C. Zachman, "Expounding Scripture and Applying It to Our Use: Calvin's Sermons on Ephesians," *Scottish Journal of Theology* 56:4, 493.

3. Donald Worster observes that Muir shamelessly stole this quote from Henry David Thoreau. See his *A Passion for Nature: The Life of John Muir* (New York: Oxford University Press, 2008), 319.

4. *Images and Shadows*, 779; *The Mind*, YE 6:357.

5. Brian Swimme, *The Universe is a Green Dragon* (Santa Fe: Bear & Co., 1984), 48.

6. See Paul Krafel, *Seeing Nature: Deliberate Encounters with the Visible World* (White River Junction, VT: Chelsea Green Publishers, 1999), 36–40.

7. See Timothy Dwight, *Travels in New England and New York*, ed. Barbara Miller Solomon (Cambridge: Belknap Press of Harvard University Press, 1969), II: 238, 139; Samuel Danforth, *A Brief Recognition of New-Englands Errand into the Wilderness* (Cambridge, MA: S. G. and M. J., 1671); Roger Williams, *A Key into the Language of America* (London: Gregory Dexter, 1643).

8. Darwin expressed this concern in a letter to Asa Gray in 1860. Quoted in Christopher Southgate, *The Groaning of Creation: God, Evolution, and the Problem of Evil* (Louisville, KY: Westminster John Knox Press, 2008), 10.

9. Southgate, Groaning of Creation, 6.

10. Southgate, *Groaning of Creation*, 16.

11. Ibid., 29, 53.

12. Holmes Rolston, "Disvalues in Nature," *The Monist* 75 (April 1992), 254.

13. Hans Urs von Balthasar, *Truth is Symphonic*, trans. Graham Harrison (San Francisco: Ignatius Press, 1987) 314–315.

14. Calvin referred to it a "magnificent theater," setting the inestimable goodness of God before the world, despite its gruesome realities. Comm. John 13:31, CO 47:317; CNTC 5:68. Edwards said that "infinite highness and infinite condescension" both met in Jesus's crucifixion. "The Excellency of Christ," YE 19:565–566; and *Religious Affections*, YE 2:258–259.

15. Holmes Rolston, *Science and Religion: A Critical Survey* (Philadelphia: Templeton Foundation Press, 2006), 144–146, and "Does Evolution Need to be Redeemed?" *Zygon* 29:2 (June 1994), 218.

16. Holmes Rolston, "Environmental Ethics: Some Challenges for Christians," *Church & Society* 86:6 (July—August 1996), 40.

17. See Irenaeus, *Adversus Haereses*, 5:20–21. Calvin says that while "the whole world is a shapeless chaos and frightful confusion," in the fullness of time God's "gathers together" (*anacephalaiosasthai*) all things in Christ. Comm. Ephesians 1:10. CO 51:294–295; CTS XXI:205.

18. A typical Puritan commentary on Romans 8:19–22 described the vivid sense of expectation pulsing through every cell and molecular structure in the cosmos. "For the whole frame of the world, even the visible heavens, with all their goodly furniture, the stars and celestial bodies, the body of the earth with her ornaments, and other elements do, by a secret instinct which God hath put into them, after a manner unknown to us, as it were long for and desire that the original perfection, in which they were first made and created, from which they are fallen and withheld through the sin of man, shall be restored to them . . . and so they do continually and earnestly, as it were with stretched out necks, and thrusting forth of their heads, expect and wait [*apokarodia* in the Greek] when both the persons of God's children, and also their glory . . . shall appear." Edward Elton, *Three Excellent and Pious Treatises . . . in Sundry Sermons upon the Whole Seventh, Eight, and Ninth Chapters of the Epistle to the Romans* (London: F. L. for Christopher Meredith, 1653), 234. Edward Elton (1569–1624) was a Puritan pastor in Bermondsey, Surrey, praised by Richard Baxter for his exegetical works and his popular *Forme of Catechizing* (1616).

19. Edwards was, in many ways, a more adventurous and speculative theologian than Calvin. The latter wrote commentaries on almost every book in the bible, but ignored the book of Revelation. By contrast, the Apocalypse was the only biblical book on which Edwards wrote an extensive commentary.

20. Jürgen Moltmann, The *Way of Jesus Christ: Christology in Messianic Dimensions* (London: SCM Press, 1990), 297. See also his *The Coming of God: Christian Eschatology*, trans. M. Kohl (Minneapolis, MN: Fortress Press, 2004), 132. Southgate discusses the eschatological hope of non-human creatures in chapter 5 of *The Groaning of Creation*, expressing this most poignantly in a poem by James Dickey, "The Heaven of Animals" (88–89).

21. See C. S. Lewis, *The Problem of Pain* (New York: Macmillan, 1944), 125–128, and *The Letters of Evelyn Underhill*, ed. Charles Williams (New York: Longmans, Green, 1943), 302.

22. "Love Dogs," in *The Essential Rumi*, trans., Coleman Barks (New York: HarperCollins, 1995), 155.

23. Arne Naess argued that "there must be identification in order for there to be compassion. . . ." Quoted in *Thinking Like a Mountain: Towards a Council of All Beings*, eds. John Seed et al. (Philadelphia: New Society Publishers, 1988), 22, 24.

24. We will always be "in a mammering," he added, until we acquire the wisdom it teaches. See Sermon xlvi on Job 12:7–16, in John Calvin, *Sermons of Maister John Calvin, upon the Booke of Job* (London: George Bishop, 1574), 214–215; CO 33:569–570.

25. In the 1850s Thoreau began a meticulous study of when plants first blossomed and leafed in the area around Concord. See *The Journal of Henry D. Thoreau*, eds. Bradford Torrey and Francis H. Allen. 14 vols. (Boston: Houghton Mifflin, 1906), 9:157–158.

26. "Of Being," YE 6:204.

27. Teilhard de Chardin, *The Divine Milieu* (New York: Harper, 1960), 15.

28. James M. Gustafson, *Ethics from a Theocentric Perspective: Theology and Ethics* (Chicago: University of Chicago Press, 1981), 106, 109. Cf. 272, 284.

29. Moltmann, *God in Creation: A New Theology of Creation and the Spirit of God* (Minneapolis: Fortress Press, 1993), 211.

30. Daniel Quinn, *Ishmael* (New York: Bantam Books, 1992), 57.

31. *Church Dogmatics*, III/3, 242. Emphasis added

32. Horace Bushnell (1802–1876) has been called the father of American liberal theology. Influenced by Coleridge's *Aids to Reflection*, his creative insights on theological language allowed him to critique the literal propositionalism of both Unitarianism and Old Calvinism, even as he censured revivalism for its lack of a communal and organic life. His emphasis on personal experience appears in his sermon on "The Immediate Knowledge of God," reprinted in David L. Smith, ed., *Horace Bushnell: Selected Writings on Language, Religion, and American Culture* (Chico, CA: Scholars Press, 1984), 218–226.

33. Horace Bushnell, *The Moral Uses of Dark Things* (New York: C. Scribner, 1869), 48. William Paley (1743–1805) was a Cambridge-trained Anglican minister who published his *Natural Theology: or, Evidences of the Existence and Attributes of the Deity, Collected from the Appearances of Nature* in 1802.

34. Bushnell, *Moral Uses of Dark Things*, 21, 57.

35. Ibid., 36.

36. Horace Bushnell, "The Power of an Endless Life," in *Sermons for the New Life* (New York: C. Scribner, 1858), 321.

37. See Robert Bruce Mullin, *The Puritan as Yankee: A Life of Horace Bushnell* (Grand Rapids: William B. Eerdmans, 2002), 184–185, 24.

38. Saying that "every word has a physical root," Bushnell argued that all abstract terms in language originated as metaphors drawn from the sensory experience of the natural world. This gave language its vitality, but also its tendency to multivalence and ambiguity. See his "Dissertation on Language" in *God in Christ* (Hartford: Brown and Parsons, 1849), 9–97.

39. *Moral Uses of Dark Things*, 222, v.

40. Ibid., 142–145, 160–162. God is not "imprisoned in his own beauty," says Bushnell, "but prefers sometimes to assert his liberty, in creating things unshapely and wild" (248).

41. Bushnell speaks of God's embrace of suffering in the cross, articulating his Moral Influence theory of the atonement, in *The Vicarious Sacrifice* (New York: C. Scribner, 1865), 1–31.

42. *Moral Uses of Dark Things*, 319, 326, 328.

43. Ibid., 329–330. Bushnell argues that many of the "insecurities, instabilities, and dark adversities of life" have a way of "pushing us on to higher points of character." Otherwise we would be "pampered and softened by the condition of ease" (378–379). He clearly exhibits here something of the "Masculine Christianity" that flourished in the late nineteenth century. Yet his concern to balance God's winsome goodness and sovereign power is characteristically Reformed.

44. For an analysis of Bushnell's thought, see Mullin, *The Puritan as Yankee*, 180–207; William A. Johnson, *Nature and the Supernatural in the Theology of Horace Bushnell* (Lund: C. W. K. Gleerup, 1963), 225–236; and Conrad Cherry, *Nature and Religious Imagination: From Edwards to Bushnell* (Philadelphia: Fortress Press, 1980), 214–230.

45. In *Nature and the Supernatural* (New York: Charles Scribner's Sons, 1877), Bushnell argued for the validity of miracles, but he defined miracles as the exercise of freedom and consciousness in a world governed by strict cause and effect. The truth is that "it is no longer necessary to go hunting after marvels, apparitions, suspensions of the laws of nature, to find the supernatural; it meets us in what is least transcendent and most familiar, even in ourselves" (43).

46. John Williamson Nevin, *The Mystical Presence* (Philadelphia: J.B. Lippincott, 1846), 155–158. Nevin (1803–1880) was a Presbyterian theologian who taught with Philip Schaff at the German Reformed Seminary in Mercersburg, Pennsylvania. For his conception of the world as a sacrament of the divine, see William DiPuccio, "Nevin's Idealistic Philosophy," in *Reformed Confessionalism in Nineteenth-Century America*, eds. Sam Hamstra and Arie Griffioen (Lanham, MD: Scarecrow Press, 1995), 43.

47. See Bushnell, *Nature and the Supernatural*, 74; Nevin's *The Mystical Presence* and Philip Schaff's *The Principle of Protestantism* (1845); and Horace Bushnell, "The Hunger of the Soul," *Sermons for the New Life* (New York: C. Scribner, 1869), 73–74.

48. Bernard McGinn, *The Foundations of Mysticism: Origins to the Fifth Century* (New York: Crossroad, 1991), xvii, 118. On the use of nature imagery in mystical writings, see Belden C. Lane, *The Solace of Fierce Landscapes: Exploring Desert and Mountain Spirituality* (New York: Oxford University Press, 1999).

49. Richard Rohr, *Everything Belongs* (New York: Crossroad, 1999). I am deeply indebted to Richard's work in many ways, as is readily apparent in this section.

50. See Robert Ellsberg, ed., *Thich Nhat Hanh: Essential Writings* (New York: Orbis Press, 2001), 53–69.

51. Gary Paul Nabhan and Stephen Trimble, The *Geography of Childhood: Why Children Need Wild Places* (Boston: Beacon Press, 1994), 5–10.

Epilogue

1. In 1980, federal law created the Superfund program, legislating taxes on chemical companies to deal with the toxic wastes they produce. It sought to identify sites of major pollution and to enforce efforts toward cleanup. The Sauget area of Dead Creek lies in

St. Clair County, Illinois, and falls under the EPA's Region 5 Superfund Division. See EPA ID# ILD980792006 (Last Update: June 2005).

2. Jonathan Kozol, *Savage Inequalities: Children in America's Schools* (New York: Crown Publishers, 1991).

3. See Ronald Rees, "The Taste for Mountain Scenery," *History Today* 25:5 (May 1975): 312; and Ramachandra Guha, "Radical American Environmentalism and Wilderness Preservation: A Third World Critique," in *The Great New Wilderness Debate*, eds. J. Baird Callicott and Michael P. Nelson (Athens: University of Georgia Press, 1998), 239.

4. H. Richard Niebuhr, *Christ and Culture* (New York: Harper, 1956), 45, 217–218.

5. Elaine Scarry, *On Beauty and Being Just* (Princeton: Princeton University Press, 1999), 4. She adds: "Beauty, as both Plato's Symposium and everyday life confirm, prompts the begetting of children: when the eye sees someone beautiful, the whole body wants to reproduce the person."

6. Elsie Anne McKee, *John Calvin: Writings on Pastoral Piety* (New York: Paulist Press, 2001), 249.

7. See Brian Tokar, "Monsanto: A Checkered History," *The Economist* 28:5 (September 1998), 254–261. Solutia, Inc., a spin-off company from Monsanto, took over its chemical business in Sauget in 1997, but the threat of bankruptcy has increasingly hindered its efforts at environmental cleanup. Since 1990, neighborhood groups in East Saint Louis have partnered with the Department of Urban and Regional Planning at the University of Illinois, Urbana-Champaign, in forming the East Saint Louis Action Research Project, addressing environmental and health concerns in the area.

8. William Spain, "Tiny Sauget, Illinois, Likes Business Misfits," *The Wall Street Journal*, Tuesday, October 3, 2006 (CCXLVIII:79), A1, A10.

9. See Allen Grimshaw, *Racial Violence in the United States* (Chicago: Aldine, 1969), 60–73, and Andrew J. Theising, *Made in USA: East St. Louis, the Rise and Fall of an Industrial River Town* (St. Louis, MO: Virginia Publishing, 2003).

10. Army Corps of Engineers (St. Louis District) Plan for Old Cahokia Creek, February 2, 2000. A few years ago the EPA ordered the Solutia Company, the spin-off of Monsanto now responsible for its Sauget operations, to spend 19 million dollars on cleaning up the creek. Several million have been put toward fencing, sediment removal, and liner installation, but Solutia has been in bankruptcy lately and it isn't at all clear what the future holds for the creek.

11. A front-page story in the *St. Louis Post-Dispatch* (September 28, 2009) recently reported on a series of lawsuits being filed against Monsanto and its cousins, charging that environmental pollution in the region has caused cancer and other medical illnesses for years.

12. Spain, "Tiny Sauget," A1. Richard Sauget, Jr., the president of the village, admits, "We were basically incorporated to be a sewer" (A10).

13. Plotinus, *Enneads*, V.8.9. See also Ronald Schenk, *The Soul of Beauty* (Lewisburg, PA: Bucknell University Press, 1992), 66–67.

14. Edwards, *Miscellanies* 293, YE 13:384.

15. Karl Barth, *Church Dogmatics*, II/1, 647–648. Barth emphasizes "man" as the "living centre" of creation to an extent that I find problematic at times. But his is a theology that gloriously sings. "The theologian who has no joy in his work is no theologian at all," he declares. "Sulky faces, morose thoughts and boring ways of speaking are intolerable in this science." Ibid., 656.

16. See William Wolf, *Thoreau: Mystic, Prophet, Ecologist* (Philadelphia: United Church Press, 1974), 42–43.

17. Richard Rohr, "The Soul, the Natural World, and What Is," a webcast teaching and compact disc from the Center for Action and Contemplation, Albuquerque, New Mexico, 2009.

18. Sharon D. Welch, *A Feminist Ethic of Risk* (Minneapolis: Fortress Press, 2000).

19. Sandra Steingraber, *Living Downstream: A Scientist's Personal Investigation of Cancer and the Environment* (New York: Vintage Books, 1998).

20. See John W. de Gruchy, "Holy Beauty: A Reformed Perspective on Aesthetics within a World of Ugly Injustice," in *Reformed Theology for the Third Christian Millennium*, ed. B. A. Gerrish (Louisville, KY: Westminster John Knox, 2003), 13–20.

21. Mary Oliver, "The Wild Geese," from her book *Dream Work* (Boston: Atlantic Monthly Press, 1986).

Index